BROWN AND BLUE

BROWN AND BLUE

Mexican Americans,
Law Enforcement,
and Civil Rights
in the Southwest,
1935–2025

BRIAN D. BEHNKEN

THE UNIVERSITY OF NORTH CAROLINA PRESS

Chapel Hill

Designed by Jamison Cockerham
Set in Scala, DIN 1451 Engschrift, and Sentinel
by Jamie McKee, MacKey Composition

Cover art: Protesters during the Dallas Disturbance, 1973.
Photograph by Jay Dickman.

Manufactured in the United States of America

LIBRARY OF CONGRESS CATALOGING-IN-PUBLICATION DATA
Names: Behnken, Brian D. author
Title: Brown and blue : Mexican Americans, law enforcement, and
    civil rights in the Southwest, 1935–2025 / Brian D. Behnken.
Description: Chapel Hill : The University of North Carolina Press, [2025] |
    Includes bibliographical references and index.
Identifiers: LCCN 2025029693 | ISBN 9781469690698 cloth alk. paper |
    ISBN 9781469690704 paperback alk. paper |
    ISBN 9781469683775 epub | ISBN 9781469690711 pdf
Subjects: LCSH: Mexican Americans—Southwestern States | Law enforcement—
    Southwestern States—History | Mexican Americans—Civil rights—
    Southwestern States | Chicano movement—Southwestern States |
    Civil rights—United States—History—20th century | Civil rights—United
    States—History—21st century | BISAC: HISTORY / United States /
    State & Local / Southwest (AZ, NM, OK, TX) | LAW / Civil Rights
Classification: LCC E184.M5 B45 2025
LC record available at https://lccn.loc.gov/2025029693

This book will be made open access within three years of publication thanks to Path
to Open, a program developed in partnership between JSTOR, the American Council
of Learned Societies (ACLS), the University of Michigan Press, and the University
of North Carolina Press to bring about equitable access and impact for the entire
scholarly community, including authors, researchers, libraries, and university
presses around the world. Learn more at https://about.jstor.org/path-to-open/.

For product safety concerns under the European Union's General Product
Safety Regulation (EU GPSR), please contact gpsr@mare-nostrum.co.uk
or write to the University of North Carolina Press and Mare Nostrum
Group B.V., Mauritskade 21D, 1091 GC Amsterdam, The Netherlands.

For my family

MONIC, BRANDIS, ELLEKA, AND AVEN

And for my adviser and friend

DR. CLARENCE WALKER

CONTENTS

ILLUSTRATIONS

ACKNOWLEDGMENTS

This book began in many ways when I came across accounts of the police killing of Santos Rodriguez, a twelve-year-old Mexican American boy executed by Dallas police officer Darrell Cain on July 24, 1973. Cain used a game of Russian roulette to try to get Rodriguez to confess to a crime he didn't commit and instead blew his brains out. I simply could not fathom the egregiousness of this case. But I wanted to know more and so I began researching the history of Mexican-origin people and law enforcement. That research took me more than a decade to complete, and it moved from Dallas to other locales in Texas and finally across the Southwest. It also expanded chronologically and kept taking me farther back in time, from the seventies and sixties and eventually all the way back to the 1830s. Such a lengthy chronology ultimately couldn't be contained in a single book, so I wrote two. The first, *Borders of Violence and Justice: Mexicans, Mexican Americans, and Law Enforcement in the Southwest, 1835–1935*, was published by the University of North Carolina Press in 2022. *Brown and Blue* is the second part of this story.

I could not complete such a lengthy process of research and writing without getting a lot of help along the way. These acknowledgments won't really do justice to all the people who have helped me, but they're a start. I will surely miss some who have assisted me, and for that I apologize. Please know that I did value your assistance.

Archivists and research librarians come first in this list of acknowledgments because none of my work would be possible without them and their staff. Many of those folks have also become my friends. At the Dallas Public

Library, I need to especially single out Carol Roark and Rachel Howe. I deeply appreciate their help and the help of all of the staff at the DPL. In San Antonio, Donna Guerra started me off on a solid footing when she worked at the San Antonio Municipal Archives. I'm blessed to say that Donna, like Carol and Rachel, also became a friend. I also received a great deal of assistance from the staff in the Texana/Genealogy Department at the San Antonio Public Library. In Austin the staff at the Austin History Center were always super helpful. I also thank the staff at Special Collections at the University of Texas, Arlington and in Houston at the Houston History Research Center at the Houston Public Library.

In New Mexico, I benefited immensely from the experts at the Center for Southwest Research and Special Collections at the University of New Mexico. I especially appreciate the help of Suzanne Schadl, Nancy Brown-Martinez, and Terry Gugliotta. I also had a wonderful experience at the Albuquerque and Bernalillo County Special Collections Library and thank Brandon Gonzalez for his help.

In Arizona, as in Texas, not only did I get to do research but I got to make more new friends. I would like to especially acknowledge my friend Christine Marin for her help. Christine for years helped researchers like me when she worked at the Chicano/a Research Collection at Archives and Special Collections at Arizona State University. I had a nice time with the Chicano/a Research Collection, where Christine and the rest of the staff made me feel very welcome.

In California, I received outstanding assistance from Lynda Claassen and the rest of the amazing staff at Special Collections and Archives at the University of California, San Diego. I also had wonderful experiences at the Special Collections Libraries at the University of California, Los Angeles. I owe a special thanks to Barbara Robinson at the Boeckmann Center for Iberian and Latin American Studies at the University of Southern California. She assisted me as if I was the only person conducting research at USC.

For assistance with photographs for illustrations, I thank Jay Dickman, whose work from his days as a news photographer in Dallas in the 1970s still has relevance today. I also gratefully acknowledge the assistance of Jasmine Torrez at the Arizona State University Library; Catie Carl at the Palace of the Governors Photo Archives in New Mexico; Molly Hults at the Austin History Center; Terri Garst at the Los Angeles Public Library; Florence Combes at ZUMA Press, Inc.; Carlos Cortéz at the University of Texas at San Antonio; Lori Podolsky at Texas A&M Corpus Christi; Chris Geherin at the University of New Mexico; Mikhaila McCray at the Houston History Research Center; and Ken Ota at RCP Publications.

For financial assistance I wish to thank Iowa State University. I received financial support for this project from my institution in the form of Small Grants from the College of Liberal Arts and Sciences and a research grant from the Center for Excellence in the Arts and Humanities. That funding gave me the ability to make multiple research trips to Southwestern archival holdings. The generosity of the LAS College is particularly appreciated. I also have a supportive group of colleagues in the Department of History, the Latino/a Studies Program, the African and African American Studies Program, and other departments and programs at Iowa State. I'd like to especially thank my chair, Dr. Simon Cordery.

I also received a lot of assistance, encouragement, guidance, and moral support from my friends and colleagues. I wish to first single out my best friend, confidant, brother from another mother, dude from another brood, relation from a different nation, and doppelgänger, Simon Wendt. Simon is a gifted intellectual, a great writer, and an excellent teacher who has always been willing to comment or question or criticize my ideas, thinking, and writing. He has also rolled out the red carpet for me to deliver talks at the University of Heidelberg and the University of Frankfurt. There, supportive and questioning crowds probed my work in ways that we academics find enormously beneficial. Simon is a kind, fun, funny, and trusted friend and I really value his friendship. Through Simon I also got to make new friends who helped me think through my own ideas, especially Fanja Razafimbelo, Fara Razafimbelo, Martin Lüthe, Peggy Preciado, and Pablo Dominguez Andersen. Thanks to you all. I am proud to call Simon my friend and owe him a huge debt of gratitude for his continued support and friendship.

In addition, friends and colleagues such as Greg Smithers, Clarence Walker, Chris Danielson, Gordon Mantler, José Angel Hernández, Max Krochmal, Jorge Mariscal, David Montejano, Jimmy Patiño, Oliver Rosales, Dan Berger, Cecilia Márquez, Brent Campney, Max Felker-Kantor, Andrew Sandoval-Strausz, Cathleen Cahill, Ben Johnson, Monica Muñoz Martinez, Annette Rodríguez, Wes Phelps, Danielle Olden, Michael Goebel, Brianna Burke, Max Viatori, Isaac Gottesman, Lora Key, Matthew Whitaker, John Mckiernan-González, Gerry Cadava, George Díaz, Santos Nuñez Galicia, Jehan Nuñez al Faisal, Katherine Thatcher, Russell Contreras, and a number of others were always willing to share a drink or a meal and listen to me go on and on about policing. I also made some new friends along the way and wish to acknowledge Brent Campney. He not only has become a friend but has also graciously shared his research material with me. I also wish thank my friend Dr. José Angel Hernández, who has for years been willing to help me out translating Spanish phrases I did not understand. I sadly learned that José died while I completed the edits on this manuscript. I will miss his friendship, colleagueship, humor, intelligence, and willingness to share a beer and a good meal.

The wonderful staff at the University of North Carolina Press once again supported this project from idea to finished manuscript. Special thanks again go out to my fabulous editor Debbie Gershenowitz, the best in the biz! In addition, the staff at UNC Press is beyond topnotch, and I wish to thank Alexis Dumain and Alyssa Brown. I would also like to single out Valerie Burton, who copyedited *Borders of Violence and Justice* and served as project editor for *Brown and Blue*. I love working with Val: she's made the production process super easy! I also wish to acknowledge Laura Jones Dooley, who copyedited the manuscript for me. Once again, UNC Press created an amazing cover and for that I thank Lindsay Starr and Patrick Holt. Finally, I thank the two anonymous readers, both of whom became known to me during the review process, Max Felker-Kantor and Robert Chase. Thanks, Max and Rob, for your insightful critiques and sage advice!

My family has always been my most consistent group of supporters. Monic, my best friend, wife, partner, and collaborator, helped with this project in numerous ways both small and large. For one, she listened to me drone on about the things I discovered while researching or writing. A lot of that became for me a way of not just debriefing but psychologically unburdening myself of the many painful things I wrote about as this book came together. That probably saved my sanity! She also always had pertinent questions and critical commentary that helped strengthen the final product. She's also an attorney, which was really helpful as I was trying to understand how the law and the criminal justice system works. I truly appreciate Monic's friendship and love and dedication to helping me produce great work. My children, too, were always there. By the time this book is published my daughter, Elleka, will be eighteen years old. She's an amazing, bright young woman who was just an infant sitting in my lap the other day. Now she's about to head off to college. My son, Aven, a wonderful, smart young man who will be sixteen by the time this book comes out, is also growing up way too fast. Not too long ago he was a preschooler yelling at squirrels. Now he's almost as tall as me (almost!). My children have always given me love and support and have even contributed to this book in their own way with their questions and commentary. I love them more than words can describe and am forever grateful to my family for their love, support, and encouragement. Finally, I write once again the name of my firstborn son, Brandis William Behnken, and in so doing speak his name into the world as a testament that he existed. Brandis only lived for two hours and died shortly after his birth, and yet his short life has affected me in ways more profound than any other human being I have ever known. I still miss him even nineteen years after his death. My family is my cornerstone. This book is dedicated to them.

Finally, this book is also dedicated to my late adviser and friend, Dr. Clarence Earl Walker. While not kin, Clarence created an environment at the University of California at Davis, when I was a doctoral student under his supervision, that was like a family. In a lot of ways, he treated me like a son. After graduate school we continued this relationship. We would speak often, and those conversations were very important for me, as I think they were for him, too. During those interactions we had lots of laughs and many a discussion of good meals we had recently enjoyed. But most importantly he continued to always demonstrate his support of my work and accomplishments, and his love for me, until his death in 2024. Clarence was, in short, a valued and trusted friend. I will miss our long conversations, his sense of humor, his massive intellect, and most of all, his steadfast and unwavering friendship.

NOTE ON TERMS

Throughout this book I have attempted to be consistent and correct in my usage of terms of ethnoracial identity. It is important to note that complete accuracy is often not possible. Some terms such as "Mexican" or "Mexican American" in part signal someone's citizenship status, but historical records don't always make it clear whether a person is a citizen of Mexico, the United States, or elsewhere. I use the terms "Mexican," "Mexican national," or "Mexican people" when it is clear that the person or persons are citizens of Mexico. I use the term "Mexican American" to describe persons of Mexican ancestry who are American citizens. When speaking of Mexican and Mexican American people as a group, I mainly rely on "Mexican-origin people" or "people of Mexican ancestry." I use other terms when chronologically important, for example, "Chicano" or "Chicana." Similarly, more modern terms like "Hispanic" or "Latino/a/x" have come to the fore only in the past four to five decades. I mainly use "Latino/a/x" when referencing people whose heritage comes from a Latin American nation as a group or when it is not possible to specifically determine their national heritage. Last, Mexican-origin people were often referred to as, or referred to themselves as, "Brown," as in the title of this book.

This book also uses a number of Spanish-language resources. In some of those sources spelling and usage of diacritical markings, especially the accent mark and tilde, are inconsistent. For names and phrases in Spanish, I follow the usage of diacritical markings as they appear in the sources or as they were preferred by the historical actors using such markings. Similarly,

Mexican-origin people usually follow Spanish naming conventions wherein an individual's first last name (paternal surname) and second last name (maternal surname) are either equally important, or they mainly use their paternal surname. In some cases, however, they used their maternal surname. For example, Jose "Joe" Campos Torres is almost always referred to as "Torres" and not "Campos." Throughout this book I use the names Mexican-origin people preferred to use. Last, I follow proper law citations and have omitted diacritical marks from titles of legal cases. All translations are my own unless otherwise noted.

The terms of ethnoracial identification for persons of European ancestry can also be problematic. While many Americans of European ancestry would be called "White" or "Caucasian" by the mid-nineteenth century, the governments of the Southwest also categorized Mexican-origin people as White. The terms "Anglo" and "Anglo American" also came to be common terms of identification for people of European heritage, even if many of those people did not originate in England. To avoid confusion, I use the term "White" throughout this book to describe individuals of European heritage only, making sure that it is clear when Mexican-origin people might also have been considered White.

For African-descent people I use the terms "Black" and "African American." For Indigenous people I use, when possible, their tribal affiliation or community attachment and, when not possible, the term "Indigenous people." Last, throughout this book I capitalize all racial and ethnic terms of identification. "White," like "Black" or "Brown," is a socially constructed racial category, and White people, like Black or Brown people, are treated as such in the pages that follow.

Many of the terms mentioned above are freighted with meaning and their usage is complex. The terms I use and how I use them are not intended to be in any way disrespectful toward the various ethnoracial communities mentioned in the pages that follow.

BROWN AND BLUE

INTRODUCTION

Joe Cedillo Jr. was only sixteen years old when Austin police officers James Johnson and Paul Looney shot him to death on the night of July 31, 1971. The officers had allegedly found Cedillo exiting a burgled convenience store and shot him in the back of the head as he fled. On the night of July 24, 1973, Dallas police officer Darrell Cain executed twelve-year-old Santos Rodriguez. Cain thought Rodriguez might have participated in a burglary, so he attempted to extract a confession from Rodriguez by using a game of Russian roulette. He shot young Santos in the head on the second pull of the trigger. In February 1978, New Mexico State Police officers Jerry Noedel and Louie Gallegos killed seventeen-year-old Frank Garcia. The officers, in plain clothes and an unmarked vehicle, had forced Garcia's car off the road and then shot him to death after he allegedly reached for a hunting rifle in the back seat. In April 1979, Los Angeles County deputy sheriff Bruce Nash shot and killed seventeen-year-old Abel Gill. Nash had pulled him over, and when Gill exited his vehicle, Nash shot him. He reported that Gill had attempted to ram him but later admitted that he had tripped and his gun had discharged.[1]

These cases, all too common in the 1970s, continued into the 1980s and 1990s, and they continue today. For me, as a writer, a researcher, and perhaps most importantly a parent, I begin this book with the killing of unarmed children because that represents one of the worst aspects of the relationship between Mexican-origin people and law enforcement in the United States. It certainly represents the powerlessness of Mexican American parents, a powerlessness that meant they couldn't protect their children from individuals and a system that takes as its very credo "to protect and serve." In all of these cases officers presumed the criminality of these Mexican American young people. All were questionable: Joe Cedillo was unarmed when police shot him; police claimed Frank Garcia reached for his rifle, but Garcia's companion denied that charge, and even if he had, I'd wager that many people might try to defend themselves if strangers forced their vehicle off the road; Bruce Nash may have accidentally killed Abel Gill, but Gill was no threat and Nash should not have had his gun drawn in the first place; the most egregious example, that of Santos Rodriguez, was a clear-cut and senseless case of police murder.[2]

Police killing of unarmed Mexican and Mexican American people—young people and adults—has an unfortunately long history. While such killings continue today, they also happened far back in the past. The cases of law enforcement–perpetrated homicide, colloquially referred to as police murder, of Mexican Americans from the mid-twentieth to the early twenty-first century motivated activism from the Mexican American community. So, too, of course, did other forms of police violence, harassment, and abuse. Mexican-origin people, their leaders, activists, and allies all fought for justice on behalf of those wronged by law enforcement. The spirit of 1960s activism helped push these responses, which in some cases produced meaningful reforms. To return to the example of the children mentioned above, protestors gathered at several demonstrations in Austin to decry the killing of Joe Cedillo. These were some of the first protests of the Chicano movement, the activist phase of the Mexican American civil rights movement, in that city. In New Mexico, activists formed an unofficial investigative unit, protested, and helped Frank Garcia's mother file a wrongful death lawsuit, but all she received was a paltry $40,000. The killing of Abel Gill and the mistreatment of others led people in Los Angeles to create the Coalition against Police Abuse, an important organization that helped marginalized communities resist police abuse. Most importantly, the murder of Santos Rodriguez led to massive protests in Dallas—one of the city's few racial uprisings—to the creation of the Dallas Police Department's Internal Affairs Division, and to new use-of-force procedures, among other reforms.

Mexican-origin people have long fought against abuses in the criminal justice system. In my first book on this subject, *Borders of Violence and Justice*, I revealed how Mexicans and Mexican Americans actively battled against extralegal justice and problematic law enforcement. Some Mexican Americans, such as New Mexico's Elfego Baca, became police officers to oppose abuse from within the ranks of law enforcement, a kind of early civil rights effort. The lynching of Mexican people in the 1800s and early 1900s led to the creation of activist groups such as La Agrupación Protectora Mexicana (Mexican Protective Group). And in the 1910s and 1920s Mexican Americans joined reform efforts aimed at professionalizing police. These examples represent early civil rights efforts on the part of Mexicans and Mexican Americans.

But it was really in the twentieth century that Mexican Americans engaged in an activist, communitywide struggle for rights. By the 1930s, the Mexican American population had grown to the point that the community had numbers sufficient enough to engage in a concerted civil rights effort. The 1930 census recorded the population of Mexican-origin people at 1.3 million. By 1950 that number had jumped to nearly 2.5 million, by 1970 to 9.1 million, and today there are approximately 37.5 million people of Mexican ancestry in the United States (about 60 percent of all Latino/a/x people).[3] That population base gave the community the necessary strength to build a civil rights movement. And the movement concentrated heavily, in many instances exclusively, on ending police abuse and reforming the justice system. This focus meant that the movement, which many people assume ended in the 1970s, continued well into the 1980s and beyond.

Brown and Blue explores the relationship between law enforcement and the broader criminal justice system and the Mexican-origin community in the US Southwest from the 1930s to the present.[4] Where issues of law enforcement and people of color are concerned, in the Southwest those issues historically have been mainly between Mexican Americans and police. The Southwest, in this book primarily Arizona, New Mexico, Southern California, Texas, and occasionally Colorado (the states where Mexicans and Mexican Americans predominated), makes for a unique case study. Its policing history is not well known. Mexican Americans experienced a lot of violence at the hands of law enforcement. But they found ways to accommodate themselves to the law enforcement situation in many parts of the Southwest while often simultaneously pushing an aggressive, sustained civil rights struggle designed to end police abuse, harassment, and murder. Mexican Americans rightly viewed the police as the first level of justice in the Southwest, and they pushed law enforcement to implement that justice fairly. Their efforts won many reforms. The community itself was therefore not antipolice—far from it. Rather, they wanted better policing and they pushed for reforms as a genuine effort to curb the long history of violence that they had experienced from the criminal justice system.[5]

In some ways, this argument demonstrates how the Mexican American community's experience with law enforcement and the criminal justice system in the Southwest differed from other locales. For one thing, understanding how Mexican Americans, the nation's second largest ethnoracial group, experienced the police and addressed problems is important. Law enforcement had historically treated Mexican-origin folks as a colonized people. Going back to the 1830s and 1840s, police existed to control the population while of course doing many of the same things law enforcement does in other parts of the country: investigate crime, protect property, render aid.[6] But the Southwest also needed Mexican Americans—as workers, as voters, as builders of community and culture. Mexican Americans also often held power in the criminal justice system in the region, as police officers or attorneys or judges, which they used to protect other Mexican people. Moreover, the nearness of Mexico often meant that Mexican Americans had an ally when problems arose. And while often segregated, Mexican Americans and White Americans often worked together, held similar positions in government (including in law enforcement), or lived near one another, which sometimes gave them an avenue for redressing wrongs. So, as I noted throughout *Borders of Violence and Justice*, the criminal justice system couldn't abuse them indiscriminately without sometimes facing a reaction or response. The Southwest by its very nature gave Mexican Americans some measure of power to confront abusive policing, especially once the civil rights movement began. To put this all a little differently, the Southwest, and the Mexican American experience there, is unique.

We know a lot about the civil rights experience of the Mexican American community. Generally speaking, in the early days of the struggle, especially in the 1940s, 1950s, and early 1960s, Mexican Americans pushed for integrated schools, for voting rights and political participation, for the desegregation of public accommodations, and in many parts of the Southwest for equality in the delivery of public services such as trash collection, the paving of roads, street lighting, and other municipal services. A big part of this period also saw fights for more inclusive policing and challenges to racism in the justice system. Another part of this early movement often included pushing for reforms based on the fact that cities, counties, states, and even the federal government classified Mexican-origin people as White. As White people, many Mexican Americans believed, segregation should not apply to them. While that focus ran counter to the efforts of progressive Mexican Americans (as well as members of the African American community), this whiteness strategy was, nonetheless, a part of the history of this period.[7]

The Chicano movement represented something different. For many Mexican Americans, and especially for young people, the tactics of the previous generation seemed hardly progressive and out of step with 1960s radicalism.

This was especially true regarding the whiteness strategy, which for many Chicanos did not comport with their lived reality—they didn't see themselves as White, nor were they treated like White people. Whiteness had seemingly won them few benefits. And the passage of the Civil Rights Act of 1964 and the Voting Rights Act of 1965 lessened the overall power of whiteness. Chicanos basically saw themselves differently. Journalist Ruben Salazar said it most plainly: "A Chicano is a Mexican American with a non-Anglo image of himself."[8] This was perhaps stated even more clearly in the Plan de Aztlán, which laid out a blueprint for Chicano organizing and activism, when it stated, "We are a bronze people with a bronze culture." Chicanos, in sum, were Brown, not White.[9]

Brownness did a lot that whiteness could not. From a practical standpoint it was more in line with the actual racial or ethnic identity of many Mexican Americans. From a more strategic perspective, it opened new doorways for securing rights, especially the use of the Fourteenth Amendment's equal protection clause. But even more than that it was an important rallying call because it allowed for much greater latitude in civil rights organizing. As people of color, as a racial minority, brownness gave Chicanos a unity and a purpose that contained a great deal of political, social, cultural, and psychological power.[10]

Nowhere was that power more important and more necessary than in Mexican American interactions with the police, especially violent interactions with law enforcement, or in violence from extralegal vigilante groups acting as law enforcement, both of which had a very long history. While in some cases this violence meant wanton killing at the hands of police, how that killing was done was equally troubling. For example, in the nineteenth century police began to kill people using what became known as the "ley de fuga" or "ley fuga," or the law of flight. Ley fuga gave law enforcement the power to kill suspects who fled by shooting them in the back. We know today that in a number of cases agents such as the Texas Rangers simply executed Mexican-origin people and then claimed they had attempted to escape.[11] Lest anyone think this kind of abusive law enforcement was a reality only in the 1800s or early 1900s, the Joe Cedillo case mentioned above was a case of ley fuga. There were many others. In most Southwestern states, police had the legal right to shoot and kill fleeing suspects, usually if they were involved in the commission of a felony, no matter their age.

Law enforcement also continued to engage in harassing and abusive behavior. Police seemingly replaced the vagrancy and loitering arrests of the late nineteenth and early twentieth centuries with the twentieth- and twenty-first-centuries version of the same thing: "papers, please" policing. "Papers, please" policing authorized law enforcement to racially profile, detain, and demand identification of anyone who appeared to be of Latino/a/x ancestry. While perhaps most famously visible in Arizona's SB 1070 legislation of 2010, "papers, please" policing originated in the 1960s. These types of laws legalize discrimination and are for the most part ineffective.

Various forms of extralegal justice also continued well into the twenty-first century. The types of violence that extralegal groups used did not simply go away in the early twentieth century; after all, the last lynching of a Mexican-origin person occurred in New Mexico in 1928. But vigilantes found new ways to exercise violence. Take, for example, the Hanigan case of 1976, wherein George Hanigan and his sons Pat and Tom captured three Mexican men, Manuel García Loya, Eleazar Ruelas Zavala, and Bernabe Herrera Mata, and brutally tortured them for crossing the Hanigans' ranchland. That type of extralegal border security also became a major organizational initiative of the Ku Klux Klan in the 1970s and 1980s, one reimagined in the twenty-first century by such groups as the Minuteman Project.

The criminal justice system also worked hard to insulate itself from criticism and change. Although this book is primarily about policing, it also has much to say about the broader criminal justice system. For example, district attorneys and law enforcement always work closely together, a collusive relationship that often protects police officers charged with wrongdoing. They found numerous ways to do so. Authorities often belittled Mexican and Mexican American victims of police abuse. They would label victims bad people, publish their criminal record if they had one, or make them seem aggressive. For example, law enforcement vilified Joe Cedillo as a juvenile delinquent. The goal of besmirching a victim was and is simple: to exonerate the officer accused of that victimization. Later in the twentieth century, concepts such as qualified immunity, which grants law enforcement protection from civil lawsuits after a case of police violence, or the "objectively reasonable" standard, which asks whether, in a case of police violence, an ordinary person would act as the police officer did (usually expressed with such phrases as "I feared for my life"), offered successful paths for exculpating law officers from sanction or punishment after they abused or killed someone.

The justice system in the Southwest was then, and is today, incredibly complex. Police agencies and the criminal justice system more generally are an interrelated series of numerous tightly bound institutions. They tend to operate similarly, to have similar organization and leadership structures, to follow similar policies and procedures, no matter the location.[12] Houston

6

and Los Angeles serve as useful examples. Each city is geographically vast, has a large population, and has numerous police agencies. In the Houston area, there are today nearly 100 police organizations, including the Houston Police Department, the Harris County Sheriff's Office, the Harris County Constables, university police at the University of Houston and University of Texas at Houston, the Houston Independent School District Police—and the list goes on. Los Angeles has a similarly massive number of police forces, considering all the closely connected cities in the LA area—Alhambra, Burbank, Glendale, Huntington Park, Inglewood, and Pasadena, among many others—as well as the numerous universities, school districts, and the like that have police. Both cities and their surrounding environs employ tens of thousands of police officers with budgets in the billions of dollars.[13]

But this is not to say that all Southwestern police departments are the same. Variations existed between departments based on locale or leadership. Houston and other Texas cities, while Southwestern, were also Southern, so their racial climate was typified by the segregation and discrimination common to the South. New Mexican cities often had a large percentage of Mexican-origin people, and police chiefs in places such as Albuquerque often knew that population well and supported reform efforts to create a better law enforcement situation. The same thing cannot be said for LA, which also had a large Mexican American population but was often the most restrictive and punitive in its policing. Differences in the structure of local governments or state laws also generated differences in policing at the local level.

Despite the similarities and differences in the Southwest's police forces, Mexican American people tended to experience and respond to policing across the Southwest in similar ways because for them abuse was abuse, police murder was murder, and justice needed to be done. From the perspective of the Mexican American community, problematic policing quite often looked and felt the same. And although Mexican American civil rights organizations may have approached policing problems in different ways depending on the group or location or time period, their goal was quite often the same: to curb police abuse, usually with reform. In some cities, for example, in South Phoenix and South Tucson in the late 1970s, Mexican Americans actually wanted more police in their communities in order to deal with crime or render aid. In other locales, such as Albuquerque, Mexican American activists worked with police to create a Police Athletic League, which local people enjoyed, as a method of improving police-community relations. And even the most radical groups simply wanted an end to police brutality and harassment. The Brown Berets pushed a fairly radical agenda, in many ways an abolitionist agenda, but as leader Carlos Montes noted, their program was an "anti-police abuse campaign," not an antipolice campaign.[14] In other words, different groups in different locations could promote different tactics, but the overall goal was often reform and the development of a more constructive relationship between police and civilians.

Police are only a part of the broader criminal justice system, which includes courts, alternative adjudication bodies, jails, and prisons. That equally complicated system grew more complex throughout the twentieth century and into the twenty-first. Whereas jails and prisons had of course been part of the Southwest's criminal justice system going back to the 1800s, many other forms of human caging—juvenile facilities, prison camps, and immigrant detention facilities, to name a few—became standard features of the system only in the twentieth century. Similarly, states began to rely heavily on private, for-profit jails mainly in the 1980s. Court systems in almost every locale are equally intricate and layered. These institutions, when coupled with the administrative authority they receive from the state and the federal government, hold a great deal of power over people in the Southwest. Mexican Americans also hoped to reform the carceral system, and they did so in important and meaningful ways.

By focusing on these systems, *Brown and Blue* shows how racism could be exercised by the criminal justice institution. The institutionalization of racism has a long history, and I discuss its origins in *Borders of Violence and Justice*. By the 1930s racism had been concretized within law enforcement and the justice system. The problem with systemic racism in the criminal justice system is that law enforcement bodies tend to treat people, and especially people of color, in wholly inappropriate ways. It also means that those who act in good faith and do not engage in abusive behavior have little power to alter the racism that they might encounter because it is systemic. This is especially true for violent behavior from police. And as readers will no doubt note, many examples of abuse came from officers of Mexican ancestry, another illustration of how institutional racism works.

Police repression and Mexican American resistance were in many ways in constant relation and communication with each another. Violence, whether extralegal or emanating from law enforcement, had to be challenged. And challenge it Mexican Americans did. Countering abusive law enforcement was one of the most important goals of the Mexican American struggle for rights. Many of the civil rights organizations that formed during the civil rights era had police reform as a part of their platform or organizational principles. Many of the protests that occurred throughout the civil rights era had some type of police reform as a goal. And reform itself was varied, differing from locale to locale and organization to organization. But, most basically, Mexican Americans wanted the police to work better and more fairly, and reforms, they thought, would help achieve that aim. If nothing else, and to put it simply, Mexican Americans wanted police to stop killing their people. To their credit, in many cases police departments responded positively to a variety of demands for reform. And when they didn't, Mexican Americans often augmented protests to keep the pressure on police.

Unfortunately, civil rights activism that led to reforms often happened only after the Mexican American community had gone through a horrible event. Although there are certainly examples of Mexican Americans pushing for reforms before an instance of violence occurred, in most cases an egregious act had to happen to generate the civil rights activism that followed. The example of Santos Rodriguez proves this point. Mexican Americans in Dallas had protested against police violence before his murder, yet it was the senseless killing of this child that produced the protests that ultimately forced reforms on the Dallas Police Department. In cases like Rodriguez's, activism attempted to try to fix the system after the damage had been done. For the Santos Rodriguezes of the world, change came too late.

But reforms did happen, and some of them transformed the criminal justice system not just for Mexican Americans but for all Americans. For example, the landmark case *Hernandez v. Texas* (1954) not only barred the exclusion of Mexican Americans from jury service but extended the Equal Protection Clause of the Fourteenth Amendment of the Constitution to all Americans. Perhaps even more well known, *Escobedo v. Illinois* (1964) and *Miranda v. Arizona* (1966) enumerated the rights of those under police custodial investigation or interrogation. The rights *Miranda* generated are well known; anyone who has watched a *Law and Order*–type TV show has seen an example of police reading someone their rights. The warning is now a verbized form of Miranda's name: to read someone their rights is to mirandize them. I think many people are probably unaware that the term came from a Mexican American litigant from Arizona.

Other reforms worked to bring law enforcement and members of the Mexican American community together. The hiring of Mexican American police officers serves as a good example. Although many communities had Mexican American officers on the force for generations, others began that process only in the mid-twentieth century. In addition, the diversification of police forces through programs usually referred to as "minority recruitment" meant the hiring of increased numbers of Mexican American officers, as well as other officers of color. These officers were viewed as go-betweens for police and the Mexican American community. Some cities launched Police Athletic Leagues as a similar bridge between police and Mexican Americans.

To secure reforms, Mexican American activists had to work with police authorities. Interestingly, in many locales police leadership proved willing to negotiate with Mexican American leaders and implement desired reforms. And in some cases, reform-minded police chiefs actually proposed or initiated reforms before violence had occurred and Mexican Americans had demanded reform. This sets some police departments apart from others. Although departments' leadership and organizational structures may be similar, the existence of sympathetic leadership in one locale could often generate reforms that a department in a city without such leadership could not accomplish. This is another aspect of Southwestern policing that makes the region unique.

In recent years, some activists have proposed "defunding" police departments, police abolition, or jail and prison abolition, all of which can serve as types of reform.[15] These concepts have been widely (and often purposefully) misunderstood. Defunding the police means redirecting police budgets for, say, mental health services away from law enforcement and to social workers or medical professionals. Defunding has also been viewed as a first step toward abolition. Those who argue in favor of police or carceral abolition often mean exactly that: getting rid of an institution altogether, in some cases with the goal of replacing it with a new one.[16] The Mexican American community did occasionally maintain an abolitionist perspective, although they did not use the word "abolition" much before the twenty-first century. For example, the Black Berets of Albuquerque understood police as an imperialist army that had occupied Mexican American neighborhoods, and they demanded an end to that occupation. While they also worked with the police to better police-community relations in Albuquerque, the Black Berets at least argued in favor of a type of abolition. Today the Mexican American community has debated abolition but often still prefers other reforms.

The problem with reforms is that they can be undone. Budgets can be cut, leading to the elimination of a reform, or police leaders opposed to certain reforms can undo the efforts of a prior leader. Sometimes the reforms proposed to solve a particular problem don't work, or subsequent reforms and other interventions supersede them. Some interventions have ended up making policing problems worse, especially over the past thirty years. For example, community policing began as an initiative that put officers at the disposal of local residents in the 1960s and 1970s. But by the 1990s it had morphed into "broken windows policing," which has been critiqued for its racial bias and as a cause of many of the policing problems we see today.[17] Perhaps even more damaging were major federal policing efforts. The War on Drugs and War on Crime serve as useful examples. But the worst culprit in this regard was Bill Clinton's Crime Bill of 1994, which led to the massive expansion of police forces, the concomitant increase in the power that those police officers have, and the significant rise in the American prison population. The protests that take place today after a case of police violence are often not just about the incident itself but also about these systematic changes to law enforcement over the past three decades.[18]

This book, then, is most importantly a history of how law enforcement treats Mexican Americans and how the Mexican American community created a civil rights struggle to oppose abuse and violence. The activism coming from the Mexican American community lasted for decades. Although some of this activism is consistent with 1960s civil rights struggles—protests, pickets, boycotts, and the like—the level of activism was remarkable. In some examples, 10,000 or 20,000 people came out to protest against police abuse. When Darrell Cain killed Santos Rodriguez, an estimated 10,000 people turned out for a protest. That demonstration also spawned a major uprising, another form of protest. Although some people decried violence as a protest tactic, it is important to note that violent behavior often produced results.[19]

Brown and Blue does not present a history that "bends toward justice," to borrow from Martin Luther King Jr.[20] Rather, it is an oscillatory history. It is a history of fits and starts. It is a history where things are bad, get better, and then get bad again. The book's chapters are organized thematically and chronologically to show these trends. The first chapter picks up where *Borders of Violence and Justice* ended. It focuses on Southwestern policing from the 1930s to the early 1960s. These years represented the nascent beginnings of Mexican American civil rights activism. Many Southwestern communities also began hiring Mexican American police officers for the first time in this period.

The second chapter explores the Chicano movement by focusing on movement participants who became victims of police abuse. From anti–Vietnam War protests to labor activism to policing protests, law enforcement often responded with a heavy hand to Chicano activism, arresting and sometimes killing movement participants. The movement responded with demands for justice and police reform, which it sometimes got. Chapter 3 explores the history of non-movement participants abused or killed by police. Numerous Mexican Americans who were not a part of the Chicano movement experienced police abuse during the movement years. That abuse gave the Chicano movement additional reasons to protest and led to further reforms. Chapter 4 details several unique—and often strange—cases that involved Mexican Americans and law enforcement. These cases reveal a great deal. For example, the Morales case—in which Castroville, Texas, police chief Frank Hayes murdered Ricardo Morales and then secretly disposed of his body—led to important modifications in how the Department of Justice reviews cases.

Chapters 5 and 6 investigate the history of reform of the criminal justice system in the Southwest. Chapter 5 looks primarily at attempts at carceral reform. This includes nationally important examples such as the *Escobedo* and *Miranda* decisions as well as the reform or attempted reform of local jails and prisons. Chapter 6 examines the many local level policing reforms won by the Chicano movement. It shows how police departments engaged with Mexican Americans and how both groups worked to develop reform efforts to better policing.

The final two chapters bring things up to the present day. Chapter 7 is about the history of the 1980s. I would guess that most people don't think of the eighties as a heyday of civil rights activism. But in many ways, it was. In fact, I argue that the Chicano movement, which many believe ended in the 1970s, continued well into the 1980s. The final chapter explores the period between the 1990s and today. This was the time that largely brought this country the policing situation we now find ourselves in. The Clinton 1994 Crime Bill and the War on Drugs and War on Crime gave us massive new police forces. These modifications to law enforcement led to some major abuses of police power and the deaths of numerous unarmed Mexican Americans, which often then triggered protests and demands for justice, which victims in most cases didn't receive.

Although I offer a succinct conclusion, the last section of this book is a coda. That coda offers ideas on how we can adjust, change, or even fix the troubling law enforcement situation in this country. We often hear about various reform ideas—more training, body cameras, defunding police, police or jail and prison abolition—without often having a complete understanding of what those things mean, how they work (or don't work), and what they can actually do. The coda, I hope, will explain these things and offer solutions.

Brown and Blue is a difficult history. Law enforcement did a lot of violence, a lot of killing, that is simply hard to imagine. But even more importantly, many of those cases of violence happened within relatively recent times, and many of the people affected by these cases are still with us and, possibly, quite probably, still feeling the effects of these events. So, this book may be difficult for some to read and will likely be painful. I want to make it perfectly plain that there is a lot of ugliness to get through as a reader turns these pages. Those in law enforcement might also find this book hard to read. They may see it as disparaging or even as an indictment on policing (which in many ways it is). But there are also people in the criminal justice system who strive every day to do good work, who want police to do better, who work daily to avoid the mistakes of the past. They, I hope, will read this book with a hopeful eye.

Reckoning with the history of Mexican-origin people and law enforcement is long overdue. I attempted with *Borders of Violence and Justice* to explain the early origins of how we got to where we are today. *Brown and Blue* concludes that examination. My sincere hope is that both books will help us not only to understand the past but, ultimately, to build a better future.

ONE

PACHUCOS AND POLICE

Mexican Americans and Law
Enforcement at Midcentury

In the 1940s, a hysteria about pachucos overtook the United States and beyond. The pachuco phenomenon, a distinct style that included dress, cultural pride, and a lingual patois, among other things, united Mexican American youths in a countercultural movement. But for others, pachucos seemed a threat. News reports from El Paso to Los Angeles to Mexico City detailed the alleged menace of Mexican and Mexican American pachucos. The reporting from Los Angeles's newspapers was particularly egregious in its inaccuracies. In August 1942, for example, the *Los Angeles Times* reported that all pachucos belonged to gangs and the police warned "the kid gloves are off!"[1] Tucson reported on a "pachuco invasion" of "hoodlums" in November 1942.[2] In El Paso, police reported that devious pachucos had developed their own language to avoid law enforcement and called them a "cult."[3] The *Austin American* translated "pachuco" to "bum."[4] Even Mexico City reported a pachuco disturbance: a wax model wearing a zoot suit. "Countrymen or not," the opinion from Mexico seemed to be, "anybody who would wear an outfit like that ought to be beaten up."[5] In all of this reporting, the prescribed solution to pachucos was expanded law enforcement.

The pachuco phenomenon represented an important moment in mid-twentieth-century Mexican American history. For Mexican-origin people this cultural style meant freedom, uniqueness, and a general sense of coolness, while simultaneously it critiqued dominant Anglo-centric cultural norms. For White folks in general, and those in positions of authority especially, pachucos caused great concern. Media interpretations almost always erroneously equated pachucos with crime, juvenile delinquency, and gangs. This generated a massive law enforcement response that culminated in 1943 in the Zoot Suit Riots, wherein US military personnel and law enforcement brutalized Mexican-origin people, as well as folks from other ethnic groups, across the United States. Law enforcement and the press produced these perceptions of criminality and delinquency in large part to control a population they disliked.[6]

The period between the late 1930s and early 1960s represented some important moments in the history of Mexican Americans and law enforcement. The police and governmental fixation on pachucos, which usually got combined with a focus on juvenile delinquency and gangs, created a lot of problems. Authorities and the public racialized both delinquency and gang affiliation as something that communities of color—and in the Southwest, Mexican-origin people especially—engaged in. Local governments once again relied on the power of law enforcement to control pachucos and zoot-suiters since they were deemed a threat to the broader city as a whole. The problem with this response, beyond its reliance on violence and racism to achieve its goals, was that in many places it was based on erroneous assumptions about Mexican American people. Both LA and Houston, quintessential examples of the police response to pachucos, had seen juvenile delinquency and gang membership decline considerably in the 1940s and into the 1950s—and they knew it. But the antipachuco response was simply too tempting for local leaders to ignore.

There were other types of violence in this period. Most notably, in Texas the notorious sheriff Robert Vail Ennis of Beeville killed three Mexican American men in 1945. But this example of violence also demonstrates the changing nature of Mexican American activism. Mexican Americans demanded that Ennis be held accountable, and the sheriff was tried but acquitted. When he ran for reelection, Mexican Americans came out hard against him. They cost him the election. He ran again; Mexican Americans voted and ensured that he lost again.

That was an important moment of activism and agency, but other important evolutions in the policing of communities of color also took place in this period. For example, numerous police departments across the Southwest began to recruit Mexican American police officers. By diversifying their ranks, these police departments hoped that they could have more fruitful, better relationships with the Mexican American community. More importantly, though, this was a time of nascent civil rights activism. Mexican Americans exerted their growing political power to alter police practices. In many ways this period set the stage for the civil rights activism that would become commonplace in the late 1960s and beyond.

For Southwestern police agencies, nothing seemed more important in the late 1930s and early 1940s than policing pachucos and zoot-suiters. Pachucos and pachucas engaged in a distinct counterculture style, called pachuquismo (literally pachuco-ism), which involved not just dress but language (pachucos had a patois called Caló), dancing, nightlife, and cultural pride. Zoot-suiters, both male and female, picked up this countercultural dress by wearing flamboyant zoot suits—high-waisted, baggy pants, a long suit jacket, an oversized tie, and a hat. The zoot suit was particularly popular among young people in the 1940s. Their style offered a criticism of American society and, especially, police brutality.[7]

Because zoot-suiters wore clothing deemed "different" by the mainstream, and because this clothing cost a substantial amount of money and used textiles deemed of value to the war effort in the 1940s, pachucos and zoot-suiters were largely maligned by American society in general and by White people specifically. Author Haldeen Braddy, for example, wrote a scathing essay in 1947 in which he described pachucos as juvenile delinquents, drug addicts, drug dealers, and effeminate (that is, gay) and commented that "their revolt against the law has had little value as a protest movement."[8] So Braddy could acknowledge their protest against police, or "revolt against the law," but he saw nothing of value in that struggle. Even sympathetic authors made problematic generalizations about pachucos. Arturo Madrid-Barela noted, "The Pachucos provoked hostility in America's press and brutality in America's police."[9] Such a statement incorrectly blames pachucos for the brutality they endured.

Most people at the time associated the pachuco–zoot suit phenomenon with Southern California. Los Angeles in particular saw a rise in this youth culture beginning in the 1930s. For young Mexican Americans, pachuquismo involved not only a style of dress and behavior but also a modest quest for dignity. Since the United States remained hostile to Mexican-origin people, pachucos crafted their own cultural style as a way to both feel comfortable and critique American society.[10] Local people and authority figures met this critique and style with a vigorous public backlash that linked pachucos with crime and delinquency.[11]

Apprehensions in LA about juvenile delinquency came to a head in the Sleepy Lagoon case. This case in many ways represented the criminal justice system run amok. It stemmed from the death of Jose Gallardo Diaz in August 1942. The circumstances of Diaz's death remain unclear, and police never solved the cased. Someone may have beaten him to death or hit him with a car; no one knows. But law enforcement in LA found Diaz's homicide of value because they could use it to railroad zoot-suiters and highlight the fictional problem of juvenile delinquency.[12] The Los Angeles Police Department (LAPD) arrested nearly 600 Mexican American young people after Diaz's death. They held forty of these youths. According to *Los Angeles Daily News* writer Ben Baeder, "the prosecution had scant evidence. But they had traviesos—troublemakers. A bunch of them."[13] That these troublemakers likely had nothing to do with the crime mattered very little; as zoot-suiters they represented a group that the criminal justice system thought needed correcting. As historian Mark Weitz has observed, in the late 1930s the LAPD "became proactive, and that aggressive stance toward crime prevention came with a system of racial profiling that in turn brought a new harshness to the way the police dealt with Mexican or Mexican Americans."[14]

Police suspicions fell heavily on Henry Leyvas and members of the 38th Street Gang. Nothing conclusively tied them to Diaz other than that Leyvas and his friends had spent time at Sleepy Lagoon the night Diaz died. Police charged twenty-two of these young people with assault and murder. The state indicted two other juveniles for lesser offenses. It is unusual in the legal profession to see such a large group tried collectively for the killing of one individual, but that was hardly the most unusual aspect of the case. For instance, the judge, Charles Fricke, seemed openly to hate Mexican-origin people. He refused to allow the youths to change clothes or get haircuts, so they appeared in court in clothes they had worn for months. He also allowed Sheriff's Lieutenant Edward Duran Ayres, who served as chief of the sheriff's foreign relations bureau, to testify as an expert witness. Ayres was no expert. Instead, he gave stereotypically racist testimony and argued that Mexican Americans had criminal proclivities, that there was a "biological basis" for this criminality, that they desired "to kill, or at least let blood," and that "the hoodlum element as a whole must be indicted as a whole."[15] Because Ayres was himself of Latin American ancestry, his words took on additional weight in the courtroom.

This stereotypical artist's depiction of a zoot-suiter appeared in the *Los Angeles Herald Examiner* on April 15, 1951. The caption for the drawing was, "A Zoot Suiter. Hoodlum? . . . or product of wartime hysteria?" Los Angeles newspapers, as well as newspapers across the Southwest, often ran such portrayals, along with numerous negative articles about zoot-suiters, which led in part to the 1940s–1950s antipachuco hysteria. *Herald Examiner Collection, Los Angeles Public Library.*

The conclusion of the case was hardly surprising. The jury convicted Henry Leyvas and two others of first-degree murder and two counts of assault. The court sentenced them to life in prison at San Quentin. The jury convicted nine other young men, including seventeen-year-old Manuel Reyes, of second-degree murder and assault and sentenced them to five years to life in prison at San Quentin. Five other youths served time in the Los Angeles County Jail for assault.[16]

While the trial took place, a number of organizations formed to help defend the accused. The Citizens' Committee for the Defense of Mexican-American Youth and the Sleepy Lagoon Defense Committee both attracted hundreds of donors and some big stars. Actor Anthony Quinn was probably the most famous member of the Sleepy Lagoon Defense Committee. Well-known labor and civil rights activists Luisa Moreno, Josefina Fierro de Bright, and Bert Corona also joined the group. A lengthy pamphlet produced by the Citizens' Committee for the Defense of Mexican-American Youth received a foreword from Orson Welles. This activism was an important example of community agency that ultimately resulted in an appeals court victory reversing the convictions and freeing the men.[17]

The so-called Zoot Suit Riots came shortly after the Sleepy Lagoon case. They occurred in early June 1943. They followed a standard pattern of race riots in the United States in that they were an angry White response to perceived transgressions by an ethnoracial community. It remains unclear what specifically spawned the violence, but US Navy service members began to congregate in downtown LA and moved from there to East Los Angeles attacking zoot-suiters specifically and Mexican-origin people more generally. These White sailors beat, stripped, and cut the hair of numerous individuals. The police encouraged this violence and arrested mainly Mexican Americans, not the White sailors who perpetrated it. After nearly a week of violence the disorder ended when the military confined all soldiers and sailors to base.[18]

Many Americans came to view the violence as a justified response of service members and the police to Mexican American cultural formations, especially the zoot suit. But when we examine the media coverage of the fictitious pachuco–zoot suit crime wave and delinquency, the Sleepy Lagoon murder trial, and the way police allowed sailors access to the Mexican American community while simultaneously arresting Mexican Americans and preventing them from fleeing or seeking aid, a different picture emerges. Of course, the police had widely publicized the "problem" of pachucos and gangs, and they had done much to punish and ridicule zoot-suiters. Police initiated the anti–zoot suit hysteria, and the sailors did the violence. In many ways, the White sailors and soldiers operated as a latter-day committee of public safety, a lynch mob that, thankfully, did not actually kill anyone. Legitimate law enforcement and military authority supported the sailors and soldiers; commanding officers had received orders not to interfere with rioting sailors. Some newspapers called the mob a "task force," which, like "committee of public safety," gave the sailors' actions an air of the official. Other papers noted that the violence had a "cleansing effect." County Supervisor Roger Jessup commented, "All that is needed to end lawlessness is more of the same action as is being exercised by the servicemen!"[19]

Most accounts of the violence focus on the abuse Mexican-origin people experienced at the sailors' hands. But the violence was not so one-sided, and numerous Mexican Americans fought back. Rudy Leyvas, the brother of Henry Leyvas, recalled how he and other Mexican Americans organized a resistance movement to counter the violence. Since the police coordinated with the sailors over the radio, Leyvas and his colleagues purchased radios and thus knew when and where attacks would take place. They staked out these locations with as many as 500 men. When the US Navy trucks arrived with the sailors, the Mexican American youths would send out a handful of individuals to act as decoys. "They started coming after the decoys," he explained, and "then we came out. They were surprised. . . . Lot of people were hurt on both sides. . . . The battle at 12th and Central lasted about half an hour. Busloads of police arrived and dozens of Mexicans were arrested. No servicemen were arrested."[20] Leyvas's account tells us a great deal. Not only did Mexican Americans organize to resist the violence they encountered, but they actually outwitted the police and naval personnel, who remained unaware that the youths spied on their radio communications.

After the Zoot Suit Riots the LA city government spent a lot of time investigating this episode. They created the Special Committee on Problems of Mexican Youth, for instance. The title of the group suggested that the committee would approach this subject from a deficit-based perspective. The problems the committee reported on, unsurprisingly, fit into the dominant narrative that Mexican American youth activity equaled juvenile delinquency. The report the committee issued began with the Jose Diaz murder and went on from there to include testimony from Sheriff Eugene Biscailuz and LA Chief of Police Clemence B. Horrall. They denied any racial component to the conflagration whatsoever. The special committee's report also focused on a group of young Mexican Americans whom the state had charged with the crime of "lynching." Despite the inflammatory nature of that word, California law defined lynching as an aggressive group who removed a prisoner from police custody. In this case, the youths "interfered with the arrest of prisoners by police officers who were endeavoring to stop a gambling game on the sidewalks at a certain corner in the City of Los Angeles." Considering that police arrested Mexican-origin people and left White people unmolested, the interference makes some sense. The name of the charge, not so much.[21]

The special committee also heard testimony from a variety of civic and political leaders, almost all of whom "pointed out the handicaps suffered by the young people of Mexican ancestry," another deficit-based perspective. The committee did note, however, that Mexican Americans "have been more sinned against than sinning, in the discriminations and limitations that have been placed on them and their families." And yet, the committee nonetheless maintained that police would play the most important role in Mexican American parts of the city—"the peace officers of the community should be heartily endorsed and supported in all efforts to apprehend and bring to justice violators of the law"—although it urged the city "to assign to districts inhabited by Mexican people only officers with special qualifications for this duty."[22]

At about the same time the Special Committee on Problems of Mexican Youth formed, juvenile court judge Robert H. Scott organized the Special Committee on Older Youth Gang Activity in Los Angeles and Vicinity to examine the "'Mexican Gang' situation."[23] Since the committee focused on gang activity, its recommendations fixated even more heavily on policing. Like the other special committee, the Special Committee on Older Youth Gang Activity "recommended that all organizations and citizens give the Sheriff and Police Department every assistance and encouragement in taking into custody anyone suspected of implication in assaults and gang activity." It also proposed new criminal laws, the most serious of which would criminalize gang involvement itself for individuals over the age of eighteen: they would be "prosecuted for contributing to the delinquency of a minor."[24]

The most honest investigations came from the California state government. The California Citizens' Committee on Civil Disturbances in Los Angeles, a group formed by Governor Earl Warren, found the consistent misrepresentation of facts, especially about zoot-suiters, by both the media and law enforcement, a key problem. "One of the causes," the committee noted, "has been the failure properly to present the facts."[25] The committee's report went on to criticize casual linkages between pachucos and crime, criminality and Mexican Americans, and the wearing of a zoot suit and gang membership. It also criticized police, noting that "mass arrests, drag-net raids and other wholesale classifications of groups of people are based on false premises and tend merely to aggravate the situation." This critiqued both media hype and the thinking of people such as Edward Ayres about Mexican American criminality. Such statements inflamed "race prejudice. . . . Any solution of the problems involves, among other things, an educational program throughout the community designed to combat race prejudice in all its forms."[26]

The California Citizens' Committee report offered a number of salient recommendations, almost all focusing on law enforcement reforms. They included: that police should make arrests for criminal or gang activity without an emphasis on race; that police officers should receive training so that they could successfully deal with people of color; that police agencies should hire officers who speak Spanish and "understand the psychology of the Spanish-speaking groups in Los Angeles"; and that the state should provide adequate detention and care facilities for juvenile offenders as well as serious offenders.[27] "The community as well as its visitors must learn that no group has the right to take the law into its own hands," the report also noted.[28]

A similar logic needed to prevail in how local officials viewed gang activity, most of which was not linked to criminal activity, and LA authorities knew it. A report from the Los Angeles County Youth Committee issued in January 1954 noted, for instance, that gangs were "best described as street corner societies. They are loosely knit organizations through which the individual members feel that they gain recognition, status and protection. Though members are frequently involved in trouble and are a thorn in the side of the police, most of their crimes cannot be classified as gang activity."[29] Despite this assertion, as well as the guidance from California Citizens' Committee, law enforcement continued to take a hard stance against juvenile delinquency and gang activity. Sheriff Biscailuz went so far as to state explicitly that so-called juvenile delinquents were "kid gangsters" and that after they become a "second or third offender" they should "be treated as an adult and given fitting punishment." The sheriff outlined what today we call three-strikes laws and pushed for the state to charge children as adults.[30]

Los Angeles County also focused on delinquency by passing a new ordinance that would ban the sale and distribution of "crime comic books." According to the county, the comics presented a "clear and present danger" because "many children have been incited to commit crimes as a consequence of looking at crime 'comic' books." No proof existed that these comics caused crimes, in much the same way that we now understand that rap lyrics or video games in the 1980s did not cause crime, but it sounded plausible and the county could sell it to the public. Of course, such an ordinance would also violate the First Amendment. When Ordinance 6633 went into effect in 1955, civil rights groups challenged it almost immediately, and in *Katzev et al. v. County of Los Angeles* the California Supreme Court struck it down in 1959.[31]

One of the other perplexing aspects of this focus on juvenile crime was that numerous police agencies in LA County had seen a substantial decrease in the amount of delinquency during the wartime and postwar periods. A study done by its probation department found that between 1945 and 1950 juvenile delinquency had declined by more than 50 percent.[32] So law enforcement knew that both gang activity and juvenile delinquency were not as serious as they had led the public to believe they were, and yet they continued to crack down on these phantom crimes. And they found new ways to do so, for example, by focusing on what they stereotypically believed led to juvenile delinquency: nightclubs and dance halls.

Dance halls and clubs were often sites of interracial contact, places where Brown, Black, and White youths comingled, and this, as well as perceptions of crime and vice at bars and dance halls, drove a heavy-handed government response.[33] The county government concentrated explicitly on how they issued dance hall permits. The county board of supervisors had previously overseen the issuing of these permits but shifted that duty to the Public Welfare Commission. The supervisors also granted the Public Welfare Commission new powers to deny licenses, basically giving the commission power to issue a denial for any reason. This gave it power to discriminate against county residents by considering "more evidence as to the moral character of the applicant than the mere existence or non-existence of a police record of such person."[34]

To make its decisions, the commission relied on reports from the LA County Sheriff's Department. This was also problematic because it meant that the institutional bias of one government agency could now influence another. The sheriff's report in 1956 demonstrated the problem with this method of data sharing. Many of the denials came from the east side. For example, the Public Welfare Commission denied the application of El Carretero Cafe in Pico Rivera because of a "police problem. Numerous arrests and uncooperative attitude of the owner toward law enforcement." This language lacked specificity. What were the arrests for? Who was arrested? In what way was the owner uncooperative? The county similarly denied El Siglo Vente [sic] Cafe's application due to a "police problem. Arrest record of owner—licensee would not comport with the public welfare." Again, the justification lacked specificity. If law enforcement had arrested the owner for, say, selling alcohol to minors, then the denial made sense. If the arrest had been for a traffic violation, then the denial did not make sense. The report did not specify. This effort, like others, had little meaningful impact on juvenile delinquency.[35]

The LA government generally tended to overemphasize the level of gang activity in the city. The various special committees and modifications in city procedures such as the dance hall permits indicated that, for the most part, the City of Los Angeles neither regretted nor hoped to change the situation that led to the unfair prosecution in the Sleepy Lagoon case or the Zoot Suit Riots. The city and its police force would continue to come down hard on Mexican Americans. Just a few years after these events, in December 1951, at least fifty officers brutally beat seven men, primarily Mexican Americans, held in the city jail. This "Bloody Christmas" incident was again met with investigations and calls for professionalization, which again did little.[36]

The City of Houston offers an interesting counterpoint to Los Angeles. Houston had seen its Mexican American population increase significantly beginning in the 1920s. Like other Southwestern cities, Houston continued to have problems with law enforcement's treatment of Mexican-origin people. Take the case of Elpidio Cortez, a Mexican national who died from injuries he received from Houston Police Department (HPD) officers R. V. Harrelson and A. H. Schomburg in early 1937. They had gone to the Cortez home after neighbors reported a domestic dispute between him and his wife. During the arrest, Schomburg repeatedly struck Cortez on the head with a blackjack. A neighbor reported that the blows rendered him unconscious. The officers then dragged Cortez to their patrol car and repeatedly slammed his legs in the car door. Cortez was booked into the city jail, where he died a few hours later from his injuries.[37]

Because Cortez was a foreign national, the Mexican government took a keen interest in this case. Mexican consular officials in Texas secured the aid of San Antonio attorney Manuel Gonzalez to assist in legal action against the two officers. Cortez's wife spurred this activity. She, with the assistance of Gonzalez, called for an investigation and the prosecution of Harrelson and Schomburg. The two men stood trial for Cortez's murder in the summer of 1937. The officers claimed that they had trouble understanding Cortez when he spoke Spanish, that he had made threatening gestures, that Schomburg had subdued him with his blackjack by striking him only on the body, and that Cortez had jumped from the patrol car in an attempt to escape, where-upon he had fallen and injured his head. Blood spatter at the Cortez home indicated that his head wound had occurred there, and the autopsy showed not only this injury but injuries to Cortez's shins, which corroborated the eyewitness account that his legs had been slammed in the car door. The jury found the two police officers not guilty.[38]

The Elpidio Cortez incident remained in the consciousness of the Mexican American community and ultimately bled into Houston's response to pachucos. The pachuco phenomenon in Houston mirrored that of Los Angeles. Houstonians of Mexican ancestry expressed their sense of pachuquismo beginning in the 1940s. In some cases, they joined local gangs, but often they simply wore zoot suits and flaunted their sense of style. As in LA, they also had violent encounters with police. John J. Herrera, who would serve as national president of the League of United Latin American Citizens (LULAC) in 1952–53, noted that Houston police frequently hassled and beat pachucos.

Others remembered a common police practice whereby officers would simply stop pachucos, handcuff them, cut their hair, and then release them. Herrera also recalled the case of Frank Sánchez, a twenty-year-old zoot-suiter police arrested for allegedly stealing a hat. Several officers brutally beat Sánchez. Jail staff later found him hanging in his cell. Police claimed he had died by suicide, but Herrera, who investigated the case, discovered that police had kicked Sánchez so violently that he probably suffocated. Herrera surmised that officers hung Sánchez after he died as a way to cover up their involvement in his death.[39]

As in LA, Houston's leaders actively linked pachucos with gang activity. Many Mexican Americans also wanted to see gang activity curbed. They hoped as well that police would work to eliminate language barriers that had frequently caused problems in the past, such as in the Elpidio Cortez case. The idea of creating a Latin American police squad seemed to give both the Mexican American community and the police department what they wanted. The HPD launched the Latin American Squad in July 1944 after hearing demands from Herrera and other Mexican American leaders who desired police accountability and officers who spoke Spanish. Police Chief Percy Heard, with the backing of Mayor Otis Massey, instead formed the group to combat pachucos, possibly in an attempt to avoid the violence that had occurred in LA. The squad was headed by Officer George Bell, who had lived in Mexico for several years and spoke Spanish. Since the HPD had few Spanish-speaking officers, the department hired Manuel Crespo, an immigrant from Spain, and several members of the local chapter of LULAC as noncommissioned officers.[40]

The Latin American Squad had several functions. It promoted understanding between the police and the Mexican-origin community by having officers who spoke Spanish patrol Mexican-dominant sections of the city, primarily the second and third wards. The squad also recruited community members who spoke Spanish for ride-alongs with non-Spanish-speaking police officers. Moreover, these ride-alongs operated as a method for Mexican Americans to monitor the police. A number of Mexican American leaders promoted the squad. Houston LULAC Council no. 60 president Dr. John Ruiz, for instance, not only supported the formation of the squad but called for its expansion. The presence of Manuel Crespo, a burgeoning leader, also mattered to the Mexican American community.[41]

For the HPD, the Latin American Squad's most important function was to combat pachucos and destroy Mexican American gangs, which the local press also fixated on. Newspapers reported on the incarceration of a number of alleged Mexican American gang members a few days after the squad's formation.[42] At the same time, word began to spread that Officer Bell had served in the Texas Rangers. For Mexican-origin people, no organization better represented anti-Mexican racism and police brutality. So Mexican American leaders began calling for the squad's dismissal. Since the HPD believed that it had decimated Mexican American gang activity, Chief Heard disbanded the Latin American Squad in 1945.[43]

Shortly after the squad's demise, Manuel Crespo resigned from the force in 1946. Although the termination of the Latin American Squad displeased him, Crespo had grown increasingly disappointed with the racism directed at him by his White colleagues. His fellow officers regularly ignored Crespo, refused to share office space with him, and on one occasion vandalized his desk, destroying important case material. The HPD did not want to investigate this harassment, so Crespo chose to leave the force and concentrate on his family's funeral home business instead.[44]

In 1947 the newly elected mayor Oscar Holcombe replaced Chief Heard with Banyon W. Payne. Chief Payne decided to try the Latin American Squad concept twice again. He founded a new squad and again appointed Officer George Bell to head the group in 1947. It might seem odd that city leaders founded another version of the squad, considering that almost all pachuco activity had ceased in Houston, but then the squad had always been based on presumptions of criminality and had worked as a form of racial control. The new squad accomplished relatively little while incurring the wrath of community leaders such as John Ruiz. He had promoted the Latin American Squad in 1944, but in 1947 he called for its disbanding. Dr. Ruiz acknowledged that Payne had "good intentions . . . but time has shown that this action [re-forming the squad] was not only unsatisfactory but detrimental to the efficiency of the Police Department." He noted that the squad had created "ill feelings" and that the HPD had "lost many Latin as well as Anglo American friends because of this Squad." Payne disbanded the squad in 1947.[45]

New gang pressures in 1950 prompted Chief Payne, with Mayor Holcombe's blessing, to announce yet another Latin American Squad. The police responded to what the *Houston Chronicle* called a "wave of Latin-American gang crimes." Officer Bell once again headed the Latin American Squad. The new squad concentrated almost exclusively on policing all Mexican Americans, not just gangs. It thus lost any semblance of community outreach and instead operated as a predatory unit in the Mexican American community.[46]

The re-forming of the squad caused a backlash from Mexican American leaders in Houston. John J. Herrera criticized the squad, calling it "discriminatory." He encouraged city leaders to hire Mexican American police, lamenting that "the city doesn't seem to want Latin-American officers on the force."[47] Herrera's critiques caused Chief Payne to backtrack almost immediately. He explained that he was not re-forming the Latin American Squad and that he had merely transferred several Spanish-speaking officers to the homicide division.[48]

Herrera also criticized how the police and local media depicted Mexican-origin people. The press especially made little distinction between Mexican American youths who wore zoot suits in the 1940s, pachucos and pachucas, gang members of the 1950s, and actual criminals. To the police and the press, they were all "thugs" and their behavior was "organized hoodlumism."[49] Herrera lashed out at this bias. "There are no organized gangs of Latin-Americans in Houston," he asserted. "The newspapers are playing up the gangsterism, while a few police officers are exaggerating it."[50] He soon announced a special meeting of LULAC members to address Mexican American and police relations, which took place on March 16, 1950. More than 400 people attended. In addition to discussing the media and police biases, the meeting focused on education, jobs, and extracurricular activities for Mexican American youth. LULACers such as Herrera offered a systematic analysis of Mexican American criminality in the Bayou City. He noted that a lack of educational equality led to a loss of job opportunities for Mexican-origin youths, while a lack of extracurricular activities led to delinquency. He hoped for more than an end to biased reporting or police behavior—he sought reform to reduce crime. Herrera didn't really get what he wanted, so LULAC in Houston in ensuing years would focus on education and outreach to accomplish what the local government would not.[51]

Houston differed from Los Angeles. Although the initial alleged gang pressures and pachuquismo, as well as the fear of a Houston zoot suit riot, were similar, Houston responded differently than LA. The idea of the Latin American Squad was novel and desired by both Mexican Americans and police leadership. It didn't go the way Mexican Americans wanted, but the idea was a good one. In the coming years, police-community relations would take on new and important roles; the Latin American Squad prefigured those efforts.

Violence committed by police agents against pachucos was matched by other instances of police abuse and killing. Perhaps no better example of law enforcement's racist and brutal violence exists than the example of Sheriff Robert Vail Ennis of Beeville, Texas.[52] Ennis had a long history of violent behavior. He had beaten a Mexican man with a heavy chain and then allegedly shot and killed this unarmed man. He also killed an African American man he had arrested in his jail cell.[53] In an even more serious incident, in 1945 Ennis killed three Mexican Americans, brothers Felix, Domingo, and Antonio Rodriguez. The Rodriguez brothers, all respected local farmers, had lived outside of Beeville for thirty years. Exactly what happened remains unclear because Ennis killed these men. He had gone to the Rodriguez farmhouse to retrieve two of their grandchildren as part of an obligation in a custody dispute. The brothers allegedly refused to let the children leave. Ennis returned to Beeville, deputized a man named Joe Walton, and contacted Texas Ranger Frank Probst. All three returned to the Rodriguez home. Ennis threw tear gas into the house, and when Felix and Domingo emerged, he shot them dead with a Thompson submachine gun. He then saw Antonio at the opposite end of the house and shot him.[54]

Sheriff Ennis claimed he acted in self-defense, but his story lack credibility and he was arrested and tried for murder. A jury acquitted him.[55] Ennis killed seven men during his time as sheriff, including four Mexican Americans and one African American. Dr. Hector P. Garcia, chair of the American GI Forum (a veterans and civic organization founded by Garcia in 1948) and forty-six other community leaders and civic organizations telegrammed Governor Allan Shivers asking that he "publicly condemn any discriminatory or segregatory acts against our American people." The signers demanded "legislation to protect our rights and to give us equal opportunity and protection under the law." Last, in wording that anticipated the psychological testing that police agencies would begin adopting in the 1960s and 1970s, they requested "that any and all public officials be interrogated as to prejudices against our people and if they show same not to be hired or allowed to occupy any public position."[56]

In many ways Dr. Garcia and the other signees responded to the sheriff with a threat. They had begun to discern that Mexican Americans had far more power than was popularly assumed. They demonstrated that power a few years later when Sheriff Ennis ran for reelection. The American GI Forum came out hard against him. The Mexican American community, angered by the sheriff's willingness to kill and disappointed by the outcome of his trial for slaying the Rodriguez brothers, voted overwhelmingly against Ennis. He lost reelection by a wide margin. Ennis tried again in 1954. Again, Mexican Americans voted against him in large numbers. He lost again.[57] The Beeville example shows that, while suffering abuse, Mexican Americans could also wield a level of power. They pushed for an investigation and trial, and they cost Ennis his bid for reelection.

Another example of senseless police violence comes from Arizona. In the small town of Tolleson in the 1940s an unnamed officer got into a fight with a man named Luis Salas. Salas beat this officer, who in turn wounded Salas in the ankle. The officer was determined to exact revenge on Salas. He later thought he saw Salas exiting a bar. Even though the man did not limp, the officer was certain it was him. So he ran him over with his patrol car, killing him. It wasn't Salas (and even if it were, running over a person isn't justice). Instead, the officer killed a farmworker named Ignacio Ruiz. The officer received no punishment for this killing.[58]

Police also continued to use stock descriptions and misnomers such as "unknown Mex" well into the mid-twentieth century.[59] For example, police agencies communicated with each other via the *Denver Police Bulletin*. The Denver Police Department produced the *Bulletin*, which they distributed across the West and Southwest. It operated as a clearinghouse for police agencies and published information from departments in numerous locales. The *Bulletin* frequently discussed Mexican-origin people, usually with references to "unknown Mexican." In February 1947 Denver police sought "Unknown, alias Tony, Mexican" in connection with a purse snatching.[60] The following month the *Bulletin* noted that police wanted two "safe burglars." The first was an "Unknown Mexican, age 28–30, 5-7-8, 150 lb., chunky build, dark complexion, dark eyes, long Black hair combed straight back, broad nose flat at base." The second was "Unknown Mexican, smaller than No.1."[61] Police tried to be slightly more specific in April when they announced that they sought "Degenerate, Unknown Mexican" who either had "one bad eye or it is missing."[62] In June 1947, the *Bulletin* listed an "Unknown Mexican" in connection with a stabbing who was "age 18, 5-10 to 6ft., 150 lb., slender build, dark comp., brown eyes, Black hair, tan pants and shirt which may be army uniform, tan cap." In all of these cases the "Unknown Mexican" could quite literally have been anyone, considering that there were no doubt thousands of eighteen-year-olds who were around six feet tall, weighing 150 pounds, slender, with black hair and brown eyes.[63]

Police also continued to arrest Mexican Americans simply to harass them. For instance, police often arrested Mexican Americans on charges of vagrancy only to release them, a common type of harassment. As I noted in *Borders of Violence and Justice*, vagrancy also led to peonage and prison labor. In one notable example, community historian Emma Moya recounted how two Albuquerque Police Department officers approached a fourteen-year-old boy playing in his own yard and then began dragging him to their squad car. When the youth yelled for help, his parents emerged from their home and demanded to know why the officers had accosted their son. They responded that they were arresting him for vagrancy. When the parents logically retorted that their son was playing in his own yard, the officers arrested all three: the child for vagrancy and the parents for interfering with an arrest. A relative bailed the parents out of jail, but the boy spent two weeks in custody.[64] These types of arrests, quotidian and widespread, contributed to bad relations between Mexican Americans and police, leading to continued distrust in the decades to come.

Perhaps nothing contributed to the degradation of relations between Mexican Americans and police more than the infamous massive deportation campaign of 1954, called Operation Wetback. Although the US government had launched a World War II–era guest worker initiative called the Bracero Program that brought millions of Mexican workers to the United States, undocumented immigration also continued in the postwar period. Thus the government's response to what many saw as an exploding Mexican population was to systematically round up and deport Mexican, or Mexican-looking, people. The US Border Patrol, assisted by local law enforcement agencies across the United States, forcibly deported nearly 1.5 million people. About 25 percent of those, or 375,000, were American citizens of Mexican ancestry.[65]

There were a number of problems with Operation Wetback. For one, it again used local law enforcement to achieve a federal purpose. Second, it was based on the same racist thinking that characterized other mass deportation campaigns—namely, that Mexican people had overrun the United States and taken jobs from the native born. Third, the government's deportation of so many Americans meant that Operation Wetback worked as a massive form of racial profiling. Anyone who happened to look "Mexican" got rounded up, including US citizens and legally authorized guest workers such as braceros. Last, as quickly as it began, it ended.[66]

While Operation Wetback continued to demonstrate the heavy-handed use of law enforcement by the federal government, again often in collusion with local law enforcement, Mexican Americans turned to policing as a form of redress. A number of groups and individuals put pressure on local police departments to hire more Mexican American officers as a method of improving relations. This is another good example that shows that Mexican Americans weren't opposed to policing itself but rather to abusive, bad policing. John J. Herrera had argued that one way the HPD could improve the degradation in the relationship between police and the Mexican American community after the failure(s) of the Latin American Squad was by hiring Mexican American officers. Police Chief Banyon Payne didn't initially respond to this demand, but Harris County sheriff Clairville V. "Buster" Kern did. Kern planned to look into hiring Mexican American officers for the sheriff's department.[67]

Houston Police Department officer Raul Martinez at the Pan America Nightclub with an unidentified man in the early 1950s. Martinez was the first of two officers of Mexican ancestry to graduate from the Houston Police Academy in July 1950. He went on to have a long and distinguished career in law enforcement in Houston. *MSS0101-0092, Houston History Research Center, Houston Public Library.*

The HPD did begin a recruiting effort designed to hire Mexican American police officers in 1950. The first Mexican Americans accepted into the police academy, Raul C. Martinez and Eddie Barrios, both graduated in July 1950. Martinez became a fixture in the local law enforcement community, received numerous promotions, and in the 1970s was appointed to the Harris County constable's office, later winning election as constable of Precinct 6. Martinez became a police officer to help the Mexican American community. "When I went to work for the Houston Police Department, I felt I owed the community this duty," Martinez noted. "I took it more as an obligation than a job." He understood the problems that affected Mexican Americans, so he viewed his police work as akin to social service. He remarked that part of his "job is to work with people and guide them in every way I can." Many times, Martinez acknowledged, when individuals, especially Mexican Americans, encountered him they expected the worst. "But all they want is someone to listen," he said, and "when someone listens, they feel better."[68]

Constable Martinez's example is a good one. But there were others. Fort Worth brought on Juan M. Gonzalez as that city's first Mexican American police officer in 1957. He served the city for twenty-eight years.[69] In Texas City, Savas Saragosa became the city's first Mexican American officer and served for forty-two years.[70] Midland hired Sid Trevino in about 1955.[71] Austin had hired its first officers of Mexican ancestry in 1920, but they did not expand this pool until the 1950s. One of the individuals hired in 1954, Leonard Flores, started out as a patrol officer and the Austin Police Department (APD) promoted him as the first Mexican American detective in 1960.[72] He had some interesting experiences. In one case, he responded to a robbery at a bar. Flores found a man standing on the porch of the establishment with a knife in one hand and a wad of cash in the other. "Drop that knife," Flores demanded. "Make me!" was the response. So, he did: "I just walked up and knocked him on the hand with my billy club," Flores said. He disarmed the man and then returned the money to the shocked bartender. Detective Flores retired in 1989 after thirty-five years on the force.[73]

The hiring of one officer led to others. John Vasquez applied to the APD in 1961, but they rejected him at first because he did not meet the height requirements. As it turned out, he did, the department simply had a habit of rejecting Mexican Americans because they believed they were short. Vasquez informed the APD of the error, and he was hired. Later, he sought to become a sergeant, and although the police administration tried to dissuade him from applying, he passed the sergeant's exam, becoming the first Mexican American sergeant in the APD's history. The department then promoted him to lieutenant and he took over leadership of the recruiting office. "I want minority men to know that I feel they not only will be hired and treated fairly, but will be promoted like any other officer," Vasquez explained.[74] He also expanded his focus beyond "minority men"; in 1976 he hired Austin's first female police officer.[75]

Victor Campos, the first Mexican American officer to serve the New Braunfels, Texas, police, also had an interesting career.[76] He got caught up in some of the tensions of the period. Campos served the New Braunfels Police Department well, but after several years of service, in 1964 he left to become head of security at the Camp Gary Job Corps training facility in neighboring San Marcos. The Job Corps was one of President Lyndon Johnson's Great Society programs; it offered technical training to economically disadvantaged young people.[77] Alas, some considered it a kind of welfare for sixties radicals. A few years later, Campos applied for a position as assistant chief with the New Braunfels police and got the job. But a number of officers protested the appointment, which the city rescinded. It seems some officers considered Campos too sympathetic to 1960s radicals.[78]

New Mexico had focused on the hiring of Mexican American police officers decades earlier than Texas.[79] In 1936 the *New Mexico Sheriff and Police* journal listed approximately 30 male Spanish-surnamed law officers out of 233 officers in the New Mexico Sheriff and Police Association. This made Spanish-surnamed officers a significant 13 percent of association members.[80] New Mexican cities also focused on hiring women as police officers. Going back to the 1920s, Albuquerque had attempted to bring more Mexican Americans into policing by focusing on women. Law enforcement had long used the services of women, but usually as volunteer workers doing dispatching or, if paid, as secretarial or clerical staff.[81] Albuquerque had unpaid female officers as far back as the 1910s. They city began a new recruiting effort to hire women—and pay them—in 1922 but ultimately could not come up with the monies to pay for female officers.[82]

By the mid-twentieth century women began to enter police forces as commissioned officers more regularly. Albuquerque's Elisa Holguin became one of the first women to serve in the Bernalillo County Sheriff's Office. She began her career in 1951 as a deputy sheriff, a "law lady," to borrow a term from the period. Deputy Holguin had a number of roles to play in the sheriff's office, some of which may sound clichéd or even sexist by today's standards. For example, the department did not allow her to walk a beat; instead, she served as the office secretary, record keeper, and jail "matron." She also had the important job of radio operator; police leadership often saw dispatch as a safe way for women to participate in law enforcement. But Holguin performed riskier roles. For example, she supervised the booking of all women into the county jail. She also helped break up a "riot" at the county's girls welfare home and then searched the girls who had revolted.[83] The Albuquerque Police Department also recruited Mexican American men and women. In 1968 the police academy graduated eighteen men and four women. Three of the men and one woman were of Mexican origin.[84]

Mexican Americans also served in other aspects of the criminal justice system in New Mexico. For many years, Felipe Sanchez y Baca served as the US marshal for the District of New Mexico. One of his duties involved keeping track of trials and federal prisoners not housed in federal prisons, a difficult and often cumbersome job that required him not only to account for these individuals but also to ensure that the state cared for them properly. In December 1935 he reported that there were thirty-nine men and one woman in prison. By January 1937 the numbers had jumped. A total of seventy-three men and four women awaited trial, three women served jail sentences, and seven men awaited transfer to a federal institution. The responsibility of caring for this growing number of individuals was no small task.[85]

Like New Mexico, Arizona had a long history of employing Mexican American police officers. Some of the state's "firsts" led to others. For example, the City of Mesa hired Ramon S. Mendoza Sr. in 1922 as the city's first Mexican American officer. Mendoza had a relatively uneventful career and retired in 1942.[86] Ramon Mendoza Jr. followed in his father's footsteps and joined the force in 1951.[87] He rose steadily through the ranks and by 1954 held the rank of captain. In 1961, the department promoted him to the newly created position of assistant chief. Mendoza was not just the first assistant chief of Mexican ancestry, he was the first assistant police chief. In 1969 the city appointed him chief of police.[88] He made a number of important reforms consistent with the climate of the 1960s. While Mendoza was not hostile to the civil rights movement, like other chiefs he expanded police training for riot situations and purchased $1,500 worth of riot gear as a response to civil rights activism.[89] Mendoza also presided over an expansion of the Mesa Police Department's facilities, which hadn't changed much since the 1930s. He also refocused the force by explicitly concentrating on police-community relations.[90] Community relations was an important part of policing in the 1960s and 1970s, and Chief Mendoza was at the forefront of this type of reform. He ultimately served thirty-six years on the Mesa police force and retired in 1978.[91]

While California cities such as Los Angeles or San Diego had long employed Mexican American officers, other smaller cities began hiring Mexican

American officers at midcentury. In Oxnard, for instance, Robert Hinostro joined the force in 1938 as an auxiliary officer, the first Mexican American to do so. He became a sworn officer in 1943. Throughout his career Hinostro advocated to bring other Mexican Americans onto the force. One of these individuals, Rodolfo Ruiz, became an auxiliary officer at Hinostro's request. But Hinostro later found out that Ruiz wasn't an American citizen, which would bar him from service. So he helped Ruiz get his citizenship, and Ruiz went on to become an officer. Hinostro climbed the ranks and even served a stint as chief in 1950. He retired in 1958 after twenty years on the force.[92]

Other smaller municipalities in California followed Oxnard. Huntington Beach hired Luis Ochoa as its first Mexican American police officer in 1965.[93] Pomona hired Robert Rodriguez as its first Mexican American officer in 1953. He was on the force for decades and retired in 1980. In 1982 he ran for a seat on the La Verne city council and won. He served in that position thirty-one years. In many ways Rodriguez epitomized the kind of policing that was like social service, so much so that he continued his public service as an elected official.[94]

Los Angeles had hired a number of Mexican American officers throughout its history, but the LAPD made additional progress in 1946 when it hired Josephine Serrano Collier, the first woman of Mexican ancestry in the force's history. Serrano Collier was one of the many Rosy the Riveters, but at the end of World War II Lockheed terminated her employment, and she needed work. When she decided to apply to the LAPD against the wishes of her fiancé, he actually ended their relationship. She persisted and applied along with 200 other women. Of that 200, the department accepted twenty-one for training, of which only nine made it through to become officers. Serrano Collier was one of these nine. She walked a beat in Lincoln Heights for fourteen years. She retired in 1960, in part because she developed a back problem, probably because she had to walk her beat in high heels.[95]

The hiring of Mexican American police officers was an important step for Southwestern police forces. That hiring came largely from the efforts of the Mexican American community. As John J. Herrera and others had argued, having Mexican Americans on police forces might help avert problematic interactions that Mexican-origin people sometimes had with police. If law enforcement and local governments viewed Mexican Americans negatively because of the popular perceptions of the time about delinquency or gangs, Mexican Americans in law enforcement might serve to counter those perceptions. This service is also another indication that the Mexican American community did not oppose or dislike police. Instead they proved willing to serve to help improve police-community relations. Despite the numbers of Mexican Americans hired by police agencies across the Southwest in this period, relatively little changed in the day-to-day operation of police departments. Hiring a couple of Mexican Americans would of course not solve policing problems.

The period between the 1940s and 1960s was an important one. It represented both a continuation of abusive police practices as well as some fundamental alterations in the policing of Mexican Americans. Certainly the hiring of Mexican American police officers signified a step in the right direction, although those officers could not singlehandedly change the relationship between local police forces and Mexican-origin people. The Latin American Squad concept had the chance of making substantive and broad change, but the fact that the program became mired in controversy limited its success. Yet its goal of having Spanish-speaking officers represented a communitywide and community-specific manner of addressing policing problems.

The police and media fixation on pachucos and zoot-suiters contributed to a degradation of police relations with the Mexican American community. The fear of pachucos, gang violence, and juvenile delinquency, most of which was overblown, meant that city governments and their police forces viewed Mexican American young people reductively as criminally prone. Criminal activity is never so simple. But that fixation led to police harassment and ultimately to the violence of the Zoot Suit Riots. The subsequent investigations, for the most part, blamed Mexican Americans for the violence they experienced and doubled down on policing yet again.

While there was also a great deal more activism in these years, from the political campaign that defeated Sheriff Ennis in Texas to the efforts to initiate reforms after the violence in Los Angeles, this period largely prefigured the days of direct action. That movement was coming, though. Much of the Mexican American struggle for civil rights focused on the police abuse and violence that Mexican-origin people had long experienced and would continue to experience in the decades to come. The Chicano movement made opposing this abuse a major component of the period's activism, especially the abuse that movement participants experienced.

TWO

LIKE KILLING A DOG

The Struggle to End Police
Violence against Chicano
Movement Participants

The groundwork laid by Mexican American individuals, activists, and leaders between the 1940s and early 1960s sowed the seeds for a sustained civil rights struggle in the decades that followed. While we generally think of the civil rights movement as a 1960s phenomenon, for Mexican Americans the struggle lasted well into the 1980s. The Chicano movement, the name of the activist phase of the Mexican American freedom struggle, saw some of the most intense protests the Southwest had ever witnessed. The movement had numerous goals: improved education and desegregation; opposition to the war in Vietnam; workers' rights; and increased political participation. But battling police abuse was at the forefront of the Chicano movement.

For Chicano activists, nothing bespoke police mistreatment better than police harassment and murder of movement participants. In Texas, Chicanos faced an old foe: the Texas Rangers. Along with local police forces, the Rangers engaged in violence to halt nascent Chicano activism. Another well-known case happened in Albuquerque when a group of law enforcement officers from several police agencies gathered themselves in an unauthorized task force and killed Black Berets Antonio Cordova and Rito Canales in 1972. Their deaths spawned a host of protests and ultimately resulted in some police reforms. When added to the generally bad law enforcement climate, as well as the killings of other Chicano activists such as Luis "Junior" Martinez in Colorado in 1973, among many others, the movement suffered a lot.

Chicanos put the criminal justice system on notice that they would no longer tolerate violence and harassment. They had reason to give that notice. While law enforcement had long been abusive toward Mexican-origin people, a movement designed in part to challenge that abuse generated additional forms of repression and abuse from police. Local governments and their police forces came to see the Chicano movement as un-American and communistic and Chicanos as latter-day pachucos who needed to be controlled. One way to control them was by arresting and imprisoning activists. Another tactic was to kill movement participants.[1] Yet, even in the face of that opposition and brutality, Chicanos still had good ideas about how to reform police. This again shows that Mexican Americans were not antipolice; they were antipolice brutality or antipolice murder. Although law enforcement did not always respond favorably to these efforts, many departments chose to work with Chicanos as opposed to continuing a hostile relationship. This helped set the stage for a better, more constructive type of policing.

The mid-1960s represented the genesis of the Chicano movement. That period saw the development of new organizations, most importantly the Brown Berets, as well as other groups, that Chicanos founded to confront police violence. Many of the organizations created in this period had challenging police abuse as a major goal. Additionally, already established groups came out strongly against police abuse. Chicanos also linked many of their protests with demonstrations against the Vietnam War. The efforts begun in this period helped to initiate some reforms in law enforcement and the broader criminal justice system. But Mexican Americans experienced a lot of pain and violence from police as the movement took off.

Police in California were particularly notorious for their heavy handedness. So, Chicanos developed one of the most important civil rights groups to emerge in this period: the Brown Berets. They arose a year after the Watts Rebellion in Los Angeles in August 1965, a six-day uprising against police violence. While the initial incident did not involve Mexican Americans, they did participate in the postrebellion investigation conducted by

Four of the original Brown Berets in Los Angeles, 1968. *From left to right:*
Fred Lopez, David Sánchez, Carlos Montes, and Ralph Ramirez. The Berets made
challenging police abuse and violence a major part of the Chicano movement. All
four men had experienced police harassment and brutality. As the Berets spread
across the Southwest, all chapters would make opposing police abuse a critical
focus of their activism. *Los Angeles Times Photographic Archive, UCLA Library Special
Collections, Los Angeles.*

the McCone Commission, which noted, "We are deeply conscious that the
Mexican-American community, which here is almost equal in size to the
Negro community, suffers from similar and in some cases more severe
handicaps than the Negro community."[2]

Mexican American didn't need the McCone Commission to tell them
what they already knew. A number of area youths, including David Sánchez, Carlos Montes, Vickie Castro, and Moctesuma Esparza, among others,
formed the Young Citizens for Community Action in Los Angeles in 1966,
the precursor to the Brown Berets, to focus on political participation and
education reform. But, as Carlos Montes noted, "We first took on the issue of
police brutality" because many in the group had experienced it.[3] In January
1968, they rebranded themselves the Brown Berets and transformed into a
self-defense group that protected the Mexican American community from
police brutality and other forms of state violence. Autonomous chapters of

the Berets spread quickly to many Southwestern communities and to cities as far away as Chicago.[4]

The Brown Berets Ten Point Program focused heavily on the criminal justice system. Four of the ten points in the program demanded policing or criminal justice reform:

- Point 3. We demand a Civilian Police Review Board, made up of people who live in our community, to screen all police officers, before they are assigned to our communities.
- Point 5. We demand that all officers in Mexican-American communities must live in the community and speak Spanish.
- Point 9. We demand that all Mexican Americans be tried by juries consisting of only Mexican Americans.
- Point 10. We demand the right to keep and bear arms to defend our communities against racist police, as guaranteed under the Second Amendment of the US Constitution.

These demands about policing and the criminal justice system accounted for 40 percent of the Ten Point Program, the most of any single topic (Points 2 and 4 were about education; 1, 6, and 7 were mainly about economics; 8 was about voting). Brown Berets made policing such a focal point of their activism because they knew how detrimental it was for the Mexican American community. Their example makes clear how central policing was to Chicano activism.[5] In fact, their first protest in LA was at a sheriff's station after a Mexican American man died in custody.[6]

The Brown Berets had additional reasons to focus on policing. Although the police had harassed them individually, Los Angeles police had begun targeting the group in early 1968. For instance, the Los Angeles Police Department arrested a number of Brown Berets for allegedly possessing an AR-15 rifle. The LAPD acted on a tip from the Federal Bureau of Investigation (FBI), which claimed that the Berets had stolen the rifle from Camp Pendleton, a nearby Marine Corps base, but this seems far-fetched, and it is unclear if the police ever located the rifle.[7] In March 1968 a group of East LA high school students engaged in massive school walkouts known as the Blowouts. The Brown Berets worked to protect the students from police, who targeted, beat, and arrested a large number of students and Berets.[8] The LAPD later arrested thirteen individuals for conspiracy to disrupt the peace, among them leaders David Sánchez, Carlos Montes, Moctesuma Esparza, and teacher Sal Castro.[9] This group, known as the Eastside 13 or East LA 13, faced over sixty

Two LAPD officers keep watch on a Chicano protest at the police headquarters building on June 2, 1968. The individuals involved were protesting the arrest of the East LA 13, which included several members of the Brown Berets and popular teacher Sal Castro. Although the district attorney later dropped all charges against the activists, law enforcement in Los Angeles would continue to monitor, infiltrate, and disrupt Chicano protests. *Herald Examiner Collection, Los Angeles Public Library.*

years in prison if convicted. The FBI called the East LA 13 "high school drop outs, dope addicts, militant racists and hoodlums." None of that was true.[10]

The arrest of the East LA 13 touched off a long series of protests by Chicano activists in Los Angeles. A large group gathered to protest at the LA Justice Building. Apparently for the FBI the protestors were an "anti-White group of American-Mexican youth."[11] Although the East LA 13 were released on bail in 1968, it took until 1970 for a judge to throw out the indictments against them. Meanwhile, the Brown Berets continued to protest. For instance, they traveled to Oxnard to protest police brutality in August 1968. Although the Berets criticized Oxnard police, allegedly calling them "White helmeted dogs," the *Oxnard Press Courier* noted that "it appears the Brown Berets have a vast potential for bettering conditions for the Mexican-American population in Oxnard."[12]

The Brown Berets also protested against the war in Vietnam, which also brought them into contact with police. Chicanos had valid concerns; the war drew them in at numbers well above their percentage of the population, resulting in a high casualty and wounded rates.[13] In July 1970, the National Chicano Antiwar Moratorium, the main Chicano antiwar group, began a protest that merged concerns about the war and police abuse. This protest stemmed from the police killings of Guillermo and Beltran Sanchez. Five LAPD officers and two other law enforcement agents raided Guillermo Sanchez's apartment seeking a robbery suspect. Sanchez had not been involved in any criminal activity, but when he opened his door, police opened fire. His cousin Beltran tried to flee, and police shot him, too. Thus, the protest, called by an antiwar group, was really about police murder. The Brown Berets noted that they protested state power that "gives law agencies a free hand to 'shoot first and make excuses later.'"[14]

The Brown Berets followed this demonstration by joining thousands of other Chicano activists in massive Moratorium protests against the Vietnam War across the Southwest in August 1970. At the Los Angeles protest nearly 30,000 activists marched through East LA and joined in a rally at Laguna Park (today Salazar Park). Officers of the LA Sheriff's Department stormed the demonstration, fired tear gas, and beat and arrested numerous marchers. They also called in reinforcements from the LAPD. Law enforcement killed four participants. A Brown Beret named Lynn Ward died after a police tear gas grenade exploded near him. Police shot Angel Gilbert Diaz to death after he allegedly tried to drive through a police barricade.[15] The killing of Gustav Montag and Ruben Salazar proved the most startling. Montag, a Jewish activist, and several Chicanos found themselves trapped in a blind alley after a police chase. As officers aimed their weapons, Montag and the others attempted to repel them by throwing bottles and rocks. LA County deputy sheriffs opened fire, killing Montag. Ruben Salazar's death was more troubling. He served as the voice of the Chicano community at the *Los Angeles Times* and had written editorials critical of police. Two deputy sheriffs found Salazar, who had taken refuge from the police onslaught at a bar, and shot him in the head with a tear gas canister.[16]

Investigations into the violence at the Moratorium march were pretty one-sided. The LAPD released flyers from a rally protesting the deaths of several Chicanos in police custody, which were supposed to show that the Brown Berets were violent. But that protest happened a month earlier and had nothing to do with the Moratorium march.[17] Police also emphasized the alleged violence of the Berets and the Moratorium by showcasing a crudely drawn picture of a Molotov cocktail. But both groups had advocated for self-defense, and few Chicanos had responded to the police with violence at the protest.[18] Last, police blamed Brown Beret leader David Sánchez for the violence, noting that his "fanatical and inflammatory oratory . . . obviously contributed to the trouble that followed." His rhetoric was no more inflammatory than that of any other speaker. Consolidating all of this conspiratorial analysis, the report concluded by noting that the Brown Berets could "best be described as being revolutionary oriented, violent in philosophy, and fanatical in the ideology of liberating the 'Chicano' people from the grip of the 'Anglo Establishment Suppressor.'"[19]

The violence at the Moratorium protest was in fact a police-instigated riot, one of many to occur during the civil rights era.[20] The National Council of La Raza used this violence to explain the continued strained relationship between Mexican Americans and police. According to the council, police violence led to a degradation in police-community relations. But it also discovered a basic disjuncture in the way police analyzed that violence: the LAPD "did not agree that killings of minorities by the police should be used to indicate the basic state of relations between police and these minorities." The National Council of La Raza noted that without altering that understanding, improving relations would prove impossible.[21]

In Texas, the Texas Rangers remained a problem for Chicano activists. While reform of the Rangers in the 1920s and 1930s had been beneficial, they still wielded great power and often acted abusively.[22] For example, when five Mexican American politicians ran for the city council in Crystal City in 1963, Texas governor John Connally dispatched Ranger captain Alfred Y. Allee to "keep the peace." Allee was a vicious racist who used his police power to brutalize people. He beat activist José Angel Gutiérrez one night after a rally.[23] The violence could not stop the election of the five Mexican American candidates, but then, their election did not stop Ranger violence either.[24] Shortly after the election, the new mayor, Juan Cornejo, demanded that the Rangers leave Crystal City. Allee responded by picking Cornejo up and banging his head against a wall. Allee was never punished, and the Rangers remained in Crystal City for several weeks.[25]

A few years later, in 1966, Mexican Americans struck to protest low wages and poor treatment in the Rio Grande Valley during the Starr County Strike, which once again saw the Rangers swing into action. Governor Connally dispatched A. Y. Allee, who, along with local law enforcement, harassed and abused strikers.[26] University of Texas professor George I. Sánchez called the Rangers "the private strong arm of the Governor."[27] He was right. In one frightening instance, police arrested strike leader Domingo Arredondo for shouting "Viva la huelga" (long live the strike) in the Rio Grande City courthouse. A deputy sheriff punched Arredondo, forced him against a wall, pointed a gun at his head, and told him that the courthouse was a "respectful place" and not to speak.[28]

Perhaps the worst example of this violence befell Magdaleno Dimas. According to court records, Dimas had left his house to go hunting when the Rangers rolled up in mid-1967. Seeing them, he dropped his .22-caliber rifle and ran back into his home. Dimas had had prior violent encounters with the Rangers, and Captain Allee specifically. The Rangers broke down the door and arrested Dimas and another Mexican American man for unspecified reasons. In what became known as the Dimas Incident, at the jail Allee and other Rangers beat these men throughout the night. Dimas later received hospital care for broken bones, internal bleeding, and a concussion. Allee claimed that the men's injuries came from colliding with a door while running back into the house during the arrest. Several doctor's reports painted a different picture: Dimas spent five days in the hospital with a concussion, multiple lacerations, and a "blow to the lower portion of his back causing the spine to curve out of shape away from the impact point."[29]

The Dimas Incident added to numerous other cases wherein law enforcement infringed on the rights of striking workers. Everyday annoyances, such as when police arrested strikers for parading without a permit even when no permit was required or when they arrested people for shouting obscenities when no one had shouted, added up over time. The Rangers also generally harassed strikers, broke a news reporter's camera, slapped a priest, and beat strikers with their shotguns.[30] In other cases the farm bosses and managers would complain to police and get instant results, but when farmworkers made a complaint, nothing happened. This "selective enforcement of the law" was not only frustrating for activists but also illegal.[31]

A good example of selective enforcement of the law came in 1967 when Ranger Allee arrested activist Francisco "Pancho" Medrano during the Starr County Strike. The United Auto Workers, of which Medrano was a member, had dispatched him to the Rio Grande Valley to observe the picketing farmworkers. Medrano was taking pictures when the Rangers arrived. A Ranger grabbed his camera and punched him in the face with it, breaking the device and ruining the film. Medrano had a second camera, which the Rangers confiscated and exposed the film inside. The Rangers also arrested Medrano and other observers. Medrano sued the Rangers and local law enforcement for violating his rights. He also asked the court to invalidate several statutes that infringed on the rights of striking workers.[32]

Medrano's case ended up in the courtroom of Judge Woodrow Seals, who ruled in Medrano's favor.[33] Seals focused his opinion on the selective nature of Ranger law enforcement: "The arrest, detentions without the filing of charges, seizures of signs, dispersals of pickets and demonstrators, the threats of further prosecutions if pro-union activities did not cease . . . disclose a pattern of action by local authorities designed to halt the strike and to discourage attempts to engage in constitutionally protected conduct in support of the strike." Seals therefore declared five Texas statutes unconstitutional, including two that prohibited picketing. The court also declared three articles in the penal code unconstitutional, including article 439, regarding unlawful assembly; article 474, regarding breach of the peace; and article 482, regarding abusive language. Finally, the court issued a permanent injunction restraining law enforcement from interfering with Medrano and the other defendants.[34] Allee appealed to the Supreme Court in 1974. His attorney argued that the permanent injunction exceeded the district court's authority. The Court disagreed, declaring that "the portion of the District Court's decree enjoining police intimidation of the appellees was an appropriate exercise of the court's equitable powers."[35]

Beginning in 1967 and continuing into 1968, Congress weighed in on the situation in Texas with series of hearings.[36] These hearings brought Texas into the national spotlight and represented a major moment in the Chicano civil rights struggle. The first meeting, conducted by the Texas Conference for the Mexican-American, met in San Antonio in 1967.[37] Another conference called by the US Civil Rights Commission also met in 1967.[38] Most importantly, the Senate Subcommittee on Migratory Labor held a series of hearings in Rio Grande City under the leadership of Harrison Williams (D-NJ) and Edward "Ted" Kennedy (D-MA). Kennedy openly criticized the Rangers. The subcommittee had invited Allee, but he refused to attend, leaving Senator Williams to joke, "Well, one thing I think we can all feel secure about, we are not going to be arrested by any Rangers today."[39] The Civil Rights Commission returned to Texas in December 1968. This hearing at Our Lady of the Lake College was well attended, and Allee finally appeared. It was an embarrassing moment for him. Activists heckled him, he was forced to account for his violence against Mexican-origin people, and he stated, shockingly, that he believed that the reputation of the Rangers among Mexican-origin people was very good.[40]

Violence toward Mexican Americans was by this point standard police practice for the Rangers. Reforms in the 1910s, 1920s, and 1930s had professionalized the Rangers somewhat, but it seems that they simply moved from

Chicano activists affiliated with MAYO and other groups protest the appearance of Texas Ranger captain Alfred Y. Allee at the US Commission on Civil Rights hearings at Our Lady of the Lake College in San Antonio on December 15, 1968. The hearings investigated abuses that Mexican-origin people experienced in many aspects of their lives, including at the hands of law enforcement. Allee had failed to attend other civil rights hearings, so Mexican Americans made sure to shame him when he attended this one. © *San Antonio Express News, University of Texas at Austin.*

killing people to beating them. Not that they weren't beating them before.[41] Ranger abuse was also augmented by local level police abuse.

The Houston Police Department serves as a good example of how local law enforcement attempted to repress the movement. The HPD operated an Intelligence Division that surveilled almost every civil rights demonstration that took place in the city. For example, intelligence officers reported on an antiwar "March for Peace" protest in November 1969. They noted the presence of 1,000 demonstrators, making sure to identify activists such as Carlos Calbillo from the Mexican American Youth Organization (MAYO) and Roy Bartee Haile, then affiliated with the Young Socialist Alliance. During the demonstration an alleged Ku Klux Klan (KKK) member slashed the tires of twenty-five vehicles and planted a bomb on a news van, but police concerned themselves only with identifying the protestors.[42] In a report from 1971 detailing a visit by Cesar Chavez, who came to Houston to promote the United Farm Workers' lettuce boycott, the HPD Intelligence Division mocked Chavez, who "rambled on and gave clumsy and loosely organized speech on solidarity."[43]

When protests of the Vietnam War came to Houston, the HPD was ready. In July 1970, 1,000 demonstrators gathered to condemn the war. Police and a group of marines disrupted the protests and beat many of the protestors.[44] In October 1973 a group called Youth against War and Fascism held a small protest against the war. More than twenty-five patrol cars responded to the demonstration, bringing nearly fifty officers to the scene. They broke up the protest, beat a number of activists, and arrested twelve protestors. Eight of those arrested were Chicanos, including Alex Rodriguez and Miguel Trujillo, who had spearheaded the protest. The other four, all White men, included Roy Bartee Haile. Rodriguez, Trujillo, Haile, and two others were charged with assault with the intent to kill a police officer.[45]

The Houston 12 Defense Committee vigorously protested these arrests. This bore some results when the prosecution dismissed the original indictments for assault with intent to kill a police officer because of bias on the grand jury. They indicted the men again, however.[46] In 1975 the trial of the Houston 12 began. The prosecution dismissed charges against Alex Rodriguez, Miguel Trujillo, and another man. Seven others were fined and released. That left only two Anglos, Bartee Haile and William Christiansen, to stand trial for assault with intent to murder a police officer. The jury convicted them on the lesser charge of aggravated assault.[47] Houston, and Texas more broadly, serves as a good example of how law enforcement attempted to railroad movement participants to destroy civil rights activism.

New Mexico had a number of important groups that challenged abusive policing, and as in LA, the most important were the Berets. In Albuquerque, Chicanos formed the Black Berets. Modeled on the LA Brown Berets (the Brown Berets had chapters in many locales; they were loosely affiliated and largely autonomous), the group was founded by Richard Moore, a local firebrand and activist, and Placido Salazar, a US Navy veteran, in 1968. They made policing a major part of their activism. The second point of the Black Berets' thirteen-point platform stated this clearly: "We demand the immediate end to the occupation of our community by the fascist police. We realize the police occupy our communities just as the US armies occupy foreign countries. Only by organizing and arming to defend ourselves can we ever hope to stop the police brutality and genocide in our communities." This was a rather clear abolitionist proposal, but the Black Berets also worked with law enforcement to end police abuse. The Berets understood police brutality because, like their counterparts elsewhere, many of them had experienced it. They also demanded "a judicial system relevant to Chicanos and therefore administered by Chicanos."[48]

The Albuquerque Berets advocated for armed self-defense: "The Black Beret organization has come to the conclusion that armed self defense is necessary in order to carry out our services to la gente & to protect them from the racist maniacs that are allowed to exist in the U.S.A. From this day on Los Berets will be armed and ready to handle any & all defensive measures necessary to protect ourselves and the people we serve."[49] They had good reason to defend themselves; police often fell on Beret activism with a heavy hand. For example, in 1971 the Black Berets organized a rally to protest the war in Vietnam as well as police brutality. About 1,000 people gathered at Roosevelt Park, next to the University of New Mexico, to participate in the rally. Activist leaders as well politicians, including Lieutenant Governor Robert Mondragon and Attorney General David Norvell, gave speeches. Several Berets spoke and made it clear that the protest, ostensibly about Vietnam, was really about police violence. Santiago Maestas, the Berets' minister of information, noted that they had made policing an issue for years and that "nothing happened. They hired Chief [Don] Byrd from Dallas. We met him, showed him, and he agreed there was harassment, but said 'give us time.' Well, he ran out of time yesterday." When the rally turned into a police-instigated riot, Byrd again asked for more time, to no avail.[50]

To disperse the growing crowd, police began to fire tear gas. Those in the rally threw the canisters back at the officers. Overwhelmed by the protestors, some police officers resorted to firing their handguns directly into the crowd. One reporter noted that he "saw one man go down, apparently shot in the back."[51] The protestors surged out of the park and began destroying nearby businesses. People then began marching downtown to the police administration building.[52] As the crowd grew, several Black Berets negotiated with Chief Byrd. After a tense meeting, Byrd evidently convinced these unnamed Berets to get the crowd to disperse. They asked people to return to the park, but that did not happen. Instead the crowd broke into smaller groups and began destroying storefronts and burning buildings.[53]

Groups of people continued to damage parts of the central business district the following day. Law enforcement had made nearly 300 arrests, but they proved incapable of containing the uprising. The next day Governor Bruce King called in the National Guard. The National Guard augmented local law enforcement and brought the violence to an end. Police arrested hundreds of people, hospitals were overrun with individuals suffering gunshot wounds, stabbings, and other injuries, and large segments of downtown Albuquerque were destroyed.[54]

As was the case with many similar disturbances, the aftermath of the conflagration tended to focus on two things: the reforms the city might make and the trials of those arrested during the disturbance. Of the hundreds of people arrested, the local court system focused on a handful of major cases. The first was that of Primitivo Trujillo Jaramillo, whom police arrested for arson. Trujillo pleaded guilty early on to a riot charge, and a jury sentenced him to nine months. The state also charged him with felony arson.[55] The Commission on Civil Disorder, established by Governor King to investigate, did little. The governor, moreover, made problematic statements that hampered the commission's work. For example, he claimed that "transient people"—his verbiage for "outside agitators"—had caused the uprising. As such, he had already deduced the cause of the disorder for the commission. When the Black Berets began to protest the governor by sitting in at his office, he pulled the plug on the commission.[56]

After these events, the Black Berets began efforts to curb police harassment by monitoring the police who patrolled the barrios, similar to operations by the Black Panthers. They had several tense encounters with the police. The Berets' "citizen's patrol" culminated in an ugly incident when four Albuquerque PD officers pulled over and arrested at gunpoint Beret leader Richard Moore. The Berets also had run-ins with police agencies in Española and Martineztown. The Berets warned that an "all-out war" might develop if the police chose not to develop reform measures. They demanded that police form a civilian review board, allow Chicanos to play a role in the hiring of the chief of police, and enact new ordinances governing police abuse.[57] Finally, the Berets got involved in carceral activism at the Penitentiary of New Mexico in Santa Fe.[58]

Two Black Berets, James Antonio Cordova and Rito Canales, became central figures in the organization's policing and carceral focus. Cordova had served a stint in the US Army, had studied journalism at the University of Utah, and had recently married his sweetheart, Anita. The Chicano newspaper *El Grito del Norte* had hired him as a photographer, and he acted as the journalist and photographer for the Berets. Cordova had firsthand experience with police brutality. He got beaten up by police after he witnessed officers arresting several Mexican American men in Española in July 1971. Cordova had seen two police cars speeding to a Standard gas station—one of them almost ran him over. The squad cars had stopped at the back of the gas station, so Cordova followed to see what was happening. He found three police cars and half a dozen police officers who had shotguns and pistols trained on an Oldsmobile. Three Mexican-origin men emerged from the car, which police began searching. They also placed the men under arrest. Officer Baltasar Archuleta then noticed Cordova and demanded to know what he was doing. When Cordova responded that he was "just watching," Archuleta told him, "I'm going to arrest you too." Cordova had his camera, and Archuleta evidently believed he had taken pictures of the arrests. When Archuleta booked Cordova at the Española police station, he punched Cordova in the face approximately eight times and viciously kicked him in the small of his back. Police later charged Cordova with public intoxication, even though he had not been drinking.[59]

After Cordova made a formal complaint about this brutality, Attorney General David Norvell investigated. Much of the investigation basically concurred with the story Cordova had told in an affidavit, except for the part about Archuleta beating him. Eight police officers witnessed Cordova's booking, but "all of these police officials claim that they neither saw nor heard any signs of violence during the period when Cordova was being booked," Norvell's report noted.[60] He found that the inconsistencies in the stories told by Cordova, the officers, and the other men arrested that night amounted to a scenario of "he said/they said." Insufficient evidence existed to corroborate Cordova's version of events or to warrant prosecuting Archuleta.[61]

Yet the attorney general's report disclosed that Archuleta had a history of violence toward civilians. He had applied for a job with the New Mexico State Police, but they would not hire him because he was "too quick with his fists." Another individual, Salomon Velasquez, had sworn an affidavit that described a violent encounter he had with Archuleta. Velasquez was walking home from a dance in June 1971 when Archuleta and Officer Ben Martinez ordered him into their squad car. They did not arrest him; they simply picked Velasquez up, then shocked him several times with a stun baton, and Martinez hit him in the face. Velasquez spent the night in jail, and police later charged him with public intoxication, even though he had not been drunk, and with resisting arrest, even though he had not been arrested. This kind of everyday police violence and arrests on trumped-up charges plagued Mexican Americans across the Southwest. Archuleta resigned from the Española police force shortly after this and the incident with Cordova.[62]

Rito Canales's life had been hard. He grew up poor in Artesia, New Mexico, and had experienced numerous painful run-ins with police. In 1962 Canales was involved in a fight with a group of men, during which an individual was shot and killed. Police singled out Canales and arrested him for the killing. He pleaded guilty to second-degree murder, and a jury sentenced him to a term of three to fifty years in prison. He spent seven years in the Penitentiary of New Mexico for the crime, and there he learned firsthand the abuses that prisoners experienced daily. For example, in 1968 another incarcerated man stabbed Canales eleven times, which he blamed on poor supervision at the facility. Prison guards also allegedly beat Canales several times.[63]

The Penitentiary of New Mexico was the subject of several investigations about conditions at the facility. The first involved prison guards who complained that administrators did not adequately protect them from the individuals they guarded. Blame fell on Warden J. E. Baker; he resigned after the New Mexico Senate declined to confirm his nomination for the post in 1970. But a few months later the prison saw a wave of resignations, including that of the new warden, Urioste Herrera.[64] A series of escapes also put the prison in an ugly light.[65] Finally, a number of people reported on abusive guards, the denial of rights, and unnecessary punishments, all persistent problems at the prison, which led to a strike and a near uprising in 1971.[66] Canales became the Berets' entry point into anticarceral activism as a result of his experiences at the prison.

Antonio Cordova and Rito Canales spoke about these issues publicly. Albuquerque's KOAT-TV news had scheduled both men for an appearance on the popular *What's the Word?* news show in January 1972. Cordova would discuss his abuse at the hands of police, and Canales planned to speak about problems at the Penitentiary of New Mexico.[67] Both men knew that police and prison staff would not appreciate their criticism. They also knew, as did the Black Berets more generally, that they were putting themselves at risk.[68]

The television appearance never happened. Instead, law enforcement killed Canales and Cordova when they allegedly attempted to steal dynamite from an Albuquerque freeway construction site atop a mesa near present-day Isleta Boulevard and Malpais Road. For reasons that remain murky, a man known as Chapa had enticed Canales and Cordova to rob the site.[69] Ten law enforcement personnel—Albuquerque PD officers Wayne Larson, Riolino Pollo, and Jose Salazar; New Mexico State Police officers Al Briggs, Bob Carroll, Ted Drennan, Ralph McNutt, and Leroy Urioste; and Bernalillo County deputy sheriffs Santos Baca and Truman Wood—staked out the construction site. Several officers came armed with their own high-powered rifles. Both Pollo and Larson each had M1 carbines, Salazar had his .243-caliber hunting rifle, McNutt and Urioste carried tactical police shotguns, and Drennan had his personal AR-180, the civilian version of the AR-18. These men positioned themselves around three storage units at the construction site, while other officers patrolled along Isleta and Malpais.[70]

At around 1:00 a.m. the six officers at the construction site saw two shadowy figures near the storage units. One carried a rifle. Officer Larson yelled, "Freeze, police officers," at which point Cordova, who had the rifle, fired several haphazard shots. Drennan, Larson, Pollo, and Salazar all returned fire, hitting Cordova, who slumped to the ground, mortally wounded. Drennan and McNutt advanced toward Cordova's body and shot him several more times as he lay prone. Canales fled down the side of the mesa and across a field. Drennan, Salazar, Pollo, and Urioste all opened fire on him from about 100 yards away, hitting him six times in the back and side. Both Canales and Cordova died at the scene.[71]

Several police agencies investigated the shootings. When local papers began reporting about the odd nature of the stakeout, the chief of the New Mexico State Police, Martin Vigil, clamped down on the reporting of the incident. The *Albuquerque Tribune* and *Albuquerque Journal* both reported that the inconsistent statements and, later, silence from the police was troubling. The *Tribune* called Vigil's actions a "ham-handed attempt to cover up the episode." Inaccuracies in the police reporting perhaps explain Vigil's caution. For example, police insisted that Canales had a .45-caliber pistol and that he had fired shots at them. But Officer Pollo, when asked if he had seen Canales fire, replied, "No, I saw flashes but I don't know who was firing. The flashes could have been mine bouncing off [the ground]." In fact, officers never located a pistol, and none of the officers could realistically claim that Canales had fired at them. In short, the reports of Canales having a gun were fiction: he had no weapon.[72]

Police Chief Don Byrd aggravated the situation further when he claimed that the Berets had "deviated from peaceful tactics to do away with our system of government and resorted to violent means."[73] The FBI also reported on the shooting, basically repeating what state officials had said. Black Beret leader Richard Moore speculated that the police had Cordova and Canales in custody and that "the men were taken to a construction site and shot. This is what we are accusing the Albuquerque police of . . . murder."[74] This fanciful assertion had no basis in reality, but it shows the level of distrust between police and the Berets.

The Bernalillo County grand jury later cleared all of the officers of wrongdoing and deemed the killings justified. It seems clear that Antonio Cordova attempted to commit felony burglary, that he went to the construction site armed, and that he fired at police. The initial shooting of Cordova, therefore, passed official muster. The secondary shooting of Cordova and the shooting of Canales did not make sense. Police had mortally wounded Cordova after they shot him the first time. Officers Drennan and McNutt claimed to have seen him lifting his rifle after they shot him, but the coroner's report showed that this was a lie. At least one of the initial bullets struck Cordova in the head, which killed him, so Cordova was already dead the second time police shot him. Their justification for shooting Cordova a second time was a fabrication.[75] So, too, was the rationale for the shooting of Canales. New Mexico had its own abhorrent ley fuga statute that allowed law enforcement to shoot a fleeing suspect if they fled a felony crime. The officers had claimed, though, that they shot Canales as he fled because he had shot at them. Later reports, of course, confirmed that Canales was not armed. The officers could have easily radioed their colleagues patrolling Malpais and Isleta to apprehend Canales. But instead they killed Canales as he ran away. Legally speaking, the killing of Rito Canales was more confusing than that of Antonio Cordova and appeared from several angles to have been unwarranted.[76]

The inconsistencies in the police officers' accounts of the killings pushed the city to ask Governor Bruce King to name a special commission to investigate these events. He tasked the state attorney general to conduct an official investigation.[77] That investigation corroborated the police version of events. Attorney General Norvell did criticize the stakeout since the officers had not gone through proper channels to form what amounted to a multiagency task force. But he declared the killing of Antonio Cordova justifiable. Cordova was not only involved in the commission of a burglary, a third-degree felony, but also shot at police. The report also justified the secondary shooting of Cordova because, as the officers had stated, "Cordova moved his rifle in a way that was reasonably interpreted as a threatening gesture."[78]

The killing of Rito Canales proved harder to legally untangle. As Norvell noted, if Canales's crime was "attempted burglary of a building," a misdemeanor, shooting him was not justifiable. However, the attorney general explained that the officers had probable cause to believe that "Canales was conspiring with Cordova to commit the felony crime of burglary." Conspiracy to commit the felony crime of burglary is a felony, which would seem to excuse the shooting of Canales. But the report stated ambiguously, "There is evidence which suggests that the use of force was not justified. There is also evidence which suggests the use of force was justified." Norvell left out that the officers had contended that Canales shot at them, their original justification for shooting him as he ran, which did not actually happen. The attorney general ignored this and instead focused on conspiracy to commit burglary in order to exonerate the officers, even though he never conclusively ruled that the killing of Canales was justified.[79]

Albuquerque attorney L. Michael Messina served on the attorney general's committee as an independent observer. He called Norvell out for the inconsistencies in his interpretation of the law and facts. Messina also ridiculed Norvell's justification for not prosecuting the officers for killing Canales, which hinged not on their culpability but on the expense of a prosecution and the damage it would do to the city. "If he is truly concerned about the impact on the community," Messina wrote, "the responsible exercise of his discretion in this case is to proceed against these police officers as against any other citizen." Moreover, Messina rightly found it incredible that after a lengthy investigation Norvell still failed "to reach a definitive conclusion as to whether or not the killing of Rito Canales was justifiable."[80] This left the killing like an open wound.

Norvell's report also raised questions about Chapa, whom the attorney general's staff failed to locate. He seemed a mysterious character in general, and perhaps a fiction altogether, and he vanished after the killing of Canales and Cordova. According to Black Beret leadership as well as activist Reies López Tijerina, Chapa was a real person. Although he had convinced Cordova and Canales to steal dynamite from the freeway construction site and had driven them there, Tijerina claimed that Chapa had also contacted him about stealing dynamite from the construction site and had offered to escort him to the location. Tijerina refused.[81]

Over time, local people learned that Chapa was in fact Tim Chapa, a police informant who had worked to implicate the Berets in a variety of crimes. When Antonio Cordova's mother, Maria, brought a wrongful death suit against the City of Albuquerque for killing her son in 1974, the press aired Chapa's full name in public for the first time.[82] A local court dismissed this case. Years later, the Cordova and Canales families again filed suit for wrongful death, asking in 2000 that the city reopen the case. Chapa told his version of the killing of Cordova and Canales that January. He acknowledged that the police had conducted the sting operation to silence Cordova and Canales and that they had forced him to entice them to rob the dynamite shed. Moreover, despite police statements that they hoped to arrest Cordova and Canales, Chapa retorted that "there wasn't no talk about . . . arresting them or breaking them. All this talk was about killing them . . . that's all they would talk about." Chapa added that he drove the two men to Malpais Road and from there they had walked to the construction site. According to Chapa, Cordova carried a rifle; Canales was unarmed.[83]

Whether Chapa had enticed the men or they went on their own accord may seem immaterial. But the nature of the stakeout clearly demonstrated that the police had it carefully planned. Indeed, the scope of the operation was pretty big, and the broad strokes of the trap they set for Canales and Cordova read more like a hunting trip than a police stakeout. In fact, the various law enforcement officers involved in the stakeout and shooting showed a troubling amount of collusion between the different police agencies. Ordinarily, the combined efforts of these officers would have come via an interagency task force with a strict mandate. In this case, the officers acted alone. No police administrator had authorized their actions, and no one in authority acknowledged the strange nature of the sting. As Joe Cordova, Antonio's brother, accurately put it, the stakeout and shootings were "just like killing a dog."[84]

Unsurprisingly, the Black Berets responded to the killings of Canales and Cordova with extreme anger. At the funeral service for Antonio Cordova, for example, Richard Moore eulogized Cordova with passion and said he "showed us the chains of oppression."[85] The Berets also exposed a number of inconsistencies in the police account of the killings and highlighted Cordova's activism opposing police brutality and Canales's antiprison activities, which the police and the local press largely chose to ignore. Moreover, the police had previously raided the headquarters of the Black Berets and claimed to have found dynamite. To muddy the waters further, investigators claimed that someone had stolen this dynamite from the same construction site where Cordova and Canales later died but also that the date numbers on the dynamite did not match the records of Wylie Brothers, the company contracted to build the freeway. Moreover, police stated contradictorily that they had lifted Cordova's fingerprints from this stolen dynamite while also admitting that because the dynamite had changed hands so many times (it had gone from allegedly being stolen to the police and then thrown in the back of a Wylie Brothers construction office before being picked up by police once more) that it was impossible to recover prints. The Berets rejected all of these accusations, a rebuttal that made even more sense when the prosecuting attorney dropped the charge of "possession of explosives" against them altogether.[86]

It seems clear that law enforcement wanted to halt Black Beret activities. Whether or not they had stolen dynamite previously—and the record is, at best, sketchy on this point—Tim Chapa had successfully lured Cordova and Canales into attempting to rob the construction site. Canales's testimony about abuse at the Penitentiary of New Mexico would have embarrassed prison officials. The strike and near uprising in 1971, and a subsequent rebellion in 1980, certainly confirmed that there were many problems at the prison. Cordova's work challenging police brutality was similarly damaging. Their scheduled news appearance would have shamed the criminal justice system in New Mexico. Their deaths meant of course that the television interview never happened. The killing of Rito Canales and Antonio Cordova represent very real examples of how law enforcement eliminated Chicano activists in an attempt to halt the movement.

Police attempted to destroy Chicano activism in Colorado as well. Colorado activists had their own history with police abuse. Rodolfo "Corky" Gonzales founded the influential Crusade for Justice in Denver in 1966 in large part to combat police brutality. Denver was a hotbed of activism throughout the 1960s: chicanismo had grown well beyond the confines of the border region.[87] Crusade members had frequent run-ins with police. For example, police clashed with Chicanos after a rally at Denver's Lincoln Park in 1969. That rally had attempted to focus attention on two questionable police killings. Police disrupted the protest and fired at the activists, badly injuring Joseph Vigil, who was shot in both legs with a shotgun.[88]

Corky Gonzales himself had dealt with police harassment, for example, when police arrested him and his teenage son Rudy on June 13, 1974. Denver police officers Jerome Powell and David Lucero accused Rudy of committing a burglary that night, even though he had been at home all evening. Rudy attempted to talk with his parents, but the officers stopped him. Corky intervened because he knew that he and his wife, Geraldine, had a legal right to assist their minor child. The officers then arrested Corky for interfering with an investigation. They also arrested Rudy. A few months later a judge threw out the case and dismissed the charges against them. Gonzales sued the city and officers for false arrest. It is unclear what happened with this suit.[89]

Whereas Corky Gonzales was critical of Denver police, for its part the Denver Police Department regarded Gonzales, members of the Crusade for Justice, and other activists as violent, antipolice radicals. Corky, however, had never advocated violence toward the police, and when accused of such, he responded with anger. He explained forthrightly, "We don't want any violence. You don't march with women and children and old people, and say we want to take on the whole armed forces."[90] He also understood police abuse analytically: brutality is "like a graph; it goes up and down. Now is one of those heavy times and brutality is on an increase. The police have adopted a military concept in dealing with Chicanos. They are going to be trigger happy in dealing with our people."[91] In one of Corky Gonzales's "Message to Aztlan" columns, which appeared in the Crusade's *El Gallo* newspaper, he asserted that police should "serve, protect and love and it can be reciprocated. Destroy, kill and treat our people with injustice and you might only receive the same in return."[92] Again, he was not antipolice; he was pro–good policing.

The police killing of Luis "Junior" Martinez further radicalized the Crusade for Justice.[93] Martinez taught dance at the Crusade for Justice's Escuela Tlatelolco. On the night of March 17, 1973, a colleague informed him that police had attempted to arrest one of the school's students for jaywalking. As it turned out, this student had seen a patrol car with Officers Carol Hogue and Stephen Snyder observing the school and several apartments owned by the Crusade. When he asked them what they were doing, the officers arrested the youth. Martinez attempted to intervene on his behalf. What happened next is unclear. Martinez fled and Officer Snyder gave chase. Martinez ran down a blind alley and Snyder shot him twice. Snyder later claimed that Martinez had shot at him first. Snyder was wounded in the altercation, but police never recovered Martinez's alleged gun. This event triggered a battle in which seventeen Chicanos and four police officers were wounded. Chicanos called this battle the St. Patrick Day Massacre.[94]

Corky Gonzales asserted that "Luis Martinez was murdered. We have at this time knowledgeable witnesses that were on the spot who will prove that young people were shot, arrested and brutalized and provoked into resistance."[95] The Justice Department investigated but soon suspended its inquiry because of a lack of formal complaints.[96] Although authorities never punished Officer Snyder, the Crusade for Justice did get the charges against most of the Chicanos dismissed.[97] The Crusade later held a massive rally to commemorate Martinez's killing. The organization also created several programs on his behalf, most importantly a nursery for movement children. "What greater monument can be erected," Crusade newspaper *El Gallo* explained, "if not that which will house the future of our people and our struggle."[98] Two years later, the Crusade joined in a tribute to Martinez at the National Day of Solidarity protest.[99]

The Crusade for Justice had other problems with police. Like Rito Canales and Antonio Cordova, in 1975 Denver police railroaded Juan Haro and Antonio Quintana, although Haro and Quintana lived through their experience. According to the Denver Police Department, Haro and Quintana allegedly planned to bomb a Denver police substation. Although they had supposedly planned to complete the bombing with a new Crusade member named Joseph Cordova, on the night of the alleged bombing Quintana drove off, leaving Haro and Cordova to transport a dynamite bomb to the police station. Police intercepted the two men and arrested them before they got to the intended target. Police later arrested Quintana on suspicion that he had also transported a bomb, although they found no bomb in his vehicle. The Crusade later learned at trial that the district attorney would rely on testimony from Joseph Cordova.[100] Even though Quintana was, at best, an accomplice in the plot, the district attorney charged him and Haro with the same crimes: unlawful use of explosives, criminal attempt to commit first-degree murder, theft, and conspiracy to commit murder.[101]

Juan Haro denied all charges against him, claimed he had not driven the car transporting the bomb, and spoke openly about a police conspiracy involving Joseph Cordova.[102] Haro's statements seemed to lack credibility until the local media discovered that Cordova was a police informant, much like Tim Chapa had been in Albuquerque. The press learned that police had arrested Cordova in connection with a number of robberies and after a high-speed chase that left several officers injured. And yet they never formally charged him with any crimes. Instead, Cordova emerged as a new Crusade for Justice member a month later.[103] This timing seemed fishy to the activists. Cordova did testify at Juan Haro's trial; a jury found Haro guilty of unlawfully possessing explosive devices in a federal trial based largely on Cordova's testimony.[104] The court sentenced him to six years' imprisonment at Fort Leavenworth.[105] However, in a later state trial, Cordova gave testimony that contradicted most of the statements he had made during Haro's federal trial. In particular, Cordova asserted that Juan Haro had never driven the vehicle with the dynamite bombs, which made him, like Quintana, an accomplice in the alleged bombing plot. The jury found Haro not guilty. The state then dropped all charges against Antonio Quintana.[106]

The case of Haro and Quintana merged with other bombings in Colorado, these the work of unknown assailants. In March 1974 the courthouse and a police station in Boulder were bombed. While there were no injuries, police speculated that Chicano activists had carried out these attacks. Then, in May 1974, six Chicanos died in two separate car bombings. They included Florencio Granado, who had witnessed the killing of Ricardo Falcón (discussed in chapter 4), and Reyes Martínez, the brother of activist Francisco "Kiko" Martínez (discussed below). Police blamed the Chicano activists for bombing themselves, but they never conclusively solved these cases.[107] The state investigated and prosecutors called the Crusade for Justice's Veronica Vigil to testify in grand jury hearings about the Boulder bombings. She invoked her Fifth Amendment rights and refused to answer questions. The state granted her immunity in order to compel her to testify, but she again refused. Judge Alfred Arraj held her in contempt of court and jailed her for the remainder of the duration of the grand jury's term, eleven months.[108]

The cases of Haro and Quintana in Denver and Cordova and Canales in Albuquerque generated a serious public discussion about the legality and morality of law enforcement entrapment. In both cases, the police had used confidential informants to orchestrate the outcome of events. In the case of Cordova and Canales, of course, the police killings of both men brought their activism to an end. The fact that Tim Chapa had set up the two men seemed to matter little. For Haro and Quintana, the establishment responded quickly with the full force of the law, but the ultimate discovery of Joseph Cordova and his criminal past just as quickly put the Denver Police Department's actions in question.[109]

An editorial in the *Rocky Mountain News* put all of these events in their proper light. It noted that it used to be easy to distinguish between "cops and robbers." Instead, police working with informant-criminals was a "criminal joint venture." "The common thread," it stated, "in many of these criminal joint ventures is the avid exploitation of the curious legal doctrine that enables an undercover agent to lawfully supply any weapon, any assistance or any other missing element needed to nourish a citizen's illicit motive into full blown crime. We find that doctrine repugnant." The editorial closed by stating, "It is government's proper function to prevent crime, without promoting it, participating in it, or resorting to it to protect government agents."[110]

A final example from Colorado demonstrates that this kind of "criminal joint venture" could manifest itself in other ways. Perhaps no other case revealed the problems with this government overreach better than that of Francisco E. "Kiko" Martínez, an activist Chicano attorney from Denver. Martínez used his legal training to defend farmworkers arrested for striking, student activists for protesting, and just about anyone else whom the system had trodden upon. He was also a witness to the killing of Ricardo Falcón in New Mexico. He later represented Priscilla Falcón, Ricardo's spouse, during subsequent trials.[111]

Kiko Martínez seemed to represent the things that Colorado's law enforcement community had come to fear: he was a tough, smart, well-educated attorney who had no compunction about speaking truth to power. It seems that Colorado authorities decided to railroad him in 1973 to remove him from activism. Denver police alleged that he had mailed bombs that year to a number of Denver officials, including Denver police officer Carol Hogue (who had been involved in the incident that led to the killing of Luis "Junior" Martinez), a city school board member named Robert Crider, and a motorcycle repair shop. Denver police found and defused these bombs. They singled out Martínez for mailing the bombs, although they never discerned a motivation or proof as to why a well-liked attorney would mail bombs (more than likely because he didn't). Denver police got a warrant for his arrest with an alleged shoot-on-sight order. That order, though patently illegal, indicated that police had already found him guilty. Martínez did the only thing that made sense to him: he fled to Mexico.[112]

In 1980, Kiko Martínez returned to the United States. Authorities arrested him at the border and sent him to Denver, where he faced nearly a dozen state and federal charges.[113] Chicanos formed the Francisco E. Martínez Defense Committee to defend him. His first trial for the attempted bombing of Officer Hogue began in 1981. It ended quickly and embarrassingly for the US government. The trial occurred in the courtroom of Judge Fred M. Winner, who expressed clear biases against Martínez, for instance claiming that "Mr. Martinez is the catalyst for bringing together four terrorist groups which have never before acted jointly," a salacious lie that had no basis in fact. But more troubling, Winner conspired with the prosecution and FBI in order to ensure a conviction. He wrote to the Justice Department—a clear example of ex parte communication—proposing that the FBI should secretly film the trial so that the court could document alleged "interference by outsiders" (Winner believed that supporters of Martínez were trying to intimidate the jury). Should the trial go badly and it appeared that Martínez would be acquitted, Winner would grant a mistrial and then prosecutors could use the evidence of "interference" to help secure a new trial. In other words, Winner hoped unethically to find a way to prevent double jeopardy from applying to Martínez. This was unconstitutional; the prosecution wisely rejected the proposal.[114]

But Winner wasn't done. He also proposed that if the case went badly for the state, the prosecution should request a mistrial—which he promised to grant—only after the defense had presented its case. That way if the state prosecuted Martínez a second time they would already know the tactics his defense would use. Thus, the conclusion of the trial would not only prevent double jeopardy but also work as a kind of one-sided discovery for the prosecution. When the prosecution asked for a mistrial after the defense had rested, Winner granted it as planned. Finally, after the mistrial he met with a group of jurors at a bar to determine what evidence they had found most compelling. He planned to share this information with the prosecution.[115]

This behind-the-scenes collusion, which became known as Winnergate, served as clear proof for Chicanos of how the criminal justice system worked via closed channels to undermine the rights of a defendant like Kiko Martínez and Chicanos more generally. It demonstrated the hollowness of the "justice" within the justice system.[116] Winner engaged in unconstitutional and prejudicial acts because he wanted Martínez convicted. As journalist David

Smythe noted, "So, as he nears 70 and prepares to step down from his august office, Fred M. Winner will leave a legacy to American jurisprudence: that a judge can exclude counsel from important meetings that affect the outcome of a trial on the thinnest suspicion that counsel is somehow connected with a crime [jury intimidation that may never have taken place]." The *American Lawyer* in 1983 declared Winner the worst judge in the Tenth Judicial Circuit. He retired in 1984. Martínez sued Winner and the prosecutors, claiming that they had violated his rights. The court rejected his case.[117]

The prosecutorial and judicial misconduct apparent in Winnergate also marred the other trials against Martínez. The second trial ended almost as quickly as the first in August 1981. In that case, Judge Alvin Lichtenstein dismissed charges that Martínez had mailed a letter bomb to Denver School Board member Robert Crider. The police had destroyed evidence, including the bomb itself, leaving the state with little material with which to try Martínez and the defense without evidence to exonerate him. In sum, Lichtenstein ruled that in destroying the bomb the police had violated Martínez's right to due process, so he dismissed the case.[118] By November 1982 the government tried again. In that case, however, Martínez was found not guilty of mailing a bomb to the motorcycle shop. A judge dismissed another bomb case after he learned that police had again destroyed much of the physical evidence.[119]

The only thing the government could pin on Martínez was using an alias and claiming Mexican citizenship when he had returned to the United States. The government tried him for perjury and making false statements to federal agents. The trial resulted in a conviction for the perjury charge only, which carried a sentence of up to five years in prison.[120] The Francisco E. Martínez Defense Committee organized a major campaign to convince Judge William Browning to set aside the conviction or release Martínez for time served. These appeals seemed to have worked. Martínez received a fairly light sentence: ninety days in prison and four and a half years of probation.[121]

While the Chicano movement boldly challenged police violence and abuse, those challenges often provoked resistance or violence from law enforcement. One of the most problematic aspects of this period was the police harassment and murder of movement participants. That abuse confirmed for many Chicanos the heavy-handed nature of Southwestern law enforcement. Chicano complaints about police were not some figment of the imagination, they were not hyperbole, and the proof was the very real incidents of violence experienced by movement participants, such as Antonio Cordova and Rito Canales and Junior Martinez. The criminal justice system also often worked to railroad movement participants, among them Juan Haro and Antonio Quintana and Kiko Martínez. Add to that the other examples of harassment that Mexican-origin people experienced and the arrests of the East LA 13, the Houston 12, and well-known figures such as Corky Gonzales, and a volatile and dangerous situation emerges.

A common denominator of this abuse was the police use of undercover agents or informants. We know that the federal government, through its Counterintelligence Program (COINTELPRO), undermined and infiltrated activist groups. But local police agencies also did this to encourage individuals to commit illegal acts and ultimately entrap them—and, in the case of Rito Canales and Antonio Cordova, to entrap and kill them. The problem with this entrapment was not only that it motivated individuals to commit crimes—crimes they otherwise might not have committed—but that the police also entrapped the individuals who encouraged those crimes. While it is unclear why Tim Chapa enticed Canales and Cordova, we know that Joseph Cordova had committed crimes and was then granted immunity from prosecution for those crimes if he agreed to entrap Juan Haro and Antonio Quintana. Thus, he was motivated or coerced into entrapping Haro and Quintana. Although such behavior from police was legal, it reinforced the perception that law enforcement had set itself against the Chicano movement.

Law enforcement had throughout the civil rights era focused on arresting or killing movement participants as a way of attempting to destroy those movements. The numerous arrests that Chicano movement participants experienced certainly bears this point out. And those participants didn't have to be involved in a protest against law enforcement. Rather, any Chicano activism brought law enforcement in to control or punish movement participants. When cases of violence against non-movement individuals, as well as cases from other ethnic communities, are combined with the information in this chapter, it's a wonder these movements survived as long as they did.

But survive they did. Chicanos persevered even in the face of police abuse and killing. And they continued to propose novel ideas for how to reform police even in the face of this relentless assault. Why? Because Mexican Americans were for the most part not antipolice. They didn't oppose law enforcement; rather, they opposed abuses within the system. Even when they engaged in abolitionist rhetoric, as the Black Berets had, they still often worked with police. Although law enforcement in some locations did attempt to work toward reform, on the whole Chicanos had to endure a lot to see any change be realized. And it wasn't just movement participants who experienced such violence. In fact, everyday violence against non-movement Mexican Americans was just as gross, if not grosser, than what movement participants experienced. The examples of everyday violence that Mexican Americans experienced at the hands of law enforcement, which in numerous cases also generated protests organized or led by Chicano movement leaders, is an important part of this history.

THREE

BLOOD ON THEIR HANDS

The Chicano Response to
Police Violence against Non-
Movement Mexican Americans

In December 1979, Arizona Department of Public Safety trooper John Bourcet pulled over Mario Diaz and Frank Guerrero for a traffic violation on the outskirts of Phoenix. When Diaz refused to extinguish a cigarette, Bourcet roughly extracted him from the vehicle and slammed him on the trunk of the car. He arrested Diaz and initially took him to the nearby town of Surprise, then to El Mirage. Meanwhile, Guerrero contacted Diaz's family, who went to the El Mirage police station. A confrontation ensued; police beat and arrested nine family members. The next day a new group, the United Front against Brutality (UFAB), organized a march and rally to protest this brutality. UFAB asserted that authorities routinely beat and harassed Mexican Americans. Officials feigned ignorance. The mayor of Surprise was, well, surprised that the march involved his city, considering that none of these events occurred there. He and the El Mirage police chief disclaimed responsibility for the incident and did nothing more. The UFAB protests ultimately ended in El Mirage and Surprise, not because anything had changed, but because other more egregious examples of police violence occurred in Arizona, which shifted their attention.[1]

The situation in Arizona proved typical for the broader Southwest. Police violence, harassment, abuse, and killing seemed to happen every day, in every town, in every state in the region. These examples of quotidian violence against Mexican-origin people were commonplace and numerous, so much so that they almost seem impossible to comprehend. When combined with the police violence meted out against movement participants detailed in the previous chapter, as well as the examples of weird and unusual violence discussed in the next, a truly horrible picture emerges. This horrible picture shows that police violence was not some aberration but was rather a standard part of police practice across the Southwest.

Part of what made this violence so gross was that it tended to happen to innocent people, bystanders, and children, as well as those suspected of a criminal offense. Sometimes it involved choking, beating (with hands or weapons), kicking, and shooting. Sometimes it involved outright police murder. A number of examples reveal the perpetuation of the old ley fuga, wherein police shot people who were running away, which was still legal. The abuse of these non-movement individuals—ordinary Mexican Americans and Mexican nationals—by law enforcement also spurred Chicano activism. Although Chicano groups such as the Brown Berets had formed in part to confront police abuse, the violent nature of the system meant that they had to confront it both for themselves and for non-movement people brutalized by police.

But confront it they did. Chicano movement participants joined with the families and friends of victims of police abuse to demand change. This meant protests, picketing, and marching, of course, but Chicanos also found new ways to challenge police violence. A number of families and their allies sued police departments after a violent encounter or death, a new, albeit not novel idea that often worked. Chicanos also demanded that the Justice Department intervene on behalf of Mexican Americans killed by police. Chicano leaders also met with city officials, including police authorities, to initiate reforms. To their credit, a number of police departments responded positively to those demands. Last, several of the most notorious cases led to violent rebellions, which also forced cities and their police forces to inaugurate change.

Arizona experienced a number of violent encounters between Chicanos and police beyond the example of Mario Diaz mentioned above.[2] Perhaps the worst, most sensational case at this time involved Jose H. Sinohui Jr. He was twenty-four at the time of his killing, a veteran of the military who was studying art and music at Pima Community College. He also worked as part of a construction crew for the state highway department. On July 2, 1977, he was killed by South Tucson police officer Christopher Dean. Sinohui was returning home from work with a friend and had stopped in at a Jack in the Box near his home for dinner. A fight broke out at the restaurant as Sinohui was leaving. Police arrived to quell this disturbance. One account suggested that Sinohui attempted to run over Dean as he drove past the restaurant, another said he attempted to run over Dean twice, and another said three times! None of these accounts proved accurate. Instead, as Sinohui passed the restaurant in his pickup, Dean was attempting to escort an arrested person across the street. Dean signaled for Sinohui to stop, but he paused and then drove on. Dean opened fire on Sinohui's departing truck. He fired at least eight times (including with two illegal armor-piercing bullets), and one bullet struck Sinohui in the back. Sinohui managed to drive two blocks to a nearby VA hospital, where he died.[3]

The local media's reporting on this case proved highly problematic. One article stated that Sinohui "was shot in the back while driving his pickup away from the scene of a riot," while another said he was killed "during a riot."[4] "Riot" had taken on a particularly negative and racialized meaning by the 1970s, so use of that word was troubling, considering that a fight is not a riot and that Sinohui was a bystander. The "driving away" part implied that Sinohui had fled the scene of a crime, which would have amounted to a criminal act. The claim that Sinohui attempted to run over Dean evolved to become the "fact" that Dean shot him for "twice running over a police officer." One account later suggested that Dean had attempted to shoot only at Sinohui's tires, a fabrication. All of this reporting suggested that Dean was justified in shooting Sinohui.[5]

The South Tucson Police Department suspended Dean while an investigation took place. When it became known that he had once served as a deputy sheriff and been terminated for abuse of power, they fired him. The state eventually tried Dean for involuntary manslaughter; the jury acquitted him. The Mexican American community was outraged and rallied around the Sinohui family. Protests were ongoing from 1977 to 1980. Activists raised money for a civil suit and pressured the federal government to prosecute Dean for violating Sinohui's constitutional rights. His parents, Jose and Lupe, filed suit, alleging that Dean acted recklessly and killed their son without provocation. Judge Ben Birdsall agreed and declared that Dean's actions were grossly negligent. He issued a judgment of $200,000 against the city and Dean. The city paid the Sinohuis $150,000, while Dean paid them $50,000 (he forfeited his home to them when he could not pay the judgment).[6]

Chicano activists continued to protest. A group of fifty affiliated with the La Raza Legal Alliance organized a demonstration in Washington, DC. They picketed the Department of Justice and demanded a federal inquiry. The Carter administration waffled. The activists asserted that the administration seemed unwilling to "seek justice where clear abuses and atrocities have been committed against the Latino community. They certainly do not reflect an aggressive civil rights policy that seeks to make equality under the law and human rights for all a reality."[7] These efforts to get a federal trial slowly petered out. The more sensational Hanigan case (discussed in chapter 4) overshadowed and distracted from the Sinohui case. A federal grand jury declined to indict Dean for violating Jose Sinohui's rights. His sister, Anna Sinohui Sanchez, criticized the grand jury decision. "For a grand jury not to respond to that [Sinohui's killing]," she stated, "is to maintain a segregated system of justice." Activist and San Antonio attorney Ruben Sandoval concurred, calling the Justice Department a "nest of weasels."[8]

The League of United Latin American Citizens demanded a new trial and dedicated its 1980 national convention to Sinohui. The group also approved a resolution demanding that Attorney General Benjamin Civiletti reopen the case.[9] Activists got some encouraging news when authorities indicated that they would reopen the case because the prosecution had failed to present some evidence during the grand jury hearings. In the end, the Justice Department declined to reopen the case.[10] Complaints went nowhere. Lupe Sinohui, Jose's mother, told Civiletti "that I didn't need his sympathy, that I need justice. So far he hasn't given me either." She would continue to be disappointed.[11]

Other cases also generated a great deal of community anger and activism in Tucson, especially after a string of police raids on homes where police made mistakes in street addresses. For instance, in August 1979 Tucson police raided the home of Margie Moraga. In what seemed like a classic seventies summer afternoon, Moraga had just finished cleaning the house while her children listened to Walt Disney songs on the record player. Garbled yelling and pounding on the front door, followed by the door flying off its hinges, disrupted the festive atmosphere. Police rushed in and proceeded to search the home for drugs while Moraga cradled her terrified children. After finding no drugs, the officers realized they had raided the wrong home and left after explaining to Moraga how she could request reimbursement for her damaged door.[12]

Tucson police followed the Moraga incident by disrupting the birthday party of Edward Montenegro at the home of his parents, Alberto and Maria, in September 1979. Someone had called the police about a fight at another house, but police wound up at the Montenegro home instead and somehow mistook the birthday party for the fight. Police arrested Maria and Alberto Montenegro, whom they beat. They also beat and arrested Edward Montenegro after he kicked at a police dog. Police knocked Javier Montenegro, another son, unconscious and then allowed a police dog to bite him. Finally, they arrested the two remaining sons, Daniel and Jose Montenegro.[13]

The state tried Maria Montenegro for hindering an officer in the execution of his duties. Her trial ended in a mistrial. At her second trial the jury found her not guilty.[14] The state tried Alberto Montenegro for misdemeanor assault. When the jury acquitted him, the state dropped an additional charge of hindering a police officer.[15] A jury acquitted Javier and Daniel Montenegro of assault charges but found Jose Montenegro guilty of misdemeanor assault against a police officer.[16] Finally, a jury acquitted Edward Montenegro of disorderly conduct.[17]

The Montenegros joined with other Tucson residents in a committee to protest the abuse the family experienced. They had a number of meetings with city officials.[18] Chief of Police William Gilkinson promised to make his department more accessible to Tucsonans but also averred speciously that brutality was "being directed against police personnel."[19] The city council founded an ad hoc group to explore developing a police-civilian review board.[20] Finally, the Montenegro family sued the police department and Tucson for $1 million.[21] It is not clear what happened with this suit, but it is doubtful the family recovered any damages.

According to the family, not only had police raided the wrong home but one officer in particular, Chester Rick II, was the aggressor.[22] Officer Rick used the media to defend his actions and cast aspersions on the Montenegro family. He claimed that police were "jumped by 12 to 15 members of a family. . . . In the process the officer's night stick is taken away and they are assaulted, the officers' guns are grabbed with such force as to rip the holster stitching completely . . . and during the altercation the family members are yelling, 'get a gun and kill them.'" Rick's language is telling. The officers were "jumped," a word commonly linked to gang behavior, "by 12 to 15 members" of a six-member family, who not only threatened the lives of the officers but attempted to take their weapons to do so. None of that happened, and the only people assaulted were members of the Montenegro family.[23]

The Montenegros continued to experience harassment from police after the events at their home in 1979. Officer Rick evidently held a grudge against the family. Police leaders had transferred Rick to another unit in the hope that he would no longer come into contact with the Montenegros, but he still somehow found ways to involve himself in their affairs. In 1981 he pulled over Edward Montenegro on several occasions. This was a common form of harassment. Rick and Sergeant Robert Fund pulled over a vehicle Montenegro rode in because they suspected the driver of being involved in a bar fight. Rick arrested the driver, Bernardino Guillen. He later filed a complaint alleging that his arrest resulted from Rick's racism; that only a field sobriety test was performed, which is not conclusive; and that although Rick's target was Montenegro, he also targeted Guillen because Guillen was scheduled to testify in the Montenegros' civil suit. From Guillen's perspective, the police were attempting to intimidate him.[24]

These cases produced ongoing protests, demands for the establishment of a police-civilian review board, and civil suits against the police. As in other parts of the country, Chicanos pushed hard for the establishment of internal affairs departments and police review agencies in Tucson and Phoenix. Tucson initially proposed what local people called a "police board" after the Moraga and Montenegro incidents. The city council approved a plan for this board in late 1979. The board would be advisory. According to the *Arizona Daily Star*, "The value of an advisory panel is its link to the community, not its ability to probe police procedures. The panel would serve the community by not permitting conflicts between police and the community to remain unresolved."[25] It would investigate but would have no say in police policy or procedure. Activists demanded an eight-member panel drawn from the city's six council districts, plus one member chosen by the mayor and one by the police.[26] That proposal went over well at city hall, until City Manager Joel Valdez urged the council to reject it. His recommendation cut because many Chicanos did not expect such a response from a Mexican American official. Valdez suggested a weaker committee that was ultimately approved.[27] Even though the board the city created disappointed many activists, it nonetheless came into existence because of their actions.[28]

Arizona had a lot of problems. Certainly the abuse Maggie Moraga or the Montenegro family experienced was bad. The killing of Jose Sinohui was so much worse. The Chicano movement, in its defense of non-movement individuals, faced stiff resistance from city governments and police forces that largely refused to change. Although Chicanos successfully pushed Tucson to found its police board, overall justice in many of these cases seemed elusive.

In California, as in Arizona, non-movement Mexican Americans also suffered a lot of violence at the hands of police. A study of police in San Diego County found widespread abuse at the local and county level. The first example dated back to 1974 in the Eden Gardens area of Solana Beach. The sheriff's department had raided a party and beat and maced a number of Mexican Americans. The raiding of parties, as in Arizona, repeated itself with some regularity. In Oceanside in 1978 police raided a party where they broke down the front door, maced, beat, and turned police dogs on partygoers, arresting fourteen people. In Spring Valley, again in 1978, sheriffs attacked partygoers and arrested eighteen individuals. In 1980 sheriffs raided a wedding party and arrested twenty-six people. In addition to these cases there were a number of other harassment allegations made in the study involving illegal searches by police, illegal ID checks on Mexican Americans and authorized resident Mexican nationals (that is, "papers, please" policing), and false imprisonment. The report ended with an account of a police killing of a Chicano youth whom they beat to death with a metal baseball bat during a softball game.[29]

In one notable shooting, mentioned in the introduction, LA County deputy sheriff Bruce Nash killed Abel Gill in 1979. Seventeen-year-old Gill and some friends were driving in Norwalk when they got into an altercation with another motorist. Gill fled and the other car gave chase. The chase continued into Commerce, where Nash began pursuing both vehicles and eventually just Gill's. For unknown reasons he pursued Gill for some time before activating the lights of his patrol car. When he did, Gill pulled over. Nash exited his vehicle with his gun drawn and, according to several witnesses, shot Gill as he stepped from his car. Nash initially claimed that Gill attempted to ram him, but when this lie didn't work he said that he tripped and his gun discharged. Despite the inconsistencies in his account, a grand jury no-billed Nash.[30]

Such violence happened to non-movement Mexican Americans in other parts of California. Two Bay Area police murders serve as useful examples. The first occurred in San Jose in 1976. San Jose police officers Don Edwards and Craig Smith shot Danny Trevino to death after a traffic stop. The officers said they opened fire on Trevino after he appeared to reach for a gun. But he was not armed. Massive protests followed. More protests occurred after a grand jury cleared both officers of wrongdoing. Thousands of people marched on city hall. In the end, Police Chief Robert Murphy was the only one punished for this event; the city fired him.[31]

The second killing was that of Jose Barlow Benavidez. Oakland police officer Michael Cogley killed him during a botched arrest also in 1976. Cogley had stopped Barlow and placed his shotgun at the back of Barlow's head while he patted him down. Barlow had evidently not spread his legs far enough apart during the pat down, so Cogley kicked his feet apart. That jostling caused the shotgun to discharge directly into Barlow's skull. He died instantly.[32] Cogley made several procedural violations in his handling of Jose Barlow Benavidez. For example, he claimed that he stopped Barlow because his car matched the description of a vehicle used in a robbery, but the two vehicles were dissimilar. He also failed to activate his lights or siren, he trained his shotgun on him for no appreciable reason, and he searched Barlow while holding a shotgun to his head, all policy violations. Cogley claimed that Barlow lunged at him, which caused the gun to discharge. Witnesses stated that Barlow cooperated fully. An internal investigation cleared Cogley of wrongdoing and ruled the killing accidental. The Oakland grand jury no-billed him.[33]

Local activists quickly formed the Barlow Benavidez Committee against Police Crimes.[34] The group had rallies and marches throughout 1976.[35] While they knew that police brutality had been ongoing for generations, they noted that police had killed sixty-three unarmed people across the Southwest between 1970 and 1975.[36] That information seemed to matter little: Cogley was never punished for killing Jose Barlow Benavidez. The California State Assembly debated revising statewide police shooting laws, which the assembly had not updated since 1872. A new law clarified the existing law by mandating that the state would only deem officer-involved shootings justified if an individual threatened death or extreme bodily harm to others or to law enforcement, a relatively minor revision.[37]

In New Mexico, police killing of non-movement people also generated a movement response. One of the first major cases involving the Albuquerque Black Berets was the police killing of Tommy Valles. On August 13, 1968, brothers Tommy and Johnny Valles and their friend Ike Saavedra were driving home in their mother's car when they noticed a squad car following them. Officer Larry Ward had received a call to look for three robbery suspects driving a blue and white 1959 Chrysler. For Ward, the Valleses' blue and white 1956 Chrysler fit the description.[38]

At this point, the accounts of the officer and Johnny Valles and Ike Saavedra began to differ drastically. Ward stated that he engaged in a high-speed pursuit of the young men for approximately two miles. According to Valles and Saavedra, Ward never activated his lights or his siren and followed them for two miles while they drove with the normal course of traffic. When Ward did activate his lights, Johnny pulled over and the three men exited the vehicle and fled. Valles and Saavedra later stated that they fled because they were

Black Beret training march in northern New Mexico, ca. 1968. The Albuquerque chapter of the Berets, as well as other New Mexico chapters, consistently protested police abuse and violence throughout the 1960s and 1970s. The Albuquerque chapter was also one of the few chapters to propose a form of police abolition in its thirteen-point program. *Reies Lopez Tijerina Papers, MSS 654 BC, Center for Southwest Research, University Libraries, University of New Mexico, Albuquerque.*

scared; Ward had followed them for some time and they didn't know why he had pulled them over. Ward apprehended Johnny Valles quickly and, after firing a "warning" shot, placed Ike Saavedra under arrest. Tommy Valles had hidden in a nearby shed. When Ward opened the shed door, he claimed that Valles threw a piece of metal at him and he shot him in the chest. Valles died immediately. A television found in the car seemed to confirm police suspicions that the men had committed a robbery.[39]

Inconsistencies in the story signaled that the city could not easily make this case go away. For the Black Berets, Ward had misidentified the men as robbery suspects, the car was not stolen, and he had killed Valles needlessly. The Berets protested by disrupting a city council meeting and demanding that the city free Valles and Saavedra, punish Ward, found a civilian review board, and psychologically test all officers for bias. The Berets noted, "Policemen must learn that they have no right to shoot people for suspicion of a minor offense."[40]

As the Berets feared, the Bernalillo County grand jury no-billed Officer Ward.[41] While the city did contemplate a civilian review board, it didn't found one. The cases against Johnny Valles and Ike Saavedra went nowhere. Albuquerque assistant district attorney James Brandenburg dismissed all charges against Ike Saavedra because no evidence linked him to any crime. The Bernalillo County grand jury did indict Johnny Valles for burglary. But the jury convicted him only of careless driving, a reduced charge from the original reckless driving charge. The court fined him fifty dollars. Accounts of a stolen television disappeared from the story.[42] In 1971 members of the Valles family sued Ward in civil court for $200,000 for "gross negligence." That case ended in a mistrial.[43]

In other cases where police abused civilians, authorities found they had trouble removing such officers. Albuquerque police chief Bob Stover discovered this in 1974 after Officers Paul Seeber and Maurice Moya beat Phillip Gallegos and Lawrence Marquez. The off-duty officers, out for a night on the town, stopped at a traffic signal next to a truck driven by Gallegos and Marquez. The officers shouted obscenities at the men, followed them to a parking lot, and assaulted Gallegos and Marquez. When Marquez fled, the officers attempted to run him over. The internal affairs office concluded that the officers wielded police power out of uniform, so Stover fired them. Seeber and Moya appealed to the city's personnel board, which reinstated them.[44]

While the Black Berets protested, the district attorney filed charges of assault, battery, and tampering with a motor vehicle against the officers. They pleaded no contest. In January 1975 Judge H. Wells Kilbourne dismissed the charges against Seeber and Moya.[45] He said that he could not determine their culpability since Gallegos and Marquez did not attend the sentencing hearing. Assistant District Attorney Joseph Jelso countered that "both [officers] had entered a guilty plea . . . which it (no contest) is in essence." He commented on the violence of the crimes, to which the judge retorted, "How is assault and battery a violent crime?" The judge followed this outrageous claim by saying that the officers had had "enough punishment." Seeber and Moya remained on the force.[46]

The judge's decision shows yet again how the justice system protects its own. It also ran counter to the law. So, District Attorney Brandenburg authorized Jelso to go before District Court Judge William F. Riordan and secure a writ of mandamus (an order from a higher court compelling a lower court to fulfill its duties) against Kilbourne. They argued that he had "failed to perform his statutory duties" since his only choice was to sentence, defer, suspend, or commit the officers. Riordan agreed.[47] Judge Kilbourne was forced to appear before the court and explain his actions. He could not. The two judges, in consultation with Jelso, agreed to change the outcome of the case to deferred. This outcome did not satisfy the community, but a deferment would give the state time to build a new case against the officers. It never did.[48]

Then there was Officer James Babich. Local people had filed a number of use of force complaints against him in the 1970s. A police investigation found that Babich had a "temper problem."[49] In 1977 Babich encountered twenty-three-year-old Andres Ramirez. Officers Babich and Ron Wuenschel went to the Ramirez home to intervene in a domestic disturbance. After talking to Andres, Babich asked him to leave the premises. He refused. Babich became irritated, withdrew his metal Kel-Lite flashlight, and hit Ramirez on the head several times. Ramirez dropped to the floor and died at a nearby hospital. Chief Stover fired Babich and the Bernalillo County grand jury indicted him for involuntary manslaughter.[50] A medical examiner determined that Ramirez had experienced a massive brain hemorrhage as a result of the bludgeoning. A study of his brain showed that he had previously had a small hemorrhage that may have caused this larger bleed. Babich testified to the grand jury that he had not hit Ramirez hard. His attorney, Leon Taylor, described the sequence of events as a "freak accident." That proved enough to convince the jury that Babich was not responsible for Ramirez's death.[51]

With the assistance of the Black Berets and a new group called People United for Justice, Andres Ramirez's mother, Maria, filed a civil suit against James Babich. San Antonio attorney Ruben Sandoval joined the case and vowed to secure justice for Ramirez.[52] At trial, Sandoval exposed Babich's previous instances of violence. He described him as a time bomb and asked for $900,000 in compensatory damages. At about the same time, a man named Jose Jesus Sedillo filed suit claiming that Babich had beaten him during an arrest. That case ended in a mistrial. It seems likely that Maria Ramirez and Ruben Sandoval thought their suit might end similarly. When the city offered her a settlement of $70,900, she accepted.[53]

The killing of Andres Ramirez did lead to some minor policy changes. Chief Stover, who was displeased to learn of Babich's history of abuse, revised departmental policy to require officers to write their supervisor a letter each time they used violence against a civilian. Three letters would trigger an automatic review.[54] Such reforms likely seemed token to Andres Ramirez's family. His death underscored the uphill battle families had to fight to get justice. The system insulated Babich. When his defense could assert that hitting someone on the head with a metal flashlight, which led to their death, was a "freak accident," they effectively used Ramirez's physiology against him and blamed him for dying because he had a hemorrhagic brain.

Other killings happened in New Mexico. Frank Garcia, mentioned in the introduction, was another child killed by police. In February 1978, seventeen-year-old Frank and his eighteen-year-old friend Eugene Aragon were driving home from target shooting near Las Vegas when an unmarked vehicle with two men in plainclothes pulled alongside and gestured for the boys to stop. Not knowing who the men were, the teens drove on, at which point the other car forced them off the road. The two men were New Mexico State Police narcotics agents Jerry Noedel and Louie Gallegos. According to the officers, Garcia retrieved a rifle from the backseat and shot at the officers. They opened fire, wounding Garcia. They rendered him no aid, and Frank Garcia slowly bled to death.[55] Aragon reported that the officers never identified themselves and that Garcia had not fired at them. An investigation could not determine if Garcia had fired at the officers because he had gunpowder residue on his hands from target shooting earlier.[56]

An unofficial citizens' police review committee formed to investigate this case. In addition, members of La Raza Unida Party demanded a state-level investigation and denied reports that Garcia shot at the officers.[57] The state met these demands with silence. A month later, the grand jury in San Miguel County no-billed Noedel and Gallegos. The New Mexico State Police reinstated them.[58] Then the state put Eugene Aragon on trial for aggravated assault. A jury convicted him in late 1978 and sentenced him to five years' probation.[59] Frank Garcia's mother, Mary, sued for $1.8 million; she ended up settling for $40,000.[60]

New Mexico demonstrated once again the quotidian nature of police violence against non-movement Mexican-origin people. The state also demonstrates some of the problems with challenging this violence. Most importantly, the justice system does a good job of shielding officers who commit violence. A police chief might fire an officer only to have a city personnel board reinstate the officer. While Chicanos protested, they also joined with families to bring suit against officers accused of violence. Those suits were, at best, moderately successful.

And now we come to Texas, which was basically unmatched in its police violence against non-movement Mexican Americans. Because of the level of violence, Texas saw some of the most intense Chicano movement protests and the creation of several new civil rights groups. Some police killings resulted in disturbances or police riots. Texas was a messy, violent place.

It is impossible to talk about Texas, law enforcement, and Mexican Americans without mentioning the Mexican American Youth Organization. Like the Brown Berets, MAYO formed for a variety of reasons, some educational, some political, but one of the most important was to combat police abuse. José Angel Gutiérrez, the young activist who was brutalized by Texas Ranger A. Y. Allee in Crystal City in 1963, spearheaded the development of MAYO in 1967. He was joined by activists Mario Compeán, Willie Velázquez, Ignacio Pérez, and Juan Patlán, known as Los Cinco out of respect for the five Crystal City candidates.[61]

MAYO activists talked openly about their frustrations with police. They also linked their concerns with the idea of armed self-defense. Yolanda Garza Birdwell of Houston's MAYO chapter explained clearly, "I don't see how we can accomplish any change by peaceable ways. I don't see how we can avoid revolution with guns." And as far as police interactions with Chicanos were concerned, Birdwell intoned, "Get a gun, get it soon . . ."[62]

One of MAYO's biggest protests came after the police killing of Dr. Fred Logan. In July 1970 San Patricio County deputy sheriff Eric Brauch shot and killed Logan after an alleged scuffle. Although Logan was not of Mexican descent, Chicanos were incensed; they regarded him as a "friend of Chicanos" and as "the Anglo who cared." At his health clinic Logan provided low-cost or no-cost services to the Mexican American community. Hundreds attended a protest against police brutality on his behalf.[63] Similarly, when Corpus Christi police killed Mario Benavides during a botched arrest, MAYO organized another massive demonstration. Benavides had only recently returned home from service in Vietnam: activists therefore carried signs that read "Fight in Vietnam, Get Killed in Corpus Christi."[64]

Similar groups also developed in San Antonio. That city also saw one of its few racial conflagrations at this time in response to police brutality and murder. For example, in 1968, San Antonio police officers James Cammack Jr. (remember that name) and four others encountered a confused African American individual named Bobby Jo Phillips, who was armed with several knives. Though the officers disarmed him, Phillips cut one officer's hand. The officers proceeded to beat Phillips, who later died from these injuries. In a subsequent trial, the jury found the officers not guilty for Phillips's death. The Black and Chicano communities rose up in anger.[65] The local chapter of the Student Nonviolent Coordinating Committee, headed by firebrand Mario Salas, protested the killing. A year later, SNCC held a major protest to commemorate Phillips's death and decry police violence, which resulted in a short riot.[66]

This situation helped produce groups such as the Brown Berets in San Antonio. They participated in protests against police abuse on a number of occasions. During one demonstration in 1971, approximately 500 people marched through San Antonio's Mexican-dominant West Side. Some marchers shouted, "Hey piggly wiggly, we're going to get you, oink oink!" at the police officers present, but the officers actually seemed amused instead of angered.[67]

Austin continued the pattern of ley fuga police killings. Austin police, for instance, killed Oscar Balboa and Valentin Rodríguez in 1968. On the night of March 23, the two had stolen a vehicle. Reports of the theft came in quickly, and numerous officers responded. They lost control of the vehicle in downtown Austin near the Colorado River. Balboa and Rodríguez fled toward the river as police arrived. Several officers gave chase and fired "warning shots." Balboa and Rodríguez both made it to the river and ran down the bank toward the First Street Bridge. Rodríguez was behind Balboa when police shot again. Several bullets hit Rodríguez, and he fell before reaching the top of the embankment and died. Balboa made it to the top of the embankment, but police shot and killed him when he turned to run across the bridge.[68]

The killing of Balboa and Rodríguez generated a great deal of local activism. This was the first police killing in a number of years, and the Austin government took it seriously. While the grand jury cleared the officers involved in the shooting of wrongdoing—they had shot Rodríguez and Balboa during the commission of a felony, which made the killing justifiable—the Austin Police Department (APD), at the behest of Chicano activists, initiated a revised gun policy. This revised policy is similar to many department policies today and included automatic suspension of the officer and an immediate investigation of the shooting. The department did nothing, however, to alter how police handled fleeing suspects. The results were hardly surprising.[69]

The sad case of Joe Cedillo Jr. (mentioned in the introduction), another ley fuga killing, also generated much community anger. On the night of July 31, 1971, Austin police responded to a burglary at a closed convenience store. Officers James Johnson and Paul Looney found Cedillo emerging from the store. When they called for him to halt, he turned and ran. The two officers opened fire, and a bullet struck Cedillo at the base of his skull, killing him instantly. Inside the store investigators found bread, lunch meat, and sandwich spread that Cedillo had dropped. He was quite literally stealing the proverbial loaf of bread. He was sixteen years old and unarmed.[70]

The APD defended the officers. They besmirched Cedillo as a juvenile delinquent who had had previous encounters with law enforcement. The press also reported that he had been suspended from school and never returned, although he had reenrolled in order to resume his eighth-grade studies when school began in August. None of this was material to his case. His family described Cedillo as quiet and unassuming. "We had no problems," Joe's mother stated.[71] Per the APD's new policies, authorities put Officers Johnson and Looney on suspended duty. Police Chief Robert Miles reinstated them the same day. The Travis County grand jury declined to indict the two officers. While the grand jury decried Texas's flight law, which it called "the remnants of frontier justice," it nevertheless also warned that "those who choose to risk death by violating those laws which provide the chance of death should recognize the risk they take."[72]

This statement incensed Mexican American leaders in Austin. A group of protestors descended on the city council to voice their frustrations with police violence and the modified shooting policy, since it seemed to have done little to change police practice. Led by local activist Gonzalo Barrientos, the group demanded that the city fire Chief Miles and Officers Johnson and Looney. That, of course, was unlikely to occur. They also demanded a revision in the state's justifiable homicide law as well as in the APD's shooting procedures. County Commissioner Richard Moya noted that "any boy can get in trouble, but I don't believe the penalty for breaking in a grocery store and stealing some sandwich meat and a loaf of bread is death." Others called for the creation of a civilian review board. None of these things happened.[73]

The border city of Pharr, Texas, also saw some ugly episodes of police violence toward non-movement people. For instance, in 1971 Sergeant Mateo Sandoval beat two men, Manuel Mata, who received two broken ribs from his beating, and Guadalupe Salinas. These types of beatings proved common, so activists began a picket in front of the Pharr police station carrying signs that read "Más justicia y menos garrotazos" (more justice and fewer clubbings) and "No necesitamos policías salvajes" (we don't need police savages). The police, Birmingham-style, dispatched the fire department to turn high-pressure hoses on the young people. As they fled, officers positioned behind a police car opened fire. While they could have killed or wounded dozens of people, it seems the police only wanted to terrorize: the bullets were blanks.[74]

Pharr police called in reinforcements from the county sheriff, the Texas Rangers, and the Texas Department of Public Safety. When the protests continued, law enforcement dispersed them by shooting at vehicles, clubbing Mexican-origin people they encountered, and making large numbers of arrests, which set off a police riot. During that violence, police killed twenty-year-old Alfonso Loredo Flores. He had been getting a haircut when the violence began and left the barbershop to check things out. Deputy Sheriff Robert Johnson shot Flores in the back of the head, either intentionally or accidentally when his bullet ricocheted into Flores.[75] Activists planned a major protest and launched a group called La Conferencia Estatal en contra Represión Policial (State Conference against Police Repression). La Conferencia organized a 1,000-person march.[76] This activism resulted in some change. Mayor R. S. Bowe and Police Chief Alfredo Ramirez resigned due to the protests and their actions in calling in the Rangers. This was a victory by itself, but a jury acquitted Johnson of negligent homicide. The tension in Pharr took years to subside.[77]

Perhaps the most distressing examples of police violence against non-movement people occurred in Texas's largest cities, Houston and Dallas. The case of Bertha and Thomas Rodriguez in Dallas in 1971 serves as a useful example. Police stormed their apartment searching for a man suspected of killing three Dallas County deputy sheriffs. They wounded Bertha and Thomas, and then they arrested Thomas and charged him with assault to murder a police officer. Dallas police later admitted that they raided the wrong apartment. Chicanos held several rallies to protest this violence and demand that the city establish a civilian review board. They also organized a Brown Berets chapter to defend the community. Brothers Ricardo and Roberto Medrano, the sons of Pancho Medrano, focused the group on community protection. The Berets also acted as an independent version of the never-established police review board. The Brown Berets denounced police violence and insisted that the city hold officers accountable for their crimes. The Berets vowed "to protect, guarantee, and serve the rights of the Chicano by 'All Means' necessary." The police eventually dropped charges against Thomas Rodriguez. But the city made no reforms and the officers went unpunished. The results proved disastrous.[78]

The inaction of city officials led to one of the most egregious examples of police murder in Southwestern history. On the night of July 24, 1973, Dallas Police Department officers Darrell Cain and Roy Arnold witnessed three individuals burglarizing a vending machine at a Fina gas station. The culprits evaded the police, but the officers thought they recognized two of the robbers as brothers David and Santos Rodriguez (mentioned in the introduction). So they drove to the Rodriguez home, awakened the boys' foster grandfather, Jose Minez, and demanded that he allow them to enter the home. Minez granted this request, explaining later, "I was afraid. What could an old man do against their guns? I was afraid they would shoot me like they shot Thomas Rodriguez."[79] Cain and Arnold roused the sleeping brothers, handcuffed them, and drove them to the gas station.

The two police officers began interrogating the Rodriguez brothers. David sat in the back seat with Arnold, while Cain sat with Santos in the front. The officers demanded that the boys confess to the burglary. They refused. In an attempt to coerce a confession, Cain began a game of Russian roulette with Santos. He withdrew his .357 magnum revolver and pressed it to Santos's head. Cain asked him to confess. Santos again refused, so Cain pulled the trigger. Nothing happened. "This time there's a bullet in there," Cain stated, "so you better confess." "Tell the truth, hombre," Arnold demanded, "because he means it, this time he's going to shoot you." Cain pulled the trigger again and the gun discharged into Santos's head. David could only watch in horror as the life quickly and irrevocably drained from his brother. Santos Rodriguez was twelve years old. According to later reports, his last words were "I'm telling the truth."[80]

The Dallas Police Department (DPD) suspended Cain and Arnold, arrested Cain, and charged him with murder. On July 26, Dallasites learned that fingerprints taken from the gas station did not match those of the Rodriguez brothers. They also learned that Cain had previously killed an unarmed African American man named Michael Morehead in 1970. Cain had shot him after an alleged burglary attempt. That shooting had caused the Black community to protest and the city to revise its shooting policy by prohibiting the use of warning shots and authorizing officers to use their weapons only when their lives were threatened. But Cain went unpunished. This information infuriated the Mexican American community because it suggested that the DPD could have prevented Rodriguez's death by removing Cain from the force for killing Morehead. That did not happen, which signaled the value police placed on their officers and the communities they were charged to protect.[81]

At the same time, Pedro Aguirre, the lone Mexican American serving on the Dallas City Council, pushed the city to institute an internal affairs office and civilian review board. Rene Martínez, the head of Dallas's informal tri-ethnic committee, also demanded that the city establish some form of police oversight commission. Aguirre, Martínez, and others also insisted that the city terminate Police Chief Frank Dyson. The city did nothing. Frustrated by this inaction, Pancho Medrano began organizing meetings with leaders in the Mexican American and African American communities. He met with Aguirre, Martínez, the Reverend Rudy Sanchez (a popular minister), and George Allen (the sole African American city council member) to organize a massive march to decry the murder of Santos Rodriguez. They hoped to send a powerful message to city leaders that communities of color would no longer tolerate police violence.[82]

At noon on Saturday, July 28, 1973, the march commenced. A group of nearly 2,000 people met at John F. Kennedy Plaza and marched peacefully through downtown Dallas to City Hall. There, Martínez, Aguirre, Reverend

A woman and other protestors run at the beginning of the Dallas Disturbance, 1973. The protest decried the police execution of twelve-year-old Santos Rodriguez and demanded police reform. The visceral, emotional expression on the woman's face shows in many ways the pain and anguish that the Mexican American community felt after Rodriguez's senseless death. *Jay Dickman Photography.*

Sanchez, and others gave speeches. A palpable anger infused the protest. Sensing this tension, the speakers began to cut their remarks short so that the marchers could return to Kennedy Plaza. When the return trek began, a reporter asked Rene Martínez how he felt about the protest. "I believe it went well. We're not trying to keep emotions down," he said, explaining the abbreviated speeches, "but [to] keep them in order."[83]

That order fell apart only moments later. Unbeknownst to Martínez, another group of approximately 500 activists had arrived late at Kennedy Plaza. Finding no one there, they assumed that police had suppressed the protest. Angered, they began their own trek to Dallas City Hall. This new group met the original group of marchers about halfway to their destination. At this point, during the heat of the day, tensions flared. Police attempted to move the protest back to Kennedy Plaza. In response, some Chicanos began taunting the police and refused to return to the plaza. Aguirre climbed atop a patrol car and attempted to calm the marchers, but his microphone failed.

At about the same time, an African American woman began yelling that the police had killed her son (a claim later proven false). The crowd erupted. The marchers attacked the police, beat several officers, and dispersed them. Several protestors set fire to a police motorcycle. They soon added a second police motorcycle to the pyre. Some people looted nearby businesses. Tactical police arrived, but their efforts often deteriorated into skirmishes with individual protestors.[84]

Dallas police ultimately did restore order. Their presence seemed to stay many of the marchers. As the police fought with individual Chicanos, others escaped down side streets and away from downtown. By 5:00 p.m. it was over. Five police officers and many more marchers were injured in the violence. Police arrested thirty-six people involved in the Dallas Disturbance, as the conflagration came to be known. But they released most of these individuals the following day. Finally, in November a jury found Darrell Cain guilty of murder and sentenced him to five years in prison. He served approximately half of that sentence.[85]

The Santos Rodriguez incident remained an ugly blight on the City of Dallas. The light sentence Cain received also irked a lot of people. So, too, did the disturbance, one of the few racial conflagrations in Dallas's history. The whole affair seemed to stun city leaders and local people, so much so that the shock actually helped calm the situation in Dallas. But Mexican Americans did not stop their push for reforms. In late 1973 the city council passed a resolution that decried the "unequal law enforcement, dual justice, and unequal treatment for the different segments of the community and different races in Dallas."[86] Throughout 1974 Chicano and Black leaders continued to demand that the DPD implement an internal affairs office, hire more officers of color, and assign Chicano and Black officers to Black and Brown parts of the city. The DPD did begin hiring more African American and Mexican American officers. The DPD also appointed its first non-White deputy police chief in 1974. And the department launched its internal affairs office that same year. Finally, in 2013 Dallas mayor Mike Rawlings publicly apologized for the murder of Santos Rodriguez.[87]

Houston had its own egregious example of police murder of a non-movement individual, that of Jose "Joe" Campos Torres. His killing, like the police murder of Santos Rodriguez, touched off a major uprising in the City of Houston. The Houston Police Department (HPD) had not made much of an effort to do the kind of community outreach, officer recruitment, and programming to improve police relations with Mexican Americans that other cities had done. Texas representative Ben Reyes noted in regards to community relations that the HPD had an "obviously weak program" and that "relatively little was done in [the] Chicano community to improve [the] image" of police. He also explained that in 1976 Chief of Police Byron G. "Pappy" Bond had promised to hire officers in proportion to their percentage of the population, but this did not happen. Instead the department appeared "to exclude and discourage minority applicants."[88]

Joe Campos Torres, a Vietnam War–era veteran, had returned to Houston after his discharge from the US Army in 1977. After recovering from a stomach ulcer, Torres began looking for work but had difficulty due to the economic slump of the late 1970s. He had also begun drinking. On the night of May 6, Torres was allegedly involved in a fight at a local bar. Houston police officers Stephen Orlando and Terry Denson, who were later joined by Officers Carless Elliott, Joseph Janish, and Louis Kinney, arrested Torres for drunk and disorderly conduct.[89]

Instead of taking Torres to jail, the officers drove him to a secluded area that police referred to as The Hole. Police frequented The Hole to gossip, drink or take drugs, and abuse suspects in custody. There, Denson, Orlando, and the other officers beat Torres. After nearly an hour of punching and kicking him, they drove him to the jail. But the desk sergeant refused to allow the officers to book Torres and ordered them to take him to the hospital. They instead drove back to The Hole and beat Torres again. They then drove him to a landing beneath the Commerce Street bridge over Buffalo Bayou, removed his handcuffs, and pushed him to the edge of the landing. Denson exclaimed, "Let's see if the wetback can swim," and pushed Torres off the landing. Torres fell about twenty feet and into the bayou. Although Denson and Orlando later claimed that they had watched Torres swim away, this statement proved a lie. Three days later a bystander spotted his body floating face down in the bayou.[90]

Local officials initially attempted to downplay this incident, but the sequence of events leading to Torres's death soon came to light. As in other cases, police sought to tarnish Torres's reputation to excuse the officers. They portrayed him as violent and as having a lengthy criminal record, which turned out to be a few arrests for public intoxication. Torres did have a drinking problem, but alcoholism is not a crime. A year later one officer testified that Torres had lashed out at police the night he died. "Pig, I'm going to kill you!" Torres allegedly shouted. Police also claimed that Torres had mastered martial arts and had threatened the officers by saying "I can kick your Adam's apple before you pull the trigger." Such comments about Torres's karate skills or drunkenness were not just ludicrous but designed to justify his killing.[91]

The HPD fired the officers involved in Torres's death and launched an investigation.[92] Mayor Fred Hofheinz expressed his frustrations with police. "I have spent political capital, I have called police chiefs on the carpet, I have had group discussions with high level officers," Hofheinz stated, "and still I leave town and find that things of this kind continue to take place in the HPD. There is no excuse for it." Hofheinz perhaps found it difficult to turn an accusatory finger toward himself. He had authorized a large increase in riot control spending and presided over a more militaristic police department. And when given the opportunity to support reforms such as police-civilian review, the mayor balked, saying, "The solution to police discipline is not a Citizen Review Board."[93] Ben Reyes pressed for a national inquiry. He wrote to Attorney General Griffin Bell and Representatives Henry B. Gonzalez and Barbara Jordan to demand justice for Torres. Mexican Americans "will not be content with a whitewash of this shocking case," he asserted.[94] These leaders responded politely but declined to get involved.[95]

Because of the Torres murder a number of groups began working with the police for reforms, while others protested the HPD. The Coalition for Responsible Law Enforcement did a great deal to push for departmental reform.[96] The group began working with Chief Harry Caldwell, who had replaced Chief Bond in June 1977. By September they could tout some results. The HPD, for example, initiated an internal affairs division. It also began looking into establishing a police-community relations bureau in the department. Although police had not killed Torres in a questionable shooting scenario, Mexican Americans wanted police shooting policies updated as well. Caldwell agreed to change department gun policies in two ways: he revised ley fuga rules by mandating that officers could only shoot fleeing suspects if their lives were in danger, and he banned police from using high-powered or modified rifles.[97]

Chicanos anxiously waited for the outcome of the state trial. The prosecution of Denson and Orlando began in September 1977. Several shocking revelations came to light during the proceedings. Orlando, for instance, admitted that he lied six times, mainly in regard to beating Torres, when first questioned about the case.[98] More significantly, Carless Elliott testified against Denson and Orlando. Although he did not witness the men push Torres into the bayou, Elliot claimed to have heard Torres fall into the water. Elliott explained his shock at the trial. "Oh my god," he claimed to have said to himself at the time, "they've really thrown him in." He also admitted that the two officers had forced him to help destroy investigative notes about Torres.[99]

Officer Louis Kinney also testified against Orlando and Denson. He admitted that he, Denson, Orlando, and Elliott had all taken turns hitting and kicking Torres. Kinney gave further evidence as to the severity of Torres's bludgeoning. He reported that at one point Orlando withdrew a metal flashlight and stated, "This is a brand new flashlight and I want to try it out. Then he [Orlando] hit him [Torres] four or five times hard on the shins." After beating Torres, Kinney testified that Orlando said, "I've got this Mexican's blood on my hands. The jail probably won't take him and we'll have to spend all night out at Ben Taub's [hospital]." To avoid taking Torres to the hospital, the officers chose to dump him in the bayou. Kinney admitted, "I bet that guy drowned."[100] Finally, Harris County medical examiner Dr. Joseph Jachimczyk confirmed what many Houston residents already knew—that Torres did not have a chance of surviving once thrown into Buffalo Bayou. He testified that Torres was "twice drunk," from the alcohol and from the beating. When asked if there was any way Torres could have survived the plunge into the bayou, Jachimczyk replied, "I wouldn't bet on him making it."[101]

The jury deliberated for several weeks and convicted Denson and Orlando of negligent homicide, a misdemeanor. Their punishment: a $2,000 fine and one-year probated jail sentences. Despite the preponderance of evidence presented by the state, including the testimony of the HPD officers, the all-White jury ultimately concluded that sufficient evidence did not exist to convict the officers of a more severe crime. Some in the HPD could see the result of the trial as a miscarriage of justice that was bad for residents, police, and the city. Lieutenant Don McWilliams, who investigated the case for the HPD, explained, "I've always maintained they were guilty of murder. I expected more, at least a manslaughter conviction." As an officer the result was additionally problematic for McWilliams because "this thing is going to come right back to the police." The lenient punishment assured there would be prolonged protests from the Chicano community.[102]

Two women became the most important leaders directing this activism. Joe Campos Torres's killing motivated his mother, Margaret, to become a leader. She denounced the officers, saying, "I'm disgusted. Killing my son like that, beating him like he was an animal and then throwing him in the bayou." She also warned, "If we don't get justice, we'll just have to try to defend ourselves." She helped plan a major protest march to express community anger over the sentences. She also supported the newly formed People United against Police Brutality, which fought against police brutality and served as a self-defense group similar to the Brown Berets. Mamie Garcia, the president of the Houston council of the League of United Latin American Citizens, also had a prominent leadership role after the trial. She met with Chief Bond and later Chief Caldwell to seek reforms such as a civilian review board. While Margaret Torres sought justice for her son, Mamie Garcia wanted policy to halt, or at least limit, police violence. The League also appealed to federal authorities. It wanted the Justice Department to prosecute the officers for violating Torres's rights. "Justice has not been done," explained Mamie Garcia, "and we will no longer sit back. We will take an active role in guaranteeing civil rights."[103]

The march engineered by Margaret Torres occurred on October 8, 1977. About 200 protesters marched to Moody Park, the heart of Houston's Northside barrio. At the protest Torres condemned the lenient sentences and called for a federal investigation. A week later, another march took place.[104] Police arrested both of Joe Campos Torres's parents after the demonstration ended. According to Joe Luna Torres, Joe's father, he and Margaret exited a community center after the protest and saw an HPD officer holding his gun to a Chicano youth's head. Torres told the officer, "He's just a kid, you got no right to shoot a kid," and Margaret Torres stated, "You can't kill him like you did my son." Police arrested and then released them a short time later.[105] Demonstrations occurred sporadically throughout late 1977. They ended when the HPD formally launched a new internal affairs division, which the Torres case had spurred into existence.[106]

A federal grand jury indicted four HPD officers involved in Torres's death, including Orlando and Denson. The federal trial largely duplicated the state trial. In February 1978 the federal court found Stephen Orlando, Terry Denson, and Joseph Janish guilty of conspiring to deprive Torres of his constitutional rights, a conspiracy that resulted in his death. Judge Ross Sterling sentenced the officers to serve one year in prison for felony misdemeanor for beating Torres and ten years for violating Torres's constitutional rights. But he suspended the harsher sentence and substituted the ten years of jail time with five years' probation. He also did not fine the officers.[107] The decision angered the Chicano community. "We never expected much more than we got out of the feds," explained Travis Morales, a Rice University student and leader in People United against Police Brutality. "There is no way to expect justice from those that don't care."[108] The Justice Department did order Judge Sterling to alter his judgment. He refused.[109] The federal government then sued to have a harsher sentence imposed on the officers, arguing that their conviction necessitated some amount of prison time. In October 1979 the Fifth Circuit Court of Appeals agreed and ordered Sterling to sentence the officers according to the law. He sentenced them to one year in prison, the lightest sentence he could give.[110]

As they had done previously, Margaret Torres, Mamie Garcia, and other activists planned a number of protests and rallies at Moody Park.[111] They first engaged in a silent march from the Northside barrio to downtown Houston on April 1, 1978. The march ended at the spot along Buffalo Bayou where the officers had pushed Torres into the water.[112] Another protest occurred about a month later on May 7, 1978, coinciding with Cinco de Mayo celebrations. A crowd of several hundred once again gathered at Moody Park. But on this occasion, a perceptible tension filled the air. The presence of a number of HPD officers only inflamed hostilities. When the officers attempted to arrest one Chicano, the crowd erupted. The protestors gathered around a police car and eventually turned it over. Amid shouts of "Get the pigs" and "Justice for Joe Torres," people surged out of the park and toward a growing contingent of police officers. The protestors destroyed almost anything in their path—a convenience store, bakery, record shop, and laundry were soon in flames. Unknown assailants fired shots at police. The police, dressed in full riot gear, marched toward the crowd, which retreated as they arrived. Despite sporadic violence throughout the night, the uprising was over in a matter of hours.[113]

The following evening protestors gathered again. Approximately 150 demonstrators met at Moody Park, but before they had the chance to hear speakers, a line of fifty HPD officers in riot gear moved in to clear them out. Young Chicanos, angered by the police presence, began throwing rocks and bricks at police. Members of the HPD SWAT team arrived on the scene and arrested eighteen individuals. Chief Caldwell wisely told his officers not to "overreact" and told the press that the aim of police "is just to contain the thing."[114] HPD leadership largely blamed Travis Morales for this violence. The local press emphasized his communist sympathies and Marxist bona fides as a way to discredit him.[115] After the second night of protests they again singled out Morales. According to witnesses, he had used a bullhorn to shout "Justice! Justice!" Evidently for police calls for "Justice!" were the same as a call to violence.[116]

While Chief Caldwell responded to these demonstrations cautiously, Houston mayor Jim McConn announced that he had considered closing Moody Park. "We can't have anarchy within the city and we don't intend to have it," he stated. McConn's words certainly resonated with some Houstonians, but the Mexican American community took them as an affront, which the mayor may well have intended. Moody Park had served as a site of recreation and community gathering for decades. Mexican-origin people thus responded negatively to this idea.[117] It took reporting from other Texas cities, especially San Antonio, to more accurately understand the disturbance.

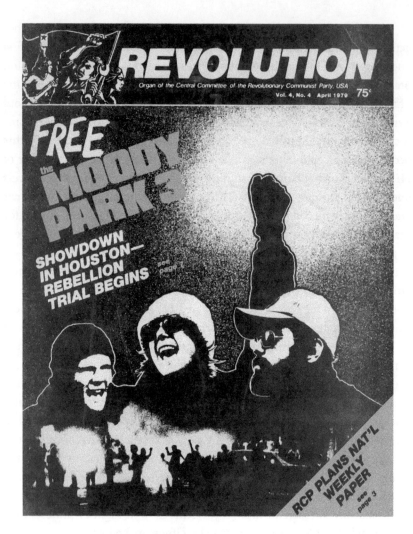

Front page of *Revolution* (April 1979) featuring a depiction of the Moody Park 3. *Pictured from left to right:* Thomas Hirsch, Mara Margolis Youngdahl, and Travis Morales. At the bottom is a scene from the Moody Park uprising. *Revolution,* the official newspaper of the Revolutionary Communist Party, USA, did consistently good reporting on all forms of civil rights activism and often had vibrant and creative cover art. © *revcom.us. In Joe Campos Torres: Handout on Police Brutality,* box 5, folder 10, HMRC Small Collections, Houston History Research Center, Houston Public Library.

The *San Antonio Express-News*, for example, commented on Houston's unfamiliarity with their growing Mexican American population as a cause of conflict.[118] They offered the wise words of Luis Cano, a longtime leader in Houston, who noted that "the biggest—and most dangerous problem is the poor relationship we've had for generations with the police department."[119]

Police arrested nearly twenty-five people for the violence at Moody Park. The weight of the justice system fell on Travis Morales, Mara Margolis Youngdahl, and Thomas Hirsch, all activists with People United against Police Brutality. Morales was an obvious target since he had helped organize the protests and been demonized in the press. Youngdahl and Hirsch had also helped organize the demonstrations. The district attorney charged them collectively with nine felony offenses, including multiple counts of criminal mischief, aggravated assault, and arson. The arson charges alone carried a maximum twenty-year sentence; if sentenced to the maximum, they could serve up to eighty years in prison.[120] Their cases resulted in the creation of Free the Moody Park 3 and the Committee to Defend the Houston Rebellion, both legal defense funds. These groups held rallies and protests to push authorities to release the Moody Park 3.[121] Brown Beret Rado Rosales explained during one of the Free the Moody Park 3 marches that "we don't need more police. We're here to defend ourselves." His bravado was matched by others, including a group of mothers who marched to protest the violence at Moody Park and the arrest of the Moody Park 3.[122] These protests also included a short play entitled *The Houston Rebellion* that recounted the murder of Joe Campos Torres and the uprising at Moody Park.[123]

The trial of the Moody Park 3 began in April 1979. The state amended the charges to inciting a riot, a felony that carried a penalty of up to five years in prison.[124] The jury of eleven White people and one Mexican American found Travis Morales and Mara Youngdahl guilty of felony riot and sentenced them to five years' probation. Morales was fined $5,000, Youngdahl $4,000. The jury convicted Tom Hirsch of misdemeanor riot and fined him $1,000. These results angered Houston Chicanos, since the penalties all seriously outweighed those that the officers who killed Torres had received. After years of legal work, activists cleared the Moody Park 3 in 1985.[125]

The Moody Park Rebellion was the outgrowth of the complicated handling of the killing of Jose Campos Torres and an expression of anger from a community that had waited patiently for justice. Various Mexican American leaders had done a great deal to implement change, including forcing the establishment of the HPD's internal affairs office and pushing the federal government to instigate its own trial of Torres's killers. But the light sentences and historic patterns of violence did little to convince Chicanos that police respected their rights. Keep in mind that the state charged and convicted the protestors of Torres's death with harsher penalties than they did Torres's killers. That said, Mexican Americans were relieved that the Fifth Circuit Court of Appeals ruled that the officers had to serve time in prison.[126]

Dallas and Houston were of course not the only big cities to see unnecessary police killings. The case of Danny Vasquez serves as a useful example. Law enforcement in El Paso killed him in January 1978. The high school senior had attended a quinceañera with his older brother, Henry, when members of the El Paso County Sheriff's Office arrived. Someone had called them to report a fight. Deputy Sheriff Sergio Guzman began to arrest Jose Zaragosa, a friend of Danny Vasquez. Both Danny and Henry explained to the officer that Zaragosa had not been fighting. Guzman ordered the boys to stop interfering and he pointed his shotgun at Danny. Vasquez pushed the weapon away, telling the officer, "Don't aim that gun at me." Guzman paused, then raised the weapon to Vasquez's chest, paused again, and shot him. Danny Vasquez lived for at least thirty minutes and begged to be taken to the hospital. None of the police rendered him aid, they prevented his friends from helping him, and he died at the scene.[127]

Police claimed the shooting was an accident. Several witnesses, however, reported that Guzman had paused, taking time to think before shooting Vasquez. A number of Chicanos also disclosed that they had had previous encounters with Guzman and that he had harassed activists involved in a group called Chicanos Unidos. Ramon Arroyos, a spokesperson for the group, explained that Guzman had arrested members of Chicanos Unidos only to release them without charging them—a common type of harassment. Danny Vasquez did not belong to this group. He had no criminal record. In fact, he was a good student, a football star at his school, and a typical high school senior.[128]

Deputy Sheriff Guzman claimed that he "was fearing for my life, I at no time intended to shoot." According to Patsy Valadez, who witnessed the shooting, "It wasn't an accident. He (Guzman) knew exactly what he was doing." The El Paso County Sheriff's Office denied the accusations but suspended Guzman pending an investigation.[129] Local people orchestrated a protest and rally. Over 300 Chicanos gathered in downtown El Paso to demand that the city prosecute Guzman for murder. They marched from the plaza to the county courthouse, where they listened to speeches from a variety of leaders. The most passionate words came from Danny's parents, Ricardo and Maria, who through tears thanked the crowd for honoring their son.[130]

Despite the organization of the Danny Vasquez Defense Committee and the enormous pressure this group put on officials to prosecute the case, the grand jury determined the case to be a justifiable homicide.[131] The defense committee and his parents appealed to President Jimmy Carter, Attorney General Griffin Bell, and Texas Governor Dolph Briscoe but received responses from no one. The Justice Department ultimately declined to pursue the case.[132] The Vasquez family filed a wrongful death suit against Guzman in federal court, arguing that he had violated their son's rights. The jury absolved Guzman of wrongdoing. Danny Vasquez became yet another non-movement youth killed by police for seemingly no reason.[133]

Police violence in Texas, from the Rangers to urban uprisings in Dallas, Houston, San Antonio, Pharr, and elsewhere, was pervasive, egregious, and ugly. It remains a sad fact that although Mexican Americans had advocated for change in Texas for generations, it often took police murders such as that of Santos Rodriguez to motivate law enforcement to change. Even after such momentous cases, police could still brutalize Mexican Americans with impunity and then be relieved of responsibility or liability by other branches of the criminal justice system, as the case of Danny Vasquez and many others make plain.

The violence against non-movement people generated some interesting responses from the Chicano movement. One thing activists did was develop defense offices, or legal defense groups that assisted Mexican-origin people whom police had abused.[134] Another idea was collecting lists of the names of those killed by police. La Raza Unida Party and the Crusade for Justice compiled a list of seventy examples of police killing that included images of the victims and a narrative describing the circumstances of their deaths.[135] When the US press ignored requests that they report on this list, activists traveled to Mexico City and held a widely attended press conference with the Mexican press. The US media then picked up the story. In other words, activists did an end run around the system that got them the attention they wanted.[136]

These actions produced some results. In May 1978 the Justice Department began a series of probes into police brutality, ultimately reviewing sixty cases.[137] That same month a group of Mexican American leaders met with Attorney General Bell in Dallas to discuss police violence. The meeting resulted in the adoption of a number of resolutions, among the most important of which was an augmented level of federal monitoring of local and state police, the formation of a presidential commission on police brutality, and a request that the US Commission on Civil Rights study police brutality against Mexican-origin people.[138] A number of leaders traveled to Washington, DC, in 1978 to meet with Bell. They asked for a specific timetable for the disposition of 192 Justice Department cases of police brutality against Mexican Americans and that the department take a position on the use of police to enforce immigration law.[139]

Activists also warned the government about the potential for violence if the Justice Department failed to prosecute cases like Jose Sinohui's. San Antonio activist Ruben Sandoval promised a "long, hot and burning summer." "What does it take to get these people off their ass?" Sandoval asked. "Does it take burning, looting, killing?"[140] His words could be seen as a warning or a promise. Chicanos had already shown a willingness to fight for their rights and had long favored working with the system for change, so these threats actually communicated a great deal.

It is important to note the Mexican American community's efforts to push the Department of Justice to secure justice for individuals wronged by law enforcement, especially when lower courts refused to do so. In many ways Mexican American activists pioneered this strategy. The Justice Department had been founded in large part to protect the rights of formerly enslaved Black people after the Civil War, but using the department for prosecuting civil rights violations, particularly at the hands of law enforcement, seemed to have been forgotten somewhere at the turn of the twentieth century. Mexican American demands were therefore very important.

Despite protests, police kept killing people. Unlike the cases involving Chicano activists discussed in the previous chapter, the cases involving everyday, non-movement people seemed particularly egregious. But of course, everyday people had experienced such violence for generations. It happened in every corner of the region. It was so commonplace that it was basically ordinary and seemed simply a standard police practice.

Chicanos responded to all forms of police violence, but the examples that got the most attention tended to be violence committed against the innocent or children (Santos Rodriguez). Even when people broke the law, like Joe Cedillo, they still deserved a fair administration of justice and not to get shot in the back of the head. The violence that non-movement individuals experienced also generated a great deal of activism. The Brown Berets had formed both to confront police violence they experienced as movement participants but also because they knew that police committed violence against non-movement folks as well.

Many of these cases simply should not have happened. But they did. They all did. And there were numerous other cases that occurred in this era. Some of those cases were really strange. Some involved police officers committing premeditated first-degree murder or police officers who shot each other in a friendly fire incident. Many resulted in meaningful and important reforms. Such cases, themselves cruel and unusual, also show just how cruel and unusual the system could be.

FOUR

CRUEL AND UNUSUAL

Strange Cases of Abuse, Activism, and Reform

In September 1975, Castroville, Texas, chief of police Frank Hayes killed Ricardo Morales. This was no accidental shooting, nor an example of an abuse of force that led to a death, nor a ley fuga killing. Instead, Hayes simply murdered Morales because he didn't like him. Not only that, Hayes employed members of his family to help dispose of Morales's body. And then he lied to authorities about what had happened in an attempt to cover up his heinous crime. Those lies ultimately undid Hayes: authorities questioned his stories, investigated, and figured out what had happened. He was convicted and sentenced to life in prison, which was somewhat unusual considering all of the deaths discussed in this book that went unpunished.

The civil rights era saw a number of appalling and, frankly, weird cases of abuse and murder. These were cases of gross violence that simply don't make sense, defy a conventional explanation or reasoning, or were just plain odd. The Hayes incident serves as a good example. But these cases are important to our understanding of law enforcement and the Mexican American community because they demonstrate aspects of policing, in some case meaningful police reforms, that complicate the history of this period. For example, the Hayes case pushed the Justice Department to modify a federal policy that allowed for such cases to be tried simultaneously at the local and federal level. That was an important modification to Justice Department policy and practice. Other cases resulted in new reforms and revisions as to how the criminal justice system does its work.

I borrow this chapter's title from the Constitution's prohibition on cruel and unusual punishment because many of these cases represented such cruelness. But many also resulted in some form of punishment, either for the aggrieved party or parties or for those who committed the aggression (sometimes both). Some of the abuse came not at the hands of law enforcement but from vigilantes who acted like law enforcement. No case better exemplifies this than the famous Hanigan case in Arizona. The work of the KKK in the late 1970s and early 1980s also fits this pattern. And finally, we have a case of a friendly fire incident wherein Tucson police officer Roy Garcia was wounded in the line of duty by a fellow officer. Such incidents are incredibly unusual for police officers, so this case is pretty remarkable. But also, Tucson's leadership handled this case poorly and basically blamed Garcia for his own shooting, which tells us something about how government agencies sometimes treat their officers.

The unusual aspects of many of these cases also often generated a concerted response from the Chicano movement. Chicano activism worked once again as a defense for those who were often defenseless. Activists wanted the justice system, and law enforcement especially, to work fairly, and so it didn't really matter to them what the circumstances of a particular case may have been or whether the people involved were unpleasant characters—and they often were—they demanded justice for the aggrieved. For example, the killing of Sheriff's Sergeant Julian Narvaez by Pete Garcia led to somewhat of a split in the Mexican American community in Albuquerque but also generated Chicano activism in support of Garcia even though he was an unsavory individual. These examples demonstrate in many ways the dexterity of the Chicano movement.

New Mexico experienced a couple of cruel and unusual cases in the civil rights period. The first was that of Pete Garcia. His example demonstrates many of the complexities of Mexican American relations with law enforcement in New Mexico. In 1969, Garcia killed Sheriff's Sergeant Julian Narvaez after a traffic stop in Albuquerque. Because the case involved a Mexican

American officer killed by a Mexican American civilian, it divided Mexican-origin people in New Mexico: some sided with Narvaez and against Garcia, while others sided with Garcia, who had prior violent run-ins with Narvaez, and against Narvaez, a troubled officer who became the face of institutional racism within local law enforcement.

Pete Garcia had a rocky life. He developed a drug addiction in his teens and first encountered the criminal justice system in his early twenties in 1959 for breaking and entering. Julian Narvaez, an eight-year veteran of the Bernalillo County Sheriff's Office, had climbed the ranks steadily and made sergeant in 1966. Garcia had a series of interactions with Narvaez beginning in the fall of 1966 when Narvaez and Deputy Cody Prestwood pulled over Garcia and his friend Eugene Aragon.[1] The officers approached the vehicle with guns drawn. Narvaez roughly removed Aragon, the driver, and threw him against the hood of the squad car and slapped him. As a passenger, Garcia had no reason to be a target of the officers, but Prestwood removed Garcia and prepared to strike him. He stopped when he noticed that Garcia had an infection on his arm. The officers arrested both men but did not charge them with a crime and released them the next day. As Garcia walked out of the jail, Narvaez arrested him again, allegedly because the vehicle from the previous evening was stolen. But the vehicle belonged to Aragon, so Narvaez released him a short time later. Two arrests in two days; this was a common form of harassment that many people of color experienced. Garcia went to attorney Gerald Goodman to make a claim of harassment. Goodman contacted the sheriff, who promised that Narvaez would cease harassing Garcia.[2]

Garcia next saw Narvaez harassing someone else, this time a man with his family. According to Garcia, the man, his wife, and their two children had their hands on the hood of a squad car as Narvaez searched them all. Narvaez hit and kicked the man. Garcia stated, "I was so disgusted that I just drove on." That response is instructive because it demonstrates one of the ways police violence works; it is designed to instill fear and cow those who might otherwise stand up to obvious examples of abuse. Garcia, himself a victim of abuse, chose to ignore the same officer exacting the same type of abuse on other people.[3]

Then, on the morning of March 26, 1969, Pete Garcia was riding with several men when Narvaez pulled them over. He removed Garcia from the vehicle, roughly patted him down, and then shoved his gun into the small of Garcia's back and shot him. "¡Ya me chingaste!" Garcia exclaimed, or "Now you fucked me!" Garcia turned and grabbed for Narvaez's gun. The two men struggled over the weapon. During this struggle Garcia's own pistol fell out of his pocket; the media later erroneously reported that he had killed Narvaez with this gun. While the two men struggled for Narvaez's gun, it discharged several more times, mortally wounding Narvaez.[4]

Pete Garcia spent two months in the hospital recuperating from his bullet wound.[5] News of Narvaez's death spread rapidly, but many of the accounts of the incident were flawed. For example, the number of guns changed from two to three then back to two. The calibers of the weapons also changed. There was also conflicting information about the shooting: some witnesses claimed that Garcia stood over Narvaez and shot him in the back, implying that Garcia had executed Narvaez; others claimed Narvaez was shot as the two men struggled. Few media outlets explained why Narvaez had chosen to harass and ultimately shoot Garcia. But by some accounts, it seems that Narvaez simply hated Garcia because he had a drug addiction.[6]

The state charged Garcia with first-degree murder and sought the death penalty. His trial began in late August 1969. The Black Berets and other groups provided legal aid to Garcia. That the Chicano movement defended Garcia showed that, from their perspective, he was simply another victim of police abuse. He pleaded not guilty and asserted at trial that he had acted in self-defense. Several witnesses explained that Narvaez had targeted Garcia because he hated drug addicts.[7] One witness told about an incident wherein Narvaez had pulled him over when he had borrowed Pete Garcia's car. Narvaez approached the vehicle with his gun drawn, but when he realized Garcia wasn't driving, he holstered his weapon. When the witness asked what he wanted with Garcia, Narvaez allegedly responded, "Every time I see that bastard Pete Garcia I'm going to have this gun in my hand, and I'm not going to need too much of an excuse to use it." A former coworker of Narvaez also noted that he had a tendency for violence.[8]

After deliberating for fourteen hours the jury deadlocked and the judge declared a mistrial.[9] The state made plans to retry Pete Garcia shortly thereafter. His second trial began in December of 1969. This time the jury convicted him of voluntary manslaughter and sentenced him to two to ten years in prison.[10] He appealed and the New Mexico Court of Appeals reversed his conviction in 1971. The court found three errors in the case, most seriously that the prosecution had erred when it introduced testimony that Garcia had a drug addiction, which unfairly prejudiced the jury against him.[11] The state tried him a third time, this time skirting the history of his drug use. The jury again found Garcia guilty of voluntary manslaughter and sentenced him to two to ten years in prison.[12] While out on bond pending an appeal, Garcia was allegedly involved in a shooting at a nightclub. A judge issued a warrant for his arrest, but Garcia failed to turn himself in. He also failed to show up for his sentencing hearing for the killing of Julian Narvaez.[13] After six months, authorities still couldn't locate Garcia. As it turned out, he had fled to Mexico. In 1974 police in Mexico City arrested him for narcotics possession. But he escaped in 1975 and thus was wanted by law enforcement in Mexico and the United States.[14] Mexican police finally collared Garcia in 1978 and returned him to New Mexico in June 1979.[15]

Just at about the time Garcia was to begin serving his two- to ten-year sentence, the New Mexico Court of Appeals again reversed his conviction in 1980. This time the court decided that the prosecution had erred when it told the jury that the state did not have to prove that Garcia had intended to kill Narvaez (New Mexico law at the time stipulated that someone charged with voluntary manslaughter had to intend to kill the victim). This was pertinent to Garcia's case both because the prosecution had misstated the applicable law and because they couldn't show that Garcia had intended to kill Narvaez.[16] The state initially planned to try Garcia a fourth time in 1981, but by now he had served enough time that by the start of a new trial he would be eligible for parole.[17] Moreover, Garcia disappeared again. This time his attorneys speculated that he might be dead. Authorities never located him.[18]

The Pete Garcia saga proved a long-running and sad affair in New Mexico. While it seemed clear that Julian Narvaez had targeted Garcia for harassment and had shot him for no reason, the resulting struggle and shooting of Narvaez seemed like self-defense. Any justice in the case was elusory. The fact that Narvaez was one of the few law officers killed in the line of duty in New Mexico seemingly got lost not only in the activist moment during which he died but also in the subsequent trials and the intrigue surrounding Garcia's flight. And the fact that both the victim and the perpetrator in this case were men of Mexican ancestry in essence pitted the Mexican American community against itself. The various ins and outs of the case, from Narvaez's initial treatment of Garcia to him shooting him in the back for no reason to Narvaez's own death and then all the subsequent trials and appeals and Garcia's flight(s), were all an ongoing series of unusual events in New Mexico.

The situation in New Mexico merged with that of Colorado and Texas in the case of Ricardo Falcón. This was another unusual case. In this example, police did not kill Falcón. Instead a gas station owner named Perry Brunson did. But for the Chicano community Falcón's death was another in a long line of "people taking the law into their own hands."[19] The various conflicting accounts of the event also made it confusing and strange. Moreover, the way the justice system worked to protect Brunson, the killer, while seeming to deny justice to Falcón, the victim, showed again whom the criminal justice system served.

Ricardo Falcón was a well-liked Chicano college student and activist in Colorado and a member of United Mexican American Students, the Crusade for Justice, and Raza Unida Party (RUP). In August 1972, he and a group of Chicanos, including Francisco "Kiko" Martínez, Florencio "Freddie" Granado, Steve Baca, and Vincent Mesa, among others, drove from Colorado to the annual RUP political convention in El Paso. Their car began to overheat between the towns of Alamogordo and Orogrande, New Mexico. They stopped on the outskirts of Orogrande for water to cool the engine at a Chevron gas station operated by Perry Brunson. The men got into an argument with Brunson when he refused to let them use his station's water. For the Chicano activists, this was a near classic kind of discrimination. According to Brunson, water was scarce and he chose not to waste it, preferring instead to simply let overheated vehicles cool down over time. An argument ensued, became heated, according to most witnesses calmed down, and then heated up again. Standing in the doorway of the station, Brunson pulled out a .38-caliber handgun. From here the details get sketchy since only Brunson lived to report on what happened next. According to him, Falcón attempted to grab the weapon. In an ensuing struggle, Brunson fired several times. These shots hit Falcón in the chest, one of which lacerated his aorta. Ricardo Falcón died on the pavement in front of the gas station.[20]

Even as Falcón lay dying, a one-sided law enforcement situation began to take shape. The police officer who initially arrived forced Falcón's friends away from him, checked him for a pulse, and then went into the station to speak with Brunson. No authority figure rendered aid to Falcón, and several of the neighboring business people refused to allow his friends to call an ambulance. Falcón did not die immediately, so refusing to render him aid seemed particularly cruel. Even though Brunson had clearly shot and killed Falcón, police did not hold or arrest him. The police officer instead threatened to arrest the other Chicano activists.[21] New Mexico authorities did arrest Perry Brunson the following day and charged him with manslaughter.[22] But the usual pattern of defaming the victim had already begun. District Attorney Norman Bloom, who later tried the case, released information that Falcón had previous encounters with police in Colorado. This was a common way of besmirching a victim and not material to the case.[23]

Brunson's trial began in late 1972. Freddie Granado, Vincent Mesa, and Steve Baca all testified about the encounter between Brunson and Falcón. According to them, Brunson had instigated the conflict with the group when they attempted to use his station's water to cool their overheated car. Brunson and Falcón had exchanged words, Brunson called the group "Chicano motherfuckers" and exhibited his firearm. But then the two men parted, Brunson to the gas station office while Falcón remained in the parking lot, and the argument settled down. However, "Brunson instigated it all over again," explained Baca, by shouting epithets at the men from the gas station office. Falcón began walking to the station. All three men stated that Brunson had pointed an object—which turned out to be his handgun—at Falcón and that Falcón had either tried to push Brunson away or had tried to grab the object in Brunson's hand. Both men fell to the ground during this tussle. Then Baca and Granado heard shots. They pulled the two apart and Granado noticed Falcón was hurt. Another patron at the gas station, Robert Rose, also testified and corroborated the testimony of Baca, Mesa, and Granado.[24]

Perry Brunson testified in his own defense. He claimed that the argument never ended and that Falcón followed him into the gas station shouting insults. He further claimed that Falcón had hit him in the face and he fell. Brunson said Falcón then stood over him menacingly. Only at that time, Brunson claimed, did he pull out his gun. He stated that he fired two warning shots and then two shots into Falcón's torso.[25] Brunson told the jury that he killed Falcón in "defense of his life" and stated, "A man can beat you to death with his fists."[26] None of the other witnesses said anything about Brunson falling down or about Falcón standing over him.

New Mexico law had stipulated in 1946, following what is commonly known as the Castle Doctrine, that shooting an unarmed person and subsequently claiming self-defense was only defensible if the shooting occurred at, or in defense of, a person's residence. Shooting someone in defense of property such as a business was not statutorily protected. Moreover, to claim self-defense an individual must not be the instigator of the confrontation, and Brunson according to several accounts had instigated the confrontation.[27] Based on this law and what clearly seemed a disparity of force, it seems that the jury should have rejected Brunson's self-defense argument and found him guilty. The jury decided instead that Brunson had acted in self-defense and found him not guilty of the charge of manslaughter.[28]

The killing of Ricardo Falcón generated a great deal of activism from RUP and other groups. RUP had made police brutality a major issue since its inception; Falcón's death was another in a long series of killings that the party protested. Party leader Kiko Martínez organized a major march from Orogrande to Alamogordo to bring attention to the case.[29] RUP also demanded a federal investigation into Falcón's killing. Party leaders had conducted their own investigation into the case and had found newly elected District Attorney Bloom's investigation into Falcón's death "sloppy." They also claimed that Bloom and Perry Brunson were friends.[30] The party also deemed the trial sloppy. Party members discovered, for instance, that Bloom had failed to challenge testimony about Falcón's consumption of alcohol the day Brunson shot him and had opened the door for testimony about Falcón's trouble with the law in his past, neither of which pertained to the case. They asserted that, based on New Mexico law, the state should have charged Brunson with first-degree murder. RUP used these criticisms of the investigation and trial to push for a federal civil rights trial.[31]

A special release from *El Grito del Norte* featured testimony from the Colorado delegation of RUP as well as from RUP's president José Angel Gutiérrez. The Colorado delegation called Falcón's killing a "racist act of cold-blooded murder." Gutiérrez, who had years of experience with police abuse going back to his beating at the hands of Texas Ranger A. Y. Allee, asked rhetorically, "Cannot an American citizen obtain emergency service in an American city without fear for his life?" The national offices of RUP through Gutiérrez demanded "an immediate federal investigation into this wanton, racist murder. The death of Ricardo Falcon cannot be justified in any way."[32] No such investigation ever occurred.

The death of Ricardo Falcón at the hands of Perry Brunson demonstrated several of the problems Mexican Americans had with the administration of justice in the Southwest. The state, in essence, put Falcón on trial even though he was the victim while they defended the perpetrator, Brunson, even though he was on trial. Moreover, Chicanos saw in the outcome of the case the systemic problems within the criminal justice system, which seemed to favor White people at the expense of people of color, especially the defaming of Falcón's character and the acceptance of Brunson's version of events despite testimony that challenged his narrative. He was allowed to equate fists with a gun, even though Falcón's use of his fists was never conclusively proved. Whether this was favoritism on the part of New Mexico officials or the selective enforcement of justice is hard to discern.

One of the cruel and unusual cases from Texas was that of Frank Hayes killing Ricardo Morales. Perhaps no example better demonstrates a wanton, calculated, disgusting example of police murder than this. Twenty-seven-year-old Ricardo Morales of Castroville, Texas, was arrested on the night of September 14, 1975, by Officer Donald McCall for suspicion of misdemeanor robbery. Morales had allegedly stolen stereo equipment, but authorities learned later that his wife had rented the stereo police accused him of stealing. Castroville police chief Frank Hayes arrived at the Morales residence, took charge, and then threatened to kill Morales. He also had McCall turn Morales over to him, ostensibly to drive him to jail. Instead, Hayes took Morales to a secluded road north of Castroville and attempted to beat a confession out of him. He failed. McCall, who stood by and watched, left after Hayes ordered him to return to the station. After he departed, Hayes withdrew a sawed-off shotgun and shot Morales in the abdomen. When he returned to the station, he told McCall that Morales had escaped. Although Hayes admitted that he shot at Morales as he fled, an inspection of the area revealed only a puddle of blood and no Morales.[33]

The exact sequence of events after McCall left the scene are impossible to reconstruct, but authorities seemed to sense that something was amiss. Indeed, it was. Hayes evidently hated Morales. According to Officer McCall, Hayes had stated that Morales was a "thieving son of a bitch" whom he had threatened to kill several times, including the night he killed him. Authorities later learned that Hayes shot and killed Morales moments after McCall had departed. After shooting him, with the assistance of his prospective son-in-law, Dennis Dunford, he loaded Morales's corpse into Hayes's vehicle. Hayes then tasked his wife, Dorothy, with transporting the body 400 miles to East Texas. She stopped to pick up her sister, Alice Baldwin, in San Antonio, and they drove to Panola County, where their brother owned land. They buried Morales's body in a shallow grave. While in the process of disposing of shovels and bloody garbage bags, local authorities apprehended the two women. Investigators found Morales's body shortly thereafter.[34]

The killing of Ricardo Morales was altogether senseless. The Medina County sheriff arrested Hayes and charged him with murder, but a friend with the San Antonio Police Department bailed him out of jail, which only exacerbated the Mexican American community's anger. Activists affiliated with Familias Unidas (Families United) had a march and rally to protest the killing. This again shows how activists got involved in such cases, although in this case the protests were limited in number.[35] Hayes did stand trial for killing Morales. At his trial he contradictorily argued that the shotgun had discharged accidentally and that he killed Morales in self-defense. The jury convicted him only of aggravated assault and sentenced him to two to ten years in prison.[36] Dorothy Hayes pleaded guilty to misdemeanor charges of tampering with evidence and received a one-year probated jail sentence. Authorities initially charged Dennis Dunford with murder, but he was apparently granted immunity in exchange for his testimony. The light sentence

Hayes received was met with anger. Congressman Henry B. Gonzalez and Texas Governor Dolph Briscoe asked the Justice Department to investigate.[37]

The Justice Department did investigate and in 1977 decided to try Frank Hayes for violating Morales's constitutional rights. This decision required some modification of the Department of Justice's "dual prosecution policy" or "Petite policy." That policy derived from a Justice Department rule from 1959 that made it impossible for a case like Hayes's to be reviewed at the federal level while a state trial also took place. Attorney General Griffin Bell, in a memo outlining a new "dual prosecution policy," stated "that each and every allegation of a violation of the civil rights laws will be evaluated on its own merits" and he modified the policy accordingly, a major reform. As such Hayes stood trial at both the state and federal level.[38] The federal trial had many of the hallmarks of how the criminal justice system treats victims of color. The prosecution, for example, publicly slandered Morales. Hayes's attorney, Marvin Miller, repeatedly asked questions during the trial about Morales's criminal past, casting aspersions on his character. Miller asked Medina County sheriff Alvin Santleben if he knew authorities wanted Morales for rape when Hayes arrested him. Santleben denied the allegation, which was untrue.[39] After a short trial, a Waco jury found Hayes guilty. They also found Dorothy Hayes and Alice Baldwin guilty of lesser charges. They sentenced Frank Hayes to life in prison.[40]

The Mexican American community protested throughout the various trials of Frank Hayes. But these protests were generally more muted than in previous episodes of police violence. Why? The answer to that question is simple. Hayes was a cold-blooded murderer whom the state quickly arrested and tried and whom the federal government also tried. The Castroville police force offered no excuse or justification for his crime because there was none. The criminal justice system made fairly quick work of Hayes and his accomplices. In short, the system actually worked as it was supposed to. If only all such cases went this way.[41]

As when Julian Narvaez shot Pete Garcia, Hayes killed Morales simply because he hated him. That made the case unusual: police don't typically kill people in cold blood. They may kill people in the line of duty under questionable circumstances or accidentally, that is certainly true, and in some of those cases officers are found guilty of a crime. But this case was odd because Hayes killed Morales with no provocation or justification, likely premeditated, and then tried to cover it up. The modification of the Justice Department's Petite policy was also unusual, important, and a direct outcome of this case.

Arizona also had a couple of cruel and unusual cases. One was that of Tucson police officer Roy Garcia. He represented a different kind of situation and another part of the problem with law enforcement in Arizona, namely that Tucson didn't seem to treat officers of color particularly well. Garcia had a distinguished record with the Tucson Police Department; he was well respected and liked by fellow officers as well as the Mexican American community. But after a friendly fire incident, the city seemed to want to cut all ties with Garcia. Friendly fire events are incredibly rare in law enforcement, which also makes this case unusual.[42]

Officer Garcia and nearly thirty-five other police officers from several agencies had responded to a disturbance at the South Tucson home of Leroy Doyle on the night October 11, 1978. Doyle suffered from schizophrenia and according to neighbors had fired a shotgun from his front porch. When police arrived, he barricaded himself in his home. Several officers approached the front door of Doyle's home. Officer Donovan Tatman recalled seeing a figure near the door and hearing a shot, and he and other officers opened fire. Doyle died during the fusillade. Tatman then heard Garcia yell, "I've been hit." Garcia was the shadowy figure Tatman had seen on the porch. Police later determined that South Tucson police officer David Novotny had accidentally shot Garcia in the back.[43]

The bullet wound left Officer Garcia paralyzed and permanently disabled. He would need care for the rest of his life. The City of South Tucson offered its sympathies and a small settlement, but also asserted that Garcia was at fault. Roy Garcia sued the city. He charged that Officer Novotny had been negligent in carrying out his duty. The city and Novotny's attorneys blamed Garcia. They claimed he put himself in harm's way when he stepped into the line of fire. The jury ultimately relieved Novotny of wrongdoing but found the city liable and awarded Garcia $3.59 million in compensatory damages.[44] He should have relished his victory, but that was hard to do considering that the city constantly whined about the settlement it had to pay. South Tucson had to file for bankruptcy in 1983 and actually blamed Garcia for its predicament. Such a response to an officer permanently injured in the line of duty was disrespectful, to say the least. The city eventually agreed to pay him $2 million over an extended period and gave him a piece of city property valued at $1 million.[45]

The shooting ruined Roy Garcia's life. He loved being a police officer, and by all accounts he was a good one. The accident, combined with the City of South Tucson's embarrassing response, was devastating for him. A weak apology and a measly settlement seem small recompense for being shot in the line of duty and paralyzed. Roy Garcia was certainly not responsible for the city's financial woes and blaming him for them only added insult to injury. And of course, friendly fire incidents are incredibly unusual among police officers. But this was not the only weird event in Arizona.

The famous Hanigan case that occurred in Arizona in 1976 was also cruel and unusual.[46] This case involved a family of ranchers who captured and tortured three Mexican nationals who had crossed the border near Douglas, Arizona, that August. Increased immigration from Mexico and Central America at this time resulted in an amplified anti-immigrant sentiment among some sectors of the American population. The incident serves as a good example of how some White Americans continued to feel justified in taking the law into their own hands. In fact, the incident feels strikingly similar to the examples of mob justice acting as law enforcement in the nineteenth century, examples that often ended in a lynching.[47] The Hanigan case as well as the KKK's so-called border security program both illustrate this phenomenon.

The Hanigan case was a disgusting example of anti-Mexican violence disguised as self-defense and the protection of personal property. George Hanigan and his sons Thomas (age nineteen) and Patrick (age twenty-two) had periodically encountered undocumented Mexicans on their 2,300-acre property near the border town of Douglas. In August 1976, Thomas Hanigan found Manuel García Loya, Eleazar Ruelas Zavala, and Bernabe Herrera Mata (all young men in their early twenties) crossing through the Hanigan's property to travel to a job in the town of Elfrida, Arizona. He took the men captive, forced them into his pickup truck, and drove them to the ranch house. His father and brother soon joined Thomas. The Hanigans accused the Mexican men of wanting to rob them, which the captives denied. After taking the men to a secluded part of their property, they verbally abused them by calling them "thieves" and "fucking Mexicans," among other slurs, and tortured them for several hours.[48]

The Hanigans bound García, Ruelas, and Herrera by their hands and feet. They kicked, hit, and stomped the men as they lay in the hot sun. Then the Hanigans cut off the men's clothing with hunting knives. While cutting off their clothes, the Hanigans discovered that each man had a small sum of money, which they took. They also used their knives to cut and rip the hair of the three men. In an incredibly sadistic manner, the elder Hanigan grabbed the genitals of each of the victims, running a knife near each man's scrotum as if he was going to castrate his captives. After scaring each man with castration, George Hanigan laughed uproariously. Pat and Tom had their own sadistic ideas and tortured García, Ruelas, and Herrera by pointing an unloaded pistol at each man's head and pulling the trigger. They also used a cattle-branding iron to make the men think they would be branded. They badly burned Ruelas's feet with this branding iron while frightening him. Like their father, Pat and Tom laughed while they tortured the men.[49] The Hanigans eventually tired of their sadism. They decided to let the men go and shoot them with birdshot as they ran. Ruelas's feet were too badly burned for him to run, so they hung him from a tree, although they cut him down and shot at him as well. Doctors later removed 125 shotgun pellets from García and forty-seven from Herrera.[50]

When word of the torture slowly seeped out, the response was bifurcated. Many Arizonans, and Americans more generally, were disgusted, outraged, and hoped justice would be done. But an equally large segment of the population defended the Hanigans, saw them as heroes, and believed them within their rights to capture the three men.[51] Many people seemed to equate the Hanigans' actions to law enforcement. García, Ruelas, and Herrera had broken the law, trespassed, and thus the Hanigan's police-like actions were understandable, even excusable. This may be part of the reason why the state and the local district attorney's office refused for some time to charge the men with a crime.[52]

In October 1976, the Cochise County sheriff finally arrested the Hanigans and charged them with three counts of kidnapping, three counts of conspiracy to kidnap, three counts of assault with a deadly weapon, three counts of conspiracy to assault with a deadly weapon, and, for Pat and Tom, two counts of robbery. They all pleaded not guilty.[53] The trial was scheduled to take place in Bisbee, the county seat of Cochise County and the site of the famous Bisbee Deportation in 1917.[54] But the prosecution requested a change of venue because too many people knew the Hanigans and a jury might be too sympathetic to them. The judge denied that request, setting the stage for a likely acquittal.[55]

George Hanigan died before his case could go to trial. Pat and Tom's trial began in September 1977. Manuel García Loya testified against the brothers and offered a particularly compelling and horrific retelling of events. He also described how the Hanigans seemed to view their actions as a police operation.[56] As a local minister noted, "It boils down to people taking justice into their own hands. . . . Some people think taking justice into their own hands is the way to do it."[57] The Hanigan brothers' attorneys offered a rather weak defense, basically impugning what they saw as inconsistencies in García's, Ruelas's, and Herrera's pretrial statements and trial testimony. For example, Bernabe Herrera Mata had trouble remembering the color of shirt that George

Hanigan had worn. The attorneys also noted the fact that the three men had discussed their testimony with Mexican consul Raúl Aveleyra Fierro even though Judge J. Richard Hannah had ordered them not to.[58] This strategy worked. An all-White jury (in a county that had a large Mexican American population) quickly acquitted Thomas and Patrick.[59]

The results of the case caused a great deal of fear and anger across the region. After the jury issued its verdicts, Consul Aveleyra declared that the criminal justice system has "just opened the hunting season for every illegal alien who comes into the United States." Aveleyra speculated that if anyone could kidnap, torture, perhaps even kill Mexican migrants, then everyone became a law enforcement official.[60] Local Mexican American leaders also began to put pressure on the Department of Justice to investigate the case.[61] Interestingly, the Justice Department initially explored prosecuting the brothers as they might police officers. "The federal government has intervened in any number of cases where police officers were accused of brutalizing illegal aliens," noted John Conroy, a deputy chief with the Justice Department's Civil Rights Division, "but the people accused in this case are private citizens."[62] Analysis from the *Tucson Citizen* echoed these points about vigilante justice but indicted all of Cochise County. The trial had exposed "the legend of Cochise County politics and justice—it's redneck, it's violent, lawless and corrupt. What law there is vigilante law—the justice, frontier style."[63]

Oddly enough, once a federal trial commenced, advocates for the Hanigans claimed that Mexican Americans, in pushing for and getting a new trial, had themselves acted as a vigilante group. They singled out in these attacks the Hanigan Case Coalition, which Mexican Americans had founded to push for a federal trial: "The coalition's vigilante behavior is reminiscent of a century past—a regrettable time when many an Hispanic met with frontier justice at the hands of a not-yet-tame society."[64] In a similar statement, a commentator called the prosecution of the Hanigans "a lynch mob atmosphere. . . . A mockery is being made of trial by jury—of our whole criminal justice system." Such statements represent another unusual aspect to this case.[65]

What the Hanigan Case Coalition actually did was work tirelessly to secure justice for Manuel García Loya, Eleazar Ruelas Zavala, and Bernabe Herrera Mata. This shows yet again the dexterity of Chicano activism in this period. The coalition wanted "the Justice Department to respond favorably to our demands for federal prosecution of Patrick and Thomas Hanigan." For the coalition, as for others, the case was from its inception about how the criminal justice system treated certain groups, and they demanded that justice be done for the three men. If Attorney General Griffin Bell and his successor, Benjamin Civiletti, proved unwilling to act, the group planned to demand their resignation.[66] Another group, the Manzo Area Council, an immigrant's rights organization founded in Tucson in 1972, sponsored a 1,500-person march and rally. The protestors also boycotted business in the Bisbee–Douglas area. They hoped the boycott would also stimulate a response from the federal government.[67]

The Justice Department took its time. In the last years of the Carter administration Attorney General Bell stepped down and in August 1979 Civiletti took over, so there were some internal bureaucratic issues that slowed a potential federal trial. But as time passed the pressure mounted as the deadline of a three-year statute of limitations approached. A number of prominent politicians demanded action. Edward Roybal (D-CA), Robert Garcia (D-NY), and Mickey Leland (D-TX), for instance, all wrote Attorney General Bell asking for action on the case.[68] State leaders such as Arizona state senator Tony Abril demanded that "justice be done" and reminded the attorney general that "brutality is brutality no matter who commits it." Arizona governor Bruce Babbitt sided with the Mexican American community, noting that "many Mexican American leaders view the case as symptomatic of the discrimination and injustices to which their people have been subjected in the Southwest." Babbitt urged the attorney general to begin a new case in order to restore "confidence in our justice system."[69]

This action produced some interesting results. Chief among them, Attorney General Bell sent then Deputy Attorney General Civiletti on a tour of the Southwest in late 1978 in an attempt to soothe tensions in the region. This was an unusual, albeit honorable, move, but Civiletti probably should have stayed in Washington, DC. A number of groups came forward to publicly shame the Department of Justice and the attorney general. Law student Antonio D. Bustamante, who had helped found the Hanigan Case Coalition, declared that "the government's claim of a full investigation of the Hanigan case represents the hypocrisy of the President's commitment to human rights." He and others demanded prosecution, not investigation.[70] In Texas local people used the tour to demand that the Justice Department reopen the Santos Rodriguez case.[71] The tour was an embarrassment for the Department of Justice; protests and anger greeted Civiletti.

The Justice Department finally decided to investigate the Hanigan case in mid-1979. A US grand jury indicted the brothers in October 1979 for six counts of robbery of García, Ruelas, and Herrera.[72] The robbery charge resulted from federal law that prohibited individuals from interfering with interstate or foreign commerce by using threats and violence, a violation of the Hobbs Act as well as the Interstate Commerce Clause.[73] The defense once again pointed out inconsistencies in García's, Ruelas's, and Herrera's recollections of events, again bringing up Bernabe Herrera Mata's misremembering of the color of George Hanigan's shirt.[74] Oddly, Patrick Hanigan's attorneys threw Thomas under the bus by arguing that Patrick was not at the ranch when the attacks occurred, an altogether ludicrous claim that no one had ever made. The prosecution did little to dispute these allegations, which were silly and easily challengeable.[75]

The most salacious testimony in the trial came from Patrick Hanigan's ex-wife, Pamela. She said that the Hanigan men often discussed "wetback hunting" and used numerous racial epithets to describe Mexican-origin people. She also commented on the law enforcement nature of their actions: "They agreed to patrol the property and make sure no one crossed." Moreover, she recalled that they had gone "looking for 'wetbacks' 14 to 16 times" before they encountered García, Ruelas, and Herrera. Pamela Hanigan ultimately described a group of angry, racist White men who decided to take the law into their own hands.[76]

While the trial took place, Mexican American activists continued to organize protests to unite the community. The National Coalition on the Hanigan Case, the revised version of the Hanigan Case Coalition, sponsored a massive March for Justice and rally in Tucson that included such speakers as Reies López Tijerina, Corky Gonzales, and San Diego leader Herman Baca. The marchers declared, "Raza Sí, Hanigans No" (People yes, Hanigans no). The protestors decried what they saw as a double standard for justice in the United States. Some, such as Samuel Delgado, chair of the National Coalition on the Hanigan Case, mocked the basis of the trial: "You can beat the hell out of any Mexican. Just don't rob him."[77]

When the first federal trial ended, many in the Chicano community expected to be disappointed. The defense had successfully excluded Mexican-origin people from the jury, leaving it all White. Although the defense made many speculative and ridiculous arguments, Mexican Americans knew that misremembering the color of someone's shirt could sow doubt in the minds of some jurors. Thus, when the jury deadlocked after deliberating for thirty hours, few Mexican Americans were surprised. Judge Richard Bilby declared a mistrial. Ruben Sandoval, one of the leaders of the National Coalition on the Hanigan Case, spoke for many when he stated, "We are not an angry people; we're sad. We're not vindictive; we're determined."[78]

Sandoval was right. Activists kept the pressure on and planned another major march and rally after the trial ended.[79] This time it did not take the

Leaflet advertising Caravana por Justicia/March for Justice, a July 24, 1980, protest against the Hanigans and their abusive and violent treatment of Manuel García Loya, Eleazar Ruelas Zavala, and Bernabe Herrera Mata. The Hanigans in many ways represented a twentieth-century version of extralegal mob justice. More than 400 people participated in this Caravana por Justicia. *Courtesy of the Chicano/a Research Collection, Arizona State University Library, Tempe.*

Justice Department as long to make a decision about a new trial. By early September 1980, Judge Bilby set a date for the third trial, to begin in October.[80] The judge eventually pushed the date back to January 1981 and moved the trial to Phoenix. Jury selection proved phenomenally slow as the judge, prosecution, and defense tried to weed out jurors who already knew too much about the case. Out of 169 possible jurors, only ten were Latino/a/x, two were African American, and one was an Indigenous person.[81] After three days Judge Bilby impaneled two juries, one for each brother, another unusual aspect to this case. As before, the juries were all White.[82] The Mexican American community once again foresaw justice slipping away.[83]

When the trials began, the prosecution introduced some new evidence that disproved Patrick Hanigan's claim that he was absent when his father and brother had tortured García, Ruelas, and Herrera. A waitress had overheard a conversation between Patrick and an unidentified woman in which he had boasted about capturing the three men and had stated, "We fixed those son-of-bitchin' wetbacks."[84] Still, his defense again argued that he was not at the ranch.[85] In a split decision, Patrick Hanigan's jury evidently did not buy his story and convicted him, while Thomas Hanigan's jury acquitted him. This split decision seemed to surprise all parties involved. As Antonio Bustamante explained, "There is no logical way one person can be found guilty and another not guilty if both are accused of the same crime."[86]

Patrick Hanigan appealed his conviction. That appeal ultimately went all the way to the US Supreme Court. The Court, however, chose not to review the case.[87] In February 1983, more than seven years after Patrick Hanigan captured, assaulted, tortured, terrorized, and robbed Manuel García Loya, Eleazar Ruelas Zavala, and Bernabe Herrera Mata, Judge Bilby sentenced him to three concurrent three-year prison terms. Bilby sent Hanigan to the Swift Trail Federal Prison Camp, a low-security federal prison, to serve his three-year sentence.[88]

Having failed to secure justice against both brothers in a criminal court, García, Ruelas, and Herrera sought justice in civil court. They sued Patrick and Thomas Hanigan as well as the estate of George Hanigan for $1,275,000 each. They filed suit in November 1977. That case lingered in the courts for years. The brothers finally settled for an undisclosed amount in May 1983.[89] The conclusion of that suit finally brought the Hanigan case to an end.

The Hanigan case was an ugly reminder of the past as well as a portent of the future. It recalled the example of frontier justice so common in the old Southwest. It also had a lot of odd features. The capture and torture of Manuel García Loya, Eleazar Ruelas Zavala, and Bernabe Herrera Mata was extreme, and their treatment at the hands of the Hanigans was cruel and unusual. The fact that many people rallied around the Hanigans largely defies logic. But a lot about this case was bizarre.

A final unusual case relates to the rise of a refocused Ku Klux Klan. While the KKK had seen its strength, membership, and influence diminish throughout the 1960s, the Klan once again reared its ugly head in the late 1970s and 1980s, this time to oppose Mexican immigration.[90] This focus coincided with a new immigration reform plan proposed by Congress and supported by President Jimmy Carter. Grand Dragon David Duke announced that the KKK would not only support these federal efforts but would also begin patrolling the US-Mexico border to apprehend undocumented border crossers, what the KKK termed its "border watch" or "border security" program. The Klan acted as an illegal border patrol that used police techniques, an old tactic that serves as a reminder of frontier extralegal "justice." Duke stated that their goal was to protect the United States from "foreign or alien influence or interest."[91]

The Klan used many of their tried and true racist tactics, including using cartoons to ridicule Mexican men as fat and lazy and women as pregnant (in one cartoon, wherein all of these stock images of Mexican-origin people appeared, they rush to board a "Grease-hound" bus, which was really a "lowered '44 Chevy"); advertisements for "Instant Greaser" powder "for liberal, White 'Freedom Marchers,' race mixers and assorted 'Spic-Symps'" who desired "cultural enrichment" (you spread this powder on the ground and "hundreds of Chicanos spring up! Little greasers, big greasers, fat jew greasers, skinny greasers. Light greasers, charcoal brown greaser[s,] greasers here, greasers there; greasers, greasers everywhere!!"); and the comic "White Power Comes to Midvale," which featured a muscular White student who arrives at "Midvale High School" to save White students from Black and Latino students and a Jewish principal.[92]

The statements that the Klan would support the government's immigration reform efforts and the KKK's patrols of the border pushed activists in Southern California and around the nation to protest. For example, in October 1977, 3,000 Chicano, African American, Indigenous, and White folks marched in San Ysidro to protest the Klan and the immigration reform proposals. The Crusade for Justice's Corky Gonzales spoke at a post-march rally, saying, "La Migra [immigration] is just as guilty, just as racist as the KKK. They are twins dressed in different uniforms who mistreat, terrorize, and brutalize our people."[93] Others railed against the immigration reform plans, which they saw as stimulating the Klan's border activities.[94]

Chicano activists also assembled at the border to prevent the Klan patrol missions. They had several small skirmishes with Klan members.[95] These activists also had numerous marches that resisted the KKK. The Klan patrols, which occurred primarily near San Ysidro, seem reminiscent of the "night rider" days of Klan activity. Immigration and Naturalization Service official Allen Clayton had actually given David Duke and Tom Metzger, the KKK grand dragon in California, a personal tour of the San Ysidro INS facility, which gave credence to Mexican American arguments that the Klan and the government were wedded over this issue.[96] Metzger had made himself known in Southern California for his racist diatribes, which tended to merge anti-Black and anti-Mexican sentiments seamlessly. For instance, he told a *Los Angeles Times* reporter that a "black hell" and "brown hordes" were trying to overrun the United States. The obvious response was Klan border patrols.[97]

The Klan patrols occurred sporadically and generally garnered the KKK bad press. In one of the most notorious incidents, four Klan members abducted a Mexican-looking individual whom they found hitchhiking near the

San Diego–Tijuana border in April 1978. They delivered this person, later identified as Juan Mendez-Ruiz, to the Border Patrol, which soon learned that Mendez-Ruiz had immigrated properly. The Klansmen knew that, too: they had taken his immigration papers and discarded them along the side of Interstate 5. The Border Patrol soon found those papers and released Mendez-Ruiz. Local FBI agents investigated, which resulted in two arrests. The Southern California grand jury indicted Klansmen Carl Shipton and Robert Cole for interfering with the rights of a lawful resident alien. Shipton pleaded guilty, but the case against Cole was dismissed due to lack of evidence.[98]

The Mendez-Ruiz kidnapping received a significant response from activists in Southern California. Groups such as the Committee on Chicano Rights, founded by San Diego activist Herman Baca, the Crusade for Justice, the National Association for the Advancement of Colored People, the San Diego chapter of the National Urban League, and the Mexican American Political Association all took an interest in the case. Baca noted that "meetings are being planned with organizational heads of the Black, Anglo, and Jewish communities to formulate strategies to ensure that such incidents do not happen again."[99] Baca wrote to INS officials, California State Assembly member Richard Alatorre, the acting US attorney in California M. James Lorenz, and others to demand an investigation.[100] San Diego City councilmember Jess D. Haro wrote to President Carter and Attorney General Bell and argued against racial profiling, stating that "individuals must not have their freedoms challenged because of their appearance." US representative Ed Roybal also wrote demanding an investigation.[101] This activism extended well into the 1980s.

As in California, the KKK also spurred a Black, Brown, and White anti-Klan activist response in Texas. They organized a massive multiethnic alliance called the Coalition for Human Dignity to plan the protests. In late 1979 the group conducted its first march and rally against the Klan in Dallas. Over 2,000 Mexican American, African American, and White people marched carrying signs that read "KKK—Scum of the Land" and "A People United Will Never Be Defeated." The marchers successfully drove away about fifty Klansmen who came out to oppose the rally.[102]

The most significant anti-Klan protests occurred in San Antonio and Austin. With its sizable Mexican American population and long history of civil rights activism, San Antonio proved a logical choice for these protests. As in Dallas, San Antonians founded an umbrella organization, aptly titled the San Antonio Coalition against the KKK, to organize the protests. The coalition announced plans for a march and rally on January 19, 1980.[103] About 500 activists marched through downtown San Antonio. At the rally, community

A group of activists gather at the San Antonio City Hall in May 1983 to protest a KKK rally at the Alamo. As in protests in other cities, including a previous one in San Antonio in 1980, the activists decried Klan racism while linking it to broader political patterns and policing problems. In this case they tied the presidency of Ronald Reagan to the KKK. The partially obscured sign reads, "Reagan and Klan Work Hand in Hand." *Photo by Lisa Davis. AR-2010-022-06-37-014, Austin History Center, Austin Public Library, Texas.*

organizer and longtime San Antonio activist Tommy "T. C." Calvert stated that "the Klan is an illegal organization and we will not tolerate them." Jaime Martinez, another well-respected San Antonio activist and a union representative for the local electrical workers union, called the Klan "scum" and a "bunch of nobodies who wave the American flag while preaching racism."[104]

A few years later, in 1983, activists in Austin had several stressful encounters with the Klan. As in Dallas and San Antonio, the KKK in Austin organized around the rallying cry of halting undocumented immigration. The Klan had reappeared in Austin with a degree of fanfare because the local media had aired several news stories depicting the Klan positively.[105]

When the Klan planned a major march in downtown Austin, the debate about allowing a parade permit aroused considerable tensions within the city council. Mayor Carole McClellan noted that while she and others "deplore, abhor, and detest the Ku Klux Klan," she supported freedom of

Chapter 4

speech. Activists argued forcefully that the KKK simply used the current anti-immigrant furor to push their racist positions. City councilmember Charles E. Urdy noted that the Klan "advocate[s] and perpetuate[s] violence against black people and other minorities." He called the freedom of speech issue a false one: "It's an issue of White supremacy, terrorism, and violence." When councilmember John Treviño, the sole Mexican American on the council, voted in favor of granting the permit, the audience erupted in shouting. Adela Mancias, a Chicano movement leader in Austin, scolded Treviño for granting rights to a group that would deny them to him. Others lambasted the council saying that it missed "the true character of the Klan" and claiming (erroneously) that they gave them "first amendment protection, which no terrorist organization ever obtained anywhere else in the world." The council granted the permit.[106]

The local chapter of the Brown Berets, which Adela Mancias, Paul Hernandez, another important Chicano leader, and others had founded in the 1970s, planned a counterprotest.[107] The Black Citizens Task Force and John Brown Anti-Klan League joined the Berets. As in Dallas, the anti-Klan demonstration was larger than the KKK protest. Approximately fifty Klan members marched to the capitol grounds, where they had a short rally. About 1,000 anti-Klan protestors lined the route of the march. They shouted, "We're fired up, won't take no more," "El pueblo unido jamás será vencido" (The united people will never be defeated), and "Hey hey, ho ho, the KKK has got to go" as the Klan members marched by.[108] Paul Hernandez stated, "We're here to let the Klan know and the police know and the city council know that the KKK, even though they may be protected by all these people [police] . . . that genocide is something we feel is directed at us, the KKK is out to do what they did to the blacks . . . that they want to do to the Mexican people now in this state, and we're not going to let them do it."[109]

The Austin Police Department and Texas Department of Public Safety had dispatched dozens of officers, which Hernandez mentioned, to protect the Klan members. After the Klan had passed, Austin police attacked a number of activists, including Adela Mancias and Paul Hernandez. Mancias believed that the police singled them out for their role in planning the anti-Klan demonstration. She also noted that the officers had removed their name tags and badges so as to avoid identification. Police beat Hernandez badly, while Mancias and activist María Limón were bloodied but not seriously injured. Police arrested all three.[110]

The Brown Berets responded to the attacks with more protests. Other groups such as the National Lawyers Guild, the UT Chicano Law Students'

Association, and the Comité para Justicia (Committee for Justice) organized to defend the arrested activists.[111] These groups developed a legal aid and redress committee. They wanted to free Paul Hernandez, Adela Mancias, and María Limón but also bring to light the unequal treatment meted out against them. While Hernandez was later convicted of resisting arrest, police released Mancias and Limón.[112]

The activist response to the KKK may not seem like a police issue, but it was. The KKK had acted like a police force since its inception. The Klan's "mission" transformed in the 1970s and 1980s to include law enforcement operations at the border. Moreover, the Klan's activities frequently brought them and the Chicanos who challenged them into conflict with the police, as the Austin example makes abundantly clear. Chicano resistance to the KKK was, therefore, a major part of the movement's goals to illuminate policing problems, one that actually generated additional abuse from law enforcement.

The KKK border patrol–police activities also fall within the category of unusual, and frankly the Klan's punitive efforts have always been cruel and unusual. But their reemergence in the late 1970s struck many observers then, and people today, as unexpected. As a kid growing up in this period, I certainly didn't have "KKK" on my bingo card. It also may seem unusual that the KKK chose to focus on border issues, given their long history of anti-Black racism. After the successes of the African American civil rights movement, such racism became less tolerable and less successful in organizing White supremacists. But anti-Mexican and anti-immigrant racism was just fine for a lot of folks. The Klan thus tapped into a somewhat hidden and largely acceptable form of racism that could attract new members. The only thing the KKK probably didn't expect was the concerted, multiracial response from activist groups, which embarrassed the Klan.

The Chicano movement period was filled with cruel and unusual events. The moments discussed in this chapter in some ways defy classification because they were so odd. A chief of police choosing to commit murder because he didn't like a person, and then trying to cover it up, seems unusual. We expect that perhaps in a TV crime drama, not in real life. Moreover, police homicide of this type is very rare. Sheriff's Sergeant Julian Narvaez similarly attempted to kill Pete Garcia because he didn't like him. That Narvaez ended up dead instead is abnormal. Both Hayes and Narvaez were high-ranking police officials, which might suggest that they should have known, or at least acted, better. But they didn't.

Friendly fire incidents are similarly very rare for law enforcement, so the shooting of Roy Garcia was fairly odd. He should have been apologized to and taken care of; instead South Tucson disrespected him and blamed him for his injuries. The Ricardo Falcón case, the Hanigan case, and rise of the KKK were all unusual in their own ways. In some aspects those cases continued the old-school, frontier style of individuals taking the law into their own hands. And in all of these examples, although the initial incident was unusual, a lot of the ins and outs that came after—be it a trial or trials, the way the criminal justice system operated, the media's reporting—also have their own unusual qualities.

But these cases were also important because they led to some meaningful activism and reforms. Certainly the modification of the Justice Department's Petite policy is a good example. Although justice was often fleeting in many of these cases, Roy Garcia, Manuel García Loya, Eleazar Ruelas Zavala, and Bernabe Herrera Mata all received some measure of legal victory. These cases also generated much activism from the Chicano movement. That activism showed once more the plastic nature and the dexterity of the movement and its leaders. Chicanos could support individuals such as Pete Garcia and Ricardo Falcón or protest against groups such as the KKK. These moments all demonstrate just how important was the Chicano movement.

FIVE

CUSTODIAL SITUATIONS

Mexican Americans
Confront the Carceral State

The Bexar County Boy's School, known as Southton due to its location
on Southton Road, was a nasty place. Although it purported to be a "reform school" for youths who committed minor offenses, it was really a
jail for teens. Abusive and uncaring administrators ran the facility. Parents complained regularly. For example, Virginia Bermea criticized the
treatment her son, Gilberto, had received at the hands of staff member
Eugene Helm in 1965. "My boy tells me," Bermea began, "that a man
who works at the school has been beating him and the other boys. He
says the man's name is Mr. Helm, and [he] kicks him to get them up
in the morning. The other day he showed me a bruise on his face that
Mr. Eugene Helm made with some keys he had on his hands when he
slapped my boy."[1] When a sympathetic caseworker brought these abuses
to the attention of the Southton superintendent, the superintendent fired
the caseworker.[2]

The United States has long had an incarceration problem. As I noted in *Borders of Violence and Justice*, in the Southwest, beginning in the 1840s, federal, state, territorial, and local governments built a web of different forms of incarceration: "White authorities fixated on erecting jails, prisons, penitentiaries, juvenile facilities, prison camps, immigrant detention facilities, and other forms of human caging going back to the first days of American control in the border region."[3] Those same governments added to their carceral facilities, or expanded existing facilities, in the late 1800s, in the 1920s and 1930s, and in the 1950s. The rise of the carceral state, which many attribute to the development of the War on Crime in the 1960s, has a much longer history than most Americans assume.[4]

The criminal justice system is a closely linked series of systems. Human caging in most instances serves as the final stop for an individual convicted of a crime. There is a kind of regrettable logic to incarceration—if you're going to adjudicate someone for a criminal offense, then you have to do something with them after they've been adjudicated. Alas, criminal justice authorities for generations have focused on the building of jail facilities as the thing to do with those adjudicated people. The huge expenditures governments spend on human caging and the lives those facilities damage or destroy means that incarceration has been anything but logical. At no time in our history has this problem been more visible than today. Prisons and jails cost the United States well over a trillion dollars each year, the United States incarcerates more people than any other nation, and communities of color have disproportionately been those incarcerated. It should also be noted that this system is linked to another one—capitalism. The linkage between criminal justice and capitalism has always existed but since the 1960s has gotten much worse as local communities, desperate for cash, vie for jail and prison contracts to help add dollars to their coffers. And of course, private jail and prisons are designed to profit from incarceration.[5]

This chapter examines incarceration broadly by focusing on numerous examples of in-custody interactions between law enforcement and the public, primarily from the 1960s to the 1980s. Custodial situations encapsulate almost all instances wherein an individual is held by members of the criminal justice system. That can include someone being detained, arrested, or interrogated by police; someone confined to a hospital or mental health facility after arrest; someone in jail while awaiting trial or being tried; and those individuals who have been sentenced to serve time in a jail or prison. All forms of custodial situations can lead to violations of a person's rights or violent encounters with law enforcement.

While the Chicano movement had from its inception been concerned about policing, the movement also focused on incarceration. Chicano activists supported those wronged by carceral facilities, protested, and demanded reform. While they fought for reforms from the outside, those incarcerated within the system developed what historian Robert Chase has accurately referred to as "the Chicano movement behind bars" and fought for change within the system.[6] In fact, Mexican Americans were quite often at the center of many reforms to the criminal justice system, in the Southwest and nationally. And to be clear, reform was most often at the center of Chicano demands. There were certainly those who wanted prison abolition, but during the Chicano period most activists focused on prison reform. Mexican Americans wanted systems of incarceration to work fairly and without abuse or violence.

The changes that Mexican Americans wrought in the criminal justice system were significant. As noted in previous chapters, the unfortunate killing of people such as Santos Rodriguez and Jose Campos Torres—both in-custody deaths—led to the formation of internal affairs departments in Dallas and Houston. Other locales focused on police-civilian review or community outreach. Such local-level reforms were important, but national-level reforms were even more meaningful, especially as they related to custody. Mexican Americans fought for fair treatment in custodial situations in the *Hernandez*, *Escobedo*, and *Miranda* Supreme Court decisions. In addition, the Chicano movement battled against a host of problems relating to police custody, especially jailhouse "suicide" deaths. Finally, incarcerated Mexican Americans, especially Dwight Duran, Eddie Sanchez, and David Resendez Ruíz, fought for prison reform from within. These are important stories.

Mexican American people pushed many of the most important, national-level reforms that modified the criminal justice system in the mid- to late twentieth century. In particular, Mexican Americans won important Supreme Court victories that transformed aspects of the entire justice system, especially as they related to incarceration and custodial interrogations. One of the first cases, *Hernandez v. Texas*, was handed down in 1954 two weeks after the famous *Brown v. Board of Education* case. *Hernandez* addressed Mexican American Fourteenth Amendment rights and jury segregation. In 1964, the Court took up an individual's Sixth Amendment right to counsel in custodial situations in *Escobedo v. Illinois*. Then, in 1966, *Miranda v. Arizona* addressed a person's right to silence during a police interrogation or when in police custody. That Mexican Americans brought all of these cases, and won, is important.

The *Hernandez* case was monumental. In 1951, farmhand Pete Hernandez got into an argument with Henry Cruz at a bar in Edna, Texas. The bar owner told Hernandez to leave, but he refused. Joe Espinoza, a local tenant farmer, intervened and helped remove Hernandez from the establishment. Hernandez left and returned with a .22-caliber rifle. He shot Joe Espinoza near the heart; Espinoza died soon thereafter. Police arrested Hernandez, and the Jackson County grand jury indicted him for murder. After a short trial an all-White jury convicted Hernandez of murder and sentenced him to life in prison.[7]

Pete Hernandez's attorney, Gustavo C. "Gus" Garcia, appealed the case. Gus Garcia is one of the most famous Mexican American lawyers in the history of the legal profession. Because the *Hernandez* case went to the Supreme Court, he holds the distinction of being the first Mexican-origin person to deliver arguments before the Court. Several other attorneys joined Garcia, including John J. Herrera, former League of United Latin American Citizens president Carlos C. Cadena, who later became chief justice of the Fourth Court of Appeals, and James DeAnda, who later became a US district court judge in Texas. They argued that the trial violated Hernandez's Sixth Amendment right to a jury of his peers as well as his Fourteenth Amendment right to equal protection. Because he didn't get those rights, he faced a lifetime of incarceration.[8] In a unanimous decision, Chief Justice Earl Warren declared that Hernandez, in asking to have his Fourteenth Amendment rights respected, did not "claim a right to have persons of Mexican descent sit on the particular juries which he faced. His only claim is the right to be indicted and tried by juries from which all members of his class are not systematically excluded—juries selected from among all qualified persons regardless of national origin or descent. To this much he is entitled by the Constitution." The Court reversed his conviction and ruled that the Fourteenth Amendment protected Mexican Americans, and by extension all Americans, from exclusion from jury service.[9]

The *Hernandez* case represented a fundamental shift in how the Court viewed Mexican Americans. In concluding that the Fourteenth Amendment applied to Mexican Americans, the Court opened a new door for civil rights activism. More importantly, the Court decreed that the exclusion of certain groups, such as people of Mexican ancestry, from jury service violated the law and often led to guilty verdicts. Thus, denial of trial rights resulted in convictions and incarceration. Hernandez was tried again in 1954. This time the jury included one Mexican American. The jury convicted him again and

Defendant Pete Hernandez (*middle*) with attorneys Gus Garcia (*left*) and John
J. Herrera (*right*) in 1954. Many scholars consider Garcia to be one of the most
important lawyers of Mexican ancestry in American history. Herrera had a lengthy
law career and served as LULAC president in 1952–1953. The *Hernandez* case, like
Escobedo and *Miranda*, secured important rights for Mexican Americans, and all
Americans. *Dr. Hector P. Garcia Papers, Special Collections and Archives, Mary and Jeff
Bell Library, Texas A&M University, Corpus Christi.*

sentenced Hernandez to twenty years in prison for killing Joe Espinoza. He
was paroled in 1960 and lived quietly until his death in the 1970s.[10]

The Supreme Court heard additional cases involving Mexican Americans
that also ushered in major changes in the criminal justice system. These
cases related specifically to custodial investigations. In *Escobedo v. Illinois*
and *Miranda v. Arizona*, the Court significantly modified several aspects of
how police do their work. Both cases involved Mexican-origin individuals
who had made incriminating statements while in police custody without
knowing their rights or having access to or, in the case of Escobedo, being
denied access to counsel.

Chicago police arrested Daniel Escobedo in the early morning of January 20, 1960, as a suspect in the murder of Manuel Valtierra, whom someone had shot to death the night before. Valtierra was married to Escobedo's sister, Grace, whom the police also took into custody. The Chicago Police Department later released both individuals. But then they booked Benedict Di Gerlando, who told police that Manuel Valtierra often beat Grace and because of that Escobedo had murdered him. Di Gerlando later amended this story to one wherein Escobedo hired him to kill Valtierra for $500.[11]

Chicago police rearrested Escobedo on January 30, 1960. They told him that they knew what happened and to "admit to this crime." He repeatedly asked to speak to his attorney, saying at one point, "I am sorry, but I would like to have advice from my lawyer." Police denied his repeated requests. Escobedo's attorney got wind of his client's arrest and went to CPD headquarters to speak with him. Officers and even the chief of police told him that he could not see his client until the police had concluded their interrogation. Escobedo even saw his attorney through the interrogation window, but police told him that he didn't want to speak to him.[12] Police instead brought Di Gerlando into the interrogation room, and he directly accused Escobedo of the murder. Escobedo retorted, "I didn't shoot Manuel, you did it." He made other incriminating statements that demonstrated he had knowledge of the crime. When the state drew up a statement for Escobedo, which amounted to a confession, he refused to sign it.[13]

In separate trials, the jury found Grace Valtierra not guilty of murdering her husband and both Danny Escobedo and Benedict Di Gerlando guilty of murder. They sentenced Di Gerlando to life in prison, Escobedo to twenty years.[14] Escobedo appealed his conviction based on the fact that police prevented him from access to his attorney during his interrogation. The Illinois Supreme Court ruled that "it does not follow that he is entitled to have someone present who, under the auspices of giving legal advice, warns and advises him against reacting to his first natural sensations to confess."[15] So Escobedo appealed to the Supreme Court.[16]

In *Escobedo v. Illinois*, Barry L. Knoll, Escobedo's attorney, explained that Escobedo had "convicted himself in that police station under an . . . accusatorial system. He convicted himself as a result of the interrogation that went on there." "In order to have the effect of assistance of counsel," Knoll stated, "you've got to have assistance at the time you need it." When Justice John Harlan asked, "Are you arguing that, in a state case, there is an absolute federal right to counsel before there can be any police interrogation once a man is under suspicion?" Knoll replied, "That is my second position, Your Honor, yes" (his first was that statements made by Escobedo were inadmissible at trial because of how police obtained them). Knoll also made issue with the "confession" Escobedo refused to sign, which the state had used during his trial. The state's attorney, James Thompson, countered that the interrogation and the trial all followed Illinois law. He further contended that any challenge to the unsigned confession should have come at trial.[17]

In June 1964 the Supreme Court declared that the State of Illinois had violated Escobedo's Sixth and Fourteenth Amendment rights. The police, in denying Escobedo access to his attorney, not only had violated his right to counsel but had, because of that violation, illegally obtained evidence that was then used to convict him.[18] The case was important because it set the standard that a state must grant individuals under custodial interrogation access to an attorney, and once they ask for an attorney all interrogation about the particular crime in question must cease. The State of Illinois decided not to retry Escobedo and released him in August 1964.[19] He was in and out of prison for the next several decades and remains there today.[20]

The Supreme Court ostensibly overruled *Escobedo* in *Miranda v. Arizona*. That case involved another Mexican American individual, Ernesto Arturo Miranda. He was born in Mesa, Arizona, in 1941. Miranda had a troubled childhood. He dropped out of school in the eighth grade and spent time in juvenile facilities before aging out in 1959. In 1962–63 he robbed and attempted to sexually assault several women in Phoenix. He did kidnap and rape Lois Jameson. Phoenix police picked him up as a person of interest in these cases. Although Jameson could not identify him as her attacker, police told Miranda that she had identified him. Miranda then said, "Well, I guess I'd better tell you about it then" and proceeded to unburden himself. He also signed a confession and verbally confessed to robbing and attempting to rape the other women.[21]

Arizona tried Miranda for all of these crimes.[22] In the first trial for the robbery of one of the women, Miranda's court-appointed attorney, Alvin Moore, brought up the manner of Miranda's custodial interrogation and confession. He asked arresting officer Carroll Cooley, "Did you say to the defendant at any time before he made the statement you are about to answer to, that anything he said would be held against him?" Cooley responded, "No, sir." "Did you warn him of his rights to an attorney," Moore asked. "No, sir," Cooley said. Moore then objected to the confession because Miranda did not voluntarily give it. Judge Yale McFate overruled the objection. The jury convicted Miranda.[23]

The following day Miranda's second trial for raping and kidnapping Lois Jameson began, again in the courtroom of Judge McFate. She gave poignant, painful testimony about the assault and identified Miranda as her attacker. When Carroll Cooley took the stand Moore again brought up the fact that Miranda had not seen an attorney. Moore: "Did you ever advise the defendant he was entitled to the services of an attorney?" Cooley: "No." Moore also objected to the admission of Miranda's confession; McFate again overruled him. The jury found him guilty.[24] McFate sentenced Miranda to twenty to thirty years in prison for each of the kidnapping and rape charges, those sentences to run concurrently, to be followed by twenty to twenty-five years for robbery.[25]

Alvin Moore appealed both of Miranda's convictions. Those appeals made it to the Arizona Supreme Court in early 1965. In the robbery case the court focused mainly on the aspects of Miranda's appeal that related to his competency to stand trial, among other issues. The court rejected the argument that Miranda was not competent to stand trial and affirmed the initial ruling. The appeal of the rape and kidnapping conviction followed. Moore again made a number of arguments that the court disposed of quickly. But one of the arguments—that the jury heard inadmissible evidence in the form of Miranda's confession—became the focus of the court. The court concluded that Miranda had freely made his confession and the fact that he did not have an attorney present did not violate his rights. They affirmed the rape and kidnapping conviction.[26]

Miranda appealed the rape and kidnapping conviction to the Supreme Court. This time Alvin Moore stepped aside and the American Civil Liberties Union (ACLU) secured the services of Phoenix attorneys John P. Frank and John J. Flynn, along with several others. Frank crafted an impressive brief, and Flynn delivered oral arguments before the Court. He argued that Miranda could not have freely made his confession because no one had advised him of his rights. Flynn also made note of Miranda's limited education as a deterrent to him understanding his rights. He argued further, citing *Escobedo*, that the state should have provided Miranda counsel. "A person in Ernest Miranda's position needs the benefit of counsel, and unless he is afforded that right to counsel he simply has, in essence, no Fifth or Sixth Amendment right, and there is no due process of law being afforded to a man in Ernest Miranda's position," Flynn concluded.[27]

The Court agreed and in a 5–4 decision overturned Miranda's conviction. *Miranda* asserted that during a custodial interrogation individuals not only had a right to counsel but had to be informed of that right before questioning began. Without such a warning individuals might incriminate themselves, as Ernesto Miranda had, which violated their Fifth Amendment rights.[28] The Court issued a set of guidelines for law enforcement to follow, and many jurisdictions responded by creating a statement, now known as a Miranda Warning, along the lines of "You have the right to remain silent. Anything you say can and will be used against you in a court of law. You have the right to an attorney. If you cannot afford an attorney, one will be provided for you."[29] Such warnings are now a standard part of all police interrogations. Further, if at any point during questioning an individual invokes their rights, either by asking for an attorney or expressing a desire to remain silent, questioning must cease until the individual has had an opportunity to confer with counsel. Miranda's name has further entered the lexicon as a verb: to read someone their Miranda rights is to mirandize them.

Miranda in many ways revolutionized how law enforcement treats individuals under interrogation. The Court made little of Miranda's ethnicity, but given that he and Ernesto Escobedo were both of Mexican ancestry, these rulings were important for the Mexican American community, as well as for all Americans. The State of Arizona did retry Miranda. His girlfriend at the time of the crimes testified that he had spoken to her about them. In February 1967 the jury convicted him based on that testimony and sentenced him to twenty to thirty years in prison, although he was paroled in 1972.[30] After prison, he mainly made a living by signing the Miranda Warning cards issued to law enforcement. In a final twist of fate, two men killed Miranda in bar fight in 1976. The state did mirandize his attackers and did not prosecute them.[31]

These Supreme Court cases represented a major shift in how the criminal justice treats in-custody individuals. *Hernandez*, *Escobedo*, and *Miranda* all resulted in major reforms to the criminal justice system, reforms that impacted not just Mexican Americans but all people in the United States. Perhaps *Miranda* is the most important, considering that Miranda rights are foundational to how police conduct investigations and are now so commonplace that police forces in other countries use them and even call them Miranda Warnings. While many people know what a Miranda Warning is, few, I would guess, know before having read this that it originated with a Mexican American individual who, when denied his rights, appealed to the Supreme Court and won.

In addition to these major, national-level cases, a number of local-level issues related to custody and incarceration plagued Mexican American people involved in the justice system. Many Southwestern communities expanded jail and prison facilities beginning at midcentury, part of the evolution of the carceral state. In Dallas in the 1950s, for example, the county constructed a new female holdover jail. The facility recorded a few Mexican-origin women. For instance, police booked Betty Martinez for theft under five dollars on

November 25, 1953. Staff recorded Martinez as "Mex."[32] The single largest booking of Mexican-origin women at one time was four—Lillian Rojo, Mary Galacio, Oleda Garcia, and Angil Rojo—all of whom police arrested the night of March 8, 1954, for disturbing the peace.[33] Dallas also expanded other jail facilities at this time.

In San Antonio the problem wasn't the expansion of the city's incarceration system but rather the condition of the existing system. The city's jails were dilapidated and a breeding ground for abuse and violence. The State of Texas had mandated jail reforms in 1957, which required modifications such as cells that allowed for the separation of first offenders from other prisoners, holding cells that could accommodate eight or fewer people, and increased security to prevent violence between the incarcerated. The Bexar County Jail had no ability to separate first offenders, and holding cells could accommodate twenty-four. The state never funded these measures, and problems mounted as the incarcerated population grew.[34]

Throughout the 1960s, several people died in custody and under questionable circumstances in San Antonio. Perhaps the worst example was that of Michael Perkins, who was beaten and raped in a holding cell by at least eight men. He later died from head injuries. Sheriff William Hauck showed little sympathy for Perkins and stated that rehabilitation began when prisoners left his jail, not while they served their time. San Antonio activists formed a group called the Ad Hoc Committee for the Safe Treatment of Prisoners (STOP) to work for reform. STOP organized several protests at the jail and submitted a list of reform ideas to Hauck, including psychiatric screenings, literacy training, and work programs for the incarcerated, all to be provided by STOP, which meant that the county would pay nothing. Sheriff Hauck refused.[35]

STOP's protests at least moved the Bexar County Commissioners Court to launch an investigation into the situation at the jail. They put Judge Solomon Casseb in charge of an investigatory committee, but Casseb seemed to think that the problems were not serious. The committee basically did nothing.[36] Hauck evidently grew tired of STOP's demonstrations and had three protestors arrested, including the Reverend Charles Sullivan, a popular minister. The deputies who arrested these individuals also beat them, meaning they suffered some of the same abuse they were protesting. Sullivan gave his Sunday sermon from his jail cell.[37] The STOP protests continued, but nothing really changed because the county refused to pay for upgrades at the jail.[38]

As noted at the beginning of this chapter, San Antonio also had problems at juvenile facilities such as the Bexar County Boy's School, or Southton.

Problems trickled down from the top. Superintendent Robert Rosa seemed to care very little about the boys in his custody, and he delegated most of the day-to-day operations of Southton to staff member Eugene Helm. In 1965 Virginia Bermea had complained about the violence her son, Gilberto, had experienced from Helm.[39] She wasn't the only parent to complain. Elisa Perez wrote to county officials also in 1965 regarding the treatment of her son, Arturo. Not only had Helm beaten and kicked Arturo, but other boys bullied him because he had a speech impediment. Arturo ran away from the facility on three occasions to avoid this abuse, but this only augmented his sentence.[40] Another parent, Velia Cardenas, added that Helm also tortured boys by having them kneel or hold the pushup position for long periods of time.[41]

Caseworker Luis Alvarado believed that problems at Southton went beyond Eugene Helm. In fact, Alvarado alleged that the problems began with Superintendent Rosa. It was the superintendent's job to monitor employees like Helm. But Alvarado noted that Rosa allowed for the use of a "wood-shed" where the abusive forms of discipline noted by the parents took place. Alvarado met with Rosa to discuss these problems and the superintendent assured him that "there was no substance to the allegations." Yet after the meeting, Rosa had Southton staff sign a memo of understanding that explicitly banned corporal punishment. When the memo was released to staff, Alvarado advised Helm that he should halt his abusive behavior. Helm then complained to Rosa about Alvarado. So Rosa terminated caseworker Alvarado![42]

In a statement about his dismissal, Alvarado cut to the heart of why the situation at Southton was so very bad: "It is very shameful that in our Great Society we cannot provide a more suitable training or treatment center which is conducive to future wholesome development of these young citizens. Perhaps their constitutional rights were taken away upon their commitment? Do they really have any rights? Is the status of these youngsters the equivalent to inmates at a penitentiary? Are our training schools really rehabilitating these youngsters? Is their new 'home' when compared to the former environment an improvement or a detriment?" In linking the school to other forms of incarceration, Alvarado asserted that Southton was no "reform school." Instead, the boys' experiences at the school probably hardened them, he argued, and maybe even set them on the path to becoming career criminals. This was a huge problem that San Antonio's officials largely chose to ignore.[43]

The deaths of incarcerated people such as Michael Perkins, and the abuse of individuals such as those at Southton, happened with some regularity across the Southwest. One of the more troubling examples of this abuse is the number of individuals who died under questionable circumstances while in police custody. Authorities almost always classified these deaths as "suicides." But Chicano activists often found that police accounts differed widely from the available evidence. So they protested to demand justice and reform.

A good example of an unusual jailhouse death comes from the case of Adan Hernandez in Houston. In 1978, Houston police had arrested him and beaten him in jail for allegedly being "belligerent." A jailer found him hanging in his cell; police told his family he died by suicide. Adan's father, Marcelino Hernandez of Mission, Texas, was suspicious, and he requested that the Brown Berets investigate. They found Adan's body badly bruised and police stories inconsistent. For instance, officers claimed that Hernandez had been in his cell for only five minutes when they found him dead, which seems implausible. The Berets also discovered that he had lingered in a coma for a week before dying. No one ever told his family he was in the hospital. The Berets organized a rally at Moody Park, a strategic choice meant to remind the city of Joe Campos Torres. Hundreds attended. While there was a sizable police presence, no violence occurred because, according to the Berets, they came armed.[44] Nothing really came of this case, which would seem to indicate that the reforms initiated after the police murder of Joe Campos Torres didn't amount to much.

Perhaps the worst in-custody death in Texas was that of Larry Ortega Lozano. On the night of January 10, 1978, twenty-seven-year-old Lozano lost control of his pickup truck in Odessa, Texas. He called for assistance, and two Ector County deputy sheriffs, Leroy Murphy and Gene Kloss, arrived. Instead of rendering aid, they demanded Lozano's identification, and when he declined, the officers attempted to take it from him. Lozano allegedly struck at Murphy, and Kloss responded by hitting Lozano "very hard" on the head with his flashlight. They arrested Lozano and took him to jail, where at least four officers beat him. He was subsequently treated at a hospital and then released to police, who returned him to the jail.[45]

Two days later, Elva Hurst, a mental health counselor with the Permian Basin Community Center for Mental Health and Mental Retardation, interviewed Lozano. She found that he "was in terrible physical condition. His face was black and blue and so swollen his eyes were shut. He kept lifting his eyelids with his fingers so he could look at me." She later testified that his face looked like "raw hamburger." A number of other medical professionals confirmed Hurst's report. They began working with Sheriff Elton Faught to have Lozano transferred to the mental health facility. He was initially transferred to a hospital but then returned to the jail. On the night of January 22, after two separate instances that indicated that Lozano's mental condition had deteriorated significantly, a jailer alleged that he found Lozano banging his head, as well as the cell's metal toilet seat, violently against the padded cell's "look through" window. Officers sprayed mace into the cell in attempt to disable Lozano, but that idea failed; the officers only incapacitated themselves. When they did finally enter the cell, a struggle ensued. Officer Randy Tenney placed Lozano in a headlock, Lozano broke free, and then Officer Jack Perkins pulled Lozano by the neck outside of the cell. Lozano began to bang his head on the floor. They tightened his restraints and Lozano stopped moving. A guard noticed that Lozano had stopped breathing and attempted to resuscitate him, but he died on the hallway floor.[46]

An initial autopsy performed by Ector County medical examiner Krishnakumari Challapalli was never released publicly. Lozano's family asked Dr. Frederick Bornstein to perform a second autopsy, and he determined that Lozano had suffocated because of excessive pressure placed on his neck. He also recorded nearly 100 distinct hematomas all over Lozano's body. The doctor determined his death to be a homicide: "It is my opinion that this man died from extensive blunt trauma such as beating, hitting and kicking as well as possible small wounds with sharp instruments." Other incarcerated people reported that staff antagonized Lozano and then beat him when he responded for the entire time he was in jail. One said he saw officers beating and kicking Lozano in the head the night he died.[47]

An inquest jury later decided that Lozano's death was accidental and cleared all the officers involved.[48] While not surprising, this still angered the Chicano community. The Brown Berets launched several protests at the courthouse.[49] They pushed for a state and federal probe of Lozano's death with the hope that the Justice Department would bring suit. Texas attorney general John L. Hill issued a report about several police killings, including Joe Campos Torres, Ricardo Morales, Danny Vasquez, and Larry Lozano, among others. He called for further legal action in the cases of Vasquez and Lozano.[50] In many ways this report was significant simply because it existed. It was the first of its kind and showed that the state's top law enforcement official agreed with Chicanos and wanted to see justice done.

The hopes for prosecution by the Justice Department quickly vanished. As in Arizona's Jose Sinohui case, the Carter administration proved unwilling to prosecute civil rights cases involving Mexican Americans. Even after Attorney General Hill's report and the preponderance of the evidence, Griffin Bell decided that insufficient evidence existed to prosecute Ector County officials and that the Justice Department would seek no indictments.[51] A number of prominent Mexican American leaders demanded a review of the case and criticized the Carter administration anew. The federal government basically stonewalled them.[52]

With the assistance of a number of activist attorneys, Lozano's family decided to sue in federal court, asserting that the officers had violated his rights. In late 1980 the case came to trial. The jury ultimately excused most of the officers involved but declared that Randy Tenney and Jack Perkins had used excessive force, which had caused Lozano's death. However, the jury also declared that these officers had performed their duties in good faith. Thus, they told the family that police had killed their son but also that the death occurred during the good faith execution of the officers' duties, which made it accidental. They awarded the family no compensation.[53]

Similar in-custody deaths happened in California. The National Council of La Raza had begun investigating suspicious deaths at jail facilities in California going back to the 1960s. A number of Mexican Americans had died under mysterious circumstances; all were classified as suicides. The Hollenbeck LAPD station was notorious in this regard; at least ten suicide deaths had occurred at the station's holding facility between 1965 and 1970. There were six suicide deaths at the Sheriff Department's Firestone Station in 1969. These stations had more cases of death by suicide than the entire California prison system. Five Mexican Americans died in this manner: Richard Hernandez, Raul Garcia, Joe Montano, Gilbert Hernandez, and a man known only as Huerta. Activists suspected that these so-called suicides were actually police murders. Police simply denied these accusations, and nothing changed.[54]

One of the most sensational in-custody deaths in Los Angeles occurred in late 1978. The LAPD picked up Reyes Martinez on November 18, 1978, for, according to one source, alleged public intoxication and, according to another, allegedly attempting to rob a van. Officers took him to the Van Nuys Division jail. Later that night police found him unconscious on the jail floor. He died the following day. When his body was returned to his family, they found it badly damaged. According to one report, he had multiple bruises and lacerations, bled from an ear, had chipped teeth, and had various cuts on his head. The coroner determined that the cause of his death was blunt force trauma to the back of the head. At a coroner's inquest, four LAPD officers and two jail supervisors refused to answer questions. Although that was their right, it muddied the waters as to what happened to Martinez. The inquest jury decided his death was not an accident but rather the result of "blunt force trauma at the hands of another person other than by accident."[55]

According to Reyes Martinez's family and activist allies, it appeared that police had beaten him throughout the night. Police claimed that Martinez had fallen out of his bunk. A number of local, small demonstrations occurred. Several months later the district attorney decided not to press charges against the officers because Martinez had "suffered the fatal blow during a fight with unknown persons a few hours before his arrest."[56]

The Reyes Martinez case proved to be a tip of a fairly large iceberg. The Coalition against Police Abuse, an activist organization focused on combatting police abuse (discussed more in chapter 7) collected data on in-custody deaths and officer-involved shootings. In a report issued in 1979 they tallied a total of fifty-six nonfatal shootings, fifteen involving White persons, sixteen of Latinos, and twenty-five of African Americans, and fourteen fatal shootings of seven Black people, five White people, and two Latinos. The most notorious of these was probably Eula Mae Love, a Black woman shot and killed by two LAPD officers. There were also three in-custody deaths that year, including one suspicious jailhouse "suicide" much like that of Reyes Martinez.[57]

When activists met to protest these killings, they demanded reform. As Carlos Ortega, who had helped found the Concerned Chicano Citizens of Canoga Park (Reyes Martinez was a resident of Canoga Park), explained, "We're not saying we don't need police—that would be stupid. But we need a certain caliber—and I don't care if he's Anglo or Chicano—of police officer." Again, as in other periods, Mexican Americans did not express antipolice sentiments, but they had a variety of demands for reforming police. In Ortega's case, he called for the hiring of officers who spoke Spanish and had some knowledge of the Mexican American community. Alas, Ortega and the other activists would have to wait. While the LAPD made a minor revision to its shooting policies after the Love case, which limited police use of deadly force to defensive action, they did nothing about in-custody deaths like Martinez's. The district attorney's office also created Operation Rollout, which required a member of the district attorney's office to be at the scene of police shootings. But the LAPD basically ignored Operation Rollout. Reform would not come until after the beating of Rodney King in 1991 and the LA Riots of 1992.[58]

In Arizona, a key problem was that those trying to reform prisons often got railroaded by the system. In essence, criticism of incarceration led to incarceration. Probably the best example of this dilemma was the case of Jesus "Jess" Lopez. He had founded the United Barrio Union in Glendale to push for civil rights. He worked hard to achieve a number of community improvements, such as the building of a local park; he ran unsuccessfully for a seat on the Glendale city council; and, most importantly, he pushed for prison reform at the Arizona State Prison at Florence. In 1976, the problem at the Florence prison, as at other American prisons, was overcrowding. In early January those incarcerated at Florence took matters into their own hands, engaging in work stoppages and sit-ins to protest conditions. According to the Arizona Department of Corrections, 90 percent of those in the middle-security section of the prison, nearly 1,300 men total, refused to turn out for breakfast or report to work. The maximum-security section of the prison had more intense demonstrations. Outside the prison walls, Jess Lopez led a group of activists who picketed the facility.[59]

The United Barrio Union approached prison staff to correct the overcrowding problem. Unfortunately, the warden had no real power to give them what they wanted. The United Barrio Union picketed the prison to draw more attention to the case, while the ACLU sued the prison system. After these events, the Arizona Department of Corrections agreed to reduce the prison population at Florence by half. That was a massive reduction and seemingly a major victory, but one accomplished via the building of new prisons.[60]

Jess Lopez's activism put him at odds with the justice system. Police made a number of unsuccessful attempts to arrest him for petty offenses. They finally collared him for allegedly firebombing a community college in Glendale in 1977.[61] The circumstances of the case reveal how law enforcement can entrap and eliminate an opponent, much as they had with other activists. Police arrested a man named Gerardo Rivera, who confessed to the firebombing. He accepted a plea deal in exchange for testifying that Lopez was his accomplice. Since Lopez had spoken critically of police, many Chicanos believed that the police had coerced Rivera into giving false testimony. Lopez's trial was itself problematic. The jury was all-White even though Maricopa County had a significant Mexican American population. The prosecution labeled Lopez a dangerous, violent individual. Prosecuting deputy county attorney Warren Smoot called Lopez a "Jekyll and Hyde. . . . [He] would appear to be a nice person until he became upset and then he would become violent."[62] A Chicano journalist called this "conditioning" of the jury.[63] Lopez's United Barrio Union colleagues retorted that he, and the United Barrio Union more broadly, were committed to nonviolence. The prosecution really had no evidence other than Rivera's testimony.[64]

Lopez's conviction inspired a good deal of new organizing. A Free Jess Lopez! legal group formed in 1977 to have his case overturned. Activists organized a series of massive rallies on his behalf.[65] Yet a jury convicted Lopez of conspiracy, second-degree arson, and depositing an explosive device with the intent to injure property based on Rivera's testimony.[66] Judge Sandra Day

O'Connor sentenced him to a mandatory five-year sentence in prison for depositing an explosive and concurrent terms of two to four years for arson and one to three years for conspiracy. Lopez would serve his time—wait for it—at the Arizona State Prison at Florence.[67]

Despite the agreement that the Florence prison would reduce its population by half, reform came slowly. In fact, even after a federal court order, a judge in 1978 called time served in the prison "cruel and unusual punishment." Violence at the prison had only grown worse. In the first seven months of 1978, seventeen inmates had been stabbed, one fatally. Activists continued to put pressure on the system.[68] Things only changed, however, after a massive prison uprising at the neighboring New Mexico State Penitentiary in Santa Fe in 1980. Arizona officials didn't want to see such an uprising in Arizona, so they expedited the reduction of the prison population at Florence. Alas, they "reduced" that population by transferring the incarcerated to new prison facilities constructed at Perryville and Tucson. That's how the prison industrial complex works.[69]

New Mexico had similar prison problems, ultimately leading to a massive uprising in 1980. Interestingly, before that a number of locales attempted several measures to address incarceration problems. Albuquerque, for instance, pioneered new types of alternative adjudication and rehabilitation programs. The city, with Police Chief Bob Stover's support, launched several programs designed to steer those with drug addictions, or those who committed crimes while under the influence, away from jail and prison facilities in 1975. One of these, the General Addictions Treatment Effort, assisted those with drug problems. The city also launched the Albuquerque Treatment Alternatives to Street Crime (ATASC), a program meant to divert nonviolent offenders with a drug addiction away from jail.[70] These types of programs were very important and would become a fixture in many communities especially in the 1980s.

In 1977 the city announced a plan to reduce the jail population by releasing incarcerated individuals convicted of misdemeanor crimes, either on their own recognizance or to the ATASC program. City officials seemed to realize that, as Judge John Brown put it, "90 per cent [of those incarcerated] simply are not people who should be in jail." The city wanted neither to house and pay for those inmates nor to do undue harm to people who did not need to be in jail. City leaders hoped to create enough of a safety net through programs such as ATASC that individuals who might recidivate would instead get treatment. The city was also building a new city jail, and city leaders hoped that with ATASC and a new facility they could shutter the city's two other jails, the Montessa Park Detention Center and the county jail.[71]

Although these reforms in Albuquerque did a good job of steering some offenders away from jail, reform of the penal system went in the opposite direction. New Mexico had, like other states, begun to expand its prison facilities—an example of the growing carceral state—in the 1930s, when the state updated the penitentiary in Santa Fe by adding a new women's quarters, and again in 1956, when the state built an entirely new prison.[72] The New Mexico State Penitentiary in Santa Fe by the 1970s was perpetually overcrowded and had a host of other problems. A series of reforms attempted to alter problems at the prison, but most ended in failure. Those failures led to a massive prison uprising in 1980.

The New Mexico State Penitentiary had a long history of troubles. Minor rebellions had occurred at the prison in 1953 and 1971. The facility had seen significant staff turnover since the early 1970s. In 1976, the new warden, Lee Aaron, abruptly quit when the prison bureaucracy stymied reform efforts the state had asked him to complete. In 1976 inmates engaged in a strike over conditions at the penitentiary, including abusive guards, rotten food, and overcrowding. Guards used tear gas and beat inmates with ax handles to halt the strike. A series of escapes and a death by suicide also caused bad press for the facility. These problems led newly appointed warden Clyde Malley to seek $27 million in 1977 to update the penitentiary and build a new medium-security facility at Los Lunas. The state did fund the construction of the new facility, which administrators hoped would ease overcrowding at the prison. It opened in 1980.[73]

In addition to these minor attempts at reform, incarcerated individuals also fought for reforms. In 1976, inmate Dwight Duran penned a nearly 100-page legal brief detailing problems at the prison. Duran was incensed when a friend died at the prison after staff denied him medical care for a year. He charged that staff routinely violated the Eighth Amendment rights of the incarcerated. His case became an ACLU class action lawsuit against Governor Jerry Apodaca in 1977. In 1979, Governor Bruce King agreed to a settlement that would allow federal oversight of the prison. *Duran v. King*, better known as the Duran Consent Decree, approved in July 1980, altered how the prison was administered. The decree may well have staved off the uprising had the various parties ratified it six months earlier.[74]

The situation in Santa Fe did not really improve despite the state appropriations and the anticipated completion of the Los Lunas facility. In 1978, the state fired Clyde Malley. Upon his departure he predicted violence. He especially lamented the cancellation of educational and recreational programs in 1975, which necessitated long periods of in-cell confinement for the incarcerated.

Governor Bruce King called in the National Guard to help end the violence at the Penitentiary of New Mexico in Santa Fe in 1980. This scene shows some of the burning prison buildings, a National Guard helicopter, and part of the soldiers' bivouac. The uprising was caused in large part because of years of budget cuts and mismanagement in the prison system. It is a good example of problems in the prison industrial complex and how they affect Mexican American people, as well as others. *Photo by Barbaraellen Koch, 1980. Courtesy Palace of the Governors Photo Archives (NMHM/DCA), negative number: HP.2014.14.27.*

The turnover at the prison continued into 1979.[75] In February 1980 the prison held 1,100 individuals; it had a capacity to hold 850. Overcrowding also meant that violent offenders could comingle with the rest of the prison population. And a problematic "snitch" system wherein staff encouraged inmates to inform on each other led to a number of abuses.[76]

These problems came to a head on the morning of February 2, 1980. A group of inmates in one dormitory took four guards hostage. Now in possession of keys and uniforms, this group, assisted by nearly 250 others, quickly took control of the prison. Guards vacated their posts to escape, while an estimated 450 inmates also fled the prison. As the incarcerated gained control of the facility, they let others out of their cells and began destroying the prison. They caught and killed a number of inmate snitches. Officials finally made contact with the leaders of the uprising on February 3. One individual who identified himself as Chopper One spoke for the group. They agreed to release an injured guard in exchange for communication with news media. They also released a detailed list of demands.[77]

The list of demands was extensive. For example, they wanted violent offenders segregated from the general prison population, an end to overcrowding, improved food, the return of educational and recreational programs, and an end to harassment, which included the snitch system. They also wanted federal officials to ensure that prison staff would not retaliate against inmates after the uprising. That demand points to the amount of distrust between the incarcerated and their incarcerators, a direct result of the failure of the state to finalize the Duran Consent Decree. They also wanted access to the media. When state leaders granted that access, Dwight Duran and Lonnie Duran (no relation) spoke for the incarcerated.[78]

The uprising ended on February 3. On February 4, New Mexico newspapers reported an initial death toll of thirty individuals (later revised to thirty-three). Many of these were prison snitches. They died horribly: inmates burned one man's face with a blowtorch until he succumbed, and they decapitated another. Many of the men killed were African Americans and Mexican Americans, although prison staff disclaimed a racial aspect to the uprising.[79] While the media seemed taken aback by the level of violence, given the dehumanization that had occurred at the prison over the past decades, the violence shouldn't have surprised anyone. A follow-up report from the attorney general's office made clear that the overcrowding, lack of control, and the snitch system, among other factors, all led to the uprising.[80]

The New Mexico State Penitentiary Riot remains one of the most violent prison uprisings in American history.[81] Although the state finalized the Duran Consent Decree in July 1980, the reforms the decree put in place came too late to halt the violence. The consent decree remained in effect until 1991 when a judge nullified many of its provisions, except those that focused on overcrowding. New Mexico approved a settlement in February 2020 that finally ended the oversight provided by the Duran Consent Decree. The settlement would continue to mandate protocols to prevent overcrowding and regular maintenance, especially pest control.[82] Little has changed in the day-to-day lives of the incarcerated. As writer Roger Morris accurately explained, "For all the money and anguish and notoriety, the causes of the riot have never been healed, and the riot itself, coursing deep in the underlying currents of prison life, has never really ended."[83]

California also had some major issues with its penal system. As in New Mexico, problems came to a head in the 1970s as prison populations grew.

Prison staff in California engaged in a number of inhumane practices. Eddie Sanchez proved this point. He had been in correctional facilities most of his life. In the 1960s prison psychiatrists began treating him with three behavioral modification treatments.[84] The first was a drug therapy using succinylcholine chloride, known by the trade name Anectine. The other two were called Special Treatment and Rehabilitation Training (START) and Control and Rehabilitation Effort (CARE).[85]

Anectine therapy was as scientifically dubious as it was awful. Psychiatric staff used the drug to sedate prisoners, leaving them in a deathlike stupor yet aware of their surroundings. Individuals reported feeling locked within their own bodies because of the muscle paralysis the drug causes, overwhelmed by feelings of asphyxiation, and consumed with the fear of death. The "therapeutic" part of Anectine treatment came from the intensely unpleasant feelings incarcerated people described, which were so painful that they would do just about anything to avoid future treatments. Also, while administering the drug, a therapist would explain that the individual could avoid future treatments if they behaved. The treatment therefore served as a kind of pharmaceutical aversion therapy. START, also an aversion therapy, employed solitary confinement. Incarcerated people held in solitary over a period of weeks could slowly obtain freedoms they had lost in exchange for good behavior. Like Anectine, START proved so horrible that prisoners would behave to avoid it. CARE also used solitary confinement and "therapy" that consisted of verbal abuse designed to "break" the individual. As historian Daniel LaChance has correctly observed, these "clumsy and cruel behavior modification programs in prisons in the late 1960s confirmed a burgeoning association between technocracy and tyranny."[86]

Prison staff at the California Medical Facility in Vacaville administered Anectine to Sanchez against his will eight times. He described the drug's effects in nightmarish detail: "My eyes closed, but I was not asleep. I could not move any part of my body, and I could not breathe at all. I thought I was dying. Then the doctor starts talking to me. He starts talking about knowing what I'm feeling and that it is not pleasant, but it was going to happen to me every time I demonstrated bad behavior in the way of violence." When Anectine didn't work, doctors recommended lobotomy. Sanchez protested, saying he was not insane. That argument had little merit—prison officials had for years used transorbital lobotomy as a punitive form of neurosurgery that they erroneously viewed as effective in eliminating criminal tendencies.[87]

Sanchez sough transfer to another prison to avoid the surgery. When that failed, he mailed a letter threatening President Richard Nixon. He was convicted of threats against the president and received a five-year federal prison sentence in 1972. Alas, the government sent him to the US Medical Center for Federal Prisoners at Springfield, Missouri, where he began treatment in the START program. He appealed and asked to have the program terminated. Prison officials then moved him to the federal penitentiary in Marion, Illinois, where staff subjected him to the Control and Rehabilitation Effort. Sanchez resisted this treatment as well.[88]

The ACLU took up Sanchez's case and a new group, the Committee to Free Eddie Sanchez, formed on his behalf. They hoped to halt the treatments he experienced.[89] In 1971 a Senate judiciary committee investigated prison therapies such as START. The negative press from the investigation caused Marion prison officials to stop the program. A congressional investigation in 1976 led to the prohibition of drug therapies such as Anectine.[90] This was largely because of Eddie Sanchez, whose suffering ultimately affected the lives of countless individuals.

The suffering of David Resendez Ruíz in Texas led to similar federal action as seen in the Duran and Sanchez cases. The Texas prison system had a lot of problems and began to reach a crisis point in the 1970s that mandated federal intervention and observation of the penal system. That intervention came because of David Ruíz. Like Sanchez and Duran, Ruíz rebelled against the abuse he experienced in prison. He had a troubled childhood and spent time in youth facilities in Texas for shoplifting. As an adult he had served time in jail for auto theft and for illegally possessing a firearm.[91] Ruíz documented overcrowding, bad food, and forced labor, but more troubling, he showed that guards and prison administrators used prisoners to torture and punish inmates they disliked at both the Ramsey Farm Unit, where he initially served time as an adult, and later at the Eastham Unit. This practice occurred in many prisons and would come to light most notably in the late 1990s at California's Corcoran State Prison.[92] Ruíz also described how prison staff beat prisoners and used work in the prison farm as punishment.[93]

For Ruíz, the debilitating farmwork he did at the Ramsey Unit and at Eastham, the frequent beatings he received from inmates as well as guards, and the long stretches he spent in solitary became too much. When staff released him from a forty-five-day stretch in solitary confinement for attempting to escape in 1968, he refused to return to work in the fields. To demonstrate his resolve, he severed his Achilles tendons with a razor. Perhaps nothing better illustrates the desperation or pitiful circumstance that inmates faced than a person brutally wounding themselves to avoid an oppressive work environment.[94]

Ruíz ultimately sued the director of the Texas Department of Corrections, William J. Estelle, in 1972 for the violation of his constitutional rights, particularly his Eighth Amendment rights. Like Dwight Duran, he penned his own legal case. In 1974, Judge William Justice combined the *Ruiz* case with several others. Those cases finally went to trial in 1978. In 1980, Justice handed down a lengthy judgment against the Texas Department of Corrections. He required them to reduce prison populations to alleviate overcrowding, to have staff undergo additional training, to have living and medical facilities brought up to code for security and safety, and to provide augmented medical and mental health care. Most importantly, the case along with subsequent legal action gave the federal government oversight of Texas prisons.[95] *Ruiz v. Estelle* fundamentally altered the prison system in Texas, destroying the old, Southern-style prison plantation system that treated the incarcerated like the enslaved.[96]

Alas, Texas in the 1990s succeeded in undoing some of the provisions established in the case, especially in reducing federal oversight. In 1996, the state attempted to terminate Judge Justice's orders. He ruled again in 1999 that Texas prisons remained cruel and unusual in their operation. But in 2002 Justice closed the case, ending federal oversight and allowing for the development of the twenty-three-hour, seven days a week lockdown prison.[97] David Resendez Ruíz sought to make the prison system in Texas more humane. Texas went in the opposite direction. Prison construction increased throughout the 1970s and 1980s. By the time Justice vacated the *Ruiz* decision, prisons in Texas had increased from 14 facilities housing 16,000 people in 1972 to 114 facilities incarcerating 150,000 people in 2002. When people speak of the rise of mass incarceration, this is what they mean.[98]

These examples of the problems with Mexican American involvement with the justice system via custodial situations proved so ubiquitous that they are hard to tabulate fully. In fact, there are numerous examples of problematic in-custody treatment of Mexican Americans in the other chapters of this book. Both Santos Rodriguez and Jose Campos Torres were, of course, in police custody when they died. It is no wonder that the Chicano movement would fight so forcefully against such treatment. In many ways, Chicanos wanted some measure of power—over their lives, their community, their futures or destinies. But in custodial situations police have all the power, and they sometimes exercised that power through violence. That is, in part, what makes being "in custody" such a predicament; whether you've done something wrong or not—and many of the examples in this chapter come from people who had really done nothing wrong—you are powerless to do anything about it. Chicanos wanted to change that dynamic.

These battles, of course, predated the Chicano period. To secure constitutional rights, Mexican Americans started early. The *Hernandez* case went back to the 1950s, but it was a portent of things to come. *Escobedo* and *Miranda* are both excellent examples of Mexican Americans fighting for the rights of those involved in a custodial interrogation, and they changed things for all Americans. During the Chicano movement itself a number of battles also took place, but as in other examples, to try to secure rights someone first had to go through a horrible situation. This was especially true for those numerous jailhouse "suicides" as well as for the treatment of people including Dwight Duran, Eddie Sanchez, and David Resendez Ruíz.

Unfortunately, with the continued growth of the carceral state throughout the civil rights era, Mexican Americans, activist or otherwise, often fought a losing battle. Abuse in custodial situations, which we know has a lengthy history and continues today, is very hard to challenge. What happens behind the walls of police stations or jails or prisons is hard for us to see. Moreover, when there is abuse, often the only thing that speaks for the dead is a body. Police and jail or prison officials tend to rally around one another, an example of the code of silence that ultimately means that the truth is muddied or never comes out. For movement participants, the body, for example of Reyes Martinez, tells a story of abuse and violence, but one that law enforcement can successfully counter or quash. Yet when we start to calculate the sheer number of in-custody cases of abuse and death, as well as their occurrences over a very long history, I think we have to start asking ourselves, are these cases aberrations? Or are they simply standard practice for police and the broader criminal justice system?

SIX

A BETTER DAY COMING?

The Chicano Movement
and Local-Level Criminal
Justice Reform

In early 1973 the Albuquerque Police Department launched its Police Athletic League (PAL). While PAL has a long history in the United States, in the 1970s it became a method for police to do community outreach to improve relations by bringing young people and police together via sports and recreational activities. PAL was supported by police and a number of civil rights groups, and it proved enormously popular in Albuquerque. In 1973 more than 300 young people participated in the program, and the track team won the New Mexico Amateur Athletic Union's Boys State Championship while the girls' softball team won the city championship.[1]

The Chicano movement boldly confronted policing problems. These challenges resulted in a number of reforms. Local and state governments inaugurated reforms not only in response to the protests they witnessed but also in anticipation of future problems that might lead to community unrest.

Understanding how police agencies responded to Chicano activism and what they were willing to do to bring about change is an important part of the history of Mexican American relations with law enforcement. Reforms, which included police-civilian review boards, human relations commissions, community-police partnerships such as PALs, police storefronts, hiring practices that sought to bring more Mexican Americans, male and female, into police work, and augmented cultural sensitivity training and psychological testing, among others, demonstrate a law enforcement commitment to improving policing. Additionally, when local level demands for reform failed, Chicanos continued to call upon the Department of Justice to investigate and prosecute officers who violated the rights of Mexican Americans.[2]

Chicano activism pushed many of the reforms of the 1960s and 1970s especially. This is yet another example that shows that Mexican Americans did not oppose law enforcement: they opposed abusive or problematic law enforcement. When police leadership responded positively to the demands of Mexican Americans—and there were good examples of leaders who did exactly that—they improved the police's relationship with the community. And a number of reforms succeeded and met the goals and expectations of city leaders and activists. It is important to note that reforms worked and to show how and why they did so. It is equally important to analyze how and why they failed, because not all reforms proved successful.

But let's be clear, there were many problems, and in a number of locales either things did not get better or they got worse before they got better. Many times, police responded to problems reactively—they might adopt a reform, but only after an instance of police abuse or murder, and law enforcement often designed these reforms to mollify the Mexican American community. Mexican Americans in many locales hoped for a more proactive response from police authorities, a response that would forestall policing problems and thereby generate a more productive relationship with police. They did not always get that response. Moreover, a number of communities resisted reform efforts that had great potential to lessen tensions after an instance of police violence, most notably the development of police-civilian review boards. Last, it is important to acknowledge that some much-touted reforms that had great potential to do good ultimately caused great harm. The best example of this is community policing efforts and the things that went along with them, such as police storefronts, which over time morphed into today's broken windows policing, a damaging police practice discussed in chapter 8.

A number of government reports highlighted the problem of police violence and the need for reform. The many meetings of US Commission on

Civil Rights, such as the San Antonio hearings in 1968, generated important studies relating to Mexican Americans and law enforcement. The most far reaching was a Commission on Civil Rights report published in March 1970 and titled *Mexican Americans and the Administration of Justice in the Southwest*. This report explored almost every aspect of the criminal justice system. The first chapter, entitled "Law Enforcement," provided a great deal of data on the ways in which police treated Mexican-origin people. The chapter contained numerous examples of abuse, mostly use of excessive force, as well as commenting on the general indecency or lack of courtesy that people received, from officers calling youths "pachuco" or "punk" to police referring to adults as "Meskin." The chapter also briefly discussed police killings of Mexican Americans.[3]

Mexican Americans and the Administration of Justice also offered reform solutions to law enforcement issues. One involved revising police complaint procedures. The report noted that many communities had outdated complaint procedures that discouraged community members from reporting problematic officers. For example, in smaller towns the police department handled complaints itself, meaning that community members had to go to the police to complain about the police. In addition, the chief of police often served as the arbiter of complaints, and many chiefs felt a duty to protect their officers. Newer automated phone or anonymous complaint procedures might eliminate many of these issues, the report asserted.[4]

The report also focused on jury service. Even after the *Hernandez* case, Mexican Americans still found themselves excluded from juries. The report also disclosed that Mexican American rarely served on grand juries. All of these issues had profound results as to how Mexican Americans perceived the criminal justice system. For example, they widely believed that the system was biased against them; those on trial for criminal offenses, even when innocent, often pleaded guilty because they believed that they would not receive a fair trial; and grand juries were biased, especially in police misconduct cases. Bail amounts, too, exceeded what the average person could pay and hindered the efforts of civil rights groups. Mexican Americans also found securing adequate counsel cost prohibitive. Some localities practiced an early version of "stop and frisk," and racial profiling proved typical.[5]

Challenging these issues in the criminal justice system was exceedingly difficult, the report noted. As one Mexican American attorney commented, "When you stand up and speak for your rights . . . they think you're infringing on their rights."[6] *Mexican Americans and the Administration of Justice* painted a depressing picture. It concluded with some harsh food for thought: "Police

Depiction of a motorcycle police officer from the US Commission on Civil Rights May 1970 report entitled *Stranger in One's Land*. The image appeared as part of chapter 6, "La Ley" (the law). That chapter offered examples of police abuse from across the region but focused heavily on Texas, labeled the Texas Rangers as "symbols of this [police] repression," and specifically criticized Ranger captain Alfred Y. Allee. Such government reports focused much-needed attention on policing in the Southwest. *US Commission on Civil Rights*, Stranger in One's Land, *Clearinghouse Publication no. 19, May 1970, Frank Sanchez Papers, MS 612 BC, Center for Southwest Research, University Libraries, University of New Mexico, Albuquerque.*

departments, courts, the law itself are viewed as Anglo institutions in which Mexican Americans have no stake and from which they do not expect fair treatment. Acts of police misconduct result in mounting suspicion and incite incidences of resistance to officers. These are followed by police retaliation, which results in escalating hostilities."[7]

The Commission on Civil Rights also published the provocatively titled *Stranger in One's Land* in May 1970. The sixth chapter, "La Ley" (the law), did a good job of synthesizing Mexican American criticisms of law enforcement practices. The most important feature of "La Ley" was how it broke down regionally important issues. For example, in California in general and in Los Angeles specifically, tension had increased after the LA Blowouts. Moreover, Mexican Americans felt disregarded by the criminal justice system and, especially, excluded from jury service. In New Mexico the report noted the issue of police overcharging young people with petty crimes. This led to lengthy rap sheets that ultimately haunted Mexican American youths after they left school or, far worse, if they committed more serious crimes later in life.[8]

Stranger in One's Land also heavily criticized police practices in Texas. The report specifically called out the Texas Rangers as "symbols of this repression." The report detailed a number of instances of Ranger brutality, especially the Magdaleno Dimas incident. Farmworker José Martinez provided a compelling explanation for why the Rangers were a problem: "Many people hate them, many people are afraid, because the majority of the Mexicans are not armed. They [Rangers] are armed. And when the Rangers are coming, then the people are afraid. They are afraid of being hit, or being pushed around. . . . The minute that you hear the Rangers are coming, everybody hides." The Ranger "La Ley" fixated on was A. Y. Allee. As has been discussed, he rightfully earned the enmity of many Mexican Americans.[9]

Stranger in One's Land acknowledged many of the problems with the policing of Mexican Americans. "Contacts with teachers, employment officials, social workers, police, and other representatives of el gobierno [the government] have, in many instances, left behind memories of mistreatment and insensitivity," the report concluded.[10] The police had been making those memories for generations and would, unfortunately, continue to make them in the years to come. So Chicano activists pushed to reform the police.

One of the most important reform ideas was police-civilian review. The basic concept involved including nonpolice members of the community in police affairs. This would give local people some measure of power in cases of police abuse or murder. The power a review board might have or who would serve on it always seemed to be sticking points for Mexican Americans, local governments, and police. If police-civilian review boards had power—to try, punish, or fire an officer—they took power from other agencies, such as city human resources departments or chiefs of police, as well as the broader criminal justice system, which would have presided over trials. As such, an idea that seemed simple was, in fact, incredibly complex.[11]

Many Southwestern communities initially followed guidance developed by the American Civil Liberties Union. The ACLU produced *Police Power and Citizens' Rights* as a guide for creating civilian review boards in 1966. But its definition of a review board was weak: a board would "have the power to hear complaints, investigate and make recommendations ONLY. Its function would be purely advisory. It would have no disciplinary powers whatever."[12] The ACLU used such language to make the idea of civilian review palatable to law enforcement, but with no power such boards would achieve little. The first review board in the nation, founded in Philadelphia in 1958, serves as a good example of the problem with this powerlessness. That board had on occasion successfully moderated disputes between officers and citizens, but even the ACLU found its effectiveness hard to determine. Its most important role, it seems, was as a "safety valve" for tensions and hostilities.[13] Other boards that had formed in New York City and Washington, DC, also suffered from the problem of powerlessness. Local governments would continue to examine review boards and their powers as the civil rights movement progressed.

In the Southwest, communities began discussing civilian review in the mid-1960s. In Arizona, Mexican Americans called for the establishment of a police-civilian review board in cities such as Phoenix early on in the Chicano period. Former police officer Richard Ruiz wanted Phoenix to found a civilian review board in 1965. "The need of a police review board is mandatory," Ruiz argued, "but it must be borne in mind that such an organization must be headed by responsible citizens free from political attachment, and conscious of the problems involving the police department and the people of Phoenix." He believed that this would establish good relations between Chicanos and police and anticipate challenges in the future.[14]

Phoenix had seen relatively few instances of police brutality before the late 1970s, so the city and police didn't favor a review board at this time. Police Chief Paul Blubaum instead created a community relations division in 1966 to promote better relations between police and communities of color. The ten-officer division did outreach by meeting with community members, giving speeches, and attending community gatherings. "Our job is not to convince minority groups to like the police," explained Lieutenant Doge Nelson, second-in-command of the division, "but to make them understand our function." The division had much work to do. Blubaum himself confirmed this point when he accused Black leaders of being "two-faced" in that they called for reform but dissuaded African Americans from becoming officers. Blubaum felt similarly about Mexican Americans. His remarks, while factually wrong, showed a lack of awareness of institutional bias in policing that kept people of color away from police work.[15]

Like Phoenix, law enforcement in Tucson also did some important work early on, especially after a protest at the University of Arizona in January 1970. That protest took place at a basketball game between UA and Brigham Young University. Arizona students protested BYU's connection to the Mormon Church and its racism toward Black people. When students disrupted the game, police beat them.[16] This response outraged the student body. Both the Tucson and UA police responded by developing community relations divisions and by holding community engagement meetings. The result seemed educational. "Cops have learned to talk kids' language," noted Lieutenant Peter

Ronstadt, who headed the Tucson PD's community relations division, "and the kids have come to understand the policeman's duty, why he must enforce the law."[17] Both the Tucson PD and the Pima County Sheriff's Department also founded internal affairs divisions in 1968 and 1971, respectively, in response to community concerns.[18]

Other Arizona communities had different experiences with law enforcement, especially developing cities that had no police force. The township of Guadalupe, near Tempe, serves as a case in point. Yaqui and Mexican-origin people had settled Guadalupe at the turn of the century. The village never incorporated, and neighboring cities such as Tempe or Phoenix never annexed it. By the 1970s, the population had reached 4,000, a sufficient number for incorporation. Township leaders hired several firms to study incorporation, including law enforcement.[19]

Before incorporation, Guadalupe received police services from the Maricopa County Sheriff's Office "in a very limited basis." One feasibility study produced by attorney Jerry Levine in September 1974 noted that Guadalupe had several options for law enforcement. The village could continue contracting with the sheriff's department, contract with a neighboring city, or establish its own police department. These suggestions had some merit but raised important questions.[20] Was a police force necessary given Guadalupe's small population and low crime rate? Weren't other parts of a developing city, say parks and schools and trash collection, as important as police? When Guadalupe incorporated in 1975, the town elected to continue its relationship with the Maricopa County sheriff. This situation was a model of how policing should develop at the local level. The townspeople debated a number of options and after careful thought and deliberation arrived at a decision they deemed best for their town.[21]

Both the Tucson and Phoenix areas had other policing problems they attempted to address. Slow police response times in South Phoenix and South Tucson also led to major community complaints. In South Phoenix, the screams of a woman outside a monastery woke up Father Michael Landry and two other priests one night in 1978. "Help! Rape!" she screamed as a male assailant attacked her. A motorist stopped and began fighting the attacker. But he was no good Samaritan. Instead, he fought with the other man to see who would "get" the woman. While the two men fought, she escaped. The police arrived more than thirty minutes later. In another case, Verna McClain called the police to report that thieves were stripping a van near her home. She called at 6:30 p.m., police did not arrive until 10:30 p.m. The burglars were long gone.[22]

In South Tucson slow response times and lack of police training in spoken Spanish caused problems. One terrible example involved a man abducted by unknown assailants in August 1978. The assailants broke both of his legs and injected him with battery acid. This individual crawled for more than a mile before coming to a mobile home. "Policía, policía," he mumbled to the mobile home owner. The owner instead called for an ambulance, but the paramedics also could not speak Spanish. They took the individual to the hospital. There the man was met by doctors and a sheriff's deputy who also spoke no Spanish. The deputy, at least, knew a Spanish-speaking colleague. When Deputy Sheriff Ralph Marmion arrived hours later, the details of the story finally emerged. Fortunately, the man recovered and the information he provided led to the arrest of the individuals who attempted to kill him.[23]

Both South Phoenix and South Tucson attempted to address these issues. South Phoenix residents put enough pressure on police that they built a new substation in the neighborhood. This victory responded directly to the needs of the community.[24] The language issue in South Tucson seemed a more difficult problem to correct. Although officers such as Ralph Marmion did the extra work of translating for non-Spanish-speaking colleagues, he noted that this could not go on indefinitely: "It just puts too much of a burden on those of us who do speak Spanish." Tucson did implement recruitment programs to hire more Mexican American officers and began Spanish-language training programs, which is good, but these efforts took years to complete.[25]

New Mexico also focused on civilian review and community relations as police reform efforts. Clovis, for example, had seen a number of instances of police brutality. In order to bolster community confidence in police and halt police brutality before it caused more damage, the city proposed establishing a community relations commission. City leaders conceived of this body broadly as one that would work toward "prohibiting discrimination in employment practices, public accommodations practices, housing practices, public contracts, and civil rights on the basis of race, sex, age, color, religion, national origin or ancestry; and providing a procedure for the conciliation of any discriminatory act prohibited hereby." The idea used "conciliation," a concept similar to restorative justice, to redress cases of discrimination. It would bring community members and law enforcement into a cooperative dialogue regarding an instance of discrimination, creating a path forward that recognized the need for the active responsibility of the offending party and their goals for making amends to the aggrieved party.[26]

The proposed commission received a boost when a group called Americans for Justice in Curry County (Clovis is the county seat of Curry County) issued a favorable statement about the community relations commission proposal. Mexican Americans had founded Americans for Justice to prevent "police harassment of Mexican-Americans in Curry County." Frank Sanchez, a local activist and education advocate, chaired the group. He worked with the New Mexico branch of the ACLU to write legally correct additions to the proposal.[27] For example, Americans for Justice added a new section that would establish a civilian review board as part of the commission's duties. They wanted the commission to have the power to "investigate, suspend or fire any member of the Clovis Police Department who is found to have participated in harassment or physical abuse of any and all citizens (White, Black or Brown) in the city of Clovis, New Mexico."[28] A group called Coalition por Derechos (Coalition for Rights) also endorsed the Clovis proposal but suggested that each city in the region—especially Roswell, Portales, Carlsbad, and Clovis—found their own community relations commissions.[29]

Despite the good intentions of its authors, as well as those of Americans for Justice and the Coalition por Derechos, the proposal generated serious resistance. One unnamed group published an editorial that said "the proposed ordinance has strong potential for 'witchhunts' and 'harassment,'" adding that "the insidious nature of the proposed law is almost without limit."[30] This visceral, anonymous response to the proposed commission found a face in local business owner Don Kennedy, who spoke before the city council in opposition to the proposal (and used language similar to that of the editorial). Several council members sided with Kennedy. While Mayor Chick Taylor Jr. favored the original proposal, he also acquiesced to some of Kennedy's demands, mainly by removing the civilian review language that Americans for Justice had added. This move signaled the city's basic unwillingness to fight for the commission, which quickly dissolved.[31] A similar proposal developed by the Criminal Justice Task Force in neighboring Roosevelt County in 1977 also offered a grim assessment of police–Mexican American relations and some well-thought-out reform ideas. That proposal also went nowhere.[32]

The most far-reaching police reform efforts in New Mexico occurred in Albuquerque. The city began to reform the Albuquerque Police Department in the late 1960s and accelerated reforms after the police violence that occurred during the Vietnam War and police protest at Roosevelt Park in 1971 and the police killings of Rito Canales and Antonio Cordova in 1972. These efforts occurred not solely because of this violence but also because Albuquerque had police chiefs willing to engage in some reform, beginning with Paul Shaver and continuing with Donald Byrd and Bob Stover. According to Byrd, police needed reform because "public apathy to police is terrific at this point . . .

people don't have confidence in police. We must build it."[33] Shaver began these efforts by founding the Community Relations Department, an internal affairs office, police storefronts, and PAL.[34] Byrd expanded the department's recruiting of Mexican American officers. Stover revised the curriculum at the academy to include cultural and language training.[35]

Police storefronts, called the Storefront Operation in Albuquerque, represented an important evolution in police procedure. The idea, which later morphed into broken windows policing in many locales, was a two-pronged approach to policing. The first prong put police at the disposal of local people for assistance, which could constitute anything from a ride to the store to the planting of a community garden. Storefronts made police into what Officer Emmett Rubio, who ran the storefront in San Jose, called "a kind of social worker."[36] The second prong fit more in line with basic law enforcement; having officers on the ground put them in a position to respond quickly to crime. Cities across the Southwest launched storefront programs.[37] The Storefront Operation in Albuquerque lasted only about a year. Although officers such as Rubio did a good job, some Mexican Americans remained distrustful of police. Albuquerque PD also had difficulty finding officers who saw policing as a public service, so they shuttered the program.[38]

The Police Athletic League proved a more welcome program. The goal of PAL was to involve barrio youths in sports and recreational activities with police officers, who served as coaches and mentors. Beginning in about 1973, PAL began offering karate, ballet, track, wrestling, baseball, and football. The Albuquerque Urban Coalition (AUC), which helped run PAL via its Police Task Force, noted that PAL was "having the community work in the behalf of the police departments and the police officer in the street becomes a good guy."[39] They called it a "fairly spectacular success."[40] The Albuquerque PD received a $5,000 grant from the Avon Foundation for equipment and to pay three youths to assist in organizing the program.[41] Chief Stover noted that the program far exceeded what the city had hoped.[42]

The AUC soon expanded the PAL program. They hired three young people, Ralph Sanchez, Theresa Holguin, and David Schuetz, to run the program with police. These were strategically sound choices; Sanchez and Holguin both hailed from the barrio and had police records, and the AUC's inclusion of a young woman was important.[43] The group also later employed another unnamed barrio youth with a police record who "expressed a desire to keep out of trouble and we [AUC] believe that the associations he will have while working with PAL will help him achieve this desire."[44] Here we see PAL's broader goals for the community at work within the organization itself. What better way to demonstrate the reformative nature of the program than by having reformed youths work there?

PAL had some impressive successes. More than 300 youths participated in the program in 1973. That year the track team won the New Mexico Amateur Athletic Union's Boys State Championship in the fourteen-to-fifteen-year-old division and came in second in the twelve-to-thirteen-year-old division. Twenty-two of the track participants qualified for the State Junior Olympics, and eighteen qualified for the Regional Boys Olympics. The girls' softball team won the city championship.[45]

PAL became an important strategic element in San Jose when tensions with that community and the police reached a critical mass. In 1974, a number of instances of police brutality occurred, especially when off-duty officers Paul Seeber and Maurice Moya beat Phillip Gallegos and Lawrence Marquez (discussed in chapter 3). The AUC held a march and rally to decry such abuse. Joe Green, who led the Concerned Citizens for Better Government (CCBG), threatened to demand "the Albuquerque Police Dept. to leave our area and we will protect our own community with responsible, dignified people of our own." A resident called the violence "police barbarism."[46] Deputy Police Chief Lou Powell, speaking on behalf of Chief Stover, agreed and blamed the city personnel board for reinstating Seeber and Moya.[47] He admitted, "We have some officers on the force who should not be wearing the uniform."[48]

The Albuquerque PD responded quickly to this situation, which came as a blow to Chief Stover, who had tried hard to mend police relations with the Mexican American community via the storefront operation and programs like PAL. The chief began investigating reopening the San Jose storefront, which had closed a year earlier. Stover also proposed expanding the PAL program as a way to strengthen police-community relations. Not only did the city expand PAL, but it got a flood of donations from local people and businesses to do so.[49]

Tensions remained high in San Jose, and then in October 1974 in nearby South Valley, six Albuquerque police officers beat sixteen-year-old Frank Zamora during an arrest for possession of marijuana. He suffered a broken nose, broken teeth, and cuts and bruises on his face. South Valley residents formed the Federación de la Raza (Federation of the People) and held a large rally. The Federación and CCBG also planned a march. Max Martinez, a leader in the Federación, demanded "an immediate stop to police brutality." South Valley resident Joe Fernandez lamented, "We can't depend on city officials and police to solve these problems for us."[50] Chief Stover did suspend the officers while internal affairs began an investigation.[51]

As the CCBG planned its march, a group calling itself Citizens for Improved Government began circulating a letter to local businesses that warned in vague terms of an impending "riot" because of this case of police brutality.[52] Unfortunately, because of the similar name, many assumed that the CCBG wrote it. Joe Green explained that the CCBG knew nothing about this letter. The intent of the letter writer was probably to remind city leaders and citizens about the police-instigated riot of 1971. Activists and city leaders began to work to defuse the situation. "Because of rumors of a riot [and] the hysterical climate in the business community regarding the march," the CCBG canceled its planned march.[53]

Chief Stover responded to the Zamora incident by expanding PAL and by championing the hiring of Mexican American police officers. This was another important goal of police agencies at this time.[54] As one report made clear, "Where officers of one group are in contact with members of the other, and where there are significant differences in beliefs and attitudes arising from cultural patterns, the result can be numerous occasions of needless friction and misunderstanding."[55] Before Chief Byrd had resigned in 1973, he met with the leaders of the AUC to flesh out a "Recruiting Team" that would increase the number of non-White officers.[56] That recruiting team, the Recruitment and Orientation of Minority Patrolmen Program (ROMP, horrible acronym), made some good suggestions as to how the department could recruit Mexican American officers. One involved a series of courses that would prepare Mexican American applicants for the training they would receive at the academy. They also appealed to local businesses to recommend capable individuals to the police force.[57]

Chief Stover presided over ROMP after Byrd created it, but he also focused on the training provided at the police academy in the 1970s. The academy revamped much of its curriculum to focus on "human relations." The cadets received forty hours of training in "minority group relations" and forty in a "Spanish language course."[58] In 1975 the academy revamped the human relations curriculum in favor of "social and psychological training," which included what today we would call "cultural competency" but also training on how to diffuse crisis situations and basic conflict resolution. The academy also extended these courses to commissioned officers as part of their continuing education.[59]

A "Police Personnel Report" conducted by the Police Foundation demonstrated the efficacy of some of these revisions. It noted that officers who received language and human relations training came to see their work as a type of public service. For White officers, many ethnoracial biases remained, from believing that communities of color presented special problems for police to experiencing anxiety when they encountered Mexican-origin people. Mexican American officers saw things differently. They were "more inclined to regard no segment of the public as presenting special law enforcement problems." They experienced little anxiety when dealing with Mexican-origin people and rated their standing in the community as high. When the report analyzed officers with some college education, it found that biases decreased further.[60]

The study also found, however, that for some officers the human relations training had the opposite results of what police leadership had envisioned. For instance, some officers who had completed the training continued to regard African Americans and Mexican Americans as having "difficult law enforcement problems." These officers also believed that communities of color "*think* they are subject to police mistreatment (but not that they actually are subject to mistreatment)." They also felt that most crimes warranted stricter penalties and that a lax judicial system accounted for a low arrest-conviction ratio. Last, while officers reported a general belief that police work had value for the city, "they feel such recognition is less prevalent among ethnic/racial minorities, youth groups, poor people, and residents of the barrios."[61] The "Police Personnel Report" offered no analysis of these responses. They unfortunately demonstrated that instead of giving officers a greater sensitivity to the issues of communities of color, officers maintained a heightened anxiety when dealing with these communities as well as negative perceptions of people of color in general and Mexican Americans in particular. A couple of things explain this. First, the human relations training in 1974 was deficient, which was why the department revised it in 1975 to focus on social and psychological training. Second, the cohort of officers who participated in the training may have presented an issue. The majority of the students were older, established police officers. They demonstrated the most deeply ingrained biases in their responses in the study, and they seemed unable to discard those beliefs. Last, this was the first attempt to offer this kind of training. That alone may explain some of the failings.

The Spanish-language training also presented some problems. University of New Mexico researcher Steven Gonzales analyzed the Spanish instruction offered to cadets and officers. He determined that those who enrolled in the training actually received more than double the hours that the academy had originally proposed, ninety-six hours for cadets and 108 hours for officers. The initial results seemed good for the officers. Out of eighteen, sixteen passed the course (with a C or higher), a pass rate of 88 percent. But that pass rate exposed a problem: thirty-five began the course, and seventeen dropped out because they were failing. The cadets did worse. Since Spanish-language instruction was part of their curriculum, they could not drop the class. Of the thirty-three cadets enrolled in the course, only thirteen passed, a pass rate of 40 percent. An intermediate Spanish class offered to cadets and officers proved more successful. Five officers and eleven cadets participated; none failed. This was largely because Mexican Americans who already knew some Spanish comprised this cohort. Gonzales noted that part of the problem with the introductory course was the textbook, a revised tourist guidebook, as well as the instructors, none of whom the academy had properly vetted. Since the proposal for Spanish instruction had not included well-defined goals, he could not conclusively deem the project a success or a failure.[62]

These results disappointed Albuquerque's police leadership, but that did not stop the forward momentum of reform. The department continued the Spanish-language instruction at the academy but also began a new program designed to use Spanish-speaking officers to teach other officers "street-language Spanish."[63] As noted, the department also revised the human relations training with social-psychological training conducted by the University of New Mexico.[64]

Another reform at this time came from Mexican American officers: the development of Chicano police associations. These officers in Albuquerque, Houston, and other cities formed these groups in the 1970s to give officers a sense of place within the police force. In Albuquerque, this group began in 1973 as the Chicano Police Officers Association, which focused primarily on labor issues. Like other officers of color, Mexican Americans often found their careers stymied by institutional racism. For example, a biased promotion exam kept officers of color from advancement. The association filed suit to have the exam revised or removed as part of the promotion process. In addition to promotion problems, the Chicano Police Officers Association alleged that biased hiring procedures kept Mexican Americans off the force. Judge H. Vern Payne granted the group a preliminary injunction to halt the use of the test but later affirmed the department's testing policy and declared it a reasonable method for determining promotions.[65]

This situation reveals some of the ways in which police departments operated as inequitable institutions. Albuquerque's government had argued that it wanted Mexican American officers but seemed unaware of the biases that might keep them away from policing or halt their advancement on the force. By leaving institutional biases in place, the city maintained the status quo while simultaneously using the Chicano Police Officers Association to promote its outreach efforts with the Mexican American community.

Albuquerque police also engaged in practices that tarnished the reform efforts they had attempted. For example, Chief Byrd augmented a police surveillance program begun by Chief Shaver called the Intelligence Division (recall that Houston had such a division, most departments did). This division kept a list of activists that included their picture, name, address, height and weight, group affiliations, and whether they were armed. The listing for Black Beret member Glen Martinez serves as a good example: "Glen Martinez, Spanish Male, DOB: 5/31/52, (NOD) [no other description], Associates with Larry Russell (Carries .22 auto in his belt). Black Berets."[66]

Chiefs Byrd and Stover also came under scrutiny for other issues that affected Mexican Americans. For example, the department regularly released reports on the number of Spanish-surnamed individuals arrested for driving while intoxicated and those who had DWI accidents. A report in 1974 tabulated that Spanish-surnamed people accounted for 54 percent of arrests for DWI accidents and 57 percent of arrests for DWI. The city did not report on other ethnic groups in this way. The data proved problematic because they implied that Mexican folks were overly prone to drink, a common stereotype, as well as the bias of this differential treatment.[67]

A variety of community groups rejected the city's reporting and data collection methods. The AUC's Police Task Force spearheaded these efforts.[68] In a major statement, the Police Task Force critiqued the city's practices, noting that police disregarded "driving while intoxicated incidents in the eastern segments of the city [the predominately White side of town] or when the culprit is Anglo, except when the police action is triggered by other traffic violations or accidents and the DWI arrest is unavoidable."[69] Deputy Chief Sam Romero defended the program, arguing that police had to attack drunk driving, but acknowledged the existence of "biased action on the part of his officers."[70]

One other aspect of this type of policing merits attention. While the Albuquerque PD engaged in this effort to reduce drunk driving, they also tied a "stop and frisk" program to it. The two ideas went hand in hand, but of course police could use stop and frisk in any interaction. The problem with stop and frisk is that police tend to abuse its power and profile people of color. The AUC noted that it led to "widespread patterns of police misconduct against Mexican Americans." Both the DWI reports and stop and frisk distinctly affected Mexican Americans.[71]

Chief Stover did a decent job responding to these and other community issues, but like Byrd, he generated controversy when the Albuquerque PD proposed purchasing police dogs and horses for a mounted patrol. Once again, the AUC protested these efforts. The group conducted an informal survey in which many people responded negatively to police dogs. "There is enough bitterness within certain communities already and the use of police dogs would only add to the disrespect people have for police officers," one individual argued. Given the historic use of police dogs against communities of color, the AUC's response to the program made sense. The AUC had a different interpretation of police horses, which they viewed positively despite the use of horses by lynch mobs or groups such as the Texas Rangers.[72]

The AUC laid out a detailed explanation of the pitfalls, as well as some potential benefits, of a K-9 unit. They averred that police dogs could aid police in drug or weapons searches. But they strongly opposed the use of dogs as a form of crowd control. They also felt that policy should prohibit police from using dogs to pursue suspects. Last, they opposed the use of dogs unless the city crafted policies to carefully govern the program. "The safeguards against the 'difficulties' [with police dogs] are adequate rules and procedures, properly monitored and enforced by supervision," James McCraw explained.[73] Notes from AUC meetings indicate that Mexican American members generally responded negatively to these ideas. AUC secretary Nina Santiago, for example, stated simply, "Police dogs, *no*, [they] only instigate the people." She also felt that the mounted patrol was "like regressing, and same thing as dogs. Mounted patrol—no." Executive committee member Vicente Ximenez stated, "Police dogs, no. Mounted Patrol, yes." Carnis Salisbury, one of the AUC's African American members, criticized the idea of a K-9 unit. She was "strongly opposed to police dogs—traditionally used in certain neighborhoods and economic areas." She did favor the mounted patrol.[74]

Chief Stover seemed taken aback by these responses. From his perspective, using canines assisted police efforts in narcotics cases. He seemed unaware of the historical perceptions people of color had about police dogs. The critiques of the mounted patrol also seemed to surprise the chief. While a mounted patrol was hardly a modern aspect of police operations, Stover thought that Burqueños would appreciate the nostalgia of a mounted patrol. After giving both dogs and horses consideration, Chief Stover launched a K-9 unit in 1975 and a mounted patrol in 1977.[75]

New Mexico, and especially Albuquerque, had attempted some important reforms. Many reforms at the local level proved much more proactive. Law enforcement and communities of color, especially Mexican Americans, attempted to work together in a number of instances. The reforms they generated, especially PAL or the new curriculum at the academy, show that police could hear community concerns and respond with well-conceived ideas.

San Antonio police officer Laura Garcia seated in her patrol car in November 1975. The San Antonio Police Department hired Garcia in 1974 among a cohort of six other women. She excelled in her work at the police academy and became the first woman of Mexican ancestry on the force. Although other police departments had made hiring women a priority going back to the turn of the century, San Antonio's efforts were very much in line with reform ideas in the 1970s. © *San Antonio Express News, University of Texas at Austin.*

Other locales also attempted or debated reforms. In Texas, San Antonio had hired Mexican American officers throughout the police force's history. In the 1960s the president of the Police Officers Association, the local police union, was Joe Mendoza.[76] As a result of Mendoza's position, San Antonio attempted to hire more Spanish-speaking officers beginning in the 1960s. Officers who could speak Spanish received special green armbands that had the words "hablo español" (I speak Spanish) printed on them.[77] The San Antonio Police Department also hired its first female officers in 1974. For instance, Laura Garcia, the first woman of Mexican ancestry admitted to the police academy, passed with flying colors. By 1983, eleven women entered the police academy, but only thirty-nine out of nearly 1,200 officers were women.[78] San Antonio suffered from problems that plagued many large police forces. In particularly, sexism on the force kept women away from police work. Some male officers regarded women as simply a "broad with a badge." Such statements dissuaded women from joining the force.[79]

Like other locales, San Antonio had programs that raised the ire of communities of color. For example, the San Antonio Police Department inaugurated a task force to combat crime in 1970. The task force was an insular body of undercover officers who "walk the city streets every day, they are bearded, long-haired and sloppily dressed. They drive beat-up old cars and carry guns." In other words, they fit certain stereotypes. Previously, the task force had been an unsanctioned "Shotgun Squad" consisting of officers who investigated cases beyond their normal duties. Now, this unofficial work became their actual job. The problem with such groups was that they gave officers power to abuse, since they operated outside of normal police parameters.[80]

Unsurprisingly, local people accused San Antonio police of corruption in part because of groups like the task force. Complaints of brutality and bribery tarnished the department's reputation. Many grievances came from officers themselves. One complained about other officers and jailers beating prisoners at the Bexar County Jail, a serious problem considering what happened at the Southton Boys Facility and the brutal beating, rape, and murder of Michael Perkins (discussed in the previous chapter). "It happens at the jail every night," this officer noted, "because police brutality is, let's say, tolerated, [and] it has severely damaged the morale of the good officers, and there are lots of them."[81] The city did nothing.

Other Texas cities did more. Dallas began a series of reforms beginning in the 1960s. This was most evident in the Dallas Police Department's *Training Manual on Community Tensions*, part of the city's broader attempt to begin desegregation.[82] The manual noted honestly that a police officer's job can be difficult because "he is a product of the same social experience to which all of us are exposed. It is likely he has absorbed some of the prejudices and hatreds toward minority groups that are so tragically widespread in our society." The officer the manual described was clearly White and male. "As an officer of the law," it warned, "his private views regarding the Negro, the Jew, the Catholic, the Oriental or the Mexican must not compromise the performance of his public duty."[83]

The manual included chapters on "The Nature of Racial Prejudices," "The Effect of Prejudice on Minorities," and "Areas of Conflict." The analysis in these chapters derived from contemporary social psychological studies. In chapter 9, "Police Preventive Measures," the manual concretized this analysis into action. It emphasized understanding: "The police must maintain a professional attitude and have professional knowledge of conditions existing in minority groups." Other points focused on maintaining a "human approach"; demanding that officers "strenuously avoid the use of insulting terms and names"; encouraging "contact with minority groups and leaders"; and noting that "on a friendly basis police can make suggestions to minority groups, and can receive suggestions from them for the improvement of law enforcement work among minority groups." In a chapter on "Quelling a Riot," the manual encouraged the establishment of a special "race relations detail" to keep lines of communication open.[84]

Not all of the manual was well conceived. The chapter "History of Racial Tension" repeated many of the stereotypes about Reconstruction, calling it "regrettable" and Black freed people "shiftless." In "Areas of Conflict" the manual conveniently left out law enforcement as one of the causes of "conflict." It also misstated some aspects of crowd control, including an insistence on having an overwhelming police "show of force" and removing key leaders to "bring the mob under control." All of these statements would tend to exacerbate problems with large crowds. They, moreover, contradicted statements made elsewhere in the manual.[85]

Dallas attempted other reform measures. The police department received a grant of $268,000 to develop a human resources program in 1971. It used the grant for the "recruitment of minority personnel."[86] The Dallas Police Department focused on recruiting officers of color throughout the late 1960s and early 1970s. The numbers of individuals applying to the police academy were low because of the city's onerous civil service exam. In 1969, out of 111 Black and Mexican American test takers, only 9—5 African Americans and 4 Mexican Americans—passed the exam. While a number of individuals pointed to testing bias and the lack of mentoring programs designed to prepare students of color for civil service, Chief Frank Dyson stated bluntly that the problem was the quality of the applicants, which certainly didn't help encourage people of color to apply.[87]

Dallas also focused on reforms via its *Goals for Dallas* project, the city's strategic plan for the future. Originally developed in 1965 by Mayor J. Erik Jonsson, in 1977 the city revised *Goals for Dallas* with *New Goals for Dallas*, and its corollary (and more verbosely titled) *New Goals for Dallas, Compared with Goals for Black Dallas and Mexican American Objectives*. This blueprint concentrated on many aspects of civic life but paid special attention to "public safety." The city was clearly concerned about policing, especially after the murder of Santos Rodriguez. City leaders hoped to "increase understanding between citizens and law enforcement" by having Mexican Americans work with police to improve relations. They also wanted to improve psychological testing and cultural proficiency training for officers and cadets.[88]

The section on the criminal and civil justice systems in *Goals for Black Dallas and Mexican American Objectives* got more specific. It demanded that all law enforcement be "duty-bound" to report civil rights violations committed by other officers and that the city augment participation of Mexican Americans on juries and grand juries, hire more Mexican American personnel, "abolish selective law enforcement toward the Mexican American community," and implement a civilian review board.[89] Such goals were lofty, but they were just goals. *Goals for Black Dallas and Mexican American Objectives* lacked specific methods by which the city might achieve them. That the publication stated them at all was important, though.

The Houston Police Department also attempted some reforms. The HPD hoped to hire more officers of color in the 1970s. It initiated a "minority recruitment program" to bring more Black and Brown officers onto the force. The department got some assistance when the HPD received a Law Enforcement Assistance Administration grant of nearly $750,000 for the recruitment program. But it stumbled when news leaked that the department planned to spend nearly a third of those dollars, $222,623, on "riot control equipment," indicating that the HPD remained focused on a draconian type of policing. The problem with this would become apparent two years later, after the killing of Joe Campos Torres and the Moody Park uprising. The HPD also initiated a series of internal reforms in 1974 after a number of scandals. The most notorious was a scandal that resulted in the indictment of twelve officers in the narcotics division, nearly 30 percent of the officers in that division. The scandal necessitated the reorganization of the entire division.[90]

Like Albuquerque, the HPD had a Chicano police group, the Chicano Squad. Mexican American officers created the squad in the summer of 1979 to help solve murder cases. But the squad's role also morphed with recruitment as the department focused on increasing trust and reducing crime in Mexican-dominant parts of the city. Its originator and director, Sergeant Jim Montero, was particularly concerned with the number of unsolved homicides of Latinos. He also understood that language could be a roadblock in policing—the same issue that had led to the development of Houston's Latin American Squad in the 1940s. As Montero noted, if a witness or suspect "spoke Spanish, we're going to investigate." Chicano Squad member Urban Hernandez confirmed this focus, saying, "Homicide kept calling us in to translate until it got to the point that we knew the cases as well, or better, than the homicide detectives." This relationship proved unusual: homicide detectives don't usually share their caseloads with beat police officers, but as squad member Jaime Escalante noted, it worked. Building trust became the Chicano Squad's most important goal. "We let them [Latinos] know that things are different here, that you don't do it your way and that there is a law and you have to respect it."[91] By 1982 the squad regularly cleared 40 percent of murder investigations—a significant number. Moreover, the community relations aspect of the squad produced good results. "People started calling in," Montero noted. "They saw we were out there to help them, and then the word got out."[92]

The HPD also changed the procedure for booking suspects after the killing of Joe Campos Torres. Previously, officers had to seek medical aid for an injured suspect before they processed the individual at the city jail. Torres's death exposed the problem with this procedure. The department revised the policy to mandate processing before an arrestee went to the hospital. Torres's killing also prompted the HPD to add an extra layer to its screening of new officers. After completing the academy work, the department would pair trainees with experienced officers who would grade the trainees on how they treated people of color; if they failed, they would be removed from the force. In 1980, the HPD initiated cultural sensitivity training for officers that included Spanish-language instruction and information that challenged stereotypes about Mexican-origin people.[93]

Mexican American civic groups were at the forefront of these reforms. As in other examples, they pushed city leaders to implement reforms and worked closely with the city to see those reforms completed. The League of United Latin American Citizens (LULAC) vowed to work with Houston police to improve relations between police and the community. Chief Harry Caldwell appointed both Texas LULAC director Ruben Bonilla and Houston Council no. 60 president Mamie Garcia to the group advising police in 1977 after the murder of Joe Campos Torres. Caldwell noted genuinely that "it is particularly valuable for the chief to have assistance from a group like LULAC." Many reforms, such as the development of the HPD's Internal Affairs Division, came from these efforts.[94]

In 1981, the HPD participated in a police fear reduction campaign sponsored by the National Institute of Justice and administered by the Police Foundation. A report produced by the National Institute of Justice noted that fear placed barriers between police and civilians and in many cases created a "fortress mentality" for both.[95] To combat this fear the department agreed to create a task force with the job of developing concepts to alleviate fear. Alas, the task force came up with some pretty lame ideas, such as a newsletter called *Community Policing Exchange* that would emphasize feel-good stories about crime prevention efforts or meritorious officers.[96]

The HPD attempted a more ambitious idea with the Community Organizing Response Team. A group of CORT officers went door to door in an undisclosed neighborhood and asked about 300 residents what they thought police should work on. The police also organized meetings with community members to implement some of these ideas. One of the most important results of these meetings was the creation of safe houses where children could go to seek assistance if they were hungry or involved in a neighborhood dispute. CORT was a good idea, but not one that the HPD could reproduce across the city because it was very expensive.[97] A related victim recontacting service, wherein police would contact crime victims to check on their well-being and see if they had additional information, also produced good results.[98]

The reform efforts in Houston were important. The development of the HPD's Internal Affairs Division proved a step in the right direction, but HPD leaders balked at more community-oriented reforms such as civilian review. The department also had less success at hiring officers of color. Other ideas such as the CORT programs had some forward-looking features but were hard to extend citywide. The HPD would only begin more serious reform efforts in the mid-1980s.

Of all the states that debated police reform, California proved the most resistant to change. Despite significant protests and cases of police violence, from the Watts Rebellion to the violence at the Chicano Antiwar Moratorium protest, the local government largely opposed reform. Los Angeles, for instance, looked into civilian review. As a *Los Angeles Times* report noted, "Isolated from civilian control or even scrutiny, the process [of police discipline in LA] is a mix of administrative machinery and personal attitudes that has brought it many critics among the public and the police."[99] The Coalition against Police Abuse argued that "the community has to control the police department, we're still not doing that." This was especially important for police shootings.[100] The LAPD resisted and ultimately stymied attempts at implementing civilian review.[101]

Los Angeles also committed a serious misstep when it authorized the destruction of twenty-five years of civilian complaints against officers. Chief Assistant Attorney Larry Hoffman, who headed LA's Civil Law Branch, believed these documents to be like an illegal secret personnel file. Chief Assistant Attorney David Perez of the Criminal Law Branch concurred and directed a law clerk to prepare a memo justifying the legality of destroying the files. That clerk wrote the memo; a subsequent investigative report noted, "Hindsight indicates that this was bad legal advice."[102] On May 5 and 7, 1976, officers shredded between 120 and 130 boxes of files of "unsustained" and "other-than-sustained" citizen complaints of excessive force by police. A conservative estimate put the number of pages between 120,000 and 130,000. City staff had to use a flatbed truck to transport these documents to their destruction.[103] The loss of information is impossible to tabulate.

The approved "Authority to Destroy Obsolete Records" form demonstrates why Los Angeles residents (not to mention historians) might have a problem with the destruction of these documents. The shredded documents included reports, notes, and memos from the Watts Rebellion, "miscellaneous files, memos, and old confidential files" from 1943 to 1966, and miscellaneous files, memorandums, and correspondence from 1971 to 1974.[104] The fact that the department specifically destroyed records pertaining to the Watts Rebellion was deeply troubling. The files from the early 1940s may well have had something to say about the Zoot Suit Riots. So, too, the documents from the early 1970s, which may have contained valuable information about the Moratorium protest and police-instigated riot in 1972. To put it bluntly, the LAPD destroyed records from some of the most intense years of police relations with communities of color, giving the public the sense that they were trying to erase ugly periods in the department's history. A better reform idea would have been to publicly release all of these documents, not destroy them.

The district attorney's office and the state attorney general's office launched an investigation and explored the possibility of criminal prosecution of those involved. The charges included destruction of evidence, a misdemeanor, and unauthorized destruction of public records, conspiracy to destroy public records without authorization, conspiracy to obstruct justice, and perjury, all felonies.[105] Their "investigation revealed ample evidence of bad judgement and some eyebrow-lifting inconsistencies in the courtroom testimony of some of those involved, [but] there is insufficient evidence to support criminal charges."[106] In essence, they forgave the LAPD.

Los Angeles also represents a good example of how police could debate reform while simultaneously engaging in problematic behavior. Like the Houston police, the LAPD was rather two-faced in its approaches to communities of color. While the department might discuss something such as civilian review, it also not only engaged in records destruction but, as historian Max Felker-Kantor has shown, instituted increasingly aggressive forms of policing. These included the Total Resources against Street Hoodlums (TRASH) program, founded in 1973, and its successor, the Community Resources against Street Hoodlums (CRASH) program, both designed to address gang activity using an incredibly violent, militarized type of policing.[107]

Southern California was pioneering in that San Diego developed one of the first civilian review boards in the Southwest. It grew out of a harrowing encounter between a motorist, Sagon Penn, and police. Penn, a twenty-three-year-old African American man, was driving with friends when San Diego PD officer Donovan Jacobs pulled him over in 1985. Jacobs said he believed Penn to be a gang member, so he radioed for backup and Officer Tom Riggs joined him. Penn was not a gang member. He complied with the officers' requests for him to exit the vehicle. When asked to produce his identification, Penn handed them his wallet. Jacobs returned the wallet and asked for his license, at which point Penn began to walk back to his vehicle. Jacobs and Riggs started beating him. He fought back and managed to acquire Jacob's revolver, opened fire, and killed Jacobs and wounded Riggs. Penn stood trial for murder and attempted murder. He argued that the officers had racially profiled him and that he acted in self-defense. Several police officers testified for the defense that Jacobs was racist. A jury acquitted Penn of all charges.[108]

Black people and Latinos engaged in a series of protests on Penn's behalf. Many had experienced similar treatment. They demanded reforms, especially the founding of a police-civilian review board. While the police department balked at such an idea, many on the San Diego City Council favored a review board. The city formed an initial police advisory panel in 1987. Not only did it provide some oversight, but it also proposed a host of new community relations and conflict resolution training sessions for San Diego police officers. The initial board gave way to a new board in 1989. The city had a referendum for a permanent board that same year, which passed. The Citizens Review Board on Police Practices was launched in late April

1989. This board reviews all complaints of police criminal activity, charges of discrimination, and excessive use of force, although it has no power to do anything about those complaints. This shows, like other locales, that review boards could get formed but also have no real control over the outcome of a case of abuse.[109]

Several important civil rights meetings relating to police reform also occurred across the Southwest. In Texas, Mexican Americans and police officials planned several gatherings to address police-community relations. One occurred in 1976 shortly after Castroville police chief Frank Hayes murdered Ricardo Morales. That killing led the Texas House of Representatives Subcommittee on Criminal Jurisprudence to hear testimony from Mexican American leaders about changing the penalty for police officers who killed suspects from life in prison to death.[110] In 1979 the "Contemporary Issues in Texas Police-Community Relations" symposium took place in San Antonio, cochaired by LULAC state director Ruben Bonilla and Dallas chief of police Frank Dyson. Police had killed at least seventeen Mexican-origin people in the preceding year, which unsurprisingly exacerbated a tense situation. "We have an opportunity to demonstrate to all Texans and all Americans that we have the capacity, the intellect, and the will to solve our problems," Bonilla noted. Although not everyone shared his optimism, such comments portended good relationship building.[111]

Similarly, meetings in San Diego led to the creation of the Mexican-American Police Command Officers Association. The group was unique in that Mexican American police officers, who hoped to recruit more Mexican Americans to do police work, organized it. Several dozen officers representing thirteen police agencies in Arizona and California met to create the group in San Diego in 1973. Lieutenant Ruben Ortega of the Phoenix Police Department, who would rise to become chief of police in Phoenix, commented that police departments had to understand that Mexican Americans have "a special value to law enforcement agencies." Ortega also noted some of the reasons Mexican Americans did not enter the law enforcement profession, including a belief that others in the community might disapprove and that they didn't understand the requirements for becoming an officer. While Ortega failed to address how police brutality may have caused Mexican Americans to shy away from policing, his overall analysis was correct. Another Mexican-American Police Command Officers Association member, Arizona Department of Public Safety captain B. D. Velasco, admittedly openly that "some of the gripes of the Black, the chicano and the anglo about law enforcement are legitimate."[112]

According to a report on Texas, the goals of the Mexican-American Police Command Officers Association to augment the hiring of Mexican American officers made sense. *Texas: The State of Civil Rights*, which longitudinally analyzed who engaged in the "Administration of Justice" from 1968 to 1978, offered a grim picture: "The administration of justice in Texas was overwhelmingly dominated by Anglo males in 1968, and that overall pattern has changed very little."[113] For example, in 1968, 1.97 percent of sheriffs were Mexican American men. That number rose to 3.5 percent in 1977. There were no female sheriffs in 1968 or 1977.[114] The report's conclusion was bleak: "Police protection in the cities and counties of Texas is dominated by Anglo men. Women are relegated primarily to traditional positions. Minority men are underutilized and disproportionately located in the lower paid positions. Minority women, however, are the most underrepresented, and virtually all are in the lowest salary classification."[115] In sum, where the hiring of Mexican American and other officers of color were concerned, Texas was woefully behind, as was much of the rest of the Southwest.

The 1970s witnessed so much discussion about reforming police that it remains difficult to tabulate it all. The debates about police-civilian review were particularly important, and although few cities actually implemented such review boards, the fact that some departments proved willing to discuss them mattered. Some of the other major reform efforts, from human relations commissions to the PALs to the recruitment of Mexican American police officers, all met with some success depending on the locale. Law enforcement agencies, given the impetus of civil rights protests and the need for better relations with Mexican-origin people, proved willing to address, discuss, and often implement important and meaningful reforms.

While the overall goal of most of these reform efforts was improved policing, it's important to remember that this goal came out of the problems and the inequities within the police profession. Corpus Christi attorney and LULAC leader Ruben Bonilla noted that "justice depends on the pigmentation of skin. And if the prisoner doesn't speak English, the law enforcement officials treat them with disdain or disrespect." And therein lay another problem: reforms often came after instances of abuse and violence. Many Mexican Americans surely wondered why people had to be brutalized or killed to get reform. Attorney and activist Ruben Sandoval had pushed for stricter sentencing laws for police who abused people. "Many people think we're pressing the charges because we're against the police," Bonilla explained, "but what we're actually trying to do is improve the administration of justice."[116]

One of the interesting things about many of these reforms was that they worked. Police reform saw the easing of tensions in many parts of the Southwest, and many programs, such as PAL, were welcomed and enjoyed by local people. The impulse among Mexican American folks and their leaders to help reform law enforcement once again demonstrates that they were not antipolice. They simply wanted better policing. And to their credit, law enforcement officers often responded positively to these reforms because they, too, wanted better policing.

Although many of these reform efforts continued into the 1980s and 1990s, many were also undone in that same period. Budget cuts in the 1980s forced cities to scrap civilian review boards and PAL programs, even though neither cuts saved cities much money. The growth in prison populations and a hard-line, tough-on-crime politics meant that prison and jail reforms would be slow in coming, if they ever came at all. And then there was the Clinton Crime Bill of 1994, which set back reform efforts for the next generation and beyond. The 1980s and 1990s were significant years as far as Mexican Americans and police were concerned.

SEVEN

THE HIDDEN EIGHTIES

Protest and Retrenchment
in a Militant Decade

Most Americans probably don't remember the 1980s as a heyday of civil rights activism. The Reagan years, the birth of MTV, Pac-Man, the rise of Blockbuster Video, the first cell phone, Michael Jackson's *Thriller*, these were but a handful of the things people may remember—civil rights, not so much. Yet a great deal of activism did occur in this period. The Chicano movement did not end in the 1970s. Rather, the movement continued into the 1980s. In fact, some of the largest and most momentous protests occurred in the eighties, almost all having something to do with challenging law enforcement abuse.

Despite the reforms of the 1970s, Mexican Americans continued to experience harassment, brutality, and murder at the hands of police in the eighties, which of course necessitated protest. One of the more notorious cases, the killing of Hector Santoscoy in San Antonio in 1980, spawned a number of protests and the involvement of the Mexican government. The AIDS crisis saw the police used in new and unfortunate ways. Numerous city governments tasked police agencies with combatting the virus, but law enforcement did so largely by cracking down on sex work. The LGBTQIA+ community, already suffering heavily because of AIDS, suffered more at the hands of police. In other noteworthy cases activists won some important victories, for example in halting an urban renewal program in the Bryant-Vanalden area of Northridge, California, that used police to racially profile area residents, in addition to such things as besting the Klan during a number of major protests, as mentioned in chapter 4. Local activists and more far-reaching regional and even national actions challenged these policing issues.

There were also a number of national level events that augmented tensions between local people and law enforcement. One notable example was immigration reform. Immigration issues had touched off problems with Mexican-origin people and the police previously; recall Operation Wetback in 1954. Immigration reform gained additional steam beginning in the 1970s and continuing into the 1980s. In 1984 the Immigration and Naturalization Service (INS) expanded border security through the formation of the Border Crime Prevention Unit. Then in 1986 Congress passed the Immigration Reform and Control Act, which augmented these border control efforts through increasingly military means. These actions, often touted as reforms, resulted in a number of deaths of Mexican immigrants, which again touched off major protests.[1]

The 1980s also saw the implementation of new crime prevention strategies. The War on Drugs and the War on Crime both revised penalties for drug crimes, and other crimes as well, that disproportionately affected Black and Brown communities. The War on Drugs originated during the presidency of Richard Nixon. In 1970 he signed the Comprehensive Drug Abuse Prevention and Control Act, which established drug "schedules" or classifications based on medicinal use and the potential for dependency. In 1971 he famously declared drugs "public enemy number one." Nixon staffers later publicly acknowledged that his focus on drugs had little to do with narcotics but was instead a political strategy designed to undercut civil rights activists and punish Black people. President Ronald Reagan greatly expanded the War on Drugs via the Comprehensive Crime Control Act of 1984, the Anti-Drug Abuse Act of 1986, and the "Just Say No" campaign. The Crime Control Act made federal sentencing guidelines harsher and augmented penalties for marijuana possession.[2]

The War on Crime has been just as damaging. The original War on Crime came from President Lyndon Johnson via the Omnibus Crime Control and Safe Streets Act of 1968. A big part of the act, the Law Enforcement Assistance

Act of 1968, identified Black men as the cause of American crime problems and increased funding to law enforcement especially for the recruiting of new officers. The War on Crime thus has its roots in institutional racism. The problem with this program is that it created a hypervigilant law-and-order approach to dealing with criminal activity that exacerbated problems rather than solved them. Communities of color, especially African Americans and Mexican Americans, suffered markedly because of these programs. The War on Crime has never worked, and authorities knew that back in the seventies. Despite rising crime statistics in the period between the late 1960s and late 1980s, neither the War on Crime nor the War on Drugs curbed criminal activity.[3]

Although these major legislative efforts did lead to violence and injustice in the Southwest, at the same time Southwestern police continued to adopt new reform innovations that attempted to reduce tensions between law enforcement and Mexican Americans. Police agencies in a number of Southwestern communities proceeded to respond both reactively and proactively to community demands. Some communities looked to Mexican American police leaders for change. Probably the best example of this was the rise of Phoenix police officer Ruben Ortega to the rank of chief of police of the Phoenix Police Department. Oddly enough, locales that had relatively good police-community relations, such as San Antonio, began to have problems in the 1980s, whereas states that initially had relatively subdued Chicano movements, such as Arizona, saw increased activism at this time.

In Arizona, police abuse and killing led to protests and then reform efforts. The case of Raymond Joya serves as a good example. Joya had attended a Christmas party with friends in 1979 in Phoenix. Several partygoers went to a nearby Circle K to buy beer when a fight broke out. Police officers from the Avondale, Goodyear, Tolleson, and Phoenix Police Departments, as well as deputies from the Maricopa County Sheriff's Office, responded. The police weighed into the fracas, and Officer David Dains shot Joya in the back twice with a shotgun. The Avondale PD contended that Joya had wrested a revolver from one officer and that Dains had shot Joya to prevent him from using that revolver. Numerous eyewitnesses denied the police account; police recovered no gun from Joya. The shotgun wounds left him paralyzed from the waist down.[4]

In early 1980, working with the United Front against Brutality, which had carried out protests in Surprise and El Mirage previously, local people in Avondale planned for a series of major demonstrations. Police charged Joya with aggravated assault; UFAB demanded that the city drop the charges. The organization also pushed Avondale to found a police-civilian review board. Further, UFAB wanted the city to prosecute Officer Dains. More than 200 people joined in the protest march that UFAB organized. In 1981, Joya filed suit against the Avondale Police Department, but his suit went nowhere. He never got his justice.[5]

The case of Robert Ramirez began with an unlawful search and arrest. Phoenix police entered Ramirez's home on March 16, 1980, searching for his uncle, who had allegedly been involved in a dispute with a taxi driver. They found the uncle and arrested him but then began a search of the home for a gun. Ramirez argued that the police had no right to search his home, at which point Officer Roger Ketelaar hit him in the face several times with the butt of his shotgun, breaking Ramirez's nose. Ketelaar placed him under arrest for resisting arrest, only to release him the following day. Police found no gun. Ramirez brought suit against Ketelaar for the illegal search and unlawful arrest. A jury sided with Officer Ketelaar, who had claimed self-defense.[6]

The Joya and Ramirez cases left a bad taste in the mouths of many Arizonans, especially those in the Mexican American community. Like so many before them, their rights had been violated by the police, whose actions were excused after the fact. Moreover, as had often been the case, police arrested and attempted to charge the individuals they had assaulted. For activists and their allies, police often used this tactic as a form of intimidation. These cases served as painful reminders for the Mexican American community that the system did not protect and serve them.

And yet, because of such encounters, some localities in Arizona began outreach programs designed to defuse tension. Mesa had its share of police problems. Everyday instances of harassment had created an untenable level of distrust between Mexican Americans and police. For example, police in riot gear and with police dogs confronted a gathering of lowriders at a park in November 1980. They sought only to show off their vehicles and had committed no crimes; the police had disturbed the festive mood and the lowriders felt harassed and intimidated. As in other cities, media bias in local reporting also proved a problem in Mesa. The media painted a dire picture of Mexican American gangs, but gang activity was in fact minimal. According to police, only three or four active gangs existed in a city of 150,000.[7]

Mesa police responded to accusations of harassment and what activist Gus Chavez, who had attended the lowrider gathering, called "selective law enforcement" by reaching out to the community. Sergeant Joe Noce, a Mexican American officer, counseled police about Mexican American concerns. So the police force tasked him and other officers, such as Lynn Bray, to work with local people. Officer Bray, a White officer, had grown up in Mesa's Escobedo barrio and still had friends and family there. He met with a number of youths, took them on tours of the police station to demystify policing, and offered them a sympathetic ear. He also began a sports program similar to the Police Athletic League. Bray soon had forty young people on his teams.[8]

In addition to these on the ground efforts, Mayor Donald Strauch met openly with community members. He had a number of "rap sessions" with Mexican American adults and youths. These meetings also included local activists such as Linda Jaurigui, the director of the Community Action Project; Gus Chavez, mentioned above; and police leadership. As the mayor noted in regards to community members and policing issues, "I always want them to feel I am available to talk about these problems when they come up. Talking about it is the beginning of solving it." The mayor also acknowledged a change in his own perspective, especially as it related to the rhetoric of gang activity. He noted that he had often used the word "gang" indiscriminately, but after someone explained to him the problem with the label, he realized it was wrong to "look at the people as gang members. These are the people we see sitting across from us at the breakfast table in the morning." "If people are better acquainted," he commented, "they see they have common goals and they get along better." Though perhaps a small step, having the top elected official in a city "get it" is important to members of marginalized communities.[9]

Police violence in the Pascua Village neighborhood of Tucson also produced some interesting results. Yaqui people had originally founded Pascua Village in the early twentieth century. Like Guadalupe (discussed in chapter 6), the village had a mainly Yaqui and Mexican American population and relied on the Tucson Police Department for law enforcement. After some violent encounters locals had with some Tucson police officers, the department initiated a community liaison patrol. Eight officers served as village liaisons. Officer Carlos Villanueva reported a typical encounter he had one evening when he came across a group of Yaqui and Mexican American men standing outside a home. Villanueva engaged one of these men, a forty-year-old Yaqui man named Manuel, asking if he needed anything. Everyone seemed nervous, but after a little chatting, Villanueva and Manuel learned that they had both served in Vietnam. This common connection broke any tension, and when Villanueva left, Manuel told him, "See you brother." This was the kind of interaction that Pascua Village residents and the Tucson Police Department hoped to have. As Villanueva understood, part of his job involved earning respect and trust: "[I'm] trying to show them that I'm coming as a friend. I'm not here to be an enemy."[10]

The City of Tempe also attempted to do community outreach in order to ease tensions. The city found a good example in Officer John Blaisdell. Blaisdell, like Mesa officer Lynn Bray, had grown up in the area and knew the community. He commented on the uniqueness of his police work and noted that he served "to help citizens of this community in whatever way they need help and to establish some rapport between the department and the people who live here." He was one of five officers who worked in the barrio and had received cultural sensitivity training.[11] Blaisdell and Bray's examples are good ones: White officers who knew Mexican American people, who did not fall prey to common stereotypes about them, and who wanted their police forces to do better. Their examples led to both improved relations and policing.

Other police officers made changes in different ways, some by attaining high positions in law enforcement. For example, Ruben Ortega served as chief of police of Phoenix after a long career on the force. When Ortega joined the Phoenix Police Department in the 1960s only six or seven Mexican American police officers worked on a force of 400. The urban uprisings of the 1960s initially drew Ortega to policing. "We [police/the city] got problems with minorities, maybe it takes a minority as an advantage," he noted. Thus he became a kind of liaison officer because of his ethnicity, a fairly common occurrence for officers of color. He found the experience draining, mainly because the Phoenix Police Department would send him and fellow officer Doge Nelson, one of the few African Americans on the force, to diffuse racial tensions. But it was a necessary part of his police work, and it gave him experience that he would rely on as he climbed the ranks. He also helped found the Mexican-American Police Command Officers Association, which also did outreach work.[12]

After his promotion to chief, Ortega worked to ensure fair representation of all groups on the force, for instance making sure that members of various ethnic communities served on the promotion board to guarantee that the "board is sensitive to the needs and concerns of minorities." He also attempted to hire officers of color equal to their percentage of the population. Further, he grasped "the enormous responsibility, the *power* that an officer has that no other city employee has . . . [including] the biggest power of all—if he feels threatened and justified in his mind—he can take your life! To me, that is awesome, awesome power and authority. When one has that kind of power and authority, you have to have strict controls." A key to good policing was understanding the breadth of this power and, perhaps more importantly, the need for those "strict controls."[13]

Like other police professionals, Chief Ortega had a "tough on crime" outlook. While he based his perspectives on crime through the lens of his own experience, he also had opinions that came from broader societal views. For instance, he believed that capital punishment served as a deterrent to crimes such as murder. He also believed that lengthier sentences and the building of new prisons deterred crime. He wanted more police and more incarceration. The data do not support these viewpoints. As such, Ortega had an analytically inaccurate view of law and order.[14]

Ortega handled many parts of his job professionally and acted quickly when his officers ran afoul of the law. In February 1982 a group of eight Phoenix PD officers and a civilian had gathered under a bridge to toast the promotion of a fellow officer. When they noticed a homeless person observing their actions, they proceeded to harass, beat, and mace this person until the individual fled. That person then called the police on the police. Chief Ortega fired the officers. While he acted in defense of a community member, Ortega terminated the officers before the internal affairs department had completed its investigation. As a result, the city reinstated them after a three-year legal battle. For his part, Ortega responded passionately about this case and others like it: "I've had to deal with several brutality cases recently. I have an officer who put a .45-caliber handgun up against a man's forehead just to scare him. It's incredible. I've tried to get rid of those who do not belong on this department. But I can't fire anybody."[15]

Ortega's critical comments about Phoenix Police Department officers aroused the ire of the Phoenix police union, the Phoenix Law Enforcement Association (PLEA), in 1986. Ortega and PLEA basically got into a public shouting match and neither side came out looking particularly good. PLEA demanded that the city investigate Ortega, but city leaders rejected that demand.[16] Ortega also made a mistake that helped end his tenure in Phoenix in 1987 when he accused players on the Phoenix Suns basketball team of using and distributing drugs. The state indicted several players, but the cases fizzled when the police could produce little evidence to back their claims.[17]

More seriously, Ortega allegedly used his own power to investigate and intimidate his opponents. One example of this was a political controversy known as AzScam. He and Maricopa County district attorney Rick Romley initiated a sting whereby an undercover agent would induce state lawmakers to take bribes to support legalized gambling in Arizona. Seven legislators took the bribes and were subsequently convicted. Ten percent of the Arizona legislature resigned in 1991 to avoid prosecution.[18] Although the sting appeared successful, Ortega faced criticism for what some saw as entrapment that began with little probable cause. City councilperson Linda Nadolski ostensibly thanked the chief for keeping citizens safe but stated, "We also need to know that we're safe from Chief Ortega." Ortega was incensed and he resigned.[19] A short time later, Salt Lake City hired him as their new chief of police, a position he held until 1999.[20]

Chief Ortega unfortunately left Phoenix under questionable circumstances, which blighted his overall record. He should receive credit, however, for his conscientious approach to law enforcement. He had served with distinction as an officer and had paved the way for other officers of color. As one of the only Mexican American police chiefs in the country, Ortega was a role model who demonstrated some of the advancements that Arizona had attempted to make in its police agencies. The community outreach programs in Mesa or Pascua Village and the open-mindedness of both police officers and Mexican Americans demonstrates a positive approach to law enforcement in the state. Ortega certainly got himself into trouble via the Phoenix Suns and AzScam scandals, but he nonetheless performed many of his duties well.

Arizona serves as a useful case study for the 1980s. With groups like UFAB we can see how Chicano protest activism continued into the eighties. Numerous police agencies also engaged in interesting and important outreach work, as the examples of Carlos Villanueva, Lynn Bray, and John Blaisdell demonstrate. Arizona was also a pioneering state in that Phoenix put Ruben Ortega in charge of its police force. Ortega was the first Mexican American to lead a major US police department, an important fact for which Arizona should be commended.

In Texas, police shootings continued to be the major issue Mexican Americans challenged. As in previous decades, the shooting of children provoked considerable community anger. One such case was that of David Medellin, a fifteen-year-old shot by police in Euless, Texas, in 1980. Police responded to a domestic disturbance at Medellin's home and, even though his father had the situation under control, broke down the door and entered the premises. Officers S. T. Cantrell, T. D. Cottle, and H. C. Westmoreland claimed Medellin threw a butcher knife at them. Medellin disputed this assertion, although he admitted he had the knife at the time police shot him. While confronting someone with a knife would certainly be frightening, Westmoreland and Cottle responded by firing half a dozen shots at Medellin, with Cottle firing five of those shots. Medellin was hit five times but survived. Civil rights groups called for protests, but members of the League of United Latin American Citizens, the Brown Berets, and La Fuerza de los Barrios (Force of the Barrios) met with police and quickly hammered out an agreement. The agreement stipulated that police would attend cultural sensitivity training and Spanish-language classes, that Chicano groups would work with the department to ensure that police policies were free of bias, and that police and Mexican Americans would push for legislation governing how police treat young people. These were important, meaningful reform efforts, and the police force and Chicano activists should receive credit for accomplishing them. Yet they still came only after a questionable police shooting.[21]

Many Mexican Americans hoped for some measure of justice for David Medellin, but the Tarrant County grand jury no-billed Officers Cottle and Westmoreland. Assistant District Attorney Charles Roach noted that he did not think the officers acted inappropriately, even though he did say that "the one officer (Cottle) who shot five shots, you might question his training." The Medellin family planned to initiate a lawsuit because the officers had violated the Medellin family's rights. They never filed a suit, though.[22]

The case of David Medellin was a major incident in Texas, but the case of Hector Santoscoy became an international incident. The twenty-five-year-old Santoscoy had come to San Antonio from Piedras Negras, Mexico, in search of work in 1980. Police alleged that he robbed a Popeyes fried chicken restaurant on December 25, 1980. Officers said they saw two suspects fleeing the Popeyes but lost sight of these individuals. Nearby residents soon alerted police to the presence of someone underneath a home. Police believed this person to be one of the burglars. They encouraged this individual, later identified as Santoscoy, to come out. When they received no response, Officer James Cammack Jr. crawled under the house. According to Cammack, Santoscoy threatened to hit him with a brick, and he shouted, "Drop that brick or I'll blow you away." According to witness Pablo Hernandez, Cammack called Santoscoy a racial epithet and then said, "I'm going to blow you away." There was then a single gunshot, followed by three or four shots. Cammack emerged from underneath the home. Police later found Santoscoy, lying on his side, dead.[23]

There was a lot to this case. If the name James Cammack Jr. sounds familiar, it should. He had previously helped beat to death Bobby Jo Phillips in 1968 (discussed in chapter 3). Cammack's involvement in the Santoscoy case immediately aroused the attention of activists who knew his name and remembered his involvement in the killing of Phillips. Police caused some problems when they initially misidentified Santoscoy as Richard Aleman.[24] This proved problematic as police later claimed that Santoscoy used the name "Aleman" as an alias, which made him appear more criminal-like. Investigators determined that he was unhoused and had been sleeping underneath neighborhood homes for shelter. The press also reported that police had recovered $2.10 from Santoscoy, so he had not burglarized the Popeyes. More-over, pictures of the crawlspace under the house indicated that the sequence of events that Cammack described were hardly plausible. Cammack stated that Santoscoy had raised his arm to throw a brick at him. But with only about eighteen inches of space between the ground and the bottom of the home, Santoscoy barely had room to move around, let alone raise an arm to throw a brick. Last, Pablo Hernandez aired concerns after hearing Cammack's claim that Santoscoy had threatened him with a brick. He stated that the officers who interviewed him after the shooting repeatedly asked about bricks. Although he denied knowing anything about bricks, Hernandez signed a statement that included information about bricks. He read English poorly and signed the form without realizing that police had added references to bricks. There was so much misinformation and contradictory stories that the FBI began investigating the Santoscoy case a few days later.[25]

Chicano activists began protesting the killing of Hector Santoscoy in February 1981. Those protests would continue, on and off, for the next year. Bernardo Eureste, one of the only Mexican Americans on the San Antonio City Council, and Ruben Sandoval, the attorney involved in many of the most prominent police brutality cases over the prior decade, organized these protests. They also brought the Mexican government into the affair, which made the Santoscoy killing an international incident. Mexican consul general Raul Gonzalez Galarza explained things from the Mexican government's viewpoint: "Irrespective of whether or not Mr. Santoscoy was involved in a burglary, you will agree with me that criminal matters should be resolved in a court of law, and not out on the streets or under a floor."[26] In a letter to San Antonio mayor Lila Cockrell, Gonzalez Galarza lamented "the attitudes and statements expressed by the authorities as to how the shooting took place." "I fail to understand," he added, "how a man can be shot twice on the right side and three times on the left side[,] when the police allege he was advancing toward the officer." Given evidence that had begun to emerge, his confusion was understandable. He asked for a new investigation: "In behalf of my government, I request you and your body of city representatives to direct that this matter be thoroughly investigated, in an impartial manner, that truth may prevail and that justice be done to all parties concerned in this incident."[27]

The Bexar County grand jury no-billed Officer Cammack and cleared him of wrongdoing.[28] Eureste, Sandoval, and many others were understandably frustrated. Consul Gonzalez Galarza stated yet again that from the Mexican government's perspective, "it would be better if the district attorney would have recommended the indictment and let the matter be settled in a public courtroom."[29] The Bexar County grand jury did look into the case a second time but decided not to reopen the case, effectively no-billing Cammack again.[30] After the second grand jury hearings, the state began investigating the case.[31]

James Cammack always maintained his innocence. He never deviated from his story that Santoscoy had attempted to throw a brick at him. When attorneys for Santoscoy called Cammack a racist, he rejected the accusation and explained that "my wife is Mexican American, and my two children are half-Mexican." However, Cammack never explained why he confronted a trapped suspect—he could have easily awaited backup—and why a brick—if there had been a brick—seemed enough of a threat to warrant shooting a man five times.[32]

Protests continued. A rally on January 31, 1981, attended by more than 300 protestors took place.[33] A large march on the county courthouse brought out 300 San Antonians from across the city. One protest sign captured the solidarity of the moment: "This is not a black, brown or white issue. This is a human rights issue." For activists, James Cammack's role in the deaths of both Bobby Jo Phillips and Hector Santoscoy made him the poster child for a racist killer cop.[34] There were more protests. On March 31, 200 people attended a march led by the Brown Berets. There was a palpable anger at this march, with signs reading "CammacKKK, Mexican Hater" and "KKKop, U Can't Hide." The crowd also carried a coffin.[35] Like others killed by police, Santoscoy was honored with a corrido. An artistic installation at Milam Park re-created the scene where he died.[36] And the Mexican American Democrats, an activist political group in San Antonio, passed a resolution demanding a full investigation and Justice Department intervention into the case.[37] Additionally, Santoscoy's mother, Alicia Santoscoy, traveled from Mexico to San Antonio to participate in the protest, saying, "I come to ask justice for the death of my son."[38] She and others pinned their hopes for justice on the results of a new autopsy.

Another autopsy did take place at the request of Hector Santoscoy's family. Former Bexar County medical examiner Dr. Ruben Santos traveled to Piedras Negras, where Santoscoy had been buried, to autopsy his exhumed body. Santos confirmed many of Bexar County medical examiner Dr. Nina Hollander's findings.[39] But he found several discrepancies in her analysis of the trajectory of the bullets and the position of Santoscoy when Cammack shot him. Hollander's analysis had shown that Santoscoy was facing Cammack when he was shot, which would seem to back up Cammack's contention that Santoscoy was advancing on him. Moreover, she supported Cammack's statement that Santoscoy had his arm raised, indicating that he was in the process of throwing something like the much-ballyhooed brick. Santos instead found that the wounds on Santoscoy's body showed that his back was to the officer. In addition, a bullet exit wound on the inside of Santoscoy's arm from a slug that passed through his body clearly showed that his arm could not have been raised. Santos contended that Cammack shot Santoscoy in the back as he lay on his side. "I'm very sure there was a murder," he stated. "There's no doubt about it."[40]

Cammack's attorney Fred Semaan dismissed Santos's findings. "I don't care what he (Santos), Hollander or the doctor in Mexico have to say about the autopsy or the exiting of bullets. What they have to say about angles has nothing to do with whether he (Cammack) was acting in self-defense," he said. But the attorney seemed to miss the point of what forensic evidence such as the angles and positions of bullet entry and exit wounds could tell investigators, which in this case indicated that Cammack had shot Santoscoy in the back.[41]

After the second autopsy, activists hoped that the federal government would investigate the case.[42] Ruben Sandoval, who represented the Santoscoy family, and a host of other leaders and groups planned another protest march to demand justice for Santoscoy.[43] The Brown Berets engaged in another protest at the downtown federal building. They hoped the protest would help convince the Justice Department to prosecute Cammack.[44] These protests finally seemed to generate some results when the Department of Justice decided to convene a special investigative hearing in San Antonio in December 1981 to determine whether the federal government should prosecute Cammack.[45] In the end, citing a lack of evidence, the Department of Justice chose not to prosecute him.[46] This decision once again provoked a great deal of anger and Santoscoy's attorneys vowed to file a civil suit against the police department and Cammack.[47]

After all of the distortions and contradictory statements, it still remains unclear why Officer Cammack killed Hector Santoscoy. Did Santoscoy threaten Cammack with a brick? If so, is a brick a weapon of sufficient force to warrant shooting someone multiple times? If Cammack was not threatened, why else would he shoot? How could the evidence—the amount of space under the home or the wounds on Santoscoy's body—all say one thing while Cammack said another? Although Cammack never deviated from his story, none of these questions were ever answered. The case and the interest it generated slowly fizzled.

San Antonio also attracted a lot of attention in the 1980s because of the so-called AIDS Panic. Texas more broadly saw a great deal of activism from the LGBTQIA+ community because of how local governments dealt with AIDS. For example, San Antonio city officials had begun to grow increasingly alarmed at the spread of the disease, and as in other locales they blamed gay men for AIDS. Even though they thought of AIDS as "the gay plague," city officials also knew it was a medical emergency that could, and already had, spread beyond the LGBTQIA+ community. The San Antonio City Council therefore tasked the police with controlling the contagion. This is another way in which cities problematically use police to control populations. Police officers are not medical professionals. Instead, as providers of law and order, the San Antonio Police Department fixated on the disease as a criminal justice issue and focused on male sex workers.

A good example of this process was the case of Carlos Villarreal. He was allegedly a cross-dressing male sex worker in San Antonio who went by the name Shirley or Shirley Ann (he identified as male but dressed as female when engaging in sex work). This "transvestite killing," as the media dubbed it, became a salacious news story. On the night of Saturday, March 31, 1984, undercover officer Robert Romero had picked up Villarreal as part of a sting operation. When Romero identified himself as a police officer and attempted to arrest Villarreal, Villarreal tried to flee. A scuffle ensued in the car, which spilled out of the vehicle, at which point Villarreal allegedly reached into his purse. Romero claimed he saw something shiny and opened fire. The shiny object was the handcuff Romero had managed to secure on one of Villarreal's wrists. Villarreal stumbled a few feet, collapsed, and quickly died from a gunshot wound to the heart.[48]

For the media, Villarreal's gender presentation and sex work were the real story. The combination of his attire and status as a sex worker made the story sensational. News reports frequently used terms such as "transvestite" or "male hooker" to describe him. They also commented on his clothing and published pictures of his belongings, particularly a high-heeled shoe and his purse, which lay on the ground near where he died.[49] Villarreal became an easy target not only for community ire through the media but for police suppression, since law enforcement believed that people like Villarreal spread the disease.

The killing of Carlos Villarreal spurred a great deal of activism. While the news media fixated on his sex work and gender-bending, activists focused on the fact that Romero had killed him under questionable circumstances. They formed the Carlos Villarreal Defense Committee and engaged in a number of demonstrations to protest his killing. For example, they organized a candlelight vigil and a nighttime march to the location where Romero killed Villarreal.[50] Other members of the LGBTQIA+ community came forward to describe their treatment at the hands of law enforcement. Besides the killing of Carlos Villarreal, a number of gay men accused the police of brutality, as well as of not investigating criminal complaints because the victim was gay.[51]

Houston saw some similar events and the collision of LGBTQIA+ rights and policing. One of the most important gay rights activists in Houston was Fred Páez.[52] He became an activist in the 1970s and got involved in police work after a gay man was murdered in 1976. He wanted to be a police officer but that proved largely impossible at the time for an out gay individual. Páez did serve a short stint as a constable. He also helped lead the Gay Political Caucus and he supported the work of the Montrose Patrol. Montrose in the 1970s became the center of gay life in Houston. By the 1980s White hoodlums from the suburbs frequently went to Montrose to seek out and attack men they encountered there. The Montrose Patrol was born to provide a measure of protection and to alert police when homophobes attacked gay people.[53]

Páez also did his own work investigating crimes in the Montrose area. He became particularly alarmed at the police killing of Gary Wayne Stock, whom HPD officer C. V. Hudson killed under questionable circumstances. Hudson had stopped Stock's vehicle for a traffic violation and claimed that he shot Stock when Stock tried to run him over.[54] The only witness, Sergeant L. L. Fulgram, backed Hudson's account. Páez began collecting data on murders of gay men, called Project Documentation, and learned that Hudson's and Fulgram's accounts of the incident did not match forensic evidence, but nothing ever came of Stock's case.

Páez met the same fate as Stock. On the morning of June 28, 1980, after doing work to prepare for the Houston Pride celebration, Officer Kevin McCoy placed Páez under arrest. During the arrest McCoy's pistol discharged, hitting Páez in the back of the head. McCoy claimed that Páez had attempted to fondle his crotch and that Páez had reached for his gun and a scuffle ensued. It is unclear why McCoy had withdrawn his weapon in the first place, or how in a scuffle Páez could have been shot in the back of the head. The only witness, Sergeant L. L. Fulgram, confirmed McCoy's story.[55]

McCoy claimed his weapon had accidentally discharged. Leaders of the gay community challenged that claim as well as Fulgram's confirmation, considering that Fulgram had also backed up Officer Hudson's account of his killing of Gary Wayne Stock. A firearms expert reported that the gun, a .45-caliber automatic pistol, could not fire accidentally, so McCoy's account seemed implausible.[56] Authorities also found cans of beer that the police officers had allegedly been drinking. They evidently continued drinking after McCoy killed Páez.[57] After pressure from the newly formed Fred Páez Task Force, the FBI began investigating the case.[58] The Gay Political Caucus also held a series of protests, one in late July 1980 that saw 1,000 people in attendance.[59] The HPD did suspend McCoy with pay and the Harris County grand jury indicted him in October 1980 on a charge of negligent homicide.[60] At trial in 1981, McCoy testified in his own defense, claiming that Páez made "a homosexual proposition" and that his gun discharged accidentally. The jury acquitted him after deliberating for four hours.[61]

Fred Páez was a good guy who wanted to work with police and to be a cop himself. As a person of Mexican ancestry, it would be nice to tie his ethnicity more fully into his activism. Unfortunately, his sexuality was evidently so repulsive to his family that they chose not to pursue justice in his case and destroyed his personal property—including the files in his Project Documentation—shortly after his death. This represented a tremendous loss of historical data and demonstrates one of the ways familial shame can blunt activism.[62]

Anti-LGBTQIA+ prejudices and policing were also evident in the Houston mayoral election in 1985, which pitted incumbent Mayor Kathryn Whitmire against former Mayor Louie Welch, who had served from 1964 to 1973. Welch aligned himself with an antigay faction running for city council called the Straight Slate. He made much of the AIDS crisis and blamed Whitmire, a popular politician and Houston's first female mayor, for the disease's spread. He also said that one way to control AIDS was "to shoot the queers." It's unclear who Welch thought might do the shooting, but he likely meant police. His homophobia cost him the election.[63]

The Houston example shows just how far LGBTQIA+ rights and homophobic sentiment had entered local politics. The policing of LGBTQIA+ people has a long history. A dozen states still have sodomy laws, despite the Supreme Court's decision in *Lawrence v. Texas* in 2003. The 1980s witnessed some important evolutions in that history because of the AIDS crisis.[64] San Antonio was not alone in its use of police to combat the virus. Los Angeles cracked down on bathhouses, while San Diego targeted female sex workers to halt the spread of the disease.[65] Of course, using police in this manner, similar to using them in situations of mental health crisis, is as problematic as it is unfair. Police officers are not doctors. The Fred Páez and Carlos Villarreal cases show that the gay rights movement was also a struggle about policing.

California also witnessed a number of highly questionable police shootings in the 1980s. Some of these ended differently than in Texas in that victims or their families in several cases won lawsuits after police killed family members. For example, LA County deputy sheriffs Sandra Jones and David Anderson killed Jildardo Plasencia on New Year's Eve in 1980. The deputies went to Plasencia's home after he allegedly fired a .22-caliber rifle into the air that night to celebrate the new year. According to Jones and Anderson, Plasencia still had the rifle, so they shot him dead and wounded his fifteen-year-old nephew and three-year-old son. Authorities later revealed that Plasencia was seated in his garage with the door (a person-sized door, not the main garage door) only slightly open, so the officers had no direct sight into the structure. They basically shot up the garage, killing Plasencia and wounding the children in the process.[66] The Mexican American community rose up in protest and the family sued. Although authorities did not punish the officers, the family won a $1.3 million judgment against the county.[67] Sandra Huchens (née Jones) went on in 2008 to become sheriff of Orange County.[68]

Such senseless killings prompted increased Chicano activism in California. Groups such as the Brown Berets worked hard to address everyday police violence. They also founded a number of new groups, such as the Coalition against Police Abuse. Activists founded CAPA in 1976 "as a result of the many Shooting[s] and Beatings by the Police and Sheriff." That activism was important. When cases like Plascencia's came along, CAPA was ready to swing into action.

In 1981 CAPA produced a longitudinal report that charted police violence from 1971 to 1981. That report also argued that "while the police demand total independence and autonomy, the people demand community control and police accountability." The worst year for police violence in Los Angeles County had been 1976, with a total of sixty-eight shooting deaths, which did not include in-custody deaths. The numbers dropped after 1976 but rose in 1980 to thirty-five and to thirty-eight in 1981.[69]

Although CAPA provided useful data in its reports, the group also advocated for community members. The group spoke generally about "mobilizing and uniting a wide base of forces into a mass movement against police abuse and racial oppression," and they also offered specific and useful advice. For example, they explained how anyone abused by police could sue. CAPA listed a group of attorneys willing to take pro bono cases. They also asked members not to ignore police abuse if they experienced it or observed it. They encouraged people to take notes and write down important information such as the time and date, the officer's badge number and name, and the victim's name. "Victims of police abuse need witnesses," the CAPA report noted in 1981, "so don't hesitate to do what has to be done and then call C.A.P.A!"[70]

Like groups in other cities, the CAPA wanted the LA city government to establish a civilian review board. They helped form a new group called the Campaign for a Citizens Police Review Board to convince the city to found such a board.[71] CAPA analyzed eighteen other cities' review boards and determined that they suffered from three common problems: city officials and residents erroneously believed that the boards were the final solution to police problems, many of the boards acted as rubber stamps, and they all lacked the power to successfully address policing problems. CAPA wanted a review board that would not have these issues. They tried for years to convince the government to form a board, without success.[72] CAPA and the Campaign for a Citizens Police Review Board did count as a victory Mayor Tom Bradley's appointment of Stephen Yslas to the Los Angeles Police Commission, the lone Latino on the five-member board that oversaw the chief of police.[73]

The CAPA attempted to do a great deal and should receive praise for trying to better police-community relations. Unfortunately, the group confronted one of the most recalcitrant police regimes in the nation. California as a whole, and Los Angeles, San Diego, and the San Francisco Bay Area more specifically, were hostile and opposed to change. The Los Angeles Police Department (LAPD) especially resisted reform. While some leaders proved willing to make minor changes, they also engaged in tactics, such as the destruction of police records, that undermined even minor reforms. In many ways the inaction of police agencies led directly to other examples of police violence in California.

In another horrible case, in November 1986 two Huntington Park police officers, William Lustig and Robert Rodriguez, tortured seventeen-year-old Jaime Ramirez in an attempt to elicit a confession. The officers had apprehended Ramirez the night of November 30 after seeing him walking down the street with a brown paper bag. The bag contained car stereo equipment that Ramirez said he had bought from another individual but that the officers suspected he had stolen. It is unclear what suspicion or probable cause the officers had to detain Ramirez, since walking with a bag is not a crime, but they did arrest him. During questioning at the jail, Lustig and Rodriguez took turns using a stun gun to shock Ramirez in an attempt to force him to confess to stealing the stereo equipment. He received at least seven 50,000-volt shocks, which resulted in electrical burns to his leg.[74]

It turned out that Lustig had a long history of abuse complaints and at least six lawsuits filed against him. The Huntington Park Police Department fired the two officers. The state tried them for felony assault under the color of law, with the enhancement of inflicting great bodily injury on Ramirez, and inhumane treatment of a prisoner, a misdemeanor. The jury convicted them on the assault and inhumane treatment charges only. Jaime Ramirez later filed a civil suit against the officers and Huntington Park. He received $300,000 in damages.[75]

These two instances of violence led to the formation of another new civil rights group, the Coalition for Law and Justice. The coalition, like CAPA, frequently spoke out against abuse and violence by law enforcement against Mexicans and Mexican Americans in the LA area and along the border, particularly near San Diego. The coalition's spokesperson, Roberto Martinez, decried the "militarization" of the border and "anti-Mexican sentiment and hysteria."[76] He listed several grievances against local and federal law enforcement agencies, including a type of "papers, please" policing used by San Diego police wherein they stopped taxis with Latino/a/x-looking individuals to check identification, a similar type of "papers, please" policing done by the San Diego County Sheriff's Office during raids on Latino/a/x bars, and the intimidation of Mexican-origin people by the Ku Klux Klan.[77] These types of harassment often caused Latino/a/x people to refrain from reporting police abuse and criminal activity, so the Coalition for Law and Justice set up a hotline for individuals to share their experiences and lodge complaints.[78] They received numerous complaints and by January 1985 could state unequivocally that "if you're brown and you look Mexican, you have a pretty good chance of getting harassed."[79]

Coalition leader Roberto Martinez appeared before the House Judiciary Subcommittee on Criminal Justice in September 1986 to testify about the abuse that Mexican-origin people faced at the border. He spoke in favor of HR 2452, the Federal Law Enforcement Review Act, which would have made abuse of force a felony. Martinez argued, "If the worst offense a federal law enforcement officer can be charged with is a misdemeanor if he injures someone, then we, the public are left virtually without protection, especially when, and if, the state declines to prosecute." Alas, his testimony didn't resonate with Congress: Representative Jim Bates, who had sponsored the legislation, withdrew it a week after Martinez testified.[80]

These issues merged into other problems at the border. In December 1987, the Border Crime Prevention Unit, a Border Patrol and San Diego Police Department task force, killed two individuals they described as "canyon bandits," resurrecting the pejorative "bandit" terminology. According to the task force, these "bandits" preyed on unsuspecting border crossers. The officers claimed that the individuals were armed with pistols and knives, but in fact the two people the Border Crime Prevention Unit killed had a pair of scissors and a toy gun.[81] Later that month this scenario played out again when members of the Border Crime Prevention Unit killed another man armed with a toy pistol. That was the ninth such killing in 1987.[82]

In 1987, 1988, and 1989 the Border Patrol came under fire for killing and injuring a number of Mexican youths. In 1987 an agent shot twelve-year-old Octavio Roma Chavez. He was in Ciudad Juárez and the agent shot him from the El Paso side of the border. Like Roma, agents shot Ignacio Mendez Pulido from the US side of the border while he was in Tijuana in December 1987. Both the Roma and Mendez incidents were crimes reminiscent of the across-the-border killing of José Maria del Valle in 1879, so these types of cases have a long history.[83] In February 1988 Immigrations and Naturalization Service agents beat seventeen-year-old Ismael Ramirez Rojas in Fresno, California. He later died from his injuries. In 1989, a Border Patrol officer in a four-wheel-drive vehicle ran over and killed a fourteen-year-old Mexican boy. Congressperson Esteban Torres and others demanded that the government hold the officers involved accountable for this abuse.[84] Alas, border agents who shoot Mexicans from the US side of the border rarely face prosecution. Only in 2018 did the government try a Border Patrol agent for such a crime. In that case Agent Lonnie Swartz fired sixteen shots from Nogales, Arizona, into Nogales, Mexico, after people allegedly threw rocks at him. He killed sixteen-year-old José Antonio Elena Rodriguez, who was shot ten times. Swartz stood trial for second-degree murder and was acquitted.[85]

Among the other policing issues Mexican-origin people have faced in recent years, beyond police murders, none has proved more serious than "papers, please" policing, which long predated Arizona's SB 1070, the most notorious example of this form of policing. In some cases, it has collided with other issues, such as urban renewal. The Bryant-Vanalden area of LA's Northridge neighborhood faced this issue in 1984. It had long been home to a bifurcated Mexican-origin and White population, with White folks living in the more affluent area of central Northridge and Latino/a/x people residing in the Bryant-Vanalden area in south Northridge. The Los Angeles City Council had proposed evicting large numbers of mainly Mexican-origin and Salvadoran-origin residents and demolishing their apartments.[86] Hundreds of White residents petitioned the city council in favor of this proposal. "We're not racist," one person explained. "This is a question of law and order, not race" another asserted. In the minds of these White nonracists, since law and order seemed lacking the obvious corrective measure involved eradicating the Latino/a/x part of the community, which made about as much sense as the claim "We're not racist."[87]

Latino/a/x residents fought back. A host of civic groups organized to protest the proposal, with city council member Ernani Bernardi emerging as its most vocal opponent. They had a protest march that ended in a demonstration at the office of council member Hal Bernson, who had proposed the measure to evict the Latino/a/x residents.[88] Like area White folks, city council members such as Art Snyder seemed shocked by the Latino/a/x opposition to the measure and charges of racism. But the opinions of White residents and the police response certainly demonstrated racism. Police, for example, initiated a type of "papers, please" policing when they began stopping Latino/a/x residents to check their identification. If the individuals could not provide identification, police handed them over to the INS. Police also worked closely with the INS to conduct raids to capture undocumented immigrants. They did this primarily to remove a portion of the city's population, which would make the urban renewal project easier to achieve.[89]

The city approved the evictions, but the protests made sure that this plan never happened. The city tried again in 1986. The city council approved a $20 million urban renewal plan, without the proposed evictions.[90] Police also did more sweeps and inspections to intimidate residents. But local people still opposed the plan because it would cause a huge increase in rents, which would, like the evictions, effectively force them out of the community. The project became fraught with cost overruns. Some minor renovations to existing apartments began in 1987. But the developer hired to perform the renewal quit in 1988. The project ultimately fizzled.[91]

The plans of local governments, community concerns, and law enforcement were clearly at odds in many parts of Southern California. Abusive law enforcement simply masqueraded as neighborhood renewal schemes in Bryant-Vanalden. While Bernson and other White people disclaimed racism, their words and deeds demonstrated otherwise. And by using police and the INS to intimidate and drive away residents, they linked their prejudice to policing in a way that clearly exposed the structural racism within California's governmental institutions.

Training in spoken Spanish was also woefully behind the times in California. Both the LAPD and the California Highway Patrol had only a handful of Spanish-speaking officers. Luis A. Murillo, a professor of Spanish at the University of Southern California, knew that this could be a barrier between police and Mexican Americans. So he began volunteering for the LAPD and the California Highway Patrol in the 1980s to assist police with translations.

CALIFORNIA HIGHWAY PATROL

El Protector Coordinator
PABLO TORRES

El
Protector
OFICIAL
PABLO TORRES
California Highway Patrol

Pablo Torres trabaja para la Unidad de Relaciones Públicas de la División del Sur del Departamento de Patrulla de Caminos de California promoviendo el Programa El Protector. Pablo es bien conocido por su estilo dinámico en sus reportes de tráfico por la radio y la televisión.

CONSEJO DE SEGURIDAD – Southern-1
Guarde su distancia del auto que esté enfrente de usted. Recuerde, que en el momento menos pensado, el tráfico se puede detener y la responsabilidad de evitar un golpe contra el auto de enfrente es suya.

A number of law enforcement agencies attempted new types of community outreach in the 1980s and 1990s. The California Highway Patrol developed the El Protector Program to educate the public, and Latino/a/x people specifically, about traffic safety and to encourage good community relations. The California Highway Patrol also produced these trading cards featuring the officers involved in the program. This card for El Protector coordinator Pablo Torres notes that he was "well known for his dynamic style in his radio and television traffic reports." The El Protector Program still exists today. *Courtesy of University of Southern California, on behalf of the USC Libraries Special Collections and the California Highway Patrol.*

He also wrote a booklet of phrases that officers could use when they encountered Spanish-speaking individuals. In a shooting situation, for example, an officer might ask, "Dónde est[á] el hombre con la pistola?" or "Where is the man with the firearm?" The booklet also contained common terms that police might need to use, such as "accomplice—cómplice" and "patrol car—carro de patrulla." "We take it for granted now," Murillo explained, "but 25 years ago, having this kind of information printed in Spanish was a new idea."[92] It seems perplexing, though, that the LA area, with its long history of Mexican settlement, had no Spanish-language guidebook before Murillo came along.

Another interesting form of police outreach came in the form of trading cards issued by the California Highway Patrol. These riffed on sports trading cards and featured Latino/a/x officers in the El Protector Program, which did outreach that emphasized education and dialogue. For example, Pablo Torres served as the El Protector coordinator for Southern California. His card featured a picture of Torres in uniform standing by his patrol car, explained that he worked for the Public Relations Unit, and noted that he "was well known for his dynamic style." His card offered sage advice, for example cautioning drivers to keep their distance from other vehicles. These cards represented a neat way of engaging with the Mexican American community.[93]

Finally, New Mexico, which had seen notable progress in police-community relations in the 1970s, experienced some regresses in the 1980s in several locales. In 1981, for instance, Roswell police raided the home of James and Sylvia Vigil for unexplained reasons, probably another clerical mistake with the address. The family contemplated suing.[94] Worse still, in 1984 they raided Pablin and Angelina Jimenez's home to recover a stolen motorcycle. Wearing ski masks and without identifying themselves, police broke down the front door, catching the elderly couple by surprise. When Pablin failed to rise quickly enough from the chair where he had been watching late-night television, officers wrestled him to the ground. Police discovered that they had raided the wrong home. The City of Roswell dragged its feet on paying for repairs to the Jimenezes' front door, so they sued the city for $2 million for violating their civil rights, property damage, and emotional distress. Their attorney, Albert Rivera, argued that the amount would not only compensate the family but also discourage police from making similar mistakes.[95]

The response from the City of Roswell was almost comical. The city blamed the mistake on bad information from a confidential informant and disclaimed any responsibility to the family. "It was a mistake," Police Chief Steven Wisniewski said, "but we didn't violate their constitutional rights." City Manager Jim Whitford was even more nonchalant: "This type of thing happens. It's certainly unfortunate, but not worth $2 million. We feel that there has been no wrongdoing on our part." They threatened to countersue the Jimenezes in order to "discourage these frivolous claims against the city," which they claimed forced the city to pay higher insurance premiums.[96] Such thoughtless statements, reminiscent of the way South Tucson responded after the friendly fire wounding of Officer Roy Garcia, did not bode well for the city's defense in the Jimenez case, because the city *had* violated the family's rights, they *had* caused physical damage to their home, and it certainly seems plausible that they *had* caused emotional distress. As it turned out, the jury in the case agreed. They awarded Pablin $50,000 in damages; Angelina received $100,000. While the amount of damages awarded to the family was far below the $2 million they sought, attorney Rivera noted that the suit had not about money but about sending a message to the police about how they tended to treat residents like the Jimenezes. The city, for its part, finally wised up and decided not to countersue Pablin and Angelina Jimenez.[97]

Like the Raymond Joya case in neighboring Arizona, New Mexico also had some issues with troubled officers. An abuse case in Roswell serves as a good example. In January 1986, Philip Gonzales and his girlfriend Kitty Lucero were driving home from a date when someone shot at their car. On arriving at his parents' home, Gonzales found a bullet hole in the vehicle and called the police to make a report. Officer Charlie White arrived and inspected the vehicle with Philip and Kitty. During this inspection, White accused Gonzales of committing a hit-and-run accident earlier in the day and began to arrest him. When White grabbed him by the elbow, Gonzales pulled away. White seized Gonzales by the neck and began choking him with one hand and punching him in the face with the other. When Philip Gonzales's parents attempted to intervene, White pointed his handgun at them. He then dragged Philip to his patrol car while continuing to hit him in the face. The Gonzales family lodged a complaint against White, but it seems nothing came of this case.[98]

This incident serves as a final example that the policing situation in the Southwest clearly remained volatile in the 1980s. Officers such as White could commit abuses for no reason and get away with it. Families like the Gonzaleses were not protected nor served by law enforcement, and their experience was not unique in the region. The number of police abuse cases, especially the numerous examples of police raiding the wrong home, as well as the Klan border patrols and the violence committed by the actual Border Patrol, generated considerable community anger. It also generated protests, proof of the continuation of Chicano activism in the 1980s. Several noteworthy examples show not only the vitality of the movement but also some of its successes.

Some locales responded well to complaints from the Mexican American community. The community outreach efforts in Mesa, Tempe, and Tucson all serve as excellent examples. Other cities also engaged in outreach or attempted to increase the number of Mexican American police officers. The hiring of Ruben Ortega as police chief in Phoenix was a step in the right direction. But just as often police failed in their dealings with Mexican-origin people. The killing of Hector Santoscoy in San Antonio, police abuse in Bryant-Vanalden, or the unfortunate evolutions in the policing of Mexican-origin members of the LGBTQIA+ community all prove this point. Using law enforcement to battle the AIDS crisis was a huge mistake. Members of the gay community and Mexican American activists had to forge new coalitions to challenge police abuse, which they did, but people such as Carlos Villarreal or Fred Páez never got their justice.

A number of governmental reports confirmed these viewpoints. For example, a "National Progress Report" produced by the American GI Forum in 1981 detailed the recent uptick in KKK and policing problems but more importantly focused on a new group called the Attorneys Committee on Police Practice, which would review instances of police abuse and provide attorneys to those affected by it. The report also emphasized the problem of deadly force and noted that between 1967 and 1976 police had killed 6,000 people, half of whom were Mexican Americans. The Department of Justice, the report opined, has "failed to enforce the laws of the land against killer cops."[99] The "National Progress Report" not only demonstrated ongoing policing problems but showed how groups such as the GI Forum brought their might to bear on this issue. Many other groups did the same. And they were joined by new groups such as the Carlos Villarreal Defense Committee. The 1980s showed that the activism of the Chicano movement endured.

EIGHT

NO JUSTICE, NO PEACE

The Problem of Policing
from the 1990s to Today

Peter Moreno stopped to watch a fight between two men in Norwalk, California, as he walked home at 1:00 a.m. on Sunday, June 5, 1990. Police soon arrived, and the fourteen-year-old Moreno ran, fearing the officers would arrest him for violating Norwalk's curfew ordinance. Alas, he ran into LA County deputy sheriff David Shriver, who grabbed him and hit him with his metal flashlight. Moreno fell to the ground and Shriver continued beating him on the legs, arms, back, and head. Shriver later admitted that he struck Moreno as hard as he could. Moreno suffered a fractured ulna, lacerations, and bruises. His family sued Shriver for violating his constitutional rights. They contended that he used excessive force contrary to federal and state law and that his subsequent arrest violated Moreno's Fourth Amendment rights since he had committed no crime and Shriver had no probable cause to believe he had. They asked for $85,000 in damages. Although he prevailed in court, Moreno received only $2,000 in compensatory damages and $3,000 in punitive damages. The LA County Sheriff's Department did not punish Deputy Shriver.[1]

The Moreno case highlights several aspects of contemporary law enforcement and how it often treats communities of color. First, he was yet another child brutalized by police. Second, Shriver beat him for no reason: Moreno had committed no criminal act, and violation of a curfew ordinance, a misdemeanor, would have at worst gotten him a citation. Third, instead of deescalating the situation Shriver chose to escalate his use of force. His heavy-handed response demonstrates the modern, hypermilitaristic policing at work in many police forces. Last, although Moreno prevailed in court, Shriver went unpunished, giving his actions official, legal sanction.

The period from 1990 to the present day represents in large part another nadir in police relations with Mexican American people.[2] The years of police reform efforts slowly unraveled as a new militaristic type of police force came to the fore. Some of this simply represented the dubious evolution of earlier reforms such as community policing. Law enforcement and communities of color in the Southwest had called for community policing in the 1960s and 1970s, which put officers, via storefronts or through liaison offices, in proximity to the Mexican American community. By the 1990s community policing morphed into broken windows policing. The theory of broken windows policing can be simplified as such: police actively look for criminal activity—a broken window thus becomes a burglary police need to investigate—and a broken window by its existence encourages other criminal activity, so dealing with the broken window means halting crime. The problem with this theory is that police tend to concentrate themselves in areas the city sees as high crime—really high-arrest areas—where they more frequently encounter people of color, like Peter Moreno, and then brutalize them.[3]

Other evolutions also took place. As noted in the previous chapter, local governments often used law enforcement to perform roles they shouldn't perform, such as fighting the AIDS crisis. Beginning in the 1990s, governments facing budget shortfalls cut social services, such as mental health services. They then tasked police to respond to these situations. Police often react to an agitated person with schizophrenia or a suicidal individual suffering from depression with deadly force. The resulting anger from the victim's community, while understandable, is often somewhat misplaced since the city forced police to do a job a mental health professional should do. Governments also tasked police with additional work, including border policing. This came mainly through the concept of "papers, please" policing, wherein police can stop anyone for any reason and demand ID.

Federal interventions exacerbated these problems. Take the Clinton Crime Law of 1994, which put billions in federal dollars behind the hiring of new police officers, among other things. The funding of those officers meant that local governments could expand police forces while other parts of a city's budget shrank. Thus, as mental health services got cut, cities simply transferred the work of those medical professionals to an expanding police force. The law also put billions toward the building of new prisons. This, at least in part, has led to the massive increase in the number of incarcerated people in the United States. In addition, the sale of surplus military equipment to police forces through initiatives such as the 1033 Program has resulted in the militarization of American police. The federal government also tried to combat drugs and gang activity, which it linked. The War on Drugs and War on Crime overpenalized drug possession and dealing, which resulted in an exploding prison population and did little to stem the flow of drugs. Moreover, American drug laws disproportionately affect Brown and Black people.[4]

Mexican Americans, and Latino/a/x people more broadly, as well as other communities, especially African Americans, responded to this situation in a variety of ways. They rose up in protest when police killed individuals under questionable circumstances. They pushed local governments to prosecute officers. They advocated for the establishment of civilian review boards. They sued. And they came up with new reform ideas, such as federal police-civilian review boards. But Latino/a/x folks often found their efforts stymied by the massive power of police forces, which resisted reform efforts and successfully defended police officers who killed people. The enormous power that police have means that they seldom have to change anything. In fact, they sometimes emerge from crises with even more power. Police and the broader justice system often use reform as a means to manage predicaments that they themselves have produced, whether that be abuse or a killing, and then emerge with more resources or authority.

One of the epicenters of police violence and institutional racism in California was the Los Angeles Police Department. The LAPD frequently stood at the forefront of regressive, draconian policing. For example, in the 1970s, the LAPD launched new antigang activities. It first created a unit called Total Resources against Street Hoodlums in the 1970s, later renamed Community Resources against Street Hoodlums. The term "hoodlum" certainly had a negative connotation that mainly applied to Black and Brown youth. "What they're doing is rounding up youths wherever they congregate, which might be gangs or youth from a block or two hanging out together," the National Council of La Raza reported. This type of policing was problematic because it meant that police hassled Mexican American youths en masse but often missed actual criminals. Such programs led directly to the Rampart Scandal, the worst example of police corruption in American history. But before Rampart was Rodney King.[5]

In what remains one of the best-known incidents of police violence, four LAPD officers, and a host of others from various police agencies who stood by and watched, repeatedly tased and beat Rodney King after a high-speed chase. The four officers went on to stand trial for assault and excessive force. When a jury acquitted them in 1992, LA erupted in a prolonged and exceedingly violent uprising. Regarding the cause of the violence, a report from the National Chicano Human Rights Council accurately noted that the video of King's beating proved "what hundreds of residents, community leaders, civil and human rights organizations had been saying for decades—that the Los Angeles Police Department, as well as the Los Angeles County Sheriff's Department and other security forces[,] were engaged in a war of attrition against marginalized communities, communities that were predominately African or Chicano/Latino."[6]

The postrebellion period proved an auspicious time to bring up the issue of police violence as it related to Latino/a/x people, since the media tended to fixate on negative encounters between Black folks and police. As had been the case in the Watts Rebellion investigations, Latino/a/x leaders played an important role in the post–Rodney King investigations. For instance, the National Chicano Human Rights Council went beyond simply making sure that the media included Latino/a/x people in an accounting of who got abused by police, focusing specifically on how police used the postrebellion period as cover to deport people. Those arrested during the uprising made easy targets for deportation. But after the rebellion, "while the rest of the country and the world were being told by the media that Los Angeles was rebuilding and healing," the National Chicano Human Rights Council reported that "the Los Angeles Police Department along with the Immigration and Naturalization Service's Border Patrol were conducting massive sweeps of predominately Latino neighborhoods, arresting thousands of people, and deporting hundreds of alleged undocumented immigrants."[7]

The timing of the deportations seems particularly cruel. The city, still in a state of disorder, had much work to do. Instead of contemplating the problem of law enforcement abuse and overreach, law enforcement chose to overreach yet again. With nearly 25,000 police, Border Patrol agents, and military personnel occupying the city, the opportunity for officials to use that force to deport unwanted people perhaps made sense to authorities.

But they committed a lot of unconstitutional acts to do it, including denial of due process, illegal searches of vehicles and homes (including homes with only children present), unlawful detentions, and the LAPD and the Border Patrol engaged in cooperative raids, a violation of LA ordinances, state, and federal law.[8]

The linking of the rebellion and deportations was not unusual. Similar things had happened in the past. So when activists proposed reforms in this period, they tended to link this aspect of the rebellion to border control. One of the more interesting reform concepts came from the Quakers. They had grown increasingly concerned with border killings, which had risen in the 1980s and 1990s, and later the Rodney King situation. The Society of Friends viewed these killings as part of the long history of border abuse that Mexicans had experienced for more than a century. In 1991 and 1993, the Society of Friends proposed that the United States should have a national civilian review board to oversee such agencies as the Border Patrol. As Friends field coordinator Jorge Hinojosa explained, "There has to be some form of civilian oversight of the Border Patrol on a local, regional and national basis." The Border Patrol rejected this idea.[9] After the rebellion the Friends tried again. They understood another facet of Mexican and Mexican American life—that "U.S. immigration authorities do not distinguish between undocumented immigrants and the larger Mexican-American population." This proved problematic because it meant that the Border Patrol and local police forces targeted all Mexican-origin people. It also caused citizens and noncitizens to distrust authorities, refrain from reporting abuse, and avoid reporting crime. The Friends again proposed a federal civilian review board, and the government again declined.[10]

The LAPD did attempt some "reforms" after the uprising of 1992. In 1995, they began a community policing program, for instance. Since community policing had come to the fore in the 1970s, the LAPD came late to the game, and its effort seemed reflexive and insincere. The department's idea of community policing meant that police would "form partnerships with all the diverse residential and business communities of the city in an effort to reduce crime and the fear of crime," but how officers might do this was not explained.[11] A subsequent community policing workbook for officers broadened some of these initial ideas. But it had problems. It opened by stating that community policing had no definition and that it "is not a program—it is a philosophy," which was basically nonsense. But the workbook also focused on "problem solving," which came from a new four-step police strategy called Scanning, Analysis, Response, and Assessment

(SARA). Scanning involved identifying a problem. The workbook used as an example "narcotic and gang activity at the S/W corner of Alvarado and 3rd, 24 hours a day 7 days a week." The Analysis part of the model allowed the officer to break the problem down further: it meant asking, "What do you want to know about the problem?" Response, while vaguer, advised officers to "design a customized response in a non-traditional manner that will effectively address the problem." Finally, the Assessment section asked them to evaluate their intervention.[12]

SARA was new in 1995, but it has since come under scrutiny. Many activists dislike its deficit-based approach to policing. Like broken windows policing, SARA anticipated and even encouraged more frequent interactions between police and civilians, especially in locations deemed "high crime areas" by police. Like other LAPD reforms, this one caused problems.[13]

Like the LAPD, the San Antonio Police Department (SAPD) came to reform later than other big cities. The department only began to initiate some minor reforms in the mid-1980s after the killing of Hector Santoscoy. For example, the department distributed to officers a first-of-its-kind operational manual in 1984. It seems odd that the SAPD would not have had such a manual until then.[14] San Antonio also developed a Police Athletic League and launched police storefronts in 1992.[15] When a group called Frontline 2000 proposed a civilian review board in 1992, the San Antonio Police Officers Association worked hard to curtail the board.[16] The review board the city eventually created had little power and, strangely, excluded civilians.[17] Activist and attorney Ruben Sandoval complained, "What we're getting is token . . . window dressing. Even if the civilians have a vote, they will always be in the minority." Of course, some police officers wanted to see civilians on the board, so neither side was pleased.[18]

Unsurprisingly, police abuse continued. In the 2000s, groups such as the San Antonio Coalition on Human and Civil Rights critiqued a rise in SAPD abuse of force complaints. Eventually the FBI began a review of the department based on these complaints. For example, officers tased Sergio Galvan after a traffic stop; he died at the scene. In a "papers, please" policing incident, Michael Olveda refused to show officers his identification. Officers beat him, and he later died from those injuries. In 2005, Officer Dean Gutierrez raped a transgender person he had taken into custody. As a result, Amnesty International investigated the SAPD and found that the department engaged in a concerted pattern of abuse, particularly for gay and transgender individuals. Given the recent cases of abuse and murders of transgender people, these instances of violence reveal an ongoing and ugly pattern.[19]

The SAPD came under fire again in 2008 after launching a new crime interdiction program, the Tactical Response Unit, which operated primarily in the city's predominantly Mexican American West and South Sides in 2007. The unit purportedly worked to curtail gang and drug activity, but instead it harassed local people for minor infractions. The case of Oscar Alvarado proved typical. While driving with his brother, Alvarado illegally passed another vehicle. The Tactical Response Unit pulled them over, and Officer Yvonne Mauricio began choking Alvarado when she claimed he attempted to swallow drugs. But there were no drugs. The unit also engaged in stop-and-frisk searches, mainly targeting Black and Brown people. Some of these searches included illegal strip and cavity searches. They also engaged in illegal "papers, please" policing.[20]

Austin had also launched a version of "papers, please" policing back in the late 1960s. Local activists resisted this program, but the Austin Police Department refused to halt it.[21] The department also opposed forming a police-civilian review board, so local activists created their own in 1981. The Community-Police Relations Advisory Council operated as civilian review "to promote positive community-police relations." Although the council saw itself as educational, it also hoped to play a role in the training of officers and in ultimately curbing police harassment and brutality.[22] A similar group, the East Austin Police Advisory Council, developed in the 1990s. This group focused specific attention on the city's Mexican-dominant east side.[23] It had the blessing of Police Chief Elizabeth Watson. She had served as Houston's first female chief of police before taking the job in Austin. Watson had previously supported community policing concepts such as Police Athletic Leagues and storefront policing, but she scrapped these programs in the mid-1990s in favor of a new idea she called the "one third model." Her idea broke a police officer's job into three parts: outreach, law enforcement, and paperwork. It might have looked good on paper, but putting it into effect and, especially, having patrol officers do community outreach proved impractical. The chief met immediate resistance from the city council. Several councilmembers balked at the idea. Mayor Bruce Todd felt that the idea simply wasn't useful.[24] Watson ultimately kept only the law enforcement part of the "one third model" and took officers who already did community outreach and reassigned them to patrol, a step in the wrong direction.[25]

The examples of "papers, please" policing in Austin and San Antonio seem quaint when compared to other parts of the Southwest, especially Chandler, Arizona. That city engaged in a massive roundup of allegedly undocumented people in 1997, known as the Chandler Roundup. Local law enforcement worked with the Immigration and Naturalization Service and Border Patrol to apprehend undocumented immigrants. Police used an augmented bicycle patrol to allow more on-the-ground contact with Chandler residents. Their tactics for discovering unauthorized immigrants were the very definition of racial profiling: officers "stopped and questioned citizens and legal residents about their legal status outside grocery stores and in parking lots, asked children for 'papers,' and [en]circled Hispanic looking individuals in public areas."[26] Some Chandler residents also believed that Mayor Jay Tibshraeny supported the roundups to push a gentrification project, much like what happened in the Bryant-Vanalden area of Northridge. Targeting the Latino/a/x community might force people out of the redevelopment zone. The raids all took place within this zone.[27]

The roundup, which the bureaucrats dubbed Operation Restoration, did more than simply racially profile people, however. It gave an important new power to law enforcement by allowing them to act as border enforcers. Police also stopped, questioned, and arrested a number of American citizens of Mexican ancestry. In a particularly ugly scene, two sisters aged seven and ten were walking home from school when three Chandler bicycle officers accosted them. The officers asked for their birth certificates and then warned the girls that they needed to keep their birth certificates with them or they risked deportation to Mexico. When they made it home, the girls reported the encounter to their mother. The incident traumatized the two children. They repeatedly told their mother, "Mom, we don't know Mexico," because like typical American citizens, they had lived their entire lives in the United States. After this incident the girls would hide if someone came to the door out of fear that "maybe it's the police." They also only went outside after this event with their birth certificates pinned to their clothes.[28]

Catalina Veloz had her own problematic encounter with Chandler law enforcement. Police pulled her over on July 29, 1997, for what she assumed was a traffic violation. The officer spoke to her in Spanish, and since she was fluently bilingual, she responded in kind. That confirmed the officer's suspicion that she was undocumented and an accompanying Border Patrol agent then asked for her papers. Although the officers let her go, she encountered another officer later that same day. This time the officer heard Veloz playing ranchera music in her car, which alerted him to her Mexican-ness. At a Chandler City Council meeting, Veloz complained and, like the two young girls, wondered, "What's next? Are they going to expect us to carry our birth certificates or papers around with us or tattoo numbers on our arms."[29]

What the two young girls, Catalina Veloz, and others experienced represents the problematic linkages that American society and the justice system have created about Mexican-origin people. Even at the tender ages of seven and ten, the Mexicanity of the young girls merited interference from police. That three officers would attempt to apprehend two children was outrageous. Police arrested 450 undocumented immigrants whom the state then deported. They also arrested and released 100 others, and probably more, who were American citizens. In almost all encounters they used flimsy excuses to justify traffic stops. They also illegally entered and searched residences, even after homeowners asked for a warrant. Chandler police also made "papers, please" inquiries without the presence of Border Patrol officers, a violation of the program. Officers also treated the individuals they arrested inhumanely, locking them in police vans for hours with no ventilation, water, or bathroom facilities (in Arizona, in July).[30]

The Chandler Roundup led to a great deal of community anger and protests. Arizona attorney general Grant Wood investigated the roundup and came down hard on the city. His investigative report faulted city leaders for tying the roundup to the redevelopment scheme; criticized the lack of a written agreement between the police and Border Patrol; condemned the civil rights violations that occurred; and rebuked the racial profiling that took place during the raids. The attorney general recommended that the city reevaluate participation in this type of program, that it acknowledge "the divisive and negative impact caused by this operation," and that it implement programs to restore trust in the community. Last, the attorney general proposed outlawing "papers, please" policing. "This joint operation by Chandler Police Department and the INS/Border Patrol and the manner in which it was executed," the attorney general's report concluded, "greatly harmed the trust relationship between the Chandler Police and many of the City's residents. There is much to be done to restore this important relationship."[31]

The Chandler Roundup also led to a series of diversity programs designed to educate city leaders and lessen tensions in Chandler. City leaders founded a Human Relations Commission, and the police department began a community outreach program. They also stopped engaging in "papers, please" policing.[32] Local residents brought a number of lawsuits against the Chandler government and police department for violating the civil rights of those ensnared by the roundup. One lawsuit brought in August 1997 sought $35 million in damages included twelve specific Chandler police officers and eight Border Patrol agents. The city settled the lawsuit in early 1999 for a paltry $400,000. The roundup remains an ugly blight on Chandler to this day.[33]

While these events transpired, several noteworthy national events occurred that affected policing at the local level. The most important was the
Violent Crime Control and Law Enforcement Act of 1994, otherwise known
as the Clinton Crime Bill/Law. The law serves as an example of how federal
initiatives can do incredible harm locally. The original bill, written by Senator Joseph Biden (D-DE) and the National Association of Police Officers,
responded to a general perception of rising crime in American cities. Lawmakers had concerns about crimes such as drug dealing and carjacking (a
1990s phenomenon; the term "carjacking" originated in 1991).[34] Politicians
also began to raise concerns about a new kind of criminal that scholar John
Dilulio called "superpredators," a term later picked up by political figures
such as Hillary Clinton that was a racist dog whistle for Black men with little
basis in reality.[35]

The biggest problem with the Clinton Crime Bill was that it responded to
a crisis that had largely abated. Crime rates, for instance, had risen throughout the 1980s but then began to drop in the 1990s. The homicide rate had
climbed from 4.6 per 100,000 in 1962 to 10.2 in 1980. But it fell steadily
throughout the 1990s, from 9.3 per 100,000 in 1991 to under 8 per 100,000
in 1994, when the Clinton Crime Bill became law, and it has for the most
part continued to decline.[36] Violent crime, which includes murder, aggravated
assault, rape, and robbery, peaked in 1991 at 758.2 per 100,000 and has declined since then. Property crimes also rose in the 1980s and then dropped.
In 1991 the property crime rate was 5,140.2 per 100,000. Today crime rates
across all categories remain at historic lows. The homicide rate was at 5.5
per 100,000 in 2023 (down from 6.3 in 2022); the violent crime rate was
at 357.9 per 100,000 in 2023 (down from 380.7 in 2022); property crime
rate was 1,876.23 per 100,000 in 2023 (down from 1,954.4 in 2022).[37] So,
by the time Congress passed the Clinton Crime Bill the crime rate across all
categories was already in a steep decline and continued to decrease for the
next two decades. The law thus anticipated a solution without a problem. It
serves as a good example of how law enforcement and its allies can use a
supposed crisis to implement "reforms" that benefit and empower police.[38]

The Clinton Crime Law did four things relevant to the analysis in this
book. First, it provided funding that allowed localities to massively expand
police forces. The law proposed hiring up to 100,000 new police officers.
Clinton had already begun augmenting the number of police officers in
1993 with new budget appropriations for the hiring of officers from the
Department of Justice.[39] The crime law furthered this process. Second, the
law adjusted sentencing guidelines for drug charges via three-strikes laws,

as well as subsequent efforts that penalized certain drugs differently, most notoriously crack versus powder cocaine. Third, it modified penal laws, for example, by expanding the death penalty by creating sixty new crimes eligible for the death penalty. Fourth, the law provided billions of dollars in funding for jails and prisons. Bill Clinton has consistently claimed credit for the drop in crime rates because of the law. Analysts have found little proof to support this assertion. Clinton is also partially responsible for the massive increase in prison populations. He prefers not to take credit for that.[40]

As far as policing is concerned, the Clinton Crime Law flooded American cities with new police officers. Houston, for instance, had already hired a number of officers for a community policing initiative in 1994 that saw no demonstrable improvement in crime rates.[41] The city added 650 new officers via the Justice Department program in 1993 while cutting the community policing initiative. Even though crime rates had decreased in Houston in the 1990s, Mayor Bob Lanier and Police Chief Sam Nuchia claimed that the hiring of these officers had led to the decline. They planned to hire 550 more officers with funding from the Clinton law.[42] In Austin the law provided $2.25 million to hire 100 officers.[43] Dallas received $5.2 million to hire seventy.[44]

In New Mexico, Gallup announced it had received a grant from the Department of Justice. The city scored $131,922 to hire two police officers. That may seem small, but at the time Gallup had a population of just under 20,000 and a police force of around 300 officers.[45] Santa Fe sought nearly $200,000 to hire three officers.[46] Rio Rancho scored big for a small town; it received $462,430 to hire seven new officers.[47] Albuquerque initially pushed to hire 300 officers by securing one of the grants from the Department of Justice.[48] Albuquerque police chief Bob Stover wanted to hire seventy-five new officers to do community policing using crime law funds.[49] Many Burqueños wanted more information as to how the city would do community policing. Albuquerque Police Officers Association president Bill Pounders wondered about the efficacy of Stover's idea, considering that it worked in some cities but not in others.[50]

Albuquerque serves as a textbook example of the expansion of a police force for no real reason. The city had throughout the 1980s and early 1990s seen its overall crime rate drop. Burglaries had fallen 26 percent between 1988 and 1993. Murder and rape had remained static throughout that five-year period. The only violent crime to increase was assault, which experts attributed to an unfortunate increase in intimate partner violence. In fact, in 1994 the total number of crimes committed in Albuquerque hit a seven-year low.[51] So why the need for all the new police?

The process seen in Texas and New Mexico repeated itself in Arizona. Mesa, for example, wanted to use federal dollars as well as a bond referendum to secure $4.2 million to rebuild a substation and hire around thirty new officers. The city also proposed building a police academy. Mesa police recruits had for years received training at the Phoenix Police Academy, but because Phoenix sought to use Clinton funds to hire 200 new officers it no longer had room for cadets from other cities. Mesa received $975,000 from the Justice Department program to hire thirteen new officers and planned to use a community college for cadet training.[52]

Phoenix jumped at the chance to hire new police officers. The city council proposed hiring thirty new officers to expand the city's gang unit in 1993. It also proposed spending $250,000 on new police cars for those new officers. The police force hoped to hire sixty officers using Clinton Crime Law funds.[53] Phoenix succeeded in receiving Clinton funds to hire fifty-two new officers. Other Arizona cities also got new officers: Scottsdale six, Tempe five. Oddly, Tucson, the second largest municipality in Arizona, received no funding for police officers.[54] Arizona differed from other Southwestern states in that its crime rate had tended to fluctuate somewhat widely from 1980 to 2000. The murder rate rose from a low of 6.7 in 1989 to a high of 10.5 in 1994 before dropping to 8.0 in 1999. The rate of rape decreased from a high of 45.7 in 1985 to 28.9 in 1999. The rate of robberies decreased from 193.6 in 1980 to a low of 131.1 in 1984 before going back up in the 1990s.[55]

Like other states, California began increasing the hiring of new police officers before the Clinton Crime Bill became law. In fact, as Max Felker-Kantor has shown, Los Angeles barely slowed its hiring from the early 1980s to the 1990s. Mayor Richard Riordan had campaigned in 1992 on significantly expanding the number of police by hiring up to 3,000 new officers.[56] The Anaheim City Council proposed shifting revenues the city received from a local hotel tax to the police force so that the city could hire an estimated ten new officers.[57] Pasadena also expanded its force before the Clinton Crime Bill was signed into law, adding eight new police officers, paid for with a half-cent sales tax.[58] California differs from other Southwestern states in that its crime rates tended to be static from 1980 to the 1990s.[59]

Shortly before the Clinton Crime Bill was enacted, Los Angeles Mayor Riordan announced the city and county would hire a whopping 4,000 new police officers. Clinton had evidently promised Riordan that funding from the new law would net LA at least 2,500 new police. The first installment of Clinton monies, about $3 million, allowed the LA County Sheriff's Department to hire thirty-three new deputies in early October 1994. By late October the county received an additional $2 million, bringing the total hiring of new deputies to fifty-two. The city also did well, initially netting funding to support the hiring of around 500 new officers, which prompted LA City Council member Richard Alarcon to suggest creating an entirely new police division in the Central San Fernando Valley.[60] In 1996, the LAPD received an additional $53 million, the largest single grant of Clinton funds up to that point, to hire another 710 officers.[61] Most California municipalities received funds to hire anywhere from three to twenty officers.[62]

The Clinton Crime Law inundated American cities with new police. While Clinton had proposed adding 100,000 new officers to police forces across the nation, the actual number of officers hired was nearly 200,000. That brought the total number of police up to 900,000.[63] For all of these new cops, the crime rate, which to reiterate had been dropping since 1990, simply continued to decline. This decline had multiple causes: changing demographics, new alternative adjudication procedures such as drug and mental health courts, or an improved economic environment.[64] Drug courts, for instance, divert offenders from traditional court processes and adjudicate them instead in a specialty court designed to offer treatment. Now, those courts do not by themselves lower crime rates—after all, people are still processed through the criminal justice system. Instead, drug courts lower rates of recidivism, thereby reducing overall crime rates.[65] Because of the Clinton Crime Law, the arrest rate for drug charges skyrocketed while arrest rates for all other categories declined. Drug arrests increased by 80 percent from 1990 to 2010.[66] Clearance rates—when an arrest leads to an indictment or prosecution—for drug-related arrests also increased. The new sentencing guidelines from the Clinton Crime Law and state-level adoption of three-strikes laws all also contributed to the growth of prison populations.[67]

The Clinton Crime Law focused on revising penalties for a variety of crimes, but especially narcotics violations, part of the War on Drugs. A big piece of this involved sentence enhancements for gang affiliation, which politicians linked to drugs. The law also created new avenues by which authorities could drug test individuals. The Anti-Drug Abuse Act of 1986 had mandated stricter sentencing for crack versus powder cocaine, called 100 to 1 (1 gram of crack equaled 100 grams of powder cocaine). When the federal sentencing commission suggested eliminating 100 to 1, Clinton doubled down, signing legislation in 1995 that rejected the sentencing commission's proposal and retained the harsher sentencing guidelines.[68]

In the Southwest the increased number of police, arrests for drug violations, and new sentencing laws had predictable results. While the data are difficult to analyze, mainly because the FBI does not treat Latino/a/x people as a distinct group in its data collection, local-level analysis shows that from 1998 to 2008 police arrested Latino/a/x folks at a higher rate than White folks and at about the same rate as African Americans. Police also arrested foreign-born Latin American immigrants at a much lower rate. As Mike Tapia has observed, "Foreign-born Latinos are the absolute least often arrested race-ethnic group, while U.S.-born Latino levels are identical to those of Blacks."[69]

The four largest Southwestern states demonstrate the result of these factors. In California, Latino/a/x people were 41 percent of those arrested in 2016 and made up 39 percent of the total population.[70] They were 44 percent of the prison population in 2018.[71] In Arizona, Latino/a/x folks were 30 percent of Arizona's population but accounted for approximately 31 percent of total arrests in 2015, a number significantly higher than the African American population (11.6 percent) but below the White arrest rate (79.2 percent).[72] Latino/a/x people also constituted 41 percent of the prison population.[73] In New Mexico, arrest rates are difficult to discern because the state does not track race or ethnicity in its criminal justice system. A study from 2019 did find that Latino/a/x people were 1.2 times more likely to be arrested than White people.[74] They were 52 percent of the prison population and 46 percent of the population.[75] Texas is the only Southwestern state where Latino/a/x people have a lower arrest and incarceration rate than their percentage of the population. They constituted 38 percent of the state's population but made up 34 percent of arrests in 2009.[76] They made up 34 percent of the prison population.[77] These statistics are largely the result of the Clinton Crime Law and other federal "reforms."[78]

One way to see the effect of these revisions to the criminal justice system is by looking at the ongoing problem of questionable police shootings. Now, it's difficult to conclusively link police hired with funds from the Clinton law to police killings, but it isn't a stretch to acknowledge that more police increase the likelihood of such encounters. One good example comes from the LAPD Rampart Scandal. The Rampart Division ran a particularly aggressive version of LAPD's Community Resources against Street Hoodlums program that engaged in beatings, shootings, killings, witness tampering, and evidence fixing. One of Rampart's many victims was Juan Manuel Saldana. In 1996 Rampart Division officer Kulin Patel killed twenty-one-year-old Saldana during a gang crackdown scheme. Several officers had raided an apartment building and Patel claimed that Saldana had fled down a hallway, turned toward the officers, and pointed a pistol at them, so Patel shot him. What really happened was that an unarmed Saldana fled down a hallway when the LAPD raided the building and Patel shot and wounded him as he ran. Patel, Sergeant Edward Ortiz, and others then concocted a story about how Saldana had threatened them. They also planted a gun on him. All the while, Saldana slowly bled to death.[79]

The LAPD quickly excused the officers who killed Juan Manuel Saldana. His life seemed to matter little: All the police had to say was that he was a gang member to justify the killing, similar to the use of the label "bandit" to excuse killings of Mexican-origin people in the past. Saldana's family and friends knew otherwise.[80] He didn't have a gun and had never shot one. Also wounded in the same attack, Oscar Peralta, Saldana's friend, stated, "Neither me or my homeboy [Saldana] ever shot a gun. We just liked to party."[81] When the city began to detail the extent of the Rampart Scandal in 1999, Saldana's story finally saw the light of day.[82] Former Rampart officer Rafael Perez gave testimony against his colleagues and explained the details of what happened the night Patel killed Saldana. According to Perez, Saldana was running down the hallway away from the officers when Patel fired. Perez, standing over the wounded Saldana, stated, "I'm looking at the guy. And I know there's no gun. There's—there's no gun." One of the other officers then placed a handgun near Saldana. All the while, a confused Saldana kept saying, "Man, what's going on?" as he slowly died. In sum, Saldana was yet another ley fuga killing.[83]

The Los Angeles government initiated a series of investigations into the Rampart Scandal, in which Saldana appeared prominently.[84] The LAPD charged officers, including Kulin Patel, with misconduct for their handling of Saldana.[85] After months of hearings, the disciplinary board in 2001 exonerated Patel and the other officers involved.[86] Saldana's family sued, but their lawsuit went nowhere. A judge declared that they didn't have standing to sue on Saldana's behalf.[87] Although many officers received various punishments, the full extent of the Rampart Scandal remains unknown. Los Angeles accepted a consent decree that gave the federal government oversight of the LAPD for five years. Juan Manuel Saldana never got justice.[88]

In Texas, Luis Alfonso Torres offers compelling evidence of how someone suffering a health crisis can fall prey to police violence. Torres, an authorized Mexican immigrant, had worked hard and eventually gained skills in metalwork that allowed him access to good jobs in Houston-area petrochemical refineries. He had visited family in Baytown in January 2002 when he began to feel ill. Torres received medical care at an area hospital, but after being discharged he began to feel sick again. His family called for medical assistance fearing he was suffering a heart attack. Torres refused this aid, telling paramedics he just needed to go for a walk. When he left for this walk, his brother called 911. Paramedics located Torres, who again refused treatment. For some reason they reported to Baytown police that he was armed and intoxicated, neither of which was true. They transformed a person experiencing a medical emergency into a dangerous threat.[89]

The communication about Torres's demeanor set the stage for how police would treat him. Four officers located him and ordered him to submit to a pat-down search. Torres backed away from the officers. They wrestled him to the ground, punched him, placed a knee on his neck, and sprayed him with pepper spray. After handcuffing Torres, the officers noticed that he wasn't moving or breathing. Paramedics then transported him to a hospital, where he died.[90]

Grainy police dash cam video caught the incident. It showed that Torres appeared to cooperate with officers and was neither violent nor resistant. Why they chose to throw him to the ground and brutalize him remains unclear. Although the information from the paramedics was wrong, the officers should have easily surmised that. The Baytown PD placed Officers Bert Dillow and Micah Aldred and Sergeant Rodney Evans, all of whom had participated in beating Torres, as well as Chad Billeaud, who arrived on the scene after the beating had ended, on paid administrative leave while the department investigated. But early on it appeared likely that the police would find the officers' actions justifiable. Baytown police chief Byron Jones, for instance, said, "There were no errors at all." He also stated that "Mr. Torres resisted to the extent that pepper spray was required to detain him." The dash cam video belied such a statement.[91]

Local people organized to protest the killing of Juan Alfonso Torres. They formed a new group called United Concerned Citizens of Baytown to monitor police and organize protests. Other groups such as the League of United Latin American Citizens joined these efforts. Activists held several protests, most notably a candlelight vigil in Magnolia Park, the center of Houston's east side Latino/a/x community.[92] The family hired attorney Michael Solar to investigate. He discovered that Chief Jones's remarks did not comport with autopsy photos, which showed that Torres had been very badly beaten. Solar and others put pressure on Baytown police to release the dash cam video, which they refused to do. That became additionally irksome when Harris County medical examiner Joye Carter declared Torres's death a "homicide caused by repeated blunt force trauma and mechanical strangulation." When the Baytown PD finally released the video, it seemed to confirm Carter's findings.[93]

Despite the medical examiner's report, the dash cam video, and the autopsy evidence, the Harris County grand jury declined to indict the officers. The Baytown PD quickly cleared and reinstated them.[94] Groups including United Concerned Citizens of Baytown put pressure on the Department of Justice to investigate the case, to no avail. Torres's widow, Yolanda, also filed a wrongful death suit against the officers. She settled for $350,000. As in other locales, not much changed, the protests petered out, and Luis Alfonso Torres received no justice.[95]

Two Houston cases followed the Torres case in 2003, both involving children needlessly killed by police. The first was fifteen-year-old Jose Vargas Jr., followed by fourteen-year-old Eli Eloy Escobar II. The slaying of Vargas happened on Halloween night in 2003. He had driven his mom's Chevy Blazer to a local movie theater. His presence aroused the suspicion of HPD officer Richard Butler, who moonlighted as a security guard at the theater. Although not on duty for HPD and out of uniform, Butler decided to follow Vargas in his own vehicle when he left the theater. When Vargas stopped at a traffic light, Butler exited his vehicle, approached Vargas's, drew his handgun, and pointed it at Vargas through his open window. Vargas put the vehicle in motion; Butler fired. That shot hit Vargas in the chest. He died at an area hospital.[96]

Eli Escobar was playing video games at a friend's house on November 21, 2003, when HPD officers Arthur Carbonneau and Ronald Olivo showed up. The officers initially went looking for a child named Oscar who had punched another kid in the face. Carbonneau knocked on the door of the apartment and demanded that the boys come outside. They did and the officers quickly determined that Escobar and his friends were not Oscar. But Carbonneau decided to illegally search the apartment and then ordered the boys to face a wall so that he could search them (also illegal). Escobar began to walk away. Carbonneau grabbed him by the shoulder and attempted to stop him, at which point Escobar said, "Leave me alone, I didn't do anything." Carbonneau and Olivo then wrestled Escobar to the ground. At some point Carbonneau withdrew his gun and pointed it at Escobar. A scared Escobar begged for his mother. As they continued to struggle, Carbonneau fired. The shot hit Escobar in the forehead and killed him instantly.[97]

Since these two killings happened within weeks of one another, involved unarmed children, and had questionable circumstances, the local media and government agencies tended to lump them together. The FBI began investigating both cases that November.[98] The Houston Police Department suspended Richard Butler while an internal investigation went forward. But it seemed pretty clear which way the tide would turn in this case. The HPD argued early on that the shooting was accidental, that the gun discharged when Vargas put the vehicle in motion and the frame of the SUV's window struck Butler's arm. In short, they blamed Vargas for the shooting. The Harris County grand jury did not indict Butler.[99] The department did fire him, but Butler appealed to the civil service commission, which reinstated him.[100] Vargas's family sued the HPD, the theater, and Butler himself. In 2008 they settled with the theater for an undisclosed amount and with the City of Houston for $45,000.[101]

As for Eli Escobar, the department suspended Carbonneau with pay while they investigated. The Harris County grand jury indicted him on a charge of murder in March 2004.[102] Escobar's parents also brought suit for the wrongful death of their child. Sadly, Eli had been their "miracle baby" after numerous miscarriages.[103] A number of police officials blamed the shooting on the poor training officers received. Carbonneau, for instance, somehow didn't receive training on when and in what circumstances he should draw his weapon, which made little sense.[104]

Arthur Carbonneau resigned from the HPD. In 2005 a jury found him guilty and convicted him of criminally negligent homicide. They sentenced him to sixty days in jail and five years of probation.[105] That light sentence angered local people, although it was somewhat unusual given that district attorneys rarely prosecute police officers for killing people.[106] In 2008, the City of Houston settled the lawsuit brought by Escobar's parents. The settlement did two things of importance: it gave the family $1.5 million for the wrongful death of their son (that is of course small recompense for the senseless killing of a child), and it implemented a new standard known as the Escobar Rule. The rule mandates that officers must holster their weapon during a struggle with an individual or, if that's not possible, keep their finger off the trigger of their gun when in a struggle. At the academy cadets learn about Eli Escobar and have to pass a test demonstrating their ability to handle a firearm during a stressful encounter. Police officers have to annually recertify their firearms competency and review the parameters of the Escobar Rule.[107]

The death of Jose Guerena in Arizona serves as a good example of the problem of militarized policing. A veteran of the US Marine Corps who had served two tours during the First Gulf War, Guerena had returned to his hometown of Tucson and found work at ASARCO's Mission Mine. He was married and had two children. On the morning of May 5, 2011, officers from a multiagency SWAT Team, which included the Sahuarita, Oro Valley, and Marana Police Departments as well as the Pima County Sheriff's Department, executed a search warrant for an alleged drug smuggling operation at

Guerena's home. His spouse, Vanessa, woke him after she saw a dark figure pass by a window. He retrieved his AR-15 rifle and secured Vanessa and their four-year-old child in a closet (their other child was at school). As Guerena investigated, the front door burst open and shots rang out. He died on the floor of his home.[108]

The initial reporting, based on statements from law enforcement, claimed that Guerena had fired at the officers and they returned fire, killing him.[109] But data soon came to light that disputed these claims. Some officers reported having heard shots or seeing muzzle flash and wood splintering around Guerena's door and thought he was shooting at them, but in fact the bullets came from other officers. Newspapers then had to explain that not only had Guerena not fired his gun but the safety was still on.[110] Other troubling facts and inconsistencies emerged. The total time from approaching his front door to shooting him was thirty-eight seconds. SWAT officers fired seventy-one times in seven seconds. Authorities originally said that police had shot Guerena sixty times, later revised to twenty-two times. He was not involved in a drug scheme; police found nothing drug related or illegal after searching his home.[111]

Matters only got worse the following week when Pima County sheriff Clarence Dupnik declined to answer questions about the killing and decided not to release any information until an investigation had concluded.[112] Things got weirder. Several of the officers involved in the botched raid hired an attorney who released information that law enforcement had found a cache of weapons and body armor at Guerena's home, that this proved he worked with a home invasion crew, and that the warrant concerned home invasion crimes *and* drugs.[113] Most of these statements were lies that only made the events leading to Guerena's killing more confusing.

Finally, after nearly a month had passed, Sheriff Dupnik released the investigative material from the raid. It turned out the sheriff's office had executed a warrant for Guerena, and several family members at several other homes, believing them to be involved in a massive marijuana smuggling scheme. The officers had banged on Guerena's front door and identified themselves, but they did so as other officers detonated flash bang grenades in the backyard, which meant that it was unlikely anyone in the house had heard SWAT identify itself. When the officers breached the front door, they saw a crouched Guerena aiming his gun at them. So they opened fire. The SWAT team didn't even make it inside the house; they shot at Guerena from just outside the front door. They then sent in a robot to make sure the home was clear. All the while Vanessa Guerena begged 911 operators and the officers for medical aid for her husband. That aid never came and likely could not have helped Jose Guerena. The SWAT team found no drugs, cash, or anything implicating him in a drug trafficking operation.[114]

A month after the killing of Jose Guerena, Sheriff Dupnik released additional information about the sting. He noted that the sheriff's department had surveilled various members of the Guerena family for twenty months but had conducted surveillance of Jose Guerena's home for two months, indicating that he was a late addition. He also revealed Guerena's brothers, Alejandro and Gerardo, as the main targets of the raid.[115] He repeated the falsehood that once officers had breached the front door, they saw muzzle flashes from Guerena. Dupnik noted that when an officer tripped and fell, some of his colleagues believed that Guerena had shot him. He said the officers feared for their lives even though they had created the situation that led to their fear. The sheriff also admitted that they had found nothing illegal in Guerena's home.[116]

The Pima County district attorney's office quickly cleared the officers involved in the killing of Jose Guerena of wrongdoing. David Berkman, the county's chief criminal deputy attorney, noted that "the officers were mistaken in believing that Mr. Guerena fired at them. However, when Mr. Guerena raised an AR-15 semiautomatic rifle in their direction, they needed to stop the deadly threat against them."[117] Attorney Christopher Scileppi, who represented Vanessa Guerena, blasted the decision, saying, "This was a biased investigation; in fact it's hardly an investigation." Vanessa Guerena filed a $20 million wrongful death suit against the law enforcement agencies involved in the raid. In 2013, she accepted a settlement of $3.4 million.[118]

Nearly a year after the raid, law enforcement finally made its first arrests of individuals suspected in the drug trafficking scheme, all family members who also had their homes raided the day police killed Guerena. They arrested Alejandro and Gerardo Guerena on a host of charges related to the drug trafficking scheme.[119] Authorities seemed to have difficulty making the charges stick, though. Most pleaded out and received probation or weekend jail sentences. Alejandro Guerena, the alleged mastermind of the drug ring, got five years' probation and 105 days in jail after he pleaded guilty to attempted possession of marijuana for sale and conspiracy to commit money laundering.[120] These lame charges and sentences indicate that law enforcement seemingly exaggerated the need for the raid. Sheriff Dupnik still found it necessary to gloat, publishing an op-ed in the *Arizona Daily Star* praising the SWAT team and defining it as a lone bulwark standing between society and lawlessness.

His words show that he might have made for a good sheriff in the nineteenth century; in the twenty-first century they were callous and wrong.[121]

The facts of the case belied the sheriff's assertions. First, the SWAT team killed Jose Guerena as he did something many Americans might do: defend their home from a potential invader. He likely did not know the people who broke down his door were law enforcement. He may have surmised it fairly quickly, though, which probably explains why he didn't fire his gun. Former SWAT member Larry Seligman noted that he believed Guerena "thought he was being home-invaded and did not know he was going to engage a SWAT team."[122] Second, the botched nature of the raid, with officers claiming to see muzzle flash or wood splintering or an officer tripping as proof that Guerena had shot at them, was almost comical. The aftermath of the raid caught officers laughing and gloating. "That was like a movie," one of them stated. "I just started boom, boom, boom, boom," another said. One officer actually noted that Guerena did not shoot, "Well, he waited, he waited and once Hector came up . . ." (Hector was the officer who fell, leading the others to think that Guerena shot him). This statement indicates officers knew Guerena had not shot at them and this could have given them a chance to announce themselves again and defuse the situation.[123] Others in law enforcement criticized the whole operation. Some critiqued the vaguely worded warrant, which described Guerena only as "the muscle" of the drug trafficking operation, and wondered how the warrant got issued and signed in the first place.[124] US Army Staff Sergeant Anthony Schiessl, who had years of experience in urban warfare, used words such as "amateur, undisciplined, unrehearsed and ineffective" to describe the raid.[125] SWAT operations have to be precise and well executed; this one was not.

The raid that killed Jose Guerena exemplified another aspect of modern policing: the militarization of police. SWAT rolled up on Guerena's home in an armored vehicle and with weapons and body armor secured through the 1033 Program. Subsequent reports showed that Pima County had received nearly $6 million in aid through the program.[126] The officers came armed for bear to track down someone described as "the muscle," which possibly predisposed them to see Guerena as more of a threat than he was. Guerena exercised "trigger discipline" because he had been trained to do so in the military. The officers did not. They had the weapons and technology of war but evidently not the training to know how and when to use them. Guerena paid for their ineptitude with his life. He was not a drug runner, not "the muscle," and had not engaged in illegal activity. Jose Guerena deserved respect for his service to the country; instead he got shot twenty-two times and died in his own home.

Other police killings show what happens when law enforcement deals with individuals suffering a mental health challenge. The killing of Anthony Nuñez in San Jose, California, in July 2016 offers a compelling example of how local governments task police with jobs such as mental health crisis intervention that they should not do. When officers respond to these emergency calls, they unsurprisingly treat these cases like police and not like health care providers. The results are often disastrous. Nuñez had a history of mental health challenges, particularly depression. On July 4, 2016, he attempted to end his life by shooting himself in the head, but he only wounded himself. A number of San Jose police officers responded and found a disoriented Nuñez walking erratically in and out of his house. The officers claimed he still had the gun. At one point, Nuñez allegedly pointed the gun at the officers, two of whom opened fire with AR-15 rifles from across the street and killed him.[127]

The family disputed police claims that Nuñez had a gun and that he had threatened officers. They stated that he was unarmed and they questioned why police refused to let them intervene to help him. A neighbor who witnessed the shooting also stated that Nuñez did not have a gun when police shot him.[128] Chief of Police Eddie Garcia denied these claims. Per standard procedure he placed the two officers, later identified as Michael Santos and Anthony Vizzusi, on paid leave. A year later the Santa Clara County district attorney cleared the officers of wrongdoing, justifying their use of force because Nuñez had pointed a gun at them.[129]

Nuñez's family sued the San Jose Police Department for excessive force and wrongful death. They claimed that a family member had taken the gun from Nuñez and hidden it, so he was unarmed when police shot him. They had a good deal of proof to back up this claim, including contradictory accounts of the shooting from police, video surveillance, and eyewitnesses. They also noted that Nuñez had shot himself twice, indicating that he was probably severely debilitated.[130] They prevailed in court. The jury determined that Officers Santos and Vizzusi had used excessive force when they shot Nuñez, that the police had lied about his threatening gestures, and that he was unarmed. The family received $2.65 million in damages.[131]

Anthony Nuñez demonstrates how police often treat individuals suffering from a mental health challenge. He needed help. He didn't get it. Deaths like this have been a consistent problem in American policing, especially over the past few decades. While city governments cut budgets by cutting health care workers, the group tasked to pick up the slack are the police. But this isn't their job, and to task them with it is inappropriate. It is also unfair to individuals such as Anthony Nuñez, who needed mental health aid and not law enforcement.

The past thirty years have represented a fundamental shift in policing in the Southwest specifically and in American policing more broadly. The years of protest and reform gave way to an increased focus on law and order, one promoted by both political parties nationally and locally. That focus meant more police officers, a more militaristic kind of policing, and new jails and prisons to house more incarcerated people. The result of all of this has been more violent encounters between police and communities of color, frequently resulting in the police killings of individuals such as Eli Escobar or Jose Guerena or Anthony Nuñez.

A chief culprit in bringing forth this modern, heavy-handed kind of policing was the Clinton Crime Law. While the addition of more than 200,000 new police officers gave American police forces an unprecedented level of new power, the other aspects of the law, as well as subsequent legislation, linked policing to the drug trade and gang activity that penalized drug crimes and gang affiliation and flooded jails and prisons with incarcerated people. None of this stopped gangs or affected the drug trade. None of it lowered crime rates, which had been dropping before these modifications to the criminal justice system and continued to do so.

Alterations to the criminal justice system uniquely hurt communities of color. In the Southwest, Mexican Americans, other Latino/a/x people, and African Americans have felt the brunt of these modifications. Arrest rates and incarceration rates have disproportionately impacted Latino/a/x people. The massive increase in police officers and police budgets meant that work done by other professionals, especially mental health workers, got shunted to police. New policing strategies such as broken windows policing and SARA actually put officers close to communities of color, which only facilitated more violent encounters.

Latino/a/x people responded to the overpolicing and violence they experienced with protests, with new reform ideas such as a national civilian review board, and with lawsuits, just to name a few. But in most cases, they received limited or no justice. The officers who killed Jose Guerena or who beat down Peter Moreno went unpunished. Of course, the families of Guerena, Moreno, and other victims won lawsuits, but that seems a small victory considering that the officers received no punishment or sanction and the law enforcement climate that caused such violence did not change. Even when justice prevailed, it seemed fairly hollow. Eli Escobar, yet another child killed by police, lost his life needlessly; Arthur Carbonneau got fired and a sixty-day jail sentence for killing a kid. Sixty days. For a convicted murderer of a fourteen-year-old, one might have expected a harsher sentence. It is good that the Houston Police Department adopted the Escobar Rule, but the fact that a child had to die to get a rule that most everyone would assume is a logical police practice is as reprehensible as it is pointless. Unlike Houston, most police forces in the Southwest successfully resisted reform efforts. Mexican Americans, and other ethnic communities, now find themselves largely incapable of overcoming a police regime that has the power to resist, subvert, or ignore their demands. Law enforcement, in essence, holds all the cards. In the Southwest, as in other parts of the country, there is no justice and there is no peace.

CONCLUSION

I began this book by detailing a series of police killings of Mexican American young people. I also noted that such killings happened in our past and that they continue to happen today. This conclusion ends on the same unfortunate note. Police continue to kill Mexican American youths, as well as young folks from other ethnoracial groups (and of course people of all ages, too) in ways that they, their parents, and their friends are powerless to stop. The occurrence of such events also happens well outside of the Southwest as the Mexican American population has grown and expanded.

One police killing of a child that garnered a great of attention and protest activism was that of Andy Lopez. In October 2013, thirteen-year-old Lopez was walking to a friend's house in Santa Rosa, California. Two Sonoma County deputy sheriffs, Erick Gelhaus and Michael Schemmel, spotted Lopez while out on patrol. He had an airsoft pellet rifle that resembled an AK-47 and was on his way to return it to his friend, to whom it belonged. Gelhaus and Schemmel approached Lopez from behind, activated their squad car's lights, and "chirped" the siren. Gelhaus exited the vehicle and ordered Lopez to drop the gun. According to the officers, Lopez turned toward them and appeared to raise the barrel of the gun. Gelhaus opened fire. He shot eight times, seven bullets hit Lopez, and he died at the scene.[1]

Evidence soon began to emerge that complicated this narrative. Whereas the officers stated that Lopez had begun to train the gun on them, eyewitnesses disputed that assertion and said that it remained pointed at the ground. The officers said that Lopez had ignored their commands, but so little time

Protestors march in Santa Rosa, California, on October 29, 2013, to decry the police killing of fourteen-year-old Andy Lopez. These young women hold signs with Lopez's likeness as well as the message "I am Andy Lopez and my life matters." That message exemplifies how the mobilizing efforts of the Black Lives Matter movement had been picked up by other communities of color. Lopez's killing later motivated the formation of IOLERO, Santa Rosa County's community outreach and civilian review body, in 2015. *Photo by Marcio Jose Sanchez, Associated Press.*

passed between their arrival and the shooting that this seemed unlikely. Since the officers approached from behind, Lopez had to turn around to face them and he barely had the time to do that. He, quite literally, wasn't given the chance to obey their commands. Gelhaus later stated that he opened fire after "a couple seconds." The estimate for how much time passed between the siren chip and the shooting was three seconds. The total amount of time from the officers' arrival to the shooting was about twenty seconds. Like the case of Tamir Rice, which occurred a year later, Gelhaus shot Lopez mere seconds after he exited his vehicle.[2]

Other contradictory evidence also came to light. Some weapons experts questioned the officers' account that they thought Lopez had a real gun. Although someone had removed the orange tip indicating that the gun was a toy, critics believed that Gelhaus should have known it was not a real AK-47 (there are noticeable differences between the toy and the real gun). Even one of the witnesses stated that they thought the gun "looked fake."[3] A trained officer should easily have noticed these details, especially one like Gelhaus, a firearms expert who had served as a shooting instructor and gun range master for his department for nearly twenty years.[4]

The Sonoma County Sheriff's Office put Gelhaus and Schemmel on administrative leave while it, as well as the FBI, launched an investigation. They also stated that Gelhaus "was fearful that he was going to be shot," setting the stage for an "objectively reasonable" defense. The Latino/a/x community didn't buy it. Hundreds turned out for major protests only days after Lopez died. Local people questioned whether Gelhaus actually feared for his life or simply didn't care about Lopez's since he was Mexican American. Others saw the police interaction as an example of racial profiling. Protests continued. On October 29, 2013, 1,000 people turned out for a march and rally. They carried signs with a likeness of Andy Lopez that said, "I Am Andy Lopez and My Life Matters."[5]

As with so many other killings of Mexican and Mexican American children, Andy's mother and father, Rodrigo and Sujey, became the faces of a campaign for justice for their son. While they joined the protests, they also filed a wrongful death suit in November 1, 2013. They did not believe that Lopez represented a threat and that the officers had not received adequate training for the use of deadly force.[6] Protestors and Lopez's parents also called for the establishment of a police-civilian review board to monitor police shootings and complaints of excessive force. Sonoma County responded by forming the Community and Local Law Enforcement Task Force to investigate founding such a committee.[7]

The Sonoma County Sheriff's Office cleared Erick Gelhaus of wrongdoing in December 2013. They found that he had followed department use of force guidelines. He returned to active duty.[8] In July 2014, District Attorney Jill Ravitch decided not to pursue charges against Gelhaus. Her reasoning mirrored other cases: she blamed Lopez for his own death because he had THC in his bloodstream, indicating that he had smoked marijuana at some point that day. For some, this makes sense, for others it seems like an excuse designed to exculpate Gelhaus without genuinely scrutinizing his actions.[9] In July 2015 the Justice Department declined to prosecute Gelhaus.[10] Andy Lopez's parents finally got some relief in 2018 when Sonoma County settled their lawsuit for $3 million, again small compensation for the death of a child.[11]

What came next mattered more. The initial Sonoma County Community and Local Law Enforcement Task Force paved the way for the formation of the Independent Office of Law Enforcement Review and Outreach (IOLERO).

Founded in 2015, IOLERO is in essence a civilian review board and a community outreach program. It investigates use of force charges, civil rights violations, and other forms of alleged police misconduct. The group formed with the support of the community, the county government, and the sheriff's office.[12]

IOLERO's quick development, its generally broad mandate, and the willingness of law enforcement and county officials to support it suggests that officials took the tragic death of Andy Lopez seriously. But I would argue that Andy Lopez should still be alive. Pedro Erik Villanueva, nineteen, killed in Fullerton in July 2016 by two plainclothes California Highway Patrol officers, should still be alive.[13] Antonio Arce, killed in Tempe on January 16, 2019, by Officer Joseph Jaen—another fake gun, ley fuga killing—should still be alive.[14] Adam Toledo, thirteen years old, killed by Chicago police on March 29, 2021, should still be alive.[15]

Such shootings continue. Take, for example, the case of Erik Cantu. On the night of October 2, 2022, the seventeen-year-old Cantu sat in his car eating a hamburger with his girlfriend when San Antonio police officer James Brennand opened the car door, his service pistol drawn, and told Cantu "get out of the car." The shocked youth, with a mouth full of food, responded "What?" while looking about nervously and putting the car in reverse. As he backed up, Brennand fired five times. Cantu continued driving away and Brennand fired five times more at the departing vehicle. Cantu was stopped minutes later by other officers and taken to a nearby hospital. He had been shot at least four times, with one bullet lodged near his heart and another that did major damage to his stomach and digestive tract. He spent seven weeks in the hospital and was released in late November, only to be readmitted to the hospital in December after suffering complications to the injuries to his digestive track.[16]

The initial news reporting on this incident followed police accounts closely. Brennand, for example, had reported to dispatch moments before he opened Cantu's car door that the vehicle was stolen and had evaded him the night before. Neither of these things was true, although Cantu's car did have a license plate registered to another vehicle. The San Antonio Police Department quickly fired Officer Brennand. While the district attorney initially planned to charge Cantu, she decided not to, although it is unclear what law, if any, he had violated. The state did bring charges of two counts of aggravated assault by a public servant and single count of attempted murder against Brennand. He was indicted on those charges, although the district attorney's office amended the attempted murder charge to deadly conduct. He is awaiting trial.[17]

The circumstances of this case, like so many others discussed in this book, would suggest that law enforcement does not care to protect and serve members of the Mexican American community. Erik Cantu couldn't even sit in his car and eat a hamburger. James Brennand "thought" the car was stolen. He perhaps should have thought a little harder before he approached a vehicle occupied by a teenage boy and his teenage girlfriend with a gun drawn. Cantu's reaction doesn't seem all that surprising: a stranger opened his car door, said, "Get out," and had a gun pointed at him. Brennand claimed Cantu's car door hit his arm, causing him to fire—five times!—but the video shows that he was never in danger. He certainly can't explain why he fired five more times at a departing vehicle. This whole unusual event seems as if it simply never should have happened; the fact that it occurred and occurred the way it did quite literally makes no sense. But it did happen and it continues to happen to other people across the country.

Mexican-origin people have had to deal with similar unusual occurrences for nearly 200 years. Much of this early history is discussed in *Borders of Violence and Justice*. In the 1930s and 1940 the wave of pachuco hysteria caused some similar strange events. The shooting death of Santos Rodriguez strikes me as pretty unusual. The police entrapment and killing of Black Berets Antonio Cordova and Rito Canales feels pretty strange. The murder of Jose "Joe" Campos Torres is as bizarre and cruel as it was unnecessary. The railroading of Francisco "Kiko" Martínez and Winnergate were obvious abuses of the system that anyone could see. The police shooting of Jose Guerena was peculiar both in its justification and in the tragically comic way it happened. At some point, these unusual occurrences can no longer be explained as unusual. After 200 years they are simply standard police practice.

The dedication and patience and decency of the Mexican-origin community in the face of this unrelenting assault is therefore admirable. Mexican Americans worked hard to try to make law enforcement work better and more fairly. Going back to the pachuco hysteria we can see Mexican American activists trying to encourage the system to act justly. In the post–Zoot Suit Riots investigations this was certainly clear. Similarly, in Houston the desire of Mexican Americans that the Houston Police Department form the Latin Squad was equally about reform and equitable treatment. Some critics argued that the Chicano movement was antipolice. But the record shows instead that they worked conscientiously for reform, and even when groups advocated for police abolition, as the Albuquerque Black Berets had, they still worked with police for reform. In the early period of the movement Chicanos simply demanded that police stop killing Mexican-origin people. Although protests in places such as Dallas led to uprisings, for example after the killing of Santos Rodriguez, the goal of those protests was reform, which did come. When Chicanos protested in the Rito Canales and Antonio Cordova cases, or the Hanigan case, or the Jose Sinohui case, or the Danny Vasquez case, or the Larry Lozano case, or the Joe Campos Torres case, or the Hector Santoscoy case, or the Fred Páez case, or the Jose Guerena case, or the Anthony Nuñez case, or the Andy Lopez case, among so, so many others, they demanded better treatment. They demanded that the system behave in a more equitable fashion. They demanded that their people not be killed over trivial things. They demanded justice.

In many cases, city governments and law enforcement responded to those demands. The level of reform and the variety of ideas that came to the fore in the 1960s and 1970s especially was impressive: revised constitutional protections that came out of the *Hernandez, Escobar,* and *Miranda* cases; the idea of community or human relations commissions; the work of outreach officers such as Lynn Bray, Ralph Marmion, John Blaisdell, and Emmett Rubio; Police Athletic Leagues; police storefronts; police-civilian review boards; modified police shooting policies; "minority recruitment programs"; the hiring of female officers of color; internal affairs departments; language and cultural training; psychological testing; jail and prison reform; reform-minded police chiefs such as Donald Byrd, Robert Stover, and Ruben Ortega; and new rules such as the Escobar Rule in Houston. The list of reforms or attempted reform ideas was remarkable. The fact that many of these reforms were implemented and worked is noteworthy.

Reforms work, until they don't. In numerous locales, city governments undid the reforms of the 1960s and 1970s when budgets tightened in the 1980s. As municipal revenues in major cities shrank, local government shifted the responsibility for the social service and psychological assistance programs that in many cases were part of the hard-won reforms of the previous decade to law enforcement. The use of police to combat the AIDS crisis in the 1980s is a clear-cut example of this shifting of duties. Cutting the budget of staff who assist people in a mental health crisis and shifting that duty to law enforcement is the late twentieth- and early twenty-first-century version of the same thing. For some reason slashing municipal budgets for social and medical workers is acceptable while cutting the budgets of police is not, which doesn't make a lot of sense. It's also not fair to law enforcement. Police, even when well trained, tend to look at a mental health crisis through a law enforcement lens. Then when they behave like police, they get blamed for acting inappropriately. That blame is somewhat misplaced in that a broader system asked law enforcement, another system, to do something it was incapable of doing.

Beginning in the 1990s things really began to get out of hand. The Clinton Crime Law created in part many of the problems we see today. The explosion in the number of police officers in this country, the huge budgets that requires, and the massive power those officers have has played a large role in many of the worst cases of police abuse and murder over the past thirty years. In many cases when people turn out to protest police abuse they are also protesting these policy changes. And yet, even after major protests over the past few years and calls for defunding or abolition of police, many major cities have instead gone in the other direction and increased funding for law enforcement. In Los Angeles, the LAPD in 2023 saw its budget climb by $123 million dollars to nearly $2 billion. While a lot of folks concerned about police power, abuse, and violence had hoped that local communities might choose to invest less in police and more in social services, as per usual LA has instead doubled down on law enforcement.[18]

Today some law enforcement agencies that worked hard to make change in the sixties and seventies are, sadly, regarded as some of the most corrupt and violent. The Albuquerque Police Department after civil rights era reforms and improvement has suffered through a number of financial scandals and cases of police violence. The city has one of the highest rates of officer-involved shootings in the country. The Albuquerque PD has been under a consent decree with the federal government since 2014 and in 2023 revised its use of force policy for the umpteenth time.[19] In fact, numerous Southwestern cities are among the worst when ranked according to the number of residents killed by police: Phoenix, San Antonio, Los Angeles, and Houston occupy the top four spots.[20] That's a pretty sad legacy, and the activists of today seem to be continuing to fight the same battles that those in the 1960s or 1970s fought. To win reform and change, often through a great deal of hardship and pain, only to lose those things in the ensuing years is disappointing, to say the least.

The activists of the sixties and seventies, like those of today, and many of their allies—as well as some of their adversaries—wanted to see things change. They sought then a brave new world, and I would argue that for a short time, in a few locales, some of them got to live in it. But as with most brave new worlds, it was fleeting. Not only did things revert to the ways they had been before, but in some ways things got worse. I don't want a brave new world. Instead I ask simply for a changed world, one where little boys aren't executed by Russian roulette, one where grown men aren't suffocated to death, one where children can make a mistake and not pay for it with their lives, one where a person can have a mental health crisis and not end up dead, one where a teenager can enjoy a hamburger in their own car without getting shot for it. To do that we must fundamentally change law enforcement, we must fix it, we must reform it.

CODA

"What can we do to fix this situation?" Whenever I speak about policing I am invariably asked this question. I wrote *Borders of Violence and Justice* and *Brown and Blue* to give the fullest picture of Mexican-origin people and their interactions with law enforcement, to tell the story from beginning to end, and, in so doing, to show how we got to where we are today. Certainly, there are important lessons to draw from this history, but such a lengthy discussion seems to me somewhat irrelevant without an additional conversation of what we should do about how law enforcement treats Mexican-origin people, other Latino/a/x peoples, African Americans, and others. This coda, based on the findings of both books, is my attempt to do that.

In the pages that follow, I want to do a few things. First, I want to explain why often-touted reforms don't work. Second, I'd like to discuss well-known but misunderstood—and sometimes maligned—ideas, such as defund the police. Third, I want to talk about reform. Last, I'd like to give the reader some concept of what we can do to change the situation between police agencies and Mexican-origin people, and other communities to be sure. This last point has some lofty ideas, many of which are probably unworkable, but let's dream big.

That Which Does Not Work

There have been a number of so-called reforms to policing practices that have proven themselves to be failures, or perhaps in some cases partial successes. What I am talking about here is the use of technology, especially police body-worn cameras and patrol car dash cams, designed to record interactions between law enforcement and civilians. It has now almost become expected that when we learn of an example of police use of force, whatever kind of force or interaction may have occurred, we hear things like "I wonder what the body camera footage will show?" And then we are often disappointed with the results or unsure of what really happened. Body cams rarely provide a clear story; it's even rarer when the information they offer leads to any kind of sanction or prosecution if it should show that an officer acted improperly.[1]

One of the big problems with body-worn cameras is that the technology can fail, work imperfectly, or be switched off. But the bigger problem with body cams is what they're actually designed to do: augment the level of trust the public has in the police. The reason the public wants police to wear such cameras is because people often don't have faith in police accounts of events. But body cameras can't create trust. Trust has to be earned by police, which takes a lot of work. My sense is that the ship has already sailed on these things—dash cams are in most patrol cars and many departments are willing to invest in body cameras despite their deficiencies.

People also call for reform in data collection and dissemination efforts, especially data about crime and police behavior. The federal government's data collection is abysmal and state and local data aren't much better. Uniform crime reporting or data on officer use of force differs from locale to locale and reporting such data to the federal government is voluntary. But data, even good data thoughtfully analyzed, mean little without changes in police policy and practice that respond to what the data show. And those changes are often not forthcoming, which makes calls for better data a somewhat meaningless technique for reform. In sum, we cannot "technology" our way out of policing problems.[2]

Defund the Police

The idea of defunding police and police abolition are often (purposefully) misunderstood. "Defunding the police" asks that governments redirect parts of police budgets that cover non–law enforcement tasks to entities that do that work, either as a method of achieving police reform or as a first step toward abolishing police. I noted in several chapters how police officers are often required to do jobs outside of the purview of law enforcement—AIDS intervention, mental health crisis response—and when they behave in these jobs like police officers and not like social workers we blame them for their actions. But they shouldn't have been charged with doing these jobs in the

Coda

first place. Instead, nurses, doctors, social workers, or therapists should be doing these jobs. In many cases, defunding the police would actually mean restoring funding to government agencies that had their budgets cut in previous decades.[3]

When public figures like former President Barack Obama say things like, "I guess you can use a snappy slogan, like 'defund the police.' But, you know, you lost a big audience the minute you say it," or when former President Joe Biden says, "We should all agree: The answer is not to defund the police. It's to fund the police," they distort what defunding the police actually means.[4] For Obama it's about messaging, which is a pretty uninspiring reason to reject an idea. For Biden the use of opposites—defund versus fund—is a misdirection of what defunding really means. We've tried funding the police; it hasn't solved our problems. And Biden, the architect of measures such as the Clinton Crime Bill, is probably the last person we should turn to for solutions.

There's been a lot of mythmaking that has perpetuated misconceptions about defunding the police. Critics argue that police protect us from violence, so defunding the police will lead to disorder and make us less safe. Similarly, some critics suggest that defunding the police will limit law enforcement's ability to prevent crime. But police aren't tasked with protecting the public from violence, and they don't prevent crime, even though the public thinks they do. About nine out of ten calls for police service are for noncriminal events such as a noise complaint or someone experiencing a mental health crisis, which public agencies and community groups could handle. But then, one of the worst criticisms of defunding is that those groups are incapable of doing the jobs that police do, which is an aspersion that has no real basis in fact.[5]

We know that defunding works because its already been implemented in certain ways in a variety of cities. Thirty years ago, Eugene, Oregon, pioneered Crisis Assistance Helping Out on the Streets (CAHOOTS), a team of medical and social workers who respond to mental health crises and behavioral issue calls for service instead of police. Today, other cities are using CAHOOTS as a model to create their own programs. For example, Honolulu has no such response team even though 10 to 30 percent of police calls are for mental health–related issues. In 2021, then Chief of Police Susan Ballard was not only receptive to this idea but noted quite honestly that most calls to the police "should be handled elsewhere. Unfortunately when nobody else steps up, and there is nowhere else to turn to, people always turn to the police to take care of whatever the problem is." The cost savings seemed the most appealing part of adopting such a program in Hawaii: Eugene's CAHOOTS reported saving its police department around $8.5 million annually and a local clinic $14 million for ambulance services in 2018. In a larger city such as Honolulu, which is roughly double the size of Eugene, those savings would be magnified.[6]

Some people call for abolishing the police as a way to solve policing problems. Abolition of police means eliminating a police department, sometimes with the goal of replacing it with another institution. Camden, New Jersey, is often used as an example of this process. In 2011, the Camden city and county governments voted to disband the city police department and create a new county-level police department in its place. Camden had a high crime rate and police had made little headway in dealing with it. The department was also regarded as corrupt, violent, and hardboiled with the public. The new Camden County Police Department had new goals and a new orientation, one geared toward community partnership and social service.[7]

My sense about defunding police is that most Americans with a clear understanding of it would be open to some of its ideas. If we respect our doctors, nurses, and social workers, then we should let them do their jobs and not ask police to do them. Keep in mind the historic failures of not allowing professionals to do their job—having police attempt to deal with the AIDS crisis or when assisting those experiencing a mental health challenge—are as real today as they were in the past. Redirecting funds from police to hospitals, crisis intervention teams, or other government agencies makes sense. It is unfortunate that our political divides prevent us from finding common ground on this issue. My sense about abolition is that most Americans simply aren't going to be in favor of it no matter how it's framed. That being said, local communities should make decisions about defunding or abolition themselves, based on data-driven discussions of what these things are and can do to benefit a community.

Reform Works

Many pundits and scholars argue that reforming police doesn't work. Such a blanket statement has both accuracies and inaccuracies. For example, poorly thought out or executed reforms often don't work, that's true. Scholars who analyze law enforcement through the lens of institutional racism are also correct in their assessment that racist institutions often cannot be reformed.[8] But this book has shown, and *Borders of Violence and Justice* did as well, that reforms often do work. Based on my research, the problem is not that reforms don't work but rather that effective reforms get eroded during times of economic stress when cities or counties cut budgets. Or, as noted especially in chapter 8, when federal measures like the Clinton Crime Law undercut local-level reforms. But that doesn't mean that we should give up on reform.[9]

It's important to note that some of the effective reforms of the 1960s and especially the 1970s are still with us today. Many departments continue to use cultural competency or awareness training, language instruction, and other types of diversity training. That's an accomplishment that civil rights activists should be proud of. Yet when some politicians cite their reform ideas, they include these things as if they don't already exist. President Biden, for example, frequently mentioned "training" as a goal, and implicit bias training was a part of his executive order of 2022 on police reform.[10] It seems silly to me to tout a reform idea as new if it is not.

There are, though, potential new ways of implementing some existing reform ideas. For example, I spoke to a police officer who suggested expanding cultural competency and implicit bias programs by using something similar to police firearm training. Police officers often get weapons instruction via the FireArms Training Simulator (FATS), a kind of virtual reality that puts an officer or a cadet in shooting scenarios. This anonymous officer suggested a FATS-like system for cultural competency. It would give police cadets and officers training in how to better understand communities of color by putting them in a virtual scenario where they, for instance, might have to interact with an individual who speaks only Spanish. Instead of having that interaction on the streets, with all the stress that might entail, they have it in a simulator.

I think it is also worth acknowledging that some civil rights–era reforms continue to be newly implemented today in departments where they never existed before. In particular, community relations commissions and police-civilian review boards still have relevancy today. As I noted in the conclusion, Sonoma County created the Independent Office of Law Enforcement Review and Outreach in 2015 after the tragic killing of Andy Lopez, which works as a civilian review board and a community outreach program. The public wanted it, the local government and law enforcement supported it, and it appears to be working. So instead of simply saying, "Reforms don't work," I think it's probably a better idea to let communities and their leaders decide which reforms they might want, as Sonoma County did.

Dreaming Big

There are a lot of major changes we could make that not only would alter the law enforcement landscape for everyone in this country but would go a long way toward altering the broader criminal justice system. In order of the likelihood that our leaders would actually implement these reforms, we have:

- Revise Police Training. Many police academies instruct cadets with what is often referred to as the "warrior" model of policing. The idea is basically one where officers see themselves as more like soldiers who are hypervigilant and in many ways suspicious of the public. This has led to numerous examples of ego-driven policing, wherein in the least problematic cases officers who feel challenged or threatened by the public engage in an escalation of hostility to demonstrate their power or dominance and in the most problematic examples officers engage in brutality or killing. Many critics blame the spate of recent police shootings in part on the idea of policing by ego and the warrior model. As noted throughout this book, police officers often justify shooting someone by claiming that they feared for their life. That fear in part comes from the warrior model, which has trained an officer to view the public as the enemy. And since concepts of criminality are highly racialized, that enemy becomes people of color. But the public isn't the enemy and we aren't in a war. To get away from the warrior mindset, many researchers have focused on augmenting training via what is known as the guardian concept of policing. The guardian model (frequently touted as new) is one where police officers act more like social servants and work with the community in partnership. This model, as noted in various chapters in this book, is one that was successfully implemented in many Southwestern locales during the civil rights era. It was then popular and appreciated by community members. It can be again. My belief is that we should end training that leads to the warrior mindset in favor of the guardian model.[11]

- Revise Sentence Enhancements. Sentence enhancers, sometimes called charging enhancements, are extra penalties to a criminal charge beyond what is ordinarily or statutorily called for in sentencing guidelines. Three-strikes laws are a well-known example, but perhaps a better one is enhancements related to gang activity. You may commit a robbery, for which there is a sentencing length, but a robbery committed as part of a gang in many states will carry a longer sentence. While the enhancement was designed to punish gang involvement in order to dissuade people from gang activity, it hasn't worked. Moreover, a robbery is a robbery: it seems unfair to penalize someone further simply because of an affiliation. Sentence enhancements have also helped increase the population of incarcerated people. Most of them have not worked and are bad law. States should seriously consider revising many sentence enhancement statutes.[12]

- End the 1033 Program. This is the federal program that allows law enforcement agencies to purchase surplus military hardware. Most police departments do not need military-grade equipment, yet small departments such as the Moundsville Police Department in West Virginia are able to buy high-dollar military machines, in this case a $1 million Mine-Resistant Ambush Protected vehicle.[13] Perhaps a large city police department might need such a vehicle as part of its drug interdiction strategy (although not if we get rid of the War on Drugs, foreshadowing!), but what a police department of around twenty officers serving a town of 8,000 people might need it for escapes me. Many of the weapons available through the program, especially assault rifles, most police departments don't need. While a good deal of contemporary police training has led to the militarization of police (see warrior mindset), it's the 1033 Program and its predecessors that actually armed police like a military. But police officers aren't soldiers and the public isn't the enemy. We need to demilitarize police, and ending the 1033 Program, at least the sale of vehicles and weapons, would help with that process.[14]

- End the War on Crime. The original idea for a War on Crime came from President Lyndon Johnson as a part of the War on Poverty in 1965. It created the close linkages we have between local-level law enforcement and the federal government. But it was racist in its inception, singling out Black men as the cause of American crime problems. The actual aspects of the War on Crime include such things as federally funded law enforcement training, grants for military equipment (LBJ's version of the 1033 Program), a linking of law enforcement with social services providers (which some critics see as making social work policing), mandatory minimum sentencing guidelines, augmented jail sentences for drug crimes, and three-strikes laws, among others. The problem with the idea of the War on Crime, beyond how it has led to mass incarceration and devastated communities of color, is that it has never worked. And they knew it back in 1968. As Attorney General Nicholas Katzenbach later noted, "It proved to be a dreadful mistake. You are meant to win wars, and the War on Crime was in a sense an unwinnable war." Katzenbach was right. The War on Crime can't be won. We should end it.[15]

- Cease Broken Windows Policing. As noted throughout this book, the broken windows theory purports that signs of social disorder or decay (graffiti, an abandoned car, the proverbial broken window) motivate further disorder, especially crime. Thus, if police monitor or investigate the broken window, they can halt the disorder (that is, crime) before it gets out of hand. This means that police are actively and always looking for criminal activity, especially in areas with said broken windows (most often areas with low socioeconomic status). There are several critiques of the broken windows theory. One, there is little to no correlation between disorder and crime. Two, it has never been clear if broken windows policing reduces crime. Three, many communities have taken the broken windows model and augmented it with more harmful programs such as stop and frisk in New York City or "papers, please" policing in Arizona. Four, the impact of broken windows policing has most often fallen on communities of color. Many of the most notorious examples of police abuse and killing over the past several decades have come from police officers engaged in broken windows policing. We should stop broken windows policing.[16]

- Overturn the "Objectively Reasonable" Standard and Qualified Immunity. Both have allowed police officers to abuse or kill members of the public and then escape accountability. The "objectively reasonable" standard came out of the *Graham v. Connor* Supreme Court decision of 1989, which determined, "All claims that law enforcement officials have used excessive force—deadly or not—in the course of an arrest, investigatory stop, or other 'seizure' of a free citizen are properly analyzed under the Fourth Amendment's 'objective reasonableness' standard, rather than under a substantive due process standard." This means that constitutional due process rights as enumerated in the Fifth and Fourteenth Amendments have no merit in such cases and instead the "objective reasonable" standard replaces them. That standard basically asks, "Given the situation under scrutiny, would a reasonable person in a similar role or capacity act in the same way?" In many cases of police brutality or a questionable shooting, law enforcement is exonerated using this test. For example, after the Pima County SWAT team killed Jose Guerena, its members were cleared by the district attorney's office because they "concluded that the use of deadly forces by the SWAT Team members was reasonable and justified under the law." In that case even though Guerena had reason to arm himself and did not fire his gun, the officers (who of course instigated the encounter) justified his killing through their fear that their lives were in danger.[17] Qualified immunity is kind of the civil version of "objective reasonableness." It shields law enforcement from personal liability for abusing or killing a person. The problem with both of these things is that they allow officers who commit egregious acts to go unpunished based on fairly flimsy excuses such as "I was afraid." These get-out-of-jail-free cards have increased the level of distrust the public has for the police. Both need revision.

- Stop "Papers, Please" Policing. We should always be concerned when states find ways to legalize discrimination. While many locales occasionally engaged in "papers, please" policing before the turn of the twenty-first century, Arizona's SB 1070 law of 2010 serves as the standout example. But there are problems beyond the racial profiling. Such laws, for example, make us less safe because they encourage communities of color not to report crime out of fear that doing so will lead to an interaction with law enforcement. We also know that many in law enforcement oppose "papers, please" policing. As I have shown throughout this book, there are numerous examples of the historic problems with "papers, please" policing. It needs to go.[18]

- Create a National Use of Force Standard. There is currently no federal standard for police use of force. Instead, state and local-level law dictates the rules regarding law enforcement's use of force. In the wake of George Floyd's murder by Derek Chauvin in 2020 many states began revising their use of force policies. For example, states have banned chokeholds and other neck restraints, have outlawed deadly force in nonviolent or misdemeanor cases, or have restricted the use of deadly force on fleeing individuals (ley fuga is still legal in many states). Many of these evolutions have also included additional measures such as de-escalation training. A federal, uniform policy for all law enforcement agencies to follow would standardize police use of force and allow for clear ramifications for breaches of that standard. All police agencies would have the same requirements and punishment wouldn't vary by jurisdiction. A federal use of force standard is long overdue.[19]

- End the War on Drugs. As noted in chapter 8, the War on Drugs has a long history. Although I have focused on the aspects of this campaign related to the United States, especially the Southwest, it is a global effort. It has been, is, and most likely will continue to be a failure. It has never curbed or reduced drug use; it has rarely restricted the supply of drugs. What it has done is led in part to a massive number of imprisonments for drug-related crimes. Like other programs, the War in Drugs is rooted in racism. It originally began as an attack on Black men and today disproportionately criminalizes people of color. It has led to the militarized, overpolicing that has plagued communities of color. Its global dimensions have caused pain and hardship in countries such as Colombia, without measurable success. There is a certain cyclical nature to the public's fear of drugs. In the 1970s it was heroin, in the 1980s crack, in the early 2000s crystal meth, and today fentanyl. In each case fear drove an overblown response that probably ended up hurting a lot more people than the drugs did. Some cities and states are already engaged in ending the War on Drugs in their communities by decriminalizing drug charges, releasing people with drug convictions, and legalizing some drugs such as marijuana. That's a start, but we need to go further. The War on Drugs is a failure of colossal proportions, and after fifty years of failure it's time for it to end.[20]

These are some ideas, but there are others out there. My vision for a modern, effective police department would be something that combines many of these ideas. It would be a department that trains along the lines of the guardian concept; it would have fewer officers than most departments have today; this smaller force would reduce costs, and those saved dollars would be invested back into the community and support social and medical workers, rehabilitation, and community-based organizations; because the department doesn't do broken windows policing and because the War on Drugs and War on Crime have ended, police officers do not see themselves as soldiers; because the 1033 Program is over, those officers don't have military weapons to act like soldiers, and because they don't see themselves as warriors they don't need or want them anyway; since they don't see themselves as warriors, because there's a national use of force standard, because the officers have been trained in de-escalation, they rarely draw their weapons; since there's no more War on Drugs and War on Crime and since sentence enhancements have gone away, prison populations have significantly declined; with the end of the

War on Drugs and War on Crime and because of decriminalization, some of the institutional racism that used to underpin the criminal justice system no longer exists; because they focus less on drugs, the police department has been able to augment its pool of detectives and they now investigate more expeditiously and clear more cases; community support programs and all of the modifications to policing have actually reduced the crime rate; there are now more cooperative interactions between the public and police, leading to better relationships and understanding; civilian confidence in and trust of police has increased, especially in communities of color; morale in the police force is high; because of all of these things people feel safe, seeing a police car or a police officer instills pride and appreciation instead of fear, and parents of little boys and little girls feel confident that when their child leaves home they'll safely return later in the day. Perhaps this all sounds like a fantasy. Maybe it is. But we've basically had the opposite of this for generations now. Perhaps let's try the fantasy.

January 6, 2025

NOTES

ABBREVIATIONS

ABCPL	Special Collections, Albuquerque Bernalillo County Public Library, NM
APL	Austin History Center, Austin Public Library, TX
ASU	Chicano Research Collection, Arizona State University, Tempe
DPL	Dallas History and Archives Division, Dallas Public Library, TX
JAFP	John Anson Ford Papers, 1928–71, Huntington Library, San Marino, CA
HPL	Houston History Research Center, Houston Public Library, TX
PTF	Police Task Force Collection, Albuquerque Urban Coalition Records
UCLA	Special Collections, University of California, Los Angeles
UCSD	Special Collections and Archives, University of California, San Diego
UNM	Center for Southwest Research and Special Collections, University of New Mexico, Albuquerque
USC	Special Collections, University of Southern California, Los Angeles
UTSA	Special Collections, University of Texas, San Antonio

INTRODUCTION

1. "Police Kill Suspect," *Austin American-Statesman*, August 1, 1971; Behnken, *Fighting Their Own Battles*, 174; "Officers Tell of Wrestling for Rifle before Shooting," *Santa Fe New Mexican*, February 16, 1978; "Fleeing 15-Year Old Shot by Police near Home of Witness under Guard," *San Bernardino County (CA) Sun*, April 27, 1979.

2. I borrow the concept of the presumption of criminality from Suddler, *Presumed Criminal*.

3. See Bureau of the Census, "We, the American Hispanics"; and Jens Manuel Krogstad, Jeffrey S. Passel, and Luis Noe-Bustamente, "Key Facts about U.S. Latinos for National Hispanic Heritage Month," Pew Research Center, September 23, 2022,

www.pewresearch.org/fact-tank/2022/09/23/key-facts-about-u-s-latinos-for-national -hispanic-heritage-month. Census data on Latino/a/x people is notoriously problematic because for many decades the Census Bureau either counted them as White or didn't count them at all.

4. Histories of law enforcement have proliferated in the past few years. For a few excellent examples, see Balto, *Occupied Territory*; Felker-Kantor, *Policing Los Angeles*; Guariglia, *Police and the Empire City*; Schrader, *Badges without Borders*; Jett, *Race, Crime, and Policing in the Jim Crow South*; and Agee, *Streets of San Francisco*.

5. On Mexican Americans/Latinos and law enforcement, see Escobar, *Race, Police, and the Making of a Political Identity*; Felker-Kantor, *Policing Los Angeles*; Urbina and Álvarez, *Hispanics in the U.S. Criminal Justice System*; Guajardo, *Milwaukee Police and Latino Community Relations*; Salinas, *U.S. Latinos and Criminal Injustice*; and Behnken, *Borders of Violence and Justice*. The argument about Mexican American desires for improved law enforcement is consistent with the experiences and hopes of other communities in the United States, especially African Americans. See, e.g., Dulaney, *Black Police in America*; Jett, *Race, Crime, and Policing in the Jim Crow South*; King, *Politics of Safety*; Forman, *Locking Up Our Own*; Fortner, *Black Silent Majority*; and Phelps, *Minneapolis Reckoning*.

6. For a somewhat similar example, see LeBrón, *Policing Life and Death*.

7. For background on this, see Behnken, *Fighting Their Own Battles*. For works on Mexican American civil rights broadly conceived, see Rosales, *Chicano!*; Brilliant, *Color of America Has Changed*; Mantler, *Power to the Poor*; Garcia, *White but Not Equal*; Orozco, *No Mexicans, Women, or Dogs Allowed*; Rivas-Rodríguez, *Texas Mexican Americans and Postwar Civil Rights*; Vargas, *Labor Rights Are Civil Rights*; and Echeverría, *Aztlán Arizona*.

8. "The Ruben Salazar Collection of Opinion Articles: 'Border Correspondent,'" California-Mexico Studies Center, August 23, 2020, www.california-mexicocenter .org/the-ruben-salazar-collection-of-opinion-articles-border-correspondent.

9. For the Plan de Aztlán, see "El Plan Espiritual de Aztlan," accessed May 21, 2023, http://websites.umich.edu/~mechaum/Aztlan.html. The literature on the Chicano movement is broad. For good starting places, see Pulido, *Black, Brown, Yellow, and Left*; Blackwell, *¡Chicana Power!*; Oropeza, *¡Raza Sí! ¡Guerra No!*; San Miguel, *Brown, Not White*; Hinojosa, *Apostles of Change*; Rodriguez, *Rethinking the Chicano Movement*; Gómez-Quiñones and Vásquez, *Making Aztlán*; and Oropeza, *King of Adobe*.

10. For good analysis of this process, see Wilson, "*Chicanismo* and the Flexible Fourteenth Amendment," 147–68.

11. Behnken, *Borders of Violence and Justice*.

12. For background on police work, see Reiner, *Politics of the Police*.

13. For information on Houston area law enforcement, see "Police Departments in Harris County, Texas," 2014–2025, CountyOffice.org, www.countyoffice.org/tx-harris -county-police-department; "Police Department—Law Enforcement—Houston Area Law Enforcement," Houston Police Department, 2025, www.houstontx.gov/police/links /txlaw.htm; and Kirkland An and Dylan McGuinness, "How Much Funding Houston's Police, Other Departments Get in the City's New $5.7 Billion Budget," *Houston Chronicle*, July 7, 2022. On the LA area, see "Municipal Police Departments Los Angeles County," Los Angeles Almanac, 1998–2025, www.laalmanac.com/crime/cr69.php; and

"LAPD Raises, Bonuses Will Cost at Least $384 Million More," *NBC Los Angeles*, August 22, 2023.

14. Montes, interview by Cline, July 27, 2016, 14.

15. There is a distinction in abolition circles between a reformist position and an abolitionist position. My contention here is simply that Mexican Americans sometimes viewed abolition as a method of changing a system with the goal of improving it . . . in other words, reform.

16. On prison abolition, see Gilmore, *Abolition Geography*; and Kaba, *We Do This 'til We Free Us*. On police abolition, see Kaba and Ritchie, *No More Police*; and Vitale, *End of Policing*. On defunding police, see Cunneen, *Defunding the Police*; and Smiley, *Defund*. See also "What Does 'Defund the Police' Mean? The Rallying Cry Sweeping the US," *The Guardian*, June 6, 2020, www.theguardian.com/us-news/2020/jun/05/defunding -the-police-us-what-does-it-mean; and Mariame Kaba, "Yes, We Mean Literally Abolish the Police," *New York Times*, June 12, 2020. Some of these works criticize reform, and rightfully so. But my research demonstrates that most Mexican Americans have histori- cally favored reform over abolition.

17. Harcourt, *Illusion of Order*, 23–40; Thompson, "Broken Policing."

18. Vitale, *End of Policing*, 129, 134. For more on prisons especially, see Alexander, *New Jim Crow*. A number of carceral scholars have critiqued reform efforts as either pur- posefully hiding continued violence or having the unintended consequence of leading to ongoing problems. See, e.g., Kohler-Hausmann, *Getting Tough*; Kohler-Hausmann, *Mis- demeanorland*; Suddler, *Presumed Criminal*; Balto, *Occupied Territory*; and Felker-Kantor, *Policing Los Angeles*. I don't disagree with this assessment; rather, I focus on reform as having the potential for good because the Mexican American community took it that way.

19. Throughout this book I attempt to be careful in my use of terms such as "riot." Historically speaking, a "riot" or "race riot" was an event wherein an angry White mob sought revenge on an ethnic community based on some perceived social or legal infrac- tion. Today, however, these terms have come to operate as a racist dog whistle coded, as Elizabeth Hinton has observed, as something "fundamentally Black." See Hinton, *America on Fire*, 4. Sometimes racial uprisings have been labeled a riot even though the event was a rebellion, an uprising, or in many cases a police-instigated riot. A number of these events have been renamed to better explain their significance. For example, the Dallas riot of 1973 is today often called the Dallas Disturbance. Yet some of these events are still termed a "riot"—for example, the Zoot Suit Riots—and in those cases in this book I label the event based on what it is called.

20. King stated during the Selma Campaign, "How long? Not long, because the arc of the moral universe is long, but it bends toward justice." "Our God Is Marching On!," March 25, 1965, Martin Luther King, Jr. Research and Education Institute, Stanford Uni- versity, accessed May 21, 2023, https://kinginstitute.stanford.edu/our-god-marching.

CHAPTER 1

1. "Gangs Warned 'Kid Gloves Off!,'" *Los Angeles Times*, August 4, 1942.

2. "Invasion of 'Pachucos' Is Seen Locally," *Tucson Daily Citizen*, November 14, 1942; "Youthful Gang in Jail after Riot Act Flops," *Tucson Daily Citizen*, November 16, 1942.

3. "Zoot-Suiters Devise Own Signs and Slang to Avoid Officers," *El Paso Herald-Post*, June 11, 1943.

4. "'Pachucos' Are Sought in Soldier Slaying," *Austin American*, January 23, 1943.

5. "Mexicans Say Zoot Suiters Should Get It," *Amarillo (TX) Globe*, July 9, 1943. For background, see Escobar, *Race, Police, and the Making of a Political Identity*, 186–202; Escobedo, *From Coveralls to Zoot Suits*, 18–21; Escobedo, "Pachuca Panic"; and Bender, *Greasers and Gringos*, 1–30.

6. The violence of this period is generally viewed as affecting Southern California, but as historian Luis Alvarez has noted, such violence occurred across the United States. See Alvarez, *Power of the Zoot*.

7. See Alvarez, *Power of the Zoot*; Escobedo, *From Coveralls to Zoot Suits*; and Escobar, "Unintended Consequences of the Carceral State."

8. Braddy, "Pachucos and Their Argot," 262. See also Griffith, "Who Are the *Pachucos?*"

9. Madrid-Barela, "In Search of the Authentic Pachuco," 33.

10. Alvarez, *Power of the Zoot*, 4–5, chap. 1.

11. "Juvenile Delinquency and Poor Housing in the Los Angeles Metropolitan Area," report prepared under the direction of the executive board of the Los Angeles County Coordinating Councils, December 1937, in Los Angeles County Government, JAFP.

12. "Sleepy Lagoon Case," publication of the Citizens' Committee for the Defense of Mexican-American Youth, June 1943, 8, in Sleepy Lagoon Defense Committee Records, 1942–45, UCLA; Escobar, *Race, Police, and the Making of a Political Identity*, 207–14.

13. Ben Baeder, "Zoot Suit Riots," *Los Angeles Daily News*, updated August 28, 2017, www.dailynews.com/2013/05/31/zoot-suit-riots-the-sleepy-lagoon-murder-case-that -helped-spur-the-wwii-era-los-angeles-race-riots.

14. Weitz, *Sleepy Lagoon Murder Case*, 30.

15. "Sleepy Lagoon Case," 14–18.

16. Weitz, *Sleepy Lagoon Murder Case*, 111–13.

17. Weitz, *Sleepy Lagoon Murder Case*, 72–73.

18. Pagán, *Murder at the Sleepy Lagoon*, 197–99; Escobar, *Race, Police, and the Making of a Political Identity*, 233–42.

19. McWilliams, *North from Mexico*, 199–201.

20. National Council of La Raza report on Los Angeles, ca. 1980, 7, in National Council de la Raza—Police Practices, 1983 folder, AFSC Records, UCSD.

21. "Report by Special Committee on Problems of Mexican Youth," part of the "Final Report of Los Angeles County Grand Jury for the Year 1942," JAFP. See also Dr. Robert A. McKibben to Honorable Robert H. Scott, December 10, 1942, JAFP.

22. "Report by Special Committee on Problems of Mexican Youth."

23. McKibben to Scott, December 28, 1942, JAFP.

24. "Summary of Recommendations & Progress to Date of the Special Committee on Older Youth Gang Activity in Los Angeles and Vicinity," ca. December 1942, JAFP.

25. "Report and Recommendations of Citizens Committee," California Citizens' Committee on Civil Disturbances in Los Angeles, June 12, 1943, 1, in FR-34 Chicano folder, ASU.

26. "Report and Recommendations of Citizens Committee," 2–4.

27. "Report and Recommendations of Citizens Committee," 5–6.

28. "Report and Recommendations of Citizens Committee," 1.

29. "The Current Juvenile Delinquency Situation," Minutes of the Regular Meeting of the Los Angeles County Youth Committee, January 20, 1954, JAFP.

30. "Current Juvenile Delinquency Situation."

31. Harold W. Kennedy (LA County counsel) to Honorable Board of Supervisors, February 14, 1955; and Ordinance No. 6633, adopted February 15, 1955, both in JAFP; *Katzev et al. v. County of Los Angeles* (1959).

32. Community Organization Section, Group Guidance Section, Staff and Community Services Division, Probation Department, County of Los Angeles, August 3, 1951, JAFP.

33. "Report of Sub-Committee Studying Dance Ordinance," November 1956, JAFP; Garcia, *World of Its Own*, chap. 6.

34. Milnor E. Gleaves (deputy county counsel) to Board of Supervisors, June 12, 1950, JAFP. See also Resolution, June 21, 1950, JAFP.

35. Deputy C. G. Broadus to Capt. J. A. Eddington, March 12, 1956, JAFP.

36. Escobar, "Bloody Christmas and the Irony of Police Professionalism."

37. "Man Dies after Being Struck by Houston Cops," *Brownsville (TX) Herald*, April 21, 1937; "Grand Jury Probe of Blackjack Killing Due," *Austin American*, April 22, 1937.

38. "Accused Policemen on Stand in Slaying Trial," *Fort Worth Star-Telegram*, June 2, 1937; "Both Policemen Declare Cortez Resisted Arrest," *Houston Post*, June 2, 1937; "Prosecution of Two Policemen Was Job No One in Office Wanted," *Houston Post*, June 4, 1937; "The Cortez Murder Trial," unknown newspaper, June 4, 1937, Mexican-American Small Collections, HPL; "Officers Acquitted in Houston Death," *Brownsville (TX) Herald*, June 3, 1937.

39. Cano, "Pachuco Gangs in Houston," 18, 20.

40. Crespo, interview by Kreneck; Crespo, interview by HPL staff.

41. Cano, "Pachuco Gangs in Houston," 19; "Police Squad to Deal with Latin-American Problems Selected," *Houston Press*, July 12, 1944; Watson, *Race and the Houston Police Department*, 111–12.

42. "Five Juvenile Gang Suspects Arrested after Girl, 15, Shot," *Houston Press*, July 6, 1944; "Court Commits 8 Youthful Gangsters to State School," *Houston Press*, July 14, 1944; "Police Seize 'Reefers' in Gang Raid," *Houston Press*, September 16, 1944.

43. "Latin-American Gangs in Houston Now Eliminated," *Houston Chronicle*, December 2, 1945.

44. Crespo, interview by Kreneck.

45. John J. Ruiz to Chief of Police H. W. Payne, March 5, 1947, and Ruiz to Mayor Oscar Holcombe, March 5, 1947, in LULAC Council #60 Papers, HPL. See also "Houston Police Latin-American Squad Disbanded," *Houston Chronicle*, ca. 1947, in LULAC Council #60 Papers, HPL.

46. "Youth Charged in Gang Slaying," *Houston Chronicle*, February 26, 1950; "Wave of Latin American Crime Stirs Calls for Fast, Efficient Action," *Houston Chronicle*, March 8, 1950.

47. "Herrera Hits Latin Squad Formation," *Houston Chronicle*, February 27, 1950.

48. "Two Councilmembers Doubt Chief Can Stop Thugs," *Houston Chronicle*, March 7, 1950.

49. See "Two Councilmembers Doubt Chief Can Stop Thugs"; and "Wave of Latin American Crime Stirs Calls for Fast, Efficient Action."

50. "Latin Americans Get Bad Deal in Public Press, Herrera Says," *Houston Chronicle*, March 9, 1950; "Letters to the Chronicle: L.U.L.A.C.'s Views," *Houston Chronicle*, March 15, 1950.

51. "Latin American Meet Hears Little on Gangs," *Houston Chronicle*, March 17, 1950.

52. James P. McCollom, "The Legend of One of the Deadliest Men in South Texas," *Texas Monthly*, November 2017, www.texasmonthly.com/articles/the-last-sheriff-in-texas.

53. "Ennis Calls GI Forum Resolution Propaganda," *Corpus Christi (TX) Times*, February 27, 1952. See also "Texas: Hellbent Sheriff," *Time*, November 24, 1947; Campney, "Police Brutality and Mexican American Families," 108–9; and McCollom, *Last Sheriff*.

54. "Beeville Sheriff Shoots Three Men," *Monitor* (McAllen, TX), July 8, 1945; "Sheriff Kills 3 Brothers in Bee County," *Fort Worth Star-Telegram*, July 8, 1945.

55. "Sheriff Faces Charge," *Marshall (TX) News Messenger*, December 5, 1945; "Sheriff Cleared of Murder Charge," *Abilene (TX) Reporter-News*, January 20, 1946.

56. Hector P. Garcia et al. to Governor Allan Shivers, telegram, December 2, 1949, Good Neighbor Commission Folder, Texas Governor Price Daniel Records, Sam Houston Regional Library and Research Center, Texas State Library and Archives Commission, Liberty.

57. "Ennis Vote Bid Fails; Duffy Wins," *Corpus Christi (TX) Times*, November 5, 1952; "Duffy Beats Ennis Again," *Corpus Christi (TX) Times*, July 26, 1954.

58. "Ignacio Fontes Ruiz," report prepared by Wilfred "Sonny" Peña, April 12, 2009, in Ignacio Fontes Ruiz folder, ASU. For other examples of violence in this period, see García, *Mexican Americans*, 91–93, 161, 220–21.

59. See Behnken, *Borders of Violence and Justice*.

60. "Purse Snatcher, Unknown, Alias Tony, Mexican," *Denver Police Bulletin*, February 22, 1947.

61. "Safe Burglars," *Denver Police Bulletin*, March 29, 1947.

62. "Degenerate, Unknown Mexican," *Denver Police Bulletin*, April 14, 1947.

63. "Stabbing, No. 2., Unknown Mexican," *Denver Police Bulletin*, June 23, 1947.

64. Emma Moya, "Old Town Training Ground for the City of Albuquerque Police Department?," n.d., Emma Moya Collection, UNM.

65. Hernández, *Migra!*, chap. 8; García, *Operation Wetback*, 225–29; Goodman, *Deportation Machine*, chap. 2. See also Blue, *Deportation Express*.

66. For a good critique of Operation Wetback, see Kang, *INS on the Line*, 165–67.

67. John J. Herrera to Mr. C. V. Buster Kern, December 15, 1948, in John J. Herrera Papers, HPL.

68. "New Constable Recalls Day He Met President Kennedy," *Texas Catholic Herald* (Dallas), ca. 1973, in Constable Raul C. Martinez Papers, HPL (first quotation); "Martinez Goes beyond Call of Duty to Serve Precinct," *Houston Chronicle*, July 26, 1981 (second quotation); "Officer Who Guarded Kennedy Remembers School Days in Goliad," *Goliad Advance-Guard* (Beeville, TX), August 30, 1973. See also Raul C. Martinez, interview by Kreneck. Eddie Barrios, it seems, did not remain on the force very long.

69. See "Juan Gonzalez Obituary," *Fort Worth Star-Telegram*, July 5, 2017, www.legacy.com/obituaries/dfw/obituary.aspx?n=juan-gonzalez&pid=185994320&fhid=11515.

70. Andy Summa, "Faces in the Crowd: Texas City Police Captain Retires after Four Decades Serving the City," *Houston Chronicle*, September 20, 2001.

71. Eddie Flores, "Sid Trevino Midland's First Hispanic Police Officer," KMID-TV (Odessa, TX), November 14, 2018, www.yourbasin.com/news/sid-trevino-midlands-first -hispanic-police-officer.

72. "In 6 Years He's Now Sergeant," *Austin Statesman*, April 13, 1960.

73. Michael Barnes, "Austin's First Hispanic Detective Saw It All," *Austin American-Statesman*, November 9, 2018. See also "No Charges Filed by Shot Man," *Austin Statesman*, July 12, 1960.

74. "John Vasquez First Chicano Lieutenant on Police Force," *La Fuerza* (Austin, TX), January 25, 1973.

75. "Mexican American Firsts: Trailblazers of Austin and Travis County Nomination Form," November 2, 2009, in John Norman Vasquez folder, APL.

76. "51 Complete Traffic Officer School Here," *Austin Statesman*, April 16, 1960.

77. Behnken, *Fighting Their Own Battles*, 106.

78. "Police Unrest Mounts," *Austin American*, June 14, 1967.

79. For background on the hiring of Mexican American and Latino officers, see Behnken, *Borders of Violence and Justice*, 81–116; Guajardo, *Milwaukee Police and Latino Community Relations*, 103–40; Urbina and Álvarez, *Latino Police Officers*, 90–112, 128–47; and Gallardo, "Thin Blue Line," 35–51.

80. *New Mexico Sheriff and Police*, 3.

81. For background, see Snow, *Policewomen Who Made History*; and Appier, *Policing Women*.

82. "Appointment of Policewoman Is Left to Chief," *Albuquerque Journal*, July 26, 1922; "How to Pat a Woman Policeman Is the Citys [*sic*] New Problem," *Albuquerque Journal*, July 27, 1922; "Curfew to Blow—Feminine Police Will Not Patrol," *Albuquerque Journal*, August 1, 1922. Los Angeles hired its first female police officer in 1913, a White woman named Alice Stebbins Well. See "Policewoman of Los Angeles to Speak Here," *Albuquerque Journal*, February 19, 1913.

83. "New Jail Matron," *Albuquerque Journal*, May 15, 1951; "Woman Official Likes to Give Helping Hand to Young People," *Albuquerque Tribune*, November 21, 1961.

84. "City Police Academy Graduates Class of 18 Men, Four Women," *Albuquerque Journal*, July 20, 1968.

85. Felipe Sanchez y Baca to Sanford Bates, March 31, 1936, includes "Federal Prisoners in Non-Federal Institutions on the Last Day of the Month" for December 1935, January 1936, and February 1936; Sanchez y Baca to Bates, July 31, 1936, and Prisoner Report; Sanchez y Baca to Bates, March 10, 1937, includes January Prisoner Report; and Sanchez y Baca to James V. Bennett, April 19, 1940, and March Prisoner Report, all in US Marshal Papers, UNM.

86. "Arizona Deaths," *Arizona Republic* (Phoenix), July 17, 1951.

87. "10-Year Span," *Arizona Republic* (Phoenix), March 2, 1952; "Mesa Police Department Honors Assistant Chief," *Arizona Republic* (Phoenix), June 5, 1967.

88. "Mesa Names Police Aid," *Arizona Republic* (Phoenix), June 14, 1961; "Mesa Policeman Serves 20 Years," *Arizona Republic* (Phoenix), June 19, 1962; "Mendoza Appointed Mesa Police Chief," *Arizona Daily Star* (Tucson), February 4, 1969.

89. "Mesa to Train Policemen with New Antiriot Gear," *Arizona Republic* (Phoenix), March 20, 1970.

90. "Mesa Annexes 475-Acre Residence Area," *Arizona Republic* (Phoenix), March 20, 1973; "11 Mesa Policemen to Be Promoted," *Arizona Republic* (Phoenix), May 31, 1973.

91. "Mesa Police Chief to Retire," *Arizona Republic* (Phoenix), January 5, 1978.

92. Timothy Hughes, "Hail to the Ex-Chief," *Los Angeles Times*, November 7, 2000; Barajas, *Curious Unions*, 188.

93. Jennifer Mena, "What a Difference 37 Years Can Make," *Los Angeles Times*, January 10, 2002.

94. Imani Tate, "Longtime La Verne Councilman Robert Rodriguez Dies at 83," *Pasadena (CA) Star-News*, July 8, 2013.

95. Nedra Rhone, "Retired Officer Chronicles Gains by Women in LAPD," *Los Angeles Times*, January 14, 2001; "The First Latina LAPD Officer," *Los Angeles Times*, March 23, 2014.

CHAPTER 2

1. For examples of this phenomenon, see Berger, *Struggle Within*.

2. See "Letter of Transmittal," in Governor's Commission on the Los Angeles Riots, *Violence in the City*; and Felker-Kantor, *Policing Los Angeles*, 20–24.

3. Montes, interview by *Fight Back!* staff, August 2, 2009; Montes, interview by Cline, June 27, 2016, 8.

4. García, *Chicano Generation*, 130–38.

5. See "Brown Beret Ten-Point Program (1968)," *Notes from Aztlán* (blog), Tumblr, April 10, 2014, www.tumblr.com/notesfromaztlan/82319768788/brown-beret-ten-point -program-1968.

6. Montes, interview by Cline, 14.

7. SAC, Los Angeles (52-11746), to Director, FBI, memo, March 8, 1968, in Brown Berets, 1968 folder, José Angel Gutiérrez Papers, UTSA.

8. García and Castro, *Blowout!*, 135–37.

9. "Brown Beret Arrests," *Los Angeles Herald Examiner*, June 1, 1968; García and Castro, *Blowout!*, 200–201.

10. W. R. Wannall to W. C. Sullivan, memo, ca. May 1968, in Brown Berets, 1968 folder, José Angel Gutiérrez Papers, UTSA.

11. Los Angeles to Director, Domestic Intelligence Division, memo, August 13, 1968, in Brown Berets, 1968 folder, José Angel Gutiérrez Papers, UTSA.

12. "Brown Berets Aggressive in Spirit, Energetic," *Oxnard (CA) Press Courier*, August 22, 1968.

13. See Oropeza, *Raza Sí, Guerra No*.

14. National Council of La Raza report on Los Angeles, ca. 1980, 13, in National Council de la Raza—Police Practices, 1983 folder, AFSC Records, UCSD; "Armed Defense and the Community," *La Raza* 1, no. 2 (1970).

15. "Anti-War Rally Erupts into East L.A. Riot," *Los Angeles Times*, August 30, 1970; "Bitter Dispute on Causes of L.A. Riot," *San Francisco Examiner*, August 31, 1970.

16. National Council of La Raza report on Los Angeles, 18–20. "The Murder of Ruben Salazar," *La Raza* 1, no. 3 (1970). For a good overview, see Oropeza, *¡Raza Sí, ¡Guerra No!*

17. "Protest 6 Deaths at E.L.A. Sheriff's Station at 4th of July Rally," flyer, ca. July 1970; and "Police Found Guilty of Murder," flyer, ca. July 1970, both in Intelligence and

Inflammatory Literature folder, LA County Sheriff's Dept's Records on the Investigation of the Homicide of Ruben Salazar, USC.

18. "Time Is Ripe for Violent Revolution," protest flyer, ca. July 1970, in Intelligence and Inflammatory Literature folder, LA County Sheriff's Dept's Records on the Investigation of the Homicide of Ruben Salazar, USC.

19. "Synopsis, Whittier Boulevard Disturbance of July 3 and 4," ca. August 1970, in Intelligence and Inflammatory Literature folder, LA County Sheriff's Dept's Records on the Investigation of the Homicide of Ruben Salazar, USC.

20. National Council of La Raza report on Los Angeles, 13.

21. National Council of La Raza report on Los Angeles, 3.

22. Behnken, *Borders of Violence and Justice*, 183–89.

23. "Los cinco candidatos" (The five candidates), *Texas Observer*, April 18, 1963; Navarro, *Cristal Experiment*, 32–33; Samora, *Gunpowder Justice*, 91–94, 102, 104–7.

24. "Crystal City Harmony Pledged," *San Antonio Light*, April 16, 1963; "Crystal City View—Town 'Taken Over,'" *San Antonio Light*, April 17, 1963; "Latin-American Takeover of Town Watched by Nation," *Southern School News*, June 1963; "The Other Texans," *Look*, October 8, 1963; Rivera, "Nosotros Venceremos," 56–64.

25. "Crystal City Officials Seek Removal of Texas Rangers," *Houston Chronicle*, May 3, 1963; "Shock Waves from Popeye Land," *Texas Observer*, May 16, 1963.

26. "The Rangers and La Huelga," *Texas Observer*, June 9, 1967; Wilson, *Rise of Judicial Management*, 143–46.

27. "George I. Sánchez to Honorable John Connally," June 1, 1967, in Judge Albert A. Peña Papers, UTSA; Medrano, interview, 66–74.

28. *Medrano et al. v. Allee* (1972), in Working File, *Medrano v. Allee*, Judge Woodrow Seals Papers, HPL.

29. "Rally Protests Rangers in Valley," *Valley Evening Monitor* (McAllen, TX), June 4, 1967; "The Dimas Incident," *Texas Observer*, June 9, 1967; "Conversation with the Captain," *Texas Observer*, June 9, 1967; "From the Day the Bridge Was Burned," *El Malcriado* (CA), ca. August 1967; "Arrests Impede the Picketing," *Texas Observer*, June 9, 1967; Testimony of Benito Rodriguez, ca. June 1967, Migrant Farm Workers Organizing Movement Collection, Special Collections, University of Texas, Arlington; US Senate, *Hunger and Malnutrition in America*, 440–46.

30. "Arrests Impede the Picketing," *Texas Observer*, June 9, 1967; "Una noche con los Rinches" (A night with the rangers), *El Malcriado* (CA), June 1967; US Senate, *Migrant and Seasonal Farmworker Powerlessness*, 1880.

31. *Medrano et al. v. Allee* (1972); "Court Knocks Out 5 Texas Laws, Raps Rangers in Farm Dispute," *Houston Chronicle*, June 27, 1972.

32. Richard Medrano, press release, May 29, 1967, Pancho Medrano Papers, Special Collections, University of Texas, Arlington; Medrano, interview, 66–74.

33. Medrano, press release; Medrano, interview, 66–74.

34. *Medrano et al. v. Allee* (1972).

35. *Allee v. Medrano*, 416 U.S. at 802; Wilson, *Rise of Judicial Management*, 186.

36. Robert E. Lucey to Joseph A. Califano, March 31, 1967; and William D. Bonilla to Califano, April 4, 1967, both in subject file box 29, WE9 4-8-67-4-19-67, White House Central Files, Lyndon Baines Johnson Presidential Library, Austin.

37. Remarks, Governor Connally, Texas Conference for the Mexican-American, April

13, 1967, in Series (5a), Texas Conference for the Mexican-American San Antonio, Texas Governor John Connally Papers, Lydon Baines Johnson Presidential Library, Austin. See also "Message from the National President," *LULAC News*, April 1967.

38. "Civil Rights Groups Takes Slap at Texas Conditions," *Dallas Morning News*, June 18, 1967.

39. "Little People's Day," *Texas Observer*, June 21, 1967 (quotations); "Bernal: Rangers Like an Appendix," *San Antonio Express*, June 12, 1967; "Senadores investigan acusaciones contra los soldados Rangers" (Senators investigate accusations against the Rangers), *El Sol de Texas* (Dallas), July 14, 1967; "Allee and Garrison Deny the Allegations," *Texas Observer*, June 21, 1967; "Capt. Allee Told to Not Testify," *San Antonio Express*, July 13, 1967; Bailey, "Starr County Strike," 58–60; "The Strike Is Beset by Woes," *Texas Observer*, June 9, 1967.

40. "Civil Rights Watchdogs Call Ranger," *San Antonio Express*, December 5, 1968; "Ranger Is Star Witness," *Corpus Christi Caller-Times*, December 15, 1968.

41. Behnken, *Borders of Violence and Justice*, chap. 6.

42. Intelligence Report, VI-41, City of Houston Police Department, November 13, 1969, in Police Reports, Mayor Louie Welch Papers, HPL.

43. Intelligence Report, VI-16, City of Houston Police Department, February 8, 1971, in Police Reports, Welch Papers, HPL.

44. "Chicanos Told to Organize, Resist," *Houston Post*, July 27, 1970; "Chicano Moratorium," *La Raza* 1, no. 3 (1970). On the antiwar movement in Houston, see Esparza, "Chale con la Guerra," 117–18, 125–29.

45. "Victory for the Houston 12 Means Victory for All Oppressed People" and "Five Facing Felony Charge Long Active in Struggle," in Free the Houston 12 newspaper, n.d., in Jose Medellin folder, Mexican-American Small Collections, HPL; "Police Brutality and the Houston 12," pamphlet, n.d., in Raza Unida Party, State Convention, Houston folder, Mexican-American Small Collections, HPL.

46. Daniel Berigan to Dear Friends, Houston 12 Defense Committee, ca. 1973, in Topics, Police Brutality—Newsclippings and Newsletters, 1950–2004, Mario Salas Papers, UTSA.

47. Gloria Rodriguez to Dear Friends, Houston 12 Defense Committee, February 28, 1975, in Topics, Police Brutality—Newsclippings and Newsletters, 1950–2004, Salas Papers, UTSA.

48. "Brown Beret 13 Point Political Program," *La Causa* (Los Angeles), February 1970. The Black Berets initially called themselves the Brown Berets.

49. "Why We Are Here," Brown Berets flyer, August 1968, in Gloria Montoya Chavez Papers, UNM; "Black Beret Organization, Why We Are Armed" (quotation), ca. 1969, in Reies López Tijerina Papers, UNM.

50. "The Rebellion," *El Grito del Norte* (Española, NM), newspaper clipping, n.d., in Chavez Papers, UNM.

51. "Rebellion" (quotation); "Newsman Pinned Down in Fighting at Park," *Albuquerque Journal*, June 14, 1971; "Afternoon Rally at Park Bred Tensions," *Albuquerque Journal*, June 15, 1971.

52. "Violence Explodes in City," *Albuquerque Journal*, June 14, 1971.

53. "Fire Bombs Touch Off 12 Blazes," unknown newspaper, n.d., in Chavez Papers, UNM.

54. "2nd Night of Terror for Albq!," *Albuquerque Tribune*, June 15, 1971; "600 Guardsmen Remain on Alert in Albuquerque," *Albuquerque Tribune*, June 16, 1971.

55. "Bond of $15,000 Set for 2 Accused of Fires at APS," *Albuquerque Journal*, June 25, 1971; "DA Reviewing Firebomb Case," *Albuquerque Journal*, June 19, 1971.

56. "Berets May Form Own Riot Investigation Unit," *Albuquerque Journal*, June 30, 1971; "King Dissolves Riot Panel; Cites 'Discord,'" *Albuquerque Tribune*, June 30, 1971; "King Warns against Disturbances in N.M.," *Albuquerque Tribune*, July 7, 1971.

57. "Black Berets Form Patrol in Valley," *Albuquerque Journal*, n.d., in NM Associations—Black Berets file, ABCPL; Antonio Cordova to Querido Camarada, September 20, 1971, in Frank I. Sanchez Papers, UNM.

58. "Black Beret Advisor Fears Nazi-Type System," *Albuquerque Tribune*, December 1, 1971; "Candlelight Vigil Held for Berets," *Albuquerque Journal*, February 2, 1972. See also "January 29—No Olvidemos" (January 29—let us not forget), *Chicano Communications Training Project*, newsletter, December 1972.

59. Appendix A (Cordova affidavit), July 20, 1971, in New Mexico Advisory Committee, *Struggle for Justice and Redress in Northern New Mexico*, 56–58. Archuleta and Cordova had had a previous encounter when Cordova photographed a protest that police had attacked. See "Valley Newsman Charges Officer with Brutality," *Santa Fe New Mexican*, July 21, 1971.

60. Appendix B (David L. Norvell investigation into Cordova affidavit), ca. July 1972, in New Mexico Advisory Committee, *Struggle for Justice and Redress in Northern New Mexico*, 60–68, 64 (quotation); "Police Brutality Charge Rejected," *Santa Fe New Mexican*, July 23, 1971; "Chief 'Welcomes' Probe of Police Department," *Santa Fe New Mexican*, July 30, 1971; "Newsman in Espanola Requesting Protection," *Albuquerque Journal*, July 21, 1971.

61. Appendix B, 66–68, 66 (quotation). See also "Meeting with Norvell/Mondragon," 1971, in Chavez Papers, UNM.

62. Salomon Velasquez affidavit, June 1971, in Chavez Papers, UNM. See also Statement by Alfred Santistevas, August 28, 1971; and Statement of Jerry Medina, August 28, 1971, both in Chavez Papers, UNM; and "Archuleta Resigns from PD," *Santa Fe New Mexican*, September 9, 1971.

63. "Court Opens Term Monday," *Carlsbad (NM) Current-Argus*, December 2, 1962; "Stab Serious for Inmate," *Santa Fe New Mexican*, August 27, 1968; "Briefs," *Alamogordo (NM) Daily News*, August 28, 1968; "Spoken Names Bring Case to Mistrial," *Santa Fe New Mexican*, August 13, 1968; *State v. Canales* (1967); *Canales v. Baker* (1969); "Why Are They Dead?," *El Grito del Norte* (Española, NM), February 18, 1972.

64. "DA Ends Prison Probe," *Santa Fe New Mexican*, July 10, 1969; "Warden Stays 'til Replaced," *Santa Fe New Mexican*, February 20, 1970; "Resignation of Warden Is Revealed," *Santa Fe New Mexican*, April 29, 1970; "Power Plays Cause Unrest at Prison," *Santa Fe New Mexican*, May 5, 1970.

65. "Have Tried to Break Prison," *Silver City (NM) Daily Press*, May 11, 1971; "Garcia Search Broadened," *Silver City (NM) Daily Press*, May 11, 1971.

66. "Prisoners Are 'Denied Rights,'" *Gallup (NM) Independent*, September 17, 1971; "State Prison Inmates Given Ultimatum," *Alamogordo (NM) Daily News*, October 7, 1971; "Guards Subdue Strikers at N.M. Prison," *Albuquerque Journal*, October 8, 1971; "State Prison 'Normal' in Wake of Disturbance," *Santa Fe New Mexican*, October 11, 1971.

67. "Slain Berets Slated for TV," *Santa Fe New Mexican*, January 31, 1972; Chicano Press Association, "Police Kill Two Chicanos in New Mexico," press release, ca. January 29, 1972, in Emma Moya Collection, UNM.

68. Press release, December 15, 1970, in Moya Collection, UNM. See also Gutierrez, *FBI Surveillance of Mexicans and Chicanos*, 227–28.

69. It remains unclear why the two men attempted to steal dynamite. Albuquerque police chief Don Byrd stated that the Black Berets wanted to "destroy our system of government," but that seems far-fetched and impossible to do with a few sticks of dynamite. See "Albuquerque Beret Killings," *New Mexico Review*, March 1972. Tim Chapa claimed that some New Mexico nightclub owners had hired the Berets to blow up several competitors' nightclubs. See Gutiérrez, *Tracking King Tiger*, 237–39. There was also speculation that the Berets were supplying the Colorado Crusade for Justice with dynamite. Tim Chapa started this rumor but also revealed that New Mexico law enforcement instructed him to do so to create a fictitious Colorado–New Mexico connection. See Bustillos, "Targeting Minorities," 42–43.

70. "Albuquerque Beret Killings."

71. "Police Slay Two Men at Dynamite Shed," *Albuquerque Journal*, January 30, 1972. The "official" police version of these events appeared in "One Beret Shot 9 Times, the Other Hit 6 Times," *Albuquerque Tribune*, February 1, 1972; and "Still No Detail in Beret Deaths, No Public Report," *Albuquerque Tribune*, February 2, 1972.

72. Emma Moya, "Notes Taken at the Federal Trial concerning Police Behavior during the Killings of Rito Canales and Antonio Cordova," January 18, 1974, 5, in Moya Collection, UNM.

73. "Byrd Blasts Berets," *Albuquerque Tribune*, February 3, 1972.

74. Albuquerque (44-927) to Director, memo, February 1, 1972, in Brown Berets, 1972 folder, Gutiérrez Papers, UTSA. Tijerina made a similar claim; see Tijerina, *They Called Me "King Tiger,"* 171.

75. Tim Chapa claimed that Officers Drennan and Urioste knew Cordova was dead and shot him "after he was down just to see him twitch or jerk or something." See Gutiérrez, *Tracking King Tiger*, 240.

76. In *Tennessee v. Garner* (1985), the Supreme Court declared that police could use deadly force only if "the officer has probable cause to believe that the suspect poses a significant threat of death or serious physical injury to the officer or others" (at *1).

77. "Beret Deaths Study Ordered," *Santa Fe New Mexican*, January 31, 1972; "Commission to Answer Slaying Questions Sought," *Albuquerque Journal*, February 5, 1972; "Commission Seeks Probe," *Albuquerque Journal*, February 8, 1972; "King Asks AG Probe in Death of Two Men," *Albuquerque Journal*, February 8, 1972.

78. Appendix C (report of David L. Norvell into the killing of Canales and Cordova), in New Mexico Advisory Committee, *Struggle for Justice and Redress in Northern New Mexico*, 70–82, 78 (quotation).

79. Appendix C, 70–82, 78–81, 78 (quotation).

80. Appendix D (statement of L. Michael Messina), in New Mexico Advisory Committee, *Struggle for Justice and Redress in Northern New Mexico*, 84–85.

81. Emma Moya, "This Happening Has More to It Than Thought," letter/statement, n.d., Moya Collection, UNM; Tijerina, *They Called Me "King Tiger,"* 171.

82. *Cordova v. City of Albuquerque* (1974); "Death Suit Dismissal Is Upheld," *Albuquerque Journal*, September 12, 1974.

83. "Suit: Activists Killed in '72 Police Plot," *Albuquerque Journal*, January 9, 2009; "Introduction Paper—Extracted and Condensed from Version of Affidavit," n.d., in Moya Collection, UNM; *Cordova v. Larsen* (2004).

84. "Beret Deaths Termed 'Like Killing a Dog,'" *Las Cruces (NM) Sun-News*, February 2, 1972.

85. "750 Attend Memorial for Slain Beret Member," *Albuquerque Journal*, February 2, 1972.

86. Chicano Press Association, "Police Kill Two Chicanos in New Mexico"; "Albuquerque Beret Killings"; "Chief Byrd Says Cordova Print on Bomb," *Albuquerque Journal*, February 9, 1972; "Coroner Gives Data on Killings," *Albuquerque Journal*, February 8, 1972.

87. Vigil, *Crusade for Justice*, 18–53; Olden, *Racial Uncertainties*, 117–20.

88. Denver 157-41 to Director, memo, March 21, 1969; and "Racial Disturbances Instigated by Crusade for Justice and Black Panther Party, Denver, Colorado, March 21, 1969," FBI summary, March 24, 1969, both in Crusade for Justice, 1968–69 folder, Gutiérrez Papers, UTSA; "Corky Gonzales on the Chicano Liberation Fight," *The Militant*, May 9, 1969.

89. "Corky Falsely Arrested," *El Gallo* (Denver), July 1975.

90. "Gonzales Denies Plotting Murders of Police," *El Gallo* (Denver), July 1976.

91. "Interview with 'Corky' Gonzales," *La Cucaracha* (Pueblo, CO), September 5, 1977.

92. "Message to Aztlan," *El Gallo* (Denver), October–November 1975.

93. Vigil, *Crusade for Justice*, chap. 11; Treviño, *Eye Witness*, 317; "Un tributo a Luis 'Jr' Martinez" (A tribute to Luis "Jr" Martinez), *El Gallo* (Denver), April–May 1976; "Denver Shoot-Out—19 Hurt," *Albuquerque Tribune*, March 17, 1973; "1 Dead in Denver Shootings," unknown newspaper, March 18, 1973, in Crusade for Justice, 1972–74 folder, Gutiérrez Papers, UTSA.

94. "One Dead, 19 Injured in Denver Shootout, Labeled 'Spontaneous,'" *Daily Sentinel* (Grand Junction, CO), March 18, 1973; "'Spontaneous Confrontation' Leaves 1 Dead, 19 Injured in Denver Incident," *Fort Collins Coloradan*, March 18, 1973; "Crusade Charges 'Trial by Press,'" *El Diario de la Gente* (Boulder, CO), April 10, 1973; "Massacre Denounced," *Arrow* (CSU Pueblo), April 26, 1973; "Solidarity Is Theme for March 17 Rally," *El Diario de la Gente* (Boulder, CO), March 8, 1974.

95. "Chicano Activist Group to Probe Denver Shooting," *Fort Collins Coloradan*, March 19, 1973.

96. "Civil Rights Investigation Is Dropped," *Greeley (CO) Daily Tribune*, April 19, 1973.

97. "Ramirez Cleared of All Charges in Crusade Massacre," *El Diario de la Gente* (Boulder, CO), September 14, 1973.

98. "March, 1973 Police Attack," *El Gallo* (Denver), May–June 1975.

99. "No mas agresion" (No more aggression), *El Gallo* (Denver), May–June 1975. See also "Tribute to Luis 'Jr' Martinez."

100. "Informant in Alleged Bomb Plot Taped Talks," *Rocky Mountain News* (Denver), September 28, 1975; "Haro & Quintana," *El Gallo* (Denver), October–November 1975.

See also the one-sided statement of McDonald, "Colorado Terrorism," in 94 Cong. Rec. H31267 (daily ed. October 1, 1975, extensions of remarks) (statement of Hon. Larry McDonald), www.congress.gov/bound-congressional-record/1975/10/01/extensions-of -remarks-section.

101. Ernesto Vigil to Denver Chicano Liberation Defense Committee, October 31, 1975, in Frank I. Sanchez Papers, UNM.

102. "Haro Denies All Charges, Claims Police Conspiracy," *Rocky Mountain News* (Denver), October 1, 1975; "Property Bond of $103,000 Posted for Haro," *Denver Post*, October 4, 1975.

103. "Informer, Denver Police Implicated in Burglary," *Rocky Mountain News* (Denver), September 30, 1975; "Denver Police Also Watched Informant in Restaurant Burglary," *Rocky Mountain News* (Denver), October 1, 1975; "Jose Cordova Jr.: An Enemy of the People," *El Gallo*, April 20, 1976.

104. "Juan . . . in Kangaroo Court," *El Gallo* (Denver), January–February 1976.

105. "Haro Sentenced to Leavenworth," *El Gallo* (Denver), September–October 1978; "Haro Starts Unjust Jail Term," *El Gallo* (Denver), January 1979.

106. "Quintana Charges Dropped, Juan Haro Not Guilty," *El Gallo* (Denver), June 1977; "Charges Dropped in Quintana Case," *La Cucaracha* (Pueblo, CO), May 1, 1977; Vigil, *Crusade for Justice*, 321.

107. "Police Probe Boulder Bombing," *Daily Sentinel* (Grand Junction, CO), May 29, 1974; "Grand Jury to Begin Investigation of Boulder Bombings That Killed 6," *Greeley (CO) Daily Tribune*, July 6, 1974; "Boulder Bombings, Others Still Unsolved," *Daily Sentinel* (Grand Junction, CO), August 19, 1974; "Los seis de Boulder" (The six of Boulder), *Boulder (CO) Weekly*, May 29, 2014.

108. "Free Veronica Vigil," *El Gallo*, October–November 1975; Free Veronica Vigil flyer, 1975, in Frank I. Sanchez Papers, UNM; Vigil, *Crusade for Justice*, 297–301.

109. A somewhat similar case of police collusion occurred when James Connely killed Dennis Lucero in Denver in 1976. Connely wasn't a police officer, but he had friends in the Denver Police Department who protected him. Police destroyed the gun used to kill Lucero, and without the gun, there was insufficient evidence to charge Connely. See "Lucero Killing, Double Standard of Justice," *El Gallo* (Denver), July 1976; and "Lucero Murderer Still Free," *El Gallo* (Denver), July 1977.

110. Editorial, "How Do We Differentiate between Today's Cops and Robbers?," *Rocky Mountain News* (Denver), October 5, 1975.

111. Francisco E. Martínez Legal Defense Fund to Dear Friend, n.d., in Francisco E. Martínez Papers, UNM; Francisco E. Martínez Defense Committee, "Chronology of Events," January 1981, in Reies López Tijerina Papers, UNM. For background, see Martínez, "'Kiko' Martínez Case"; and Barrera, "Political Repression of a Chicano Movement Activist."

112. Barrera, "Political Repression of a Chicano Movement Activist"; Nieto, "Running the Gauntlet," 365–78; Francisco E. Martínez Defense Committee, "Martínez Saga," newsletter, October 1986, in Frank I. Sanchez Papers, UNM; Martínez, " 'Kiko' Martinez Case."

113. There was a great deal of incorrect reporting about Martínez. For example, after he fled to Mexico he was accused of being a drug runner and having been arrested in a drug raid, both falsehoods.

114. Judge Winner's letter was reprinted in the *Francisco "Kiko" Martínez Defense Committee Newsletter*, May 1981, in Reies López Tijerina Papers, UNM.

115. *Francisco "Kiko" Martínez Defense Committee Newsletter*, May 1981.

116. *Francisco "Kiko" Martínez Defense Committee Newsletter*, May 1981. See also Peter Waack, "Litigating *Martinez v. Winner* Ten Years Later," ca. 1991; and Francisco "Kiko" Martínez Defense Committee, "Free Kiko, Stop Repression against Chicanos," flyer, ca. 1981; and "Aplastemos al Estado Todos a la Corte" (Crush the state, everyone to the court), flyer, ca. 1981, all in Martínez Papers, UNM.

117. "Judicial Jujitsu," *Westword* (Denver), September 17, 1981; "Magazine Dubs Utah Judge Best in 10th U.S. Circuit," *Salt Lake City Tribune*, July 25, 1983; *Martinez v. Winner* (1985).

118. "Judge Rejects Bomb Data in Martinez Case," *Denver Post*, August 8, 1981.

119. Francisco "Kiko" Martínez Defense Committee, "2d Trial: Not Guilty," press release, November 1982, in Martínez Papers, UNM; Francisco E. Martínez Defense Committee, "26 de octubre, 1986," press release, October 26, 1986, in Frank I. Sanchez Papers, UNM; Barrera, "Political Repression of a Chicano Movement Activist."

120. "Chicano Activist Freed of Indictment," *Arizona Daily Star* (Tucson), May 9, 1985; "U.S. Holds Vendetta, Hispanic Activist Says," *Rocky Mountain News* (Denver), October 7, 1986; "Chicano Activist Convicted of False Claim, Using Alias," *Arizona Daily Star* (Tucson), October 10, 1986.

121. Francisco E. Martínez Defense Committee, "October 26, 1986," update, in Frank I. Sanchez Papers, UNM; "Activist Who Lied to Judge Is Sentenced," *Arizona Republic* (Phoenix), December 16, 1986. See also "Francisco 'Kiko' Martinez, a Symbol of Chicanismo"; and "Press Conference Statement," both in *FUCK*, November 1973. I found this *FUCK* newspaper in Martínez Papers, UNM.

CHAPTER 3

1. "Officers Accused of Brutality," *Phoenix Gazette*, December 7, 1979; "Stop Police Brutality!," flyer, December 6, 1979, in Police Brutality folder, ASU; "Officials Are Confused," *Peoria Times* (Tempe, AZ), December 10, 1979.

2. For examples of police abuse leading up to the Sinohui case, see Lawrence Koslow, "The Chicano and the Police in Phoenix, Arizona: Some Comments and Observations," manuscript, April 1971, 4, in Lawrence Koslow folder, ASU; "Arrests at Debutante Party Sparks Battle in Phoenix," *Tucson Daily Citizen*, September 27, 1976; "Youths, Parents Claim 'Excessive Force' at Party," *Phoenix Gazette*, September 28, 1976; "Police Overly Forceful, Council Is Told," *Arizona Republic* (Phoenix), September 29, 1976.

3. "Officers Kill Man in Drive-In Melee," *Tucson Citizen*, July 2, 1977; "Victim's Family 'Can't Understand,'" *Arizona Daily Star* (Tucson), July 3, 1977; "Suspect Is Killed in Tucson," *Arizona Republic* (Phoenix), July 3, 1977.

4. "Hanigan, Sinohui Case, Hispanic Rights Denied," *Tucson Citizen*, November 5, 1980; "The Dean Case: Why Do We Seek Vengeance," *Tucson Citizen*, December 1, 1980.

5. "Officer Says Shooting Victim Tried to Ram Him with Truck," *Arizona Daily Star* (Tucson), July 3, 1977; "Witnesses Contradict Policeman," *Arizona Daily Star* (Tucson), July 5, 1977; "Witnesses Say No Attempt to Hit Officer," *Tucson Citizen*, July 5, 1977;

"Fatal Shot Aimed at Tire of Truck, Ex-Officer Says," *Arizona Republic* (Phoenix), October 19, 1979.

6. "Officer Suspended in Shooting Once Fired for Abuse of Power," *Arizona Daily Star* (Tucson), July 4, 1977; "Sinohui's Parents File Civil Suit in Son's Death," *Tucson Citizen*, October 5, 1979; "Opposing Views of Sinohui Killing Launch Trial in $5 Million Lawsuit," *Arizona Daily Star* (Tucson), October 5, 1979; "Judge Will Make Decision in Suit over Sinohui Death," *Tucson Citizen*, November 23, 1979; "Sinohuis Given $200,000 in Shooting Death of Son by Policeman," *Arizona Daily Star* (Tucson), March 29, 1980.

7. "50 Hispanics Demand Prosecution in Slaying," *Arizona Republic* (Phoenix), April 18, 1980.

8. "Sinohuis 'Crippled,' Says Lawyer," *Tucson Citizen*, March 27, 1980; "Sinohuis Won't Lose Grief, Attorney Says," *Arizona Daily Star* (Tucson), March 27, 1980; "Hanigans, Sinohuis Lose in Court," *Tucson Citizen*, October 18, 1980; "Sinohui Case Closed, Hanigans Lose Appeal," *Arizona Daily Star* (Tucson), October 18, 1980 (quotations).

9. "LULAC Recalls Sinohui," *Tucson Citizen*, June 27, 1980.

10. "U.S. to Evaluate Any New Data in Sinohui Case," *Arizona Daily Star* (Tucson), October 22, 1980; "Sinohui Probe May Be Revived," *Tucson Citizen*, October 22, 1980; "Sinohui Reprobe Is Urged," *Tucson Citizen*, November 11, 1980.

11. "Hispanic Rights Denied," *Tucson Citizen*, November 5, 1980.

12. "Violent Narcotics Raid Rattles Family but Net No Drugs," *Tucson Citizen*, August 17, 1979; "5 Claim Excessive Force; Cops Cite Mass Attack," *Arizona Daily Star* (Tucson), September 25, 1979.

13. "6 in Fight at Party Jailed," *Tucson Citizen*, September 22, 1979; "Montenegro Incident, Group Calls for Talks with Tucson Officials," *Arizona Daily Star* (Tucson), September 28, 1979; "7 Charged in Ruckus between Cops, Family," *Arizona Daily Star* (Tucson), October 17, 1979.

14. "Prosecutors Appealing Jury Trial for Montenegro," *Arizona Daily Star* (Tucson), January 8, 1980; "Defense Case Pre-Empted by Montenegro Mistrial," *Arizona Daily Star* (Tucson), January 19, 1980; "Retrial of Montenegro Scheduled for Feb. 13," *Tucson Citizen*, January 23, 1980; "Second Montenegro Is Found Not Guilty," *Tucson Citizen*, February 14, 1980; "Jose Montenegro Convicted," *Tucson Citizen*, February 22, 1980; "City Wins One, Loses One in Montenegro Litigation," *Tucson Citizen*, February 26, 1980.

15. "First Montenegro Cleared in Assault," *Arizona Daily Star* (Tucson), February 1, 1980; "Montenegro's Charges Dropped after 3 Officers Fail to Testify," *Arizona Daily Star* (Tucson), February 27, 1980.

16. "City Court Jury Finds First Montenegro Guilty on Reduced Charge," *Arizona Daily Star* (Tucson), February 22, 1980; "Third Acquittal in Montenegro Incident," *Arizona Daily Star* (Tucson), February 20, 1980.

17. "Magistrate Acquits Last Montenegro," *Arizona Daily Star* (Tucson), April 8, 1980.

18. "Minorities Meet to Back Family in Police Complaint," *Tucson Citizen*, September 25, 1979; "Group Calls for Talks with Tucson Officials," *Arizona Daily Star* (Tucson), September 28, 1979.

19. "Gilkinson to Chart Easier Access on Police Problems." *Arizona Daily Star* (Tucson), September 29, 1979.

20. "Panel to Check Police-Civilian Relations," *Arizona Daily Star* (Tucson), October 2, 1979; "Panel on Police Nearer," *Tucson Citizen*, October 8, 1979.

21. "Montenegros File $1 Million Lawsuit," *Arizona Daily Star* (Tucson), October 6, 1979; "Montenegros Sue Police, City over Arrests at Party," *Tucson Citizen*, October 6, 1979.

22. "7 Charged in Ruckus between Cops, Family."

23. "Officer Denies 'Prejudiced' Arrest," *Tucson Citizen*, February 13, 1982; "City Denies Racism in Drunken-Driving Arrest," *Arizona Daily Star* (Tucson), February 20, 1982.

24. Field sobriety tests are not conclusive in most states, which require a blood-alcohol test. "Racial Prejudice Alleged in Drunken-Driving Case," *Arizona Daily Star* (Tucson), February 10, 1982.

25. "Police Panel Necessary," *Arizona Daily Star* (Tucson), November 9, 1979.

26. "Minorities Want 8-Member Panel to Watch Police," *Arizona Daily Star* (Tucson), December 8, 1979.

27. "Valdez Urges Weaker Police Review Board," *Tucson Citizen*, December 13, 1979.

28. "City, Minorities Agree on Police Advisory Panel," *Arizona Daily Star* (Tucson), November 1, 1979; "Minority Groups Reject Proposal for Police Panel," *Tucson Citizen*, November 2, 1979; "Police Board Ok'd for Study," *Tucson Citizen*, December 19, 1979; "Tucson OKs Weakened Version of Police-Review Board," *Arizona Republic* (Phoenix), February 26, 1980.

29. "A Chronological History of Abuse and Discrimination of Chicanos in San Diego County," ca. 1982, in U.S.-Mexico Border Violence, 1983–2005 folder, Roberto Martinez Papers, UCSD.

30. "Abell [sic] Gill Defense Committee," *El Gallo* (Denver), April–May 1979; "Fleeing 15-Year Old Shot by Police near Home of Witness under Guard," *San Bernardino County (CA) Sun*, April 27, 1979; "Coalition Protests Handling of Police Shooting Probes," *Los Angeles Times*, June 27, 1979.

31. "Trevino Slain: Cops Cleared," *El Gallo* (Denver), April–May 1976; "Police Shooting Reminds Family of Earlier Tragedy," Recordnet.com, September 4, 1995, updated January 7, 2011, www.recordnet.com/article/19950904/a_news/309049977.

32. "The Facts," flyer, n.d., in Frank I. Sanchez Papers, UNM; "100 Protest Shooting Death," *San Francisco Examiner*, June 19, 1976.

33. "The Cop's Terrible Dilemma: When to Pull the Trigger," *San Francisco Examiner*, December 25, 1977.

34. "Garbage Rates Going Up in Oakland," *San Francisco Examiner*, June 30, 1976.

35. "100 Protest Shooting Death," *San Francisco Examiner*, June 19, 1976.

36. BBCAPC flyer, n.d., in Frank I. Sanchez Papers, UNM.

37. "The Cop's Terrible Dilemma," *San Francisco Examiner*, December 25, 1977.

38. "City Policeman Kills Suspect after Chase," *Albuquerque Journal*, August 14, 1968; "Albuquerque Man Killed," *Las Vegas Optic*, August 14, 1968. The 1950s-style rear fins on the 1959 Chrysler were taller, the blue paint was darker, and the 1959 vehicle had double headlights, differences a police officer would know.

39. "Data on Death of Suspect Goes to DA," *Albuquerque Journal*, August 15, 1968.

40. Brown Berets, "Why We Are Here," flyer, August 1968; and "The Murder of Tommy Valles," flyer, ca. August 1968, both in Reies López Tijerina Papers, UNM;

Brown Berets, "We Demand of Our City Commission," flyer, August 1968, in Gloria Montoya Chavez Papers, UNM; "Berets Make Demands," *Santa Fe New Mexican*, August 20, 1968 (first quotation); "Review of Police Demanded in City," *Albuquerque Journal*, August 20, 1968 (second quotation).

41. "Policeman Faces Threats Alone," *Albuquerque Journal*, August 25, 1968; "Berets Reject City Report on Shooting," *Albuquerque Journal*, August 27, 1968.

42. "Johnny Valles Is Indicted in Burglary," *Albuquerque Journal*, November 1, 1968; "Valles Fined $50 on Driving Count," *Albuquerque Journal*, September 6, 1968.

43. "Policeman Sued for Death," *Albuquerque Journal*, July 24, 1971; "Mistrial Is Ruled in Shooting Case," *Albuquerque Journal*, September 14, 1973.

44. "Resigned Policemen Say Action Possibly Forced," *Albuquerque Journal*, July 6, 1974; "City Policemen Fired," *Albuquerque Journal*, September 24, 1974; "Policeman Allowed Job Back," *Albuquerque Journal*, October 10, 1974.

45. "Complaint Filed against Officers," *Albuquerque Journal*, October 23, 1974; "Charges Are Dismissed against Two Policemen," *Albuquerque Journal*, January 1, 1975.

46. "Charges Are Dismissed against Two Policemen"; "Order of Dismissal Filed for Police Case," *Albuquerque Journal*, January 16, 1975.

47. "Officers Sentence Ruled," *Albuquerque Journal*, January 14, 1975.

48. "Judge Changes Order to Defer Police Case," *Albuquerque Journal*, January 18, 1975.

49. "Police Didn't Heed 'Warning Signs' on Babich," *Albuquerque Tribune*, March 8, 1979.

50. "Man Dies in Police Struggle," *Las Vegas Optic*, November 11, 1977; "Babich Held for Trial on Manslaughter," *Las Vegas Optic*, December 29, 1977; "Officer Fired in Beating Death," *Santa Fe New Mexican*, November 16, 1977; "Ex-Policeman Ordered to Stand Trial for Death," *Albuquerque Journal*, December 30, 1977.

51. "'Mild Blow' Testimony Heard in Babich Trial," *Santa Fe New Mexican*, February 23, 1978; "Babich Describes Act of Swinging Flashlight," *Albuquerque Journal*, February 24, 1978.

52. "Lawyer to Pursue Babich Case," *Albuquerque Journal*, September 24, 1978.

53. "Man Files Suit," *Santa Fe New Mexican*, September 20, 1978; "Mistrial Declared," *Roswell (NM) Daily Record*, September 24, 1978; "City Pays $72,900 in Babich Case," *Albuquerque Journal*, February 28, 1979.

54. "Stover Gets Police Letters on Force Use," *Albuquerque Journal*, March 9, 1979.

55. "Officers Tell of Wrestling for Rifle before Shooting," *Santa Fe New Mexican*, February 16, 1978.

56. "Jury Probes Boy's Death," *Albuquerque Journal*, March 31, 1978; "Las Vegas Tragedy Tale Still Varies with Teller," *Albuquerque Journal*, May 21, 1978.

57. "Agentes de la Policia Asesinan a Frank Garcia" (Police agents murder Frank Garcia), *Justicia*, September 1978, in Reies López Tijerina Papers, UNM; "Raza Unida Wants Shooting Probe," *Albuquerque Journal*, February 22, 1978.

58. "San Miguel Jury Declines to Indict State Policemen," *Albuquerque Journal*, April 4, 1978.

59. "Assault Trial Jury Starts Deliberations," *Albuquerque Journal*, November 17, 1978; "Vegas Man Guilty of Assault," *Albuquerque Journal*, November 18, 1978.

60. "Mother Sues State Police, Two Officers," *Albuquerque Journal*, May 8, 1979; "Wrongful Death Settled," *Santa Fe New Mexican*, October 7, 1981.

61. "M.A.Y.O. Jefe Raps," *El Deguello*, June 1969; "New Wind from the Southwest," *The Nation*, May 30, 1966; Gutiérrez, interview; Navarro, *Mexican American Youth Organization*. Willie Velázquez is an interesting figure in Chicano history. His untimely death in 1988 is widely and correctly viewed as a tragedy. See Sepúlveda, *Life and Times of Willie Velásquez*; and "Willie Velasquez, 1944–1988," *Texas Observer*, July 29, 1988.

62. "MAYOs Here Fold; New Group Foreseen," *Houston Post*, March 2, 1971.

63. "FBI Will Probe Slaying in Mathis," *Houston Chronicle*, July 15, 1970; "Friend of Chicanos-Doctor's Death Stirs Town," *Dallas Morning News*, July 19, 1970; "No Mathis Hearings, Says Dies," *San Antonio Express*, July 21, 1970; "MAYO to Protest Shooting of Doctor," *Houston Post*, July 21, 1970; "Death Stirs Mathis Talks with MAYO," *Houston Post*, July 22, 1970; Truan, interview.

64. "Crowd Faces Police, Demands Resignation," *Corpus Christi Caller*, October 9, 1970.

65. "Black San Antonio III: They Call It Police Brutality," *San Antonio Express*, February 15, 1972; "Black San Antonio V: Political Inroads," *San Antonio Express*, February 17, 1972; "Bobby Jo Phillips Investigative File 1968," in box 10, folder 4, Mario Salas Papers, UTSA; Salas, interview.

66. Salas, interview; Behnken, *Fighting Their Own Battles*, 168.

67. "500 Peacefully Protest Alleged Police Misconduct," *San Antonio Express*, November 21, 1971; for background on the San Antonio Brown Berets, see Montejano, *Sancho's Journal*.

68. "Death Called 'Near Execution,'" *Odessa (TX) American*, March 29, 1968; "3 Austin Policemen Cleared in Shooting," *Corpus Christi Caller-Times*, March 29, 1968; Joseph P. Witherspoon, "The Austin Police, a Tragic Violation of the Law, and Recommendations," April 11, 1968, in Mario G. Obledo Papers, Special Collections Department, University of California, Davis; James F. Dear and Jeffrey M. Friedman, brief, April 25, 1968; and Haver C. Currie to Mayor Akin, April 30, 1968, both in Haver C. Currie, "Papers Concerned with Mexican-Americans in Austin and Travis County," APL.

69. "Police under New Gun Rule," unknown newspaper, July 26, 1968; "New Police Policy Is Changed," unknown newspaper, September 25, 1968; and Witherspoon, "Austin Police," all in Obledo Papers, Special Collections Department, University of California, Davis.

70. "Police Kill Suspect," *Austin American-Statesman*, August 1, 1971.

71. "Slain Boy Stayed out of Spotlight," *Austin American*, August 2, 1971.

72. "Policemen's Guns Due Tests in Cedillo Shooting Probe," *Austin American*, August 3, 1971; "Inquiry into Boy's Death Held," *Austin American*, August 4, 1971; "Youth's Death 'Justified,'" *Austin American*, August 6, 1971.

73. "Pickets to Protest Death of Young Boy," *Austin American*, August 5, 1971; "East Side Killing Protested," *Austin American*, August 6, 1971.

74. "Full Scale Rioting Sweeps Pharr Streets," *Valley Morning Star* (McAllen, TX), February 7, 1971; "Poncho Flores Is Dead," *Texas Observer*, February 26, 1971; Robles, "'It Was Us against Us,'" 136–39; Robles, "Chicano Revolt and Political Response," 126–27.

75. "Man Injured in Pharr Riot Dead of Bullet Wound," *Valley Morning Star* (McAllen, TX), February 8, 1971; "Poncho Flores Is Dead"; Flores, interview; Robles, "Chicano Revolt and Political Response," 116.

76. "Conferencia estatal en contra represión policial," ca. March 1971, in Reies López Tijerina Papers, UNM.

77. "Hidalgo County Deputy Sheriff Found Innocent of Negligent Homicide in Pharr Riot Death," *El Paso Times*, February 9, 1973; "Pharr Riots' Anniversary Marks Watershed Moment in Valley History," *The Monitor* (McAllen, TX), February 6, 2016, l; Campney, "'Bunch of Tough Hombres.'"

78. "Chicanos, Anglos, y Negros protestaron" (Chicanos, whites, and Blacks protest), *El Sol de Texas* (Dallas), March 5, 1971; "The Rodriguez Story," *Dallas News*, March 10–24, 1971; "Chicanos Protest Shooting," *Dallas News*, March 10–24, 1971; "Guzman y Lopez por tres muertes" (Guzman and Lopez for three deaths), *El Sol de Texas* (Dallas), March 12, 1971; "Chicanos y Negros preparan fuerte boicot" (Chicanos and Blacks prepare for strong boycott), *El Sol de Texas* (Dallas), March 19, 1971; "Chicanos March in Protest of Rodriguez Treatment," *El Sol de Texas* (Dallas), March 26, 1971; "Dallas Latins March in Protest," *El Sol* (Houston), April 2, 1972; "Brown Berets forman comite" (Brown Berets form committee), *Papel Chicano* (Houston), September 2, 1971; "One Year Later—Rodriguez Family Still Survives," *Iconoclast*, February 25–March 3, 1972; "The Law Fails Rodriguezes," *Iconoclast*, March 31–April 7, 1972; Behnken, *Fighting Their Own Battles*, 174–75; Behnken, "'We Want Justice!,'" 196–200; Bynum, "Civil Rights in the 'City of Hate.'"

79. "Santos Rodriguez," *Tejano News Magazine*, August 2–16, 1974.

80. "Questioning of Brothers Ends in Dallas Tragedy," *Dallas Times Herald*, July 24, 1973; "Policeman Involved in Previous Shooting," *Dallas Morning News*, July 25, 1973; "Fingerprints Don't Match," *Dallas Morning News*, July 26, 1973; "Minorities Hope Child's Death Will Bring Change," *Iconoclast*, August 3–10, 1973. See also Hernández, "¡Justicia for Santos!," 78–106.

81. "Morehead Death Tightened DPD's Firearm Policy," *Dallas Times Herald*, July 25, 1973; "Minorities Hope Child's Death Will Bring Change"; Achor, *Mexican Americans in a Dallas Barrio*, 148–53; Payne, *Big D*, 416–18.

82. "Santos Rodriguez," *Tejano News Magazine*, August 2–16, 1974.

83. As quoted in "March Began in Peace, Ended in Violence," *Dallas Times Herald*, July 29, 1973.

84. "March Began in Peace, Ended in Violence"; "Angry Crowd Burns and Loots in Downtown Dallas Rampage," *Dallas Times Herald*, July 29, 1973; "City March Dissolves into Random Violence," *Dallas Morning News*, July 29, 1973; Behnken, "'We Want Justice!,'" 199–200.

85. "Police Security Guards against Disturbance Repeat," *Dallas Times Herald*, July 30, 1973; "Downtown Area Guarded," *Dallas Morning News*, July 30, 1973; *Cain v. State* (1977).

86. As quoted in Williams and Shay, *And Justice for All*, 148.

87. "New Deputy Chiefs," *Dallas Morning News*, August 23, 1973; "Police Shakeup," *Dallas Morning News*, January 22, 1974; Dulaney, "Whatever Happened to the Civil Rights Movement in Dallas, Texas?," 88–89; Taylor Danser and Dianne Solis, "40 Years after Son's Death, Bessie Rodriguez Surprised by Mayor's Apology," *Dallas Morning News*, September 21, 2013.

88. "Notes on HPD Problems," June 2, 1977, in Relations, Police, Community, Correspondence, Brochure, 1977–78 folder, Ben T. Reyes Papers, HPL. See also Guzmán Hays, "Brown Bodies and Police Killings," 51–74.

89. For information on the Houston Police Department, see Watson, *Race and the Houston Police Department*. Steven Wilson examines the Torres case in Wilson, *Rise of Judicial Management*, 247–71. See also Watson, "Murder on the Bayou," 57–68; and Rodriguez, "Racial Injustice in Houston, Texas," 96–157.

90. "Police Officer Charged with Murder of Man," *Houston Chronicle*, May 10, 1977; "Slain Man's Brother Asks 'Why' of Death," *Houston Post*, May 11, 1977; "The Hole," *Houston Chronicle*, May 14, 1977; "Torres," *Houston Chronicle*, May 15, 1977; "The Torres Case," *Texas Observer*, June 17, 1977; "'Oh, My God, They've Really Thrown Him In,'" *Houston Post*, September 16, 1977. This was a major story across the United States. See "5 Houston Police Officers Suspended in Beating, Drowning of Mexican-American," *Los Angeles Times*, May 13, 1977; "Police in Houston Pictured as Brutal and Unchecked," *Washington Post*, June 13, 1977; and "Houston Fighters Spread Rebellion," *The Worker*, January 6, 1979.

91. "Past Torres Violence Alleged," *Houston Post*, September 30, 1977; "Torres Violent When Drunk," *Houston Post*, September 30, 1977. See also "New Gang in Town," *Texas Monthly*, September 1977.

92. "Bond Moving to Fire 6 Officers Linked to Alleged Murder," *Houston Chronicle*, May 12, 1977; "Bond Fires Five Officers in Torres Death Case," *Houston Chronicle*, May 12, 1977; "5 of 6 Officers Fired in Torres Death Case," *Houston Post*, May 13, 1977; "U.S. Probe of Torres Death Is Sought," *Houston Chronicle*, May 13, 1977.

93. Mayor Fred Hofheinz news conference; and Mayor Fred Hofheinz news conference excerpts, May 16, 1977, both in Fred Hofheinz—Speech Transcripts folder, Mayor Fred Hofheinz Papers, HPL.

94. Representative Ben T. Reyes, press release, May 11, 1977, in Reyes Papers, HPL.

95. For a variety of appeals written on behalf of Torres by local leaders, see Ben T. Reyes to Drew S. Days III, May 19, 1977; Days to Reyes, June 1, 1977; Hilda D. Garcia to Griffin Bell, May 11, 1977; Henry B. Gonzalez to Reyes, May 18, 1977; Texas Representative Joe L. Hernandez to Bell, May 19, 1977; Texas Representative Arnold Gonzales to Bell, May 19, 1977; and Congresswoman Barbara Jordan to Bell, May 23, 1977, all in Reyes Papers, HPL.

96. See Coalition for Responsible Law Enforcement proposal, n.d., in Relations, Police, Community, Correspondence, Brochure, 1977–78 folder, Reyes Papers, HPL.

97. Coalition for Responsible Law Enforcement newsletter, September 1977, in Relations, Police, Community, Correspondence, Brochure, 1977–78 folder, Reyes Papers, HPL. The second revision was most likely a response to the police killing of Black Power leader Carl Hampton—whom plainclothes police snipers had killed in 1970. On Hampton, see Behnken, *Fighting Their Own Battles*, 163–64.

98. "Orlando's Story Has Variations," *Houston Post*, September 28, 1977; "Orlando Says He Lied When First Queried," *Houston Post*, September 29, 1977.

99. "Police Officer Charged with Murder of Man"; "Police Officers' Defense: Five Expected to Contend Bayou Drowning Not Intentional," *Houston Post*, May 13, 1977; "Police Rookie Recounts Arrest of Joe Torres," *Houston Post*, September 15, 1977; "Torres Case"; "'Oh, My God, They've Really Thrown Him In.'"

100. "Ex-Officer Admits Beating Torres," *Houston Chronicle*, September 20, 1977; "'To Save My Hide,'" *Houston Post*, September 21, 1977. See also "Police Story: Two Hard Towns," *Time*, September 19, 1977.

101. "Body Bruised, Autopsy Shows," *Houston Post*, May 15, 1977; "Official Says Torres Had Little Chance," *Houston Post*, September 23, 1977.

102. "Jury Set to Begin Deliberating Today in Trial of Officers," *Houston Post*, October 4, 1977; "Torres Case Jury Deliberates," *Houston Post*, October 5, 1977; "Negligent Homicide Is Verdict in Torres Case, " *Houston Chronicle*, October 6, 1977; "Bitterness Greets Verdict," *Houston Post*, October 7, 1977; "Politics, Moving of Trial Hurt Case, Prober Thinks," *Houston Post*, October 7, 1977 (quotations); "Orlando, Denson Get Probated Sentence," *Houston Post*, October 8, 1977; "No Evidence, Jurors Claim," *Houston Post*, October 8, 1977; "LULAC Leader Calls Torres Case Verdict 'Unconscionable,'" *Houston Informer*, October 15, 1977. For some reason, the fine the officers received was reported to have been one dollar. This seems to be a mistake, possibly due to a misstatement from Houston Police Department Chief Bond when he said, "To think that a human life is worth one dollar and a probated sentence is tragic and it offends me." See "Torres Sentences Sharply Criticized," *El Paso Herald-Post*, October 8, 1977.

103. "2 Ex-Officers Convicted," *Houston Post*, October 7, 1977 (first quotation); "Federal Trial Still Possible," *Houston Post*, October 7, 1977; "Mexican-American Groups Looking to Federal Process," *Houston Post*, October 7, 1977 (second quotation); "LULAC Will Lobby for Civil Rights Law," *Houston Post*, October 9, 1977. See also "LULAC Director to Ask U.S. Probe of Alleged Police Murder of Torres," *Houston Chronicle*, May 11, 1977; and Paul Moreno to Griffin Bell, October 18, 1977; and Henry Gonzalez to Ben Reyes, October 18, 1977, both in Reyes Papers, HPL.

104. "About 200 Protest Torres Case Verdict," *Houston Post*, October 9, 1977; "Protests May Bring U.S. into Mexican-American Civil Rights Cases," *Arizona Daily Star* (Tucson), October 13, 1977; "March, Rally in City Protest Verdicts of Torres Case Jury," *Houston Chronicle*, October 16, 1977; "400 Chicanos March to Demand 'Houston Police, Out of Our Community!,'" *El Gallo*, November 1977; "Communities March in Unity against Police Brutality," "Demonstrate!," and "Justice for Joe Torres!!!," protest flyers, ca. October 1977, in Reyes Papers, HPL.

105. "Parents of Torres Charged, Beating by Police Alleged," *Houston Post*, October 10, 1977; "Police, Witnesses Differ on Arrest of Torres' Parents," *Houston Post*, October 11, 1977; "Torres' Parents Jailed, Claim Cop Brutality," *Houston Informer*, October 15, 1977.

106. Watson, *Race and the Houston Police Department*, 116. See also Houston Crime Commission, "Internal Affairs Board," Fifth Annual Report, December 1962, in Houston Crime Commission Report folder, Mayor Louie Welch Papers, HPL.

107. "The Torres Case," *Houston Post*, October 21, 1977; "Mayor Lauds Officers' Indictments," *Houston Post*, October 22, 1977; "Torres Case Goes to Jury," *Houston Post*, February 7, 1978; "Many Will Await Sentencing to See If Justice Served," *Houston Post*, February 9, 1978; "3 Former Officers Convicted of Violating Torres' Rights," *Houston Post*, February 9, 1978.

108. "Torres' Mother Unhappy," *Houston Post*, March 29, 1978; "Many Critical of Punishment and Comments by the Judge," *Houston Post*, March 29, 1978 (quotation); "Chicano Leaders Say Sterling Is Prejudiced," *Houston Informer*, April 29, 1978.

109. "Justice Dept. Assails Judge in Houston Drowning Case," *Los Angeles Times*, April 6, 1978.

110. United States v. Denson, 588 F.2d 112 (5th Cir. 1979); United States v. Denson, 603 F.2d 1143 (5th Cir. 1979); "1-Year Sentences Imposed in Houston Brutality Case," *Washington Post*, October 31, 1979.

111. People United to Fight Police Brutality, "Jail Joe Torres' Murderers for Life!," flyer, March 28, 1978, Joe Camps Torres folder, Small Collections 47, HPL.

112. "McConn Supports Protest," *Houston Post*, March 30, 1978; "McConn Says Police to 'Assist' March," *Houston Chronicle*, March 31, 1978; "Demonstrators Protest Torres Case Sentences," *Houston Post*, April 3, 1978; "End of the Rope," *Time*, April 17, 1978.

113. "Chicano Fete Erupts in Violence," *Houston Informer*, May 13, 1978; "Morales, 2 Others Held on Riot Charges," *Houston Post*, May 13, 1978.

114. "More Violence Flares Up on Houston's North Side," *Houston Chronicle*, May 9, 1978.

115. "Anti-Police Protester Says His Outlook Is Communist," *Houston Chronicle*, May 10, 1978; "Chicano Charged in Riot Defends Marxist Views," *Dallas Times Herald*, June 4, 1978.

116. "Old Injustices Called Fuel for Park Rioting," *Houston Chronicle*, May 9, 1978.

117. "North Side Group Urges Open Park, Increasing Police Patrols," *Houston Chronicle*, May 10, 1978.

118. "Houston Unrest Outcropping of Ethnic Growth," *San Antonio Express-News*, May 13, 1978.

119. "Houston Police Hit for Not Using Force," *San Antonio Express-News*, May 14, 1978; "Barrios Are Festering Blot on Houston," *San Antonio Express*, May 15, 1978.

120. "Morales' Lawyers Try for Lower Bond," *Houston Chronicle*, May 14, 1978.

121. See "On Cinco de Mayo It's Right to Rebel," flyer, May 13, 1978, in Moody Park Riot folder, Reyes Papers, HPL.

122. "Morales' Lawyers Try for Lower Bond," *Houston Chronicle*, May 14, 1978; "Mothers Hold Peace March to Moody Park," *Houston Chronicle*, May 15, 1978.

123. "The Houston Rebellion," flyer, ca. May 1978, in Moody Park Incident folder, Mexican-American Small Collections, HPL. Gil Scott-Heron also memorialized Torres in his "Poem for Jose Campos Torres."

124. "Moody Park 3 Trial Begins," *Revolution*, April 1975.

125. "Criminal Verdict Hits Moody Park 3!," *Revolutionary Worker*, May 18, 1979; "Echoes of the Moody Park Rebellion," *Revolutionary Worker*, June 7, 1998; "Support for Houston Rebellion Grows," protest flyer, ca. 1978; "Free the Moody Park 3," ca. 1978; "Demonstrate October 29," protest flyer, ca.1978; and "Trial Bulletin, Railroad Starts Monday April 16, Free the Moody Park 3!," ca. 1979, all in Moody Park Riot Papers, HPL.

126. "U.S. Panel Begins Review of Houston Police Reforms," *Arizona Republic* (Phoenix), September 11, 1979; "Jail Terms Ordered for 3 Officers," *Arizona Republic* (Phoenix), October 5, 1979; "Hispanics Upset with Sentence in Man's Death," *Phoenix Gazette*, October 31, 1979.

127. "Youth Shot to Death," *El Paso Times*, January 23, 1978; "Death of Moon City Youth Called 'Intended, Senseless,'" *El Paso Times*, January 24, 1978; "Brother Shooting 'Cold-Blooded,'" *El Gallo* (Denver), March–April 1978.

128. "Brother Shooting 'Cold-Blooded'"; "Harassing by Officers Charged," *El Gallo* (Denver), March–April 1978.

129. "Death of Moon City Youth Called 'Intended, Senseless'"; "Intentional Harassing of Youths Denied by Sheriff's Department," *El Paso Times*, January 25, 1978.

130. "Moon City Citizens Call for DA Probe," *El Paso Times*, January 27, 1978; "E. P. Deputy Murders Chicano Youth," *El Gallo* (Denver), March–April 1978; "LULAC, City Trying to Keep Lid on South Side," *El Paso Times*, May 14, 1978.

131. "Vasquez Killing 'Justifiable Homicide,'" *El Paso Herald*, March 8, 1978; "Danny Vasquez Defense Committee," *El Gallo* (Denver), January 1979.

132. "Justice Won't Pursue Action against Deputy," *El Paso Times*, February 8, 1979; "Justice Dept. Ignores Danny's Murder," *El Gallo* (Denver), April–May 1979; Danny Vasquez Justice Committee to Griffin Bell, n.d.; and "Justicia para Danny Vasquez," flyer, n.d., both in "Justice for Danny Vasquez" file, Herman Baca Collection, UCSD, https://library.ucsd.edu/dc/object/bb3755590p/_1.pdf.

133. "Danny Vasquez Case Protested," *El Paso Times*, May 24, 1979; "Suit in Shooting Goes to Jury Today," *El Paso Times*, February 27, 1981; "Jury Absolves Deputy in Death of Teen-Age Boy," *El Paso Times*, February 28, 1981.

134. Defense Office, "What to Do If You Get Busted," flyer, n.d., in Martínez Papers, UNM; Hector P. Garcia, statement, 1978, in American G. I. Forum (1959, 1960, 1966, 1973–74, 1976–79) folder, Samuel Garcia Papers, Genealogy, Local History and Archives, Fort Worth Public Library, TX.

135. See, e.g., US House of Representatives, "Brutality by Law Enforcement Agencies," in Reies López Tijerina Papers, UNM.

136. "Group Will Air Rights Abuses in Mexico," *El Paso Times*, June 8, 1978; "67 Chicanos asesinados en EU, denuncia L. Tijerina" (67 Chicanos murdered in US, alleges L. Tijerina), unknown newspaper, June 16, 1978, in Reies López Tijerina Papers, UNM.

137. "U.S. Probes Alleged Brutality to Hispanics," *San Antonio Express*, May 15, 1978; "Chicanos Want U.S. Panel to Probe Police Brutality," *Houston Chronicle*, May 24, 1978.

138. "Mexican-Americans Call for Police Brutality Study," *Tucson Citizen*, May 25, 1978; Vilma S. Martinez to President Jimmy Carter, May 31, 1978, in Reies López Tijerina Papers, UNM; "Mexican-American Leaders Police Brutality Told," *San Antonio Express-News*, May 20, 1978.

139. MALDEF, press release, June 21, 1978, in Reies López Tijerina Papers, UNM.

140. "Hispanics Warn of Long, Hot Summer," *Arizona Republic* (Phoenix), May 24, 1980 (first quotation); "Hispanic Coalition: U.S. Slow to Prosecute Police Excess," *Tucson Citizen*, May 24, 1980; "Miami Riots Should Rekindle Efforts for New Sinohui Case, Group Says," *Arizona Daily Star* (Tucson), May 24, 1980 (second quotation). See also "Hispanic Tide Keeps Rolling," *Phoenix Gazette*, June 27, 1980; Lentzner et al., *Hispanic Victim*; and "An Unequal Society," *Washington Post*, March 28, 1978.

CHAPTER 4

1. Prestwood was likely the officer with Narvaez—they had worked together previously—but the record in regards to the incident with Narvaez is not clear. See "Veteran Continental Pilot Lands on Mesa," *Albuquerque Tribune*, August 15, 1966.

2. "Pete Garcia Trial Notes," n.d., in Gloria Montoya Chavez Papers, UNM; "Man Critical after Police Shooting," *Santa Fe New Mexican*, March 27, 1969.

3. "Pete Garcia Trial Notes."

4. "Pete Garcia Trial Notes"; "Man Charged in Slaying of Officer," *Albuquerque Journal*, March 27, 1969. In a more colloquial sense, Garcia's "ya me chingaste" could be translated as something along the lines of "fuck, now you really got me."

5. "Suspect in Murder Listed as Serious," *Albuquerque Journal*, March 30, 1969.

6. "Man Charged in Death in 'Good' Condition," *Albuquerque Journal*, April 10, 1969; "Innocent Plea Entered in Slaying of Lawman," *Albuquerque Journal*, May 10, 1969; "Defense to Claim Deputy Violent Man," *Clovis (NM) News-Journal*, August 29, 1969; "Self-Defense Plea Backed," *Albuquerque Journal*, September 30, 1969.

7. "Jury Selection Continues," *Santa Fe New Mexican*, August 26, 1969; "Defense to Claim Deputy Violent Man"; "Witnesses Tell of Struggle in Garcia Trial Testimony," *Albuquerque Journal*, August 29, 1969; "Dramatic Peak Reached in Trial," *Clovis (NM) News-Journal*, September 1, 1969; "Pete Garcia Trial Notes."

8. "Self-Defense Plea Backed"; "Trial Defense Will Conclude," *Santa Fe New Mexican*, September 3, 1969.

9. "Jury Scheduled to Get Garcia Case Today," *Albuquerque Journal*, September 4, 1969; "Murder Trial Is Deadlocked," unknown newspaper, n.d., in Chavez Papers, UNM; "Mistrial Declared in Garcia Case," *Santa Fe New Mexican*, September 7, 1969.

10. "Garcia Retrial Set for Oct. 6," *Albuquerque Journal*, September 9, 1969; "Garcia's Second Trial for Murder Starts Today," *Albuquerque Journal*, December 2, 1969; "Pete Garcia Shot Officer; State's Witness Affirms," *Albuquerque Journal*, December 6, 1969; "Prosecution Rests Case in Garcia Murder Trial," *Albuquerque Journal*, December 10, 1969; "Witness Testifies Garcia Was Beaten by Sergeant," *Albuquerque Journal*, December 11, 1969; "Psychologist Testifies Garcia Shot Narvaez 'Instinctively,'" *Albuquerque Journal*, December 12, 1969; "Garcia Ruled Guilty by Jurors," *Clovis (NM) News-Journal*, December 14, 1969; "Garcia Gets 2 to 10 Years; Released on $10,000 Bond," *Albuquerque Journal*, December 18, 1969; "Tried and Retried and Still No Justice," *El Grito del Norte* (Española, NM), December 24, 1969.

11. *State v. Garcia* (1971); "Garcia Conviction Reversed," *Albuquerque Tribune*, July 31, 1971.

12. "New Garcia Trial Set for Oct. 13," *Albuquerque Journal*, August 12, 1971; "Prosecution Rests in Garcia Trial," *Albuquerque Journal*, December 15, 1971; "Self-Defense Claimed in Garcia Trial," *Albuquerque Journal*, December 16, 1971; "Garcia Found Guilty in Shooting of Deputy," *Albuquerque Journal*, December 18, 1971; "White Amerika Finds Pedro Garcia Guilty," *El Grito del Norte* (Española, NM), December 1971.

13. "Garcia Sought in Shooting," *Santa Fe New Mexican*, January 7, 1972; "Bench Warrant Issued for Garcia," *Albuquerque Journal*, January 11, 1972; "Warrant Issued," *Santa Fe New Mexican*, January 24, 1972.

14. "Police Still Searching for Pete, Mary Garcia," *Albuquerque Journal*, July 7, 1972; "Pete Garcia Jailed by Mexican Police," *Albuquerque Journal*, February 23, 1974; "Shooting Suspect in Mexico City Jail," *Albuquerque Journal*, February 25, 1974; "Mexicans Seeking Pete Garcia," *Albuquerque Journal*, July 25, 1975; "Bail Jumpers' 'Ghosts' Still Haunt U.S. Authorities," *Albuquerque Journal*, May 16, 1977.

15. "Authorities to Return Fugitive Today," *Albuquerque Journal*, June 8, 1979; "Fugitive Comes Home," *Albuquerque Journal*, June 10, 1979.

16. "Man Faces Fourth Trial in 1969 Slaying of Deputy," *Albuquerque Journal*, June 18, 1980.

17. "Possibilities of Retrying Accused Killer Dwindle," *Albuquerque Journal*, January 10, 1981.

18. "Officials Believe Suspect in '69 Slaying Is Dead," *Albuquerque Journal*, January 27, 1981; "Attorney Believes Client Dead," *Carlsbad (NM) Current-Argus*, January 27, 1981; "Delay Asked for Retrial of Pete Garcia," *Albuquerque Journal*, April 3, 1981.

19. "Verdict Is In—Brunson 'Not Guilty' in Slaying," *Albuquerque Tribune*, December 6, 1972; Navarro, *Raza Unida Party*, 98.

20. Dr. Thomas E. O'Brien, Autopsy of Richard Falcon, August 31, 1972, in Francisco E. Martínez Papers, UNM; Vigil, *Crusade for Justice*, 187–88.

21. "Contents of Petition in Chevron Gas Station Operated by Perry Brunson, Oro Grande, New Mexico, in Window on September 1, 1972," in Martínez Papers, UNM; MALDEF, "At the Hands of Anglo-American, a Summary of Richard Falcon Shooting Case," n.d., in Martínez Papers, UNM; Vigil, *Crusade for Justice*, 187–89.

22. "Raza Unida Delegate Shot in Orogrande," *Gallup (NM) Independent*, August 31, 1972.

23. See Robert N. Miller (district attorney in Greeley, CO) to Mr. Joe Muskrat, September 7, 1972, in Francisco E. Martínez Papers, UNM.

24. Statements of Daniel Luevano, September 6, 1972; and Supplementary or Progress Report from Jerry Hamilton, New Mexico State Police, September 1, 1972, both in Martínez Papers, UNM; "Testimony Reveals Death Fight," *Albuquerque Journal*, December 5, 1972; Colorado Delegation of La Raza Unida Party, Statement on the Death of Ricardo Falcon, ca. 1972, in National RUP Convention, 1972 folder, Judge Albert A. Peña Papers, UTSA.

25. Supplementary or Progress Report from John Cunningham, New Mexico State Police, August 30, 1972; and Statement of Perry Brunson, n.d., both in Martínez Papers, UNM.

26. "Brunson Takes Stand as Trial Moves to a Close," *Alamogordo (NM) Daily News*, December 5, 1972.

27. *State v. Couch* (1946); New Mexico Supreme Court, Committee on Uniform Jury Instructions, *New Mexico Uniform Jury Instructions*, 14-51/1, 14-51/81, Romero, "Sufficiency of Provocation for Voluntary Manslaughter in New Mexico."

28. "Verdict Is In—Brunson 'Not Guilty' in Slaying," *Albuquerque Tribune*, December 6, 1972; "Orogrande Station Owner Found Innocent Today," *Las Vegas Optic*, December 6, 1972; "Jury Acquits Station Man in Death Case," *Albuquerque Journal*, December 7, 1972.

29. Justicia Para Falcón Comité, "Do You Remember Ricardo Falcon?," letter, n.d., in Martínez Papers, UNM; "Demonstrations Expected Monday," *Alamogordo (NM) Daily News*, December 3, 1972; "La Raza March Gets Under Way Quietly," *Alamogordo (NM) Daily News*, December 3, 1972.

30. "Federal Probe Is Sought in Chicano Activist Slaying," *Rocky Mountain News* (Denver), September 3, 1972.

31. MALDEF, "At the Hands of Anglo-American, a Summary of Richard Falcon Shooting Case," investigation report, n.d., in Martínez Papers, UNM.

32. "Another Chicano Murdered by Racists in New Mexico," *El Grito Special Bulletin* (Española, NM), September 1, 1972, in Frank I. Sanchez Papers, UNM; "La Raza Unida Declares Murder Trial 'Whitewash,'" *Santa Fe New Mexican*, December 8, 1972.

33. "Memorandum of Law," 1975, in Subject Files, Herman Baca Collection, UCSD; "Hondo Marchers Urge Probes of 2 Deaths," *San Antonio Express*, September 28, 1975; *United States v. Hayes* (1979); Campney, "Most Turbulent and Most Traumatic Years," 38–39, 50–52.

34. *United States v. Hayes* (1979). The warrant for Morales's arrest was about stolen cows, but Hayes had dispatched McCall to search Morales's home for the stolen stereo.

35. "Hondo Marchers Urge Probes of 2 Deaths," *San Antonio Express*, September 28, 1975.

36. "Civil Rights Charges Asked," *Corpus Christi Times*, July 23, 1976.

37. "Ricardo Morales Cases Opens Bitter Dispute," *Del Rio (TX) News-Herald*, August 11, 1976; "U.S. Urged to Enter Case in Castroville," *Corpus Christi Times*, August 23, 1976.

38. Griffin Bell to all United States attorneys and all heads of offices, divisions, bureaus and boards of the Department of Justice, memo, ca. April 1978, in Moody Park Incident folder, Mexican-American Small Collections, HPL; *United States v. Hayes* (1979).

39. "Hayes' Day on Stand Due," *San Antonio Light*, n.d., in Police Brutality, 1977 folder, José Angel Gutiérrez Papers, UTSA.

40. "Life Imprisonment Facing Hayes," *Corpus Christi Times*, September 30, 1977; "U.S. Attorney General to Pursue Dual Prosecution Policy," *Forumeer*, October 1977; "Hayes Given Life Sentence," *Del Rio (TX) News-Herald*, February 19, 1978; "Ex-Police Chief Convicted in Civil Rights Case," unknown newspaper, n.d., in Police Brutality, 1977 folder, Gutiérrez Papers, UTSA.

41. "Briscoe Greeted with Protest," *Austin American Statesman*, July 27, 1976; "Equality & Justice for All," *El Servidor* (Seguin, TX), August 1976; "Morales Killing Still Stirs Ire," *San Antonio Express*, October 20, 1976; Ruben Sandoval to Honorable Edward H. Levi, July 13, 1976, in Richard Morales Murder Case, 1976, Judge Albert A. Peña Papers, UTSA.

42. According to FBI data, between 2014 and 2018, three officers out of 241 total officers were accidentally killed in "Crossfire" or "Mistaken for offender" situations, which is as close to friendly fire as the FBI comes. That's 1.24 percent. See FBI: UCR, "2018 Law Enforcement Officers Killed & Assaulted," table 67, Law Enforcement Officers Accidentally Killed, 2018, https://ucr.fbi.gov/leoka/2018/topic-pages/tables/table-67.xls.

43. *Garcia v. City of South Tucson* (1981); "Sniper Hits 2 Cops, Dies in Siege," *Arizona Daily Star* (Tucson), October 12, 1978; "Policeman Was Shot by Fellow Officer," *Tucson Citizen*, October 13, 1978; "1978 Shooting Still Haunts Tucson Officer," *Tucson Citizen*, May 18, 2004 (quotation).

44. *Garcia v. City of South Tucson* (1981); *Garcia v. South Tucson* (1983); "Jury Is Told Wound Isn't Only to Flesh," *Tucson Citizen*, September 18, 1980; "Garcia Asks $5.2 Million in Shooting by Fellow Cop," *Arizona Daily Star* (Tucson), October 9, 1980; "Paralyzed Officer Wins Record $3.59 Million," *Arizona Daily Star* (Tucson), October 11,

1980; "$3 Million Award in Police Shooting Could Break City," *Tucson Citizen*, October 11, 1980.

45. "$4.5 Million in Debt, City Files for Bankruptcy," *Washington Post*, September 10, 1983; "S. Tucson OKs Bonds to Settle Ex-Officer's Suit," *Arizona Republic* (Phoenix), November 21, 1984.

46. On the Hanigan case, see Marin, "They Sought Work and Found Hell"; and Cadava, *Standing on Common Ground*, chap. 5.

47. See Behnken, *Borders of Violence and Justice*, esp. chap. 2.

48. "The Hanigan Torture Case," *El Gallo* (Denver), January 1979; National Coalition on the Hanigan Case, "The Hanigan Case: A Chronology," ca. 1978, in Hanigan Case, Vol. 2, ASU. For an excellent recent account of the Hanigan case, see Elmore, "Shadow of the Law."

49. National Coalition on the Hanigan Case, "Summary of Hanigan Case," n.d., in Reies López Tijerina Papers, UNM.

50. National Coalition on the Hanigan Case, "Summary of Hanigan Case," n.d.; and "Mexicans Tortured outside of Douglas," flyer, both in Reies López Tijerina Papers, UNM; "Prepared Statement of Antonio D. Bustamante," in US Senate, "Civil Rights Improvements Act of 1977," 70–71, 77–78.

51. "Due to Burglaries, Many Back Bisbee Defendants," *Arizona Republic* (Phoenix), September 17, 1977.

52. "Hanigan Torture Case."

53. "Rancher and Two Sons Deny Guilt in Alleged Mexico-Alien Torture," *Arizona Republic* (Phoenix), October 8, 1976; "Alleged Torture, Rancher, Sons Trial March 29," *Tucson Citizen*, January 8, 1977.

54. See Behnken, *Borders of Violence and Justice*, 179–80.

55. "Cochise Seeks Change of Venue in Beating Trial," *Arizona Republic* (Phoenix), March 5, 1977; "Venue Change Denied in Alien-Torture Case," *Arizona Republic* (Phoenix), May 5, 1977.

56. "Mexican Tells Jury of Torture," *Arizona Republic* (Phoenix), September 17, 1977.

57. "Acquittal: Bad Day in Bisbee," *State Press* (Tempe, AZ), October 19, 1977.

58. "Hanigan Case Discussed, Alien Says," *Arizona Daily Star* (Tucson), September 28, 1977; "Testimony Ends in Trial of Hanigans," *Arizona Daily Star* (Tucson), October 5, 1977; "Defense Rests Case in Trial of Douglas-Area Brothers," *Arizona Republic* (Phoenix), October 5, 1977.

59. "Jury Acquits Hanigans on All Charges," *Arizona Daily Star* (Tucson), October 8, 1977; "Acquittal: Bad Day in Bisbee."

60. "Freeing Douglas Pair Has Opened Hunting Season, Consul Says," *Phoenix Gazette*, October 8, 1977.

61. "Probe Sought on Illegal Alien Mistreatment," *Arizona Republic* (Phoenix), October 9, 1977; "Cowan to Ask U.S. to Retry Hanigans," *Arizona Daily Star* (Tucson), October 9, 1977.

62. "Odds against U.S. Action on Hanigans, Official Says," *Arizona Daily Star* (Tucson), October 13, 1977.

63. "Hanigan Trial Uproar Bares the Soul of Cochise County," *Tucson Citizen*, October 26, 1977.

64. "Vigilante Tactics," *Arizona Republic* (Phoenix), July 11, 1980.

65. "Should the Hanigan Brothers Be Tried a Third Time? Con," *Arizona Daily Star* (Tucson), September 7, 1980.

66. Hanigan Case Coalition Meeting notes, May 18, 1979, in Reies López Tijerina Papers, UNM. For President Carter's response, see "Carter Vows Action in Hispanics' Deaths," *Arizona Republic* (Phoenix), June 18, 1978.

67. "Boycott Urged over Hanigan Acquittal," *Arizona Daily Star* (Tucson), October 17, 1977; "Boycoteo," protest flyer, October 16, 1977, in Hanigan Case, Vol. 1, ASU; Cadava, *Standing on Common Ground*, 186–87.

68. Edward R. Roybal to the Honorable Griffin B. Bell, June 15, 1979; Mickey Leland to Bell, June 12, 1979; and Robert Garcia to Bell, June 6, 1979, all in Hanigan Case, Vol. 2, ASU.

69. Tony Abril to the Honorable Griffin B. Bell, June 20, 1979; and Bruce Babbitt to Bell, December 21, 1978, both in Hanigan Case, Vol. 2, ASU. See also "Statement of the National Coalition on the Hanigan Case regarding the Justice Department's Decision to Initiate an Investigation into the Hanigan Case," *El Mundo* (Las Vegas), July 13, 1979.

70. "Hispanics Warn U.S.," *Tucson Citizen*, November 30, 1978.

71. "Key U.S. Official Hopes to Close Rifts between Hispanics, Police in Southwest," *Arizona Republic* (Phoenix), November 26, 1978.

72. National Coalition on the Hanigan Case, press release, June 26, 1979, in Hanigan Case, Vol. 2, ASU; "U.S. Indicts Hanigans in Alien Robbings," *Arizona Daily Star* (Tucson), October 11, 1979; "Sinohui Case Closed; Hanigans Lose Appeal," *Arizona Daily Star* (Tucson), October 18, 1980; "Hispanic Rights Denied," *Tucson Citizen*, November 5, 1980.

73. On the Hobbs Act, see Department of Justice, Criminal Resource Manual, "2402. Hobbs Act—Generally," accessed May 21, 2023, www.justice.gov/archives/jm/criminal-resource-manual-2402-hobbs-act-generally.

74. "Hanigans' Trial Begins," *Tucson Citizen*, June 26, 1980; "Mexican Admits Conflicting Stories in Hanigan Case," *Arizona Republic* (Phoenix), July 2, 1980; "Hanigan Defense Presses Credibility Attack," *Arizona Daily Star* (Tucson), July 3, 1980.

75. "Hanigan Prosecution Called Poor," *Arizona Republic* (Phoenix), July 4, 1980; "Witnesses Say Hanigan Not at Site," *Phoenix Gazette*, July 23, 1980.

76. "Hanigan Brothers Hunted 'Wetbacks,' Ex-Wife Tells Jury," *Arizona Republic* (Phoenix), July 5, 1980; Doty, *Law into Their Own Hands*, 27–28.

77. "Caravana por justicia," flyer, ca. 1980, in Hanigan Case, Vol. 3, ASU; "Demonstrators Ask Justice, 'Human Rights,'" *Arizona Daily Star* (Tucson), July 25, 1980.

78. "Judge Declares Hanigan Mistrial," *Arizona Daily Star* (Tucson), July 30, 1980; "Hanigan Jurors Give Up," *Tucson Citizen*, July 30, 1980; "The Hanigan Saga," *New Times Weekly*, August 6–12, 1980.

79. "March for Justice in Phoenix," protest flyer, August 2, 1980, in Hanigan Case, Vol. 3 folder, ASU; "40 Marchers Urge Revival of Hanigan, Sinohui Cases," *Arizona Daily Star* (Tucson), August 2, 1980.

80. "Judge Denies Hanigan Acquittal, Sets Oct. 7 Trial," *Arizona Daily Star* (Tucson), September 3, 1980.

81. "Selection of Hanigan Jury Begins with Panel of 169," *Arizona Daily Star* (Tucson), January 21, 1981.

82. "Two Jury Panels Are Seated in Trial of Hanigan Brothers," *Tucson Citizen*, January 24, 1981; "Anglo Juries Picked for Hanigan Retrials," *Arizona Daily Star* (Tucson), January 24, 1981.

83. "Hanigan Juries' Makeup Assailed," *Arizona Republic* (Phoenix), January 27, 1981; "Chicano Students Rally against Hanigan Case," *State Press* (Tempe, AZ), February 10, 1981.

84. "Jury Told of Patrick Hanigan Boast," *Arizona Republic* (Phoenix), February 13, 1981.

85. "Closing Arguments Given to 1 Hanigan Jury," *Arizona Daily Star*, February 20, 1981.

86. "Hanigan Juries' Verdicts Differ; Patrick Guilty," *Arizona Daily Star* (Tucson), February 24, 1981.

87. "Supreme Court Gets Final Hanigan Appeal," *Arizona Daily Star* (Tucson), December 1, 1982.

88. "Patrick Hanigan Is Ordered to Prison," *Arizona Daily Star* (Tucson), May 25, 1983.

89. "Three Aliens in Hanigan Case File Lawsuit Seeking Damages," *Tucson Citizen*, November 2, 1977; "Hanigan Settlement Undisclosed," *Arizona Daily Star* (Tucson), May 27, 1983.

90. For more, see Behnken, "Next Struggle."

91. "Strengthen America," Klan flyer, n.d. [ca. 1977], in Baca Collection, UCSD; "KKK Racists to Begin Border Patrol," *El Gallo* (Denver), November 1977.

92. See "Grease-Hound Bus Lines, Inc.," "Instant Greaser," "White Power Comes to Midvale," and "White Man Wake Up!," Klan cartoons, ca. 1977, in Baca Collection, UCSD.

93. "Community Unites in San Diego," *CCR Newsletter*, October 19, 1977.

94. "3000 Protest KKK," *El Gallo* (Denver), November 1977.

95. "From Night Riders to Border Patrolmen" and "Actions Kick Sheets Out of KKK," *The Worker*, n.d., in Baca Collection, UCSD; "Secuestro de Chicanos por el KKK" (Seizure or kidnapping of Chicanos by the KKK), unknown newspaper, n.d., in Baca Collection, UCSD.

96. "KKK—enemigo del pueblo . . ." (KKK—enemy of the people), *El Obrero*, n.d., in Baca Collection, UCSD; "When the KKK and the INS Are on the Same Side," *CCR Newsletter*, October 29, 1977.

97. "On Guard against the Hordes, Klan Dragon Fears an Invasion," *Los Angeles Times*, April 16, 1978.

98. KGTV News transcript, April 4, 1978; Charles C. Sava to Herman Baca, May 3, 1978; US Attorney Michael H. Walsh to Baca, February 1, 1979; and "News Release" from Walsh, January 29,1979, all in Baca Collection, UCSD. See also "2 Men Indicted on Charges of Violating Alien's Rights," *San Diego Union*, November 4, 1978; and "Mexicano Apprehended by KKK," *El Gallo* (Denver), May–June 1978.

99. "Mexicano Apprehended by KKK"; "La Raza against the KKK," *El Gallo* (Denver), May–June 1978. See also "Police Terror in San Diego," *El Gallo* (Denver), September–October 1978.

100. Baca to Walsh, April 12, 1978; M. James Lorenz to Baca, April 21, 1978; and Richard Alatorre to Baca, April 26, 1978, all in Baca Collection, UCSD.

101. Jess D. Haro to Attorney General Griffin Bell, April 19, 1978 (quotation); Jess D. Haro to the Honorable Jimmy Carter, April 20, 1978; and Edward Roybal to Walsh, April 12, 1978, all in Baca Collection, UCSD.

102. "Abajo con el KKK" (Down with the KKK), *El Pueblo*, December 1979.

103. "March against the Ku Klux Klan," *El Pueblo*, January 1980.

104. "El pueblo unido—the Fight against Racism," *El Pueblo*, February 1980; "500 marchan contra el racismo en S.A." (500 march against racism in S.A.), *El Pueblo*, February 1980.

105. Brown Berets Central Texas Region, "No marcharan!," flyer, February 3, 1983, http://renerenteria.files.wordpress.com/2013/04/austinbrownberets_march272013_19 .jpg.

106. "The Day the Klan Marched," YouTube, accessed May 21, 2023, www.youtube .com/watch?v=FttayZRBcGE (the video is now private).

107. "Brown Berets Allege Local Police Brutality," *Daily Texan* (Austin), November 14, 1977.

108. On the Klan march and anti-Klan demonstration, see "Austin City Council Minutes," February 24, 1983, www.austintexas.gov/edims/document.cfm?id=16431.

109. For recent commentaries on the Brown Berets' activism in Austin, see the online interviews of Susana Almanza by René Rentería: "Austin Brown Berets—Insights, Reflections and Discussion," *René Rentería Photography Blog*, April 9, 2013, https:// renerenteria.wordpress.com/2013/04/09/austin-brown-berets-insights-reflections-and -discussion. See also "Day the Klan Marched."

110. Raymond, "Mexican Americans Write toward Justice in Texas," 131–32. See also "A '60s Voice Grows Quiet," *Austin American-Statesman*, April 5, 2008.

111. Brown Berets and Comite para Justicia, "Police Violence and Racism in Perspective: What the TV News Isn't Showing," flyer, April 18, 1983, in Mexican Americans, Brown Berets folder, APL.

112. See Comite para Justicia, Brown Berets, and Prison Coalition, "Benefit," flyer, ca. November 1983, in Mexican Americans, Brown Berets folder, APL.

CHAPTER 5

1. Sworn Statement of Virginia Bermea, November 1965, in Bexar County Boys School, 1965 folder, Judge Albert A. Peña Papers, UTSA.

2. Statement by Luis Alvarado (Institutional Caseworker) concerning His Dismissal from the Bexar County Boy's School, November 1965; and Statement by Luis Alvarado concerning His Dismissal as Institutional Caseworker at Southton, November 20, 1965, both in Bexar County Boys School, 1965 folder, Judge Albert A. Peña Papers, UTSA.

3. Behnken, *Borders of Violence and Justice*, 221.

4. See Hinton, *From the War on Poverty to the War on Crime*.

5. See Wang, *Carceral Capitalism*, for a good overview of this subject.

6. Chase, "Cell Taught, Self Taught," 849. See also Chase, *We Are Not Slaves*; and Escobar, "Unintended Consequences of the Carceral State."

7. "Slaying Leads Edna Grand Jury List," *Victoria (TX) Advocate*, September 16, 1951; "2 Murder Cases Will Be Called in Edna on Monday," *Victoria (TX) Advocate*, October

7, 1951; "Edna Laborer Draws Life in Slaying," *Victoria (TX) Advocate*, October 12, 1951; García, *White but Not Equal*, 28–30.

8. García, *White but Not Equal*, 54–55.

9. *Hernandez v. Texas* (1954), at 482; Haney López, "Retaining Race," 279–96. See also Olivas, *Colored Men and Hombres Aquí*; García, *White but Not Equal*; and "Hernandez Tried Again," *G.I. Forum Bulletin*, February–March, 1956.

10. "New Indictment in Murder Case," *Austin American*, September 24, 1954; "Lighter Sentence at Second Trial," *Corpus Christi Times*, December 28, 1955; Olivas, "*Hernandez v. Texas*," 221; García, *White but Not Equal*, 194.

11. "Hired Killer Leads Police to Gun Cache," *Chicago Daily Tribune*, February 1, 1960; "Has Admitted He Was Hired to Kill Man," *De Kalb (IL) Daily Chronicle*, February 1, 1960. Di Gerlando's name is often spelled "De Gerlando."

12. "4 Held to Jury in Murder for Hire Slaying," *Chicago Daily Tribune*, February 2, 1960; *Escobedo v. Illinois* (1964), at 481–82; Dowling, "Escobedo and Beyond," 144.

13. Dowling, "Escobedo and Beyond," 144–45. See also Moore, *Political Roots of Racial Tracking*, 89–90; Valencia et al., *Mexican Americans*, chap. 8.

14. "Wife Freed," *Chicago Daily Tribune*, July 9, 1960.

15. "Court OK's Secrecy for Dope Informers," *Chicago Tribune*, May 28, 1963.

16. "High Court to Sift Chicago Murder Case," *Chicago Tribune*, November 13, 1963.

17. Oral arguments available at "Escobedo v. Illinois," Oyez, accessed May 21, 2023, www.oyez.org/cases/1963/615; *Escobedo*, at 479–88.

18. "U.S. High Court Voids Murder Decision, 5–4," *Chicago Tribune*, June 23, 1964; *Escobedo*, at 490–92.

19. "Convict Freed after 4 Years; Reject Retrial," *Chicago Tribune*, August 8, 1964.

20. Escobedo would seem to fit the pattern of a life-course-persistent offender. See Moffitt, "Adolescence-Limited and Life-Course-Persistent Antisocial Behavior." He was convicted of multiple crimes from the late 1960s to the early 2000s. See "$100,000 Bail Is Set for Escobedo," *Chicago Tribune*, September 23, 1967; "Dan Escobedo Is Sentenced to 22 Years," *Chicago Tribune*, February 21, 1968; "Escobedo . . . ," *Southern Illinoisan* (Carbondale), January 29, 1975; "Escobedo on Trial, Accused of Molesting Teen," *Southern Illinoisan* (Carbondale), September 28, 1984; "High Court Protagonist Gets 11 Years," *The Dispatch* (Moline, IL), March 5, 1987; "Escobedo Handed 62 Month Sentence," *Chicago Tribune*, November 3, 1995; "Escobedo Arrested in Mexico," *The Pantagraph* (Bloomington, IN), June 22, 2001; and "Escobedo Gets 40 Years in Killing of Merchant," *Chicago Tribune*, August 28, 2003.

21. Stuart, *Miranda*, 6.

22. "23-Year-Old Miranda Faces Kidnap Charge," *Arizona Republic* (Phoenix), March 15, 1963.

23. Stuart, *Miranda*, 11–15.

24. Burgan, *Miranda v. Arizona*, 19–21; Stuart, *Miranda*, 17–19; "Jury Convicts Phoenician," *Arizona Republic* (Phoenix), June 21, 1963.

25. "Phoenician Sentenced," *Arizona Republic* (Phoenix), June 28, 1963; Stuart, *Miranda*, 22.

26. *State v. Miranda* (1965).

27. For oral arguments, see "Arizona v. Miranda," Oyez, accessed May 21, 2023, www.oyez.org/cases/1965/759; "State Joins in Appeal on Confessions," *Arizona Daily Sun*

(Flagstaff), March 1, 1966; "Arizonan's Conviction Reversed," *Arizona Daily Star* (Tucson), June 14, 1966.

28. Miranda v. Arizona, 384 U.S. 436, 468–69 (1966).

29. "What Are Your Miranda Rights?," MirandaWarning.org, accessed May 21, 2023, www.mirandawarning.org/whatareyourmirandarights.html.

30. "Date Set for Miranda's Retrial," *Tucson Daily Citizen*, August 11, 1966; "Miranda Convicted Second Time," *Tucson Daily Citizen*, February 25, 1967; "Miranda Gets Sentence of 20–30 Years," *Tucson Daily Citizen*, March 1, 1967; "Miranda Granted Parole; Landmark Case Figure," *Arizona Daily Star* (Tucson), December 12, 1972.

31. "Ernesto Miranda Is Killed; Subject of Landmark Case," *Arizona Republic* (Phoenix), February 1, 1976; "Miranda Slaying Suspect's 'Miranda Rights' Observed," *Tucson Citizen*, February 2, 1976; Stuart, *Miranda*, 96–101.

32. Betty Martinez arrest, November 25, 1953, in Arrest/Jail Log Books (female), Women's Holdover, 11/20/1953–5/31/1954, DPL.

33. Lillian Rojo, Mary Galacio, Oleda Garcia, and Angil Rojo arrests, in Arrest/Jail Log Books (female), Women's Holdover, 11/20/1953–5/31/1954, DPL. Dallas had a high murder rate in the twentieth century, but Mexican Americans barely register in these numbers. In 1955, for example, there were seventy-four murders in Dallas, of which Mexican American committed three. In 1961, ninety-nine murders occurred in Dallas, nine of which involved Mexican-origin suspects. Thus, contrary to popular opinion, Mexican people were not the killers many Americans took them to be. See "Dallas Murders Description, 1955–1956"; "Murder: 1955," comparison chart; and "List of Murders, 1955," all in Murders—1955–56 folder, Dallas Police Archives, DPL; and "Analysis of Murders, Dallas, Texas, 1961," Dallas Police Department Reports, 1961, DPL.

34. "'Safe Jail Law' Still Not Enforced," *San Antonio Express*, August 22, 1969.

35. Ad Hoc Committee for the Safe Treatment of Prisoners, Synopsis of Bexar County Jail Conditions, February 6, 1970, in Topics, Police Brutality—Newsclippings and Newsletters, 1950–2004, Mario Salas Papers, UTSA.

36. "Casseb Heads Jail Committee," *San Antonio Express*, August 21, 1969; "Jail Study Committee Needs Resources for Comprehensive Job," *San Antonio Express-News*, August 30, 1969; "County Eyes Funds to Examine Jails," *San Antonio Express*, August 30, 1969; "Jail Panel to Get Suggestions," *San Antonio Express*, October 2, 1969.

37. "This Is a Statement Made by Three People Arrested While Demonstrating Friday Night, February 12, in Front of the Bexar County Jail," ca. 1969, in Topics, Police Brutality—Newsclippings and Newsletters, 1950–2004, Salas Papers, UTSA; "Protesters Seek Changes at Jail," *San Antonio Express*, September 29, 1969.

38. "Protestors Plan Sunday Vigil at Jail," *San Antonio Express*, February 14, 1971.

39. Sworn Statement of Virginian Bermea, November 1965, in Bexar County Boys School, 1965 folder, Judge Albert A. Peña Papers, UTSA.

40. Sworn Statement of Elisa Perez, November 1965, in Bexar County Boys School, 1965 folder, Judge Albert A. Peña Papers, UTSA.

41. Velia C. Cardenas to Commissioner Albert A. Peña, ca. 1965, in Bexar County Boys School, 1965 folder, Judge Albert A. Peña Papers, UTSA.

42. Statement by Alvarado concerning Dismissal from Bexar County Boy's School and Statement by Alvarado concerning Dismissal as Institutional Caseworker at Southton.

43. Statement by Alvarado concerning Dismissal.

44. "Alleged Slaying Protested at Rally," *Victoria (TX) Advocate*, November 19, 1978; "10 Brown Berets Arrested in Houston," *El Paso Herald-Post*, November 20, 1978; "Free Houston 7," *El Gallo* (Denver), April–May 1979.

45. "Pecos Man Faces Assault Charges," *Odessa (TX) American*, January 11, 1978; "Minor Accident Beginning of End for Odessa Inmate," *Dallas Morning News*, February 12, 1978.

46. "Federal Complaint Filed in Death of Jail Inmate," *Odessa (TX) American*, January 26, 1978; *Lozano v. Smith* (1983).

47. Medical Examiner's Autopsy #36-78, Lozano, Larry Ortega (27), January 26, 1978, in Herman Baca Collection, UCSD, https://library.ucsd.edu/dc/object/bb89774813/_1.pdf (quotation); "Second Autopsy Performed after Death of Prisoner Here," *Odessa (TX) American*, January 27, 1978; "Ector County Jail Suicide Ruling Challenged," *El Paso Times*, February 9, 1978; "Cellmate Claims Jail Mistreatment," *San Angelo (TX) Standard Times*, January 29, 1978.

48. "Death of Lozano Ruled Accidental," *Houston Post*, April 15, 1978.

49. Zapata, "South-by-Southwest Borderlands' Chicana/o Uprising"; "Non-Violent Display of Solidarity Shown during Saturday Motorcade," *Odessa (TX) American*, February 26, 1978.

50. Texas Attorney General's Office, *Summary of Civil Rights Investigations*; "Hill: 3 Chicano Deaths by Police Unjustified," *Dallas Times Herald*, December 29, 1978.

51. Justice Department memo, June 22, 1979, in Baca Collection, UCSD, https://library.ucsd.edu/dc/object/bb89774813/_1.pdf; "Shock, Anger Follow Lozano Death Ruling," *San Antonio Express-News*, June 23, 1979; "Prosecutors Drop Lozano Death Case," *Dallas Morning News*, June 23, 1979.

52. See the numerous letters in Baca Collection, UCSD https://library.ucsd.edu/dc/object/bb89774813/_1.pdf.

53. *Lozano v. Smith* (1983).

54. National Council of La Raza report on Los Angeles, ca. 1980, 11–12, in National Council de la Raza—Police Practices, 1983 folder, AFCS Papers, UCSD.

55. "Officers Refuse to Give Testimony during Inquest," *Los Angeles Times*, February 23, 1979; "Inmates Death Not an Accident, Inquest Jury Says," *Los Angeles Times*, February 18, 1979; National Council of La Raza report on Los Angeles, ca. 1980, 31–32.

56. "D.A. Clears Police in Death of Prisoner," *Los Angeles Times*, December 12, 1979.

57. C.A.P.A., Report for 1979, in Coalition against Police Abuse folder, Rosalio Muñoz Papers, UCLA.

58. "Chicano Group Flexes Muscle at Builders, Politicians and Police," *Los Angeles Times*, July 22, 1979; "D.A. Rollout Program Never Worked, and Never Will," *Los Angeles Times*, October 11, 1999; Felker-Kantor, "Coalition against Police Abuse," 67–70.

59. "11 in Race for Glendale Mayor and City Council Seats," *Arizona Republic* (Phoenix), January 20, 1974; "Glendale Oks Bid Calling for Building," *Arizona Republic* (Phoenix), April 26, 1974; "Half of Prison's Inmates Refuse to Work," *Arizona Republic* (Phoenix), January 6, 1976.

60. "Why Are You Paying to Send This Man to Jail?," newspaper-like publication supporting Jess Lopez, Human Rights Defense League, 1978, in Police Brutality folder, ASU.

61. "2 Accused of Arson at Glendale College," *Arizona Republic* (Phoenix), June 30, 1977.

62. "Activist Is Sentenced to 5 Years for Role in Bombing at College," *Arizona Republic* (Phoenix), November 24, 1977.

63. "Jess Lopez Railroaded to Prison," *El Mestizo* (Austin, TX), October 1977.

64. "Chicano Group Says Activist Was Framed in Arson Case," *Arizona Republic* (Phoenix), October 10, 1977; "Judge Rejects Plea for Retrial in Arson Case," *Arizona Republic* (Phoenix), November 1, 1977; "Prosecutor Accuses College of Apathy in Building Bombing," *Phoenix Gazette*, November 24, 1977.

65. "Free Jess Lopez!," protest flyer, December 17, 1977, in Police Brutality folder, ASU. See also Free Jess Lopez! materials in Baca Collection, UCSD.

66. "Activist Group Leader Guilty in College Fire," *Arizona Republic* (Phoenix), October 15, 1977; "Activist Jess Lopez Files for Mistrial," *Para la Gente* (Austin, TX), November 1977.

67. "Activist Is Sentenced to 5 Years for Role in Bombing at College."

68. "Humane and Sensible Punishment," *Arizona Daily Star* (Tucson), April 5, 1978; "Despite Changes, Violence Goes On," *Arizona Daily Star* (Tucson), August 20, 1978.

69. "Prison Construction Could Threaten Suit Settlement," *Arizona Daily Sun*, March 20, 1980; "Prison Double-Bunks Urged by Legislator," *Tucson Citizen*, December 24, 1981.

70. "GATE to Expand Services to Aid Women Alcoholics," *Albuquerque Journal*, June 19, 1975. For background on alternative adjudication methods, see Behnken, Arredondo, and Packman, "Reduction in Recidivism in a Juvenile Mental Health Court"; and Ojmarrh et al., "Assessing the Effectiveness of Drug Courts on Recidivism."

71. "Plan Would Reduce Jail Population," *Albuquerque Journal*, November 23, 1977.

72. Behnken, *Borders of Violence and Justice*, 145, 210–11.

73. "Aaron Resigns in Santa Fe; Calls Prison Reform Failure," *Gallup (NM) Independent*, May 29, 1976; "Prison Dorm Fight Quelled by Tear Gas," *Albuquerque Journal*, June 17, 1976; "Escapees Elude Police," *Clovis (NM) News-Journal*, July 27, 1976; "Inmate Reported Missing," *Santa Fe New Mexican*, August 29, 1976; "Hanged Man Vowed to Kill Self, Police Say," *Albuquerque Journal*, September 1, 1976; "Three Prison Escapees Elude Capture," *Clovis (NM) News-Journal*, December 13, 1976; "Prison," *Santa Fe New Mexican*, January 2, 1977; "Judicial Committee Favors New Prison," *Albuquerque Journal*, January 27, 1977; "New Light Security Prison Building Near," *Alamogordo (NM) Daily News*, September 11, 1977.

74. *Duran v. Apodaca* (1977); *Duran v. King* (1980); "Dwight Duran Led the Charge for Prison Reform," *Albuquerque Journal*, January 26, 2020.

75. "Santa Fe," *Santa Fe New Mexican*, March 23, 1978; "Heads Roll at New Mexico State Prison," *Roswell (NM) Daily Record*, December 21, 1979; "Warden Says Becknell Wanted 2 Firings," *Albuquerque Journal*, January 16, 1980.

76. Morris, *Devil's Butcher Shop*, 15, 87–88.

77. "Inmates Riot, Control Prison—11 Hostages Alive, Fate Unclear," *Albuquerque Journal*, February 3, 1980; "Prison Report," *Albuquerque Journal*, February 3, 1980; "King Puts Negotiators in Contact with Rioters," *Albuquerque Journal*, February 3, 1980.

78. "The 11 Demands," *Albuquerque Journal*, February 3, 1980; "Riot-Torn Prison Recaptured; 32 Dead, but Hostages Safe," *Albuquerque Journal*, February 4, 1980.

79. "Inmate: 'They Wiped Them Out,'" *Santa Fe New Mexican*, February 3, 1980; "35 Dead in Prison Riot," *Deming (NM) Headlight*, February 4, 1980; "Death Toll in Prison Rampage Hits 33 as Cleanup Wears On," *Albuquerque Journal*, February 5, 1980.

80. "New Mexico Penitentiary Violence All Too Familiar," *Albuquerque Journal*, February 3, 1980; "Prison a Site of Past Strikes, Sit-Ins, Violence," *Santa Fe New Mexican*, February 3, 1980; "Forecasts of the Rioting Given in Recent Years," *Albuquerque Journal*, February 5, 1980; "Saenz: Conditions Sparked Riot," *Santa Fe New Mexican*, February 5, 1980; "Overcrowding Led to Siege, Corrections Director Claims," *Santa Fe New Mexican*, February 5, 1980; Office of the Attorney General of the State of New Mexico, *Report of the Attorney General*, parts 1 and 2.

81. "Cost of Damage Was $21 Million," *Carlsbad (NM) Current-Argus*, February 5, 1980; "Santa Fe Prison Damage Estimated at $20 Million," *Deming (NM) Headlight*, February 5, 1980.

82. "Legacy of New Mexico Prison Riot Costs Still Linger Today," Associated Press, February 1, 2020, https://apnews.com/6eccb9deaf88c38681e79367c4b5b7e5; Phaedra Haywood, "Federal Judge Approves Duran Decree Settlement," *Santa Fe New Mexican*, February 14, 2020, updated March 21, 2021, www.santafenewmexican.com/news/local_news/federal-judge-approves-duran-decree-settlement/article_a8abcb14-4f8b-11ea-9d2c-e76695894d9c.html; "Judge Approves Penal Reform Settlement in New Mexico," Associated Press, February 15, 2020, https://apnews.com/9d1616eeec267f4a5836f86ab4743d48.

83. Morris, *Devil's Butcher Shop*, 230.

84. Aynes, "Behavior Modification"; Floyd, "Administration of Psychotropic Drugs to Prisoners."

85. Committee to Free Eddie Sanchez, "A Lifetime in Prison: The Case of Eddie Sanchez," pamphlet, n.d., in Frank I. Sanchez Papers, UNM.

86. LaChance, *Executing Freedom*, 60–61. See also "Bizarre Realities," *VIVA*, October 25, 1973.

87. Johnson, *American Lobotomy*, 44.

88. Committee to Free Eddie Sanchez, "Lifetime in Prison."

89. "Inmates Hearing Awaits Report," *Kansas City (MO) Times*, March 26, 1975.

90. US House of Representatives, *Prison Inmates in Medical Research*; LaChance, *Executing Freedom*, 62; Hornblum, *Acres of Skin*, 110–14.

91. "Grand Jury Finds Murder Indictment against Evant Man," *Gatesville (TX) Messenger and Star-Forum*, June 5, 1955; "Man Held in Austin Robberies," *Austin American*, January 15, 1968.

92. For some background on Corcoran, see Parenti, "Guarding Their Silence," 252–57.

93. Perkinson, *Texas Tough*, 252–54; Chase, *We Are Not Slaves*, 277–82.

94. "Ruiz Indicted by Vengeful Texas Officials," *El Gallo* (Denver), January 1979; "Petition and Letter Drive to Free Ruiz," *El Gallo* (Denver), April–May 1979; Prisoner Solidarity Committee, "Prisoners Resist Texas Prison Slave System," brochure, September 1978, in Mexican-American Small Collections, HPL.

95. Consent Decree, *Ruiz v. Estelle*, in William Wayne Justice Papers, Tarlton Law Library, University of Texas School of Law, Austin; Perkinson, *Texas Tough*, 251–85, chap. 7; Justice, "Origins of *Ruiz v. Estelle*"; *Ruiz v. Estelle* (1980).

96. See *Ruiz v. Collins* (1992); *Ruiz v. Scott* (1998); Chase, "We Are Not Slaves," 78–79; and "The Prisoner Dilemma," *The Baffler*, July 2019, https://thebaffler.com/salvos/the-prisoner-dilemma-gottschalk.

97. *Ruiz v. Johnson* (2001); Chase, *We Are Not Slaves*, chap. 11; Perkinson, *Texas Tough*, 325–27.

98. Perkinson, *Texas Tough*, 357–65.

CHAPTER 6

1. Nick Bachus, PAL report, in Agreement between AUC & PAL file, PTF, ABCPL.

2. See Walker, *Critical History of Police Reform*.

3. Commission on Civil Rights, *Mexican Americans and the Administration of Justice*, 8–10.

4. Commission on Civil Rights, *Mexican Americans and the Administration of Justice*, 20–22.

5. Commission on Civil Rights, *Mexican Americans and the Administration of Justice*, 10–11, 36–46, 48–52, 54–59.

6. Commission on Civil Rights, *Mexican Americans and the Administration of Justice*, 2.

7. Commission on Civil Rights, *Mexican Americans and the Administration of Justice*, 87.

8. "La Ley," in Commission on Civil Rights, *Stranger in One's Land*, 40, 41.

9. "La Ley," 41–42. See also Commission on Civil Rights, *Mexican Americans and the Administration of Justice*, 16–17.

10. "La Ley," 45 (quotation), 46–47.

11. See Perino, *Citizen Oversight of Law Enforcement*; and Prenzler and Heyer, *Civilian Oversight of Police*.

12. Gross and Reitman, *Police Power and Citizens' Rights*, 2.

13. Gross and Reitman, *Police Power and Citizens' Rights*, 34.

14. "Police Board Mandatory," *Arizona Republic* (Phoenix), December 6, 1965.

15. "Police: 'The Man's' Agent Bends," *Arizona Republic* (Phoenix), May 19, 1968. See also "Chicanos Discuss Problems of Bias," *Arizona Daily Star* (Tucson), September 1, 1972.

16. "Black Protesters Rush at BYU–U of A Game," *Arizona Republic* (Phoenix), January 9, 1970.

17. "Police-Youth Rapport Replacing Antagonism," *Arizona Daily Star* (Tucson), November 30, 1972.

18. "'Policing the Police' Is Unpleasant Job Assigned to Internal Affairs Officers," *Arizona Daily Star* (Tucson), July 5, 1973.

19. "The Status and Direction of the Unincorporated Village of Guadalupe," September 1, 1974, in Guadalupe, Arizona folder, ASU.

20. "Status and Direction of the Unincorporated Village of Guadalupe."

21. Raymond G. Zylla, "Guadalupe: Was Incorporation Best?," November 1977, in Guadalupe, Arizona folder, ASU.

22. "Police Accused of Slighting S. Phoenix," *Arizona Republic* (Phoenix), July 13, 1978.

23. "It's a Hassle When Policemen No Hablan Español," *Tucson Citizen*, August 11, 1978.

24. "Police Accused of Slighting S. Phoenix."

25. "It's a Hassle When Policemen No Hablan Español."

26. Ordinance No. _____, February 1977, in Frank I. Sanchez Papers, UNM; "Powerful Rights Law under Study by City," *Clovis (NM) News-Journal*, April 28, 1977. On restorative justice, see Umbreit and Armour, *Restorative Justice Dialogue*.

27. Brook Boroughs to Frank Sanchez, October 13, 1976; and Spencer Coxe, "Police Abuses," paper prepared for the 1976 ACLU Biennial Conference, both in Frank I. Sanchez Papers, UNM.

28. Manuel Chavez, "Proposal on Clovis Human Rights Commission to Clovis City Commission," Americans for Justice in Curry County, February 20, 1977, in Frank I. Sanchez Papers, UNM.

29. Coalition por Derechos to Estimado Pueblo de Roswell, ca. April 1977, in Frank I. Sanchez Papers, UNM. The group used the English word "coalition" instead of the Spanish "coalición."

30. "A 'Golden Rule' Ordinance for Clovis?," *Clovis (NM) News-Journal*, May 1, 1977.

31. "City to Draft New Ordinance," *Clovis (NM) News-Journal*, May 5, 1977.

32. Dolores Penrod, "Report by the Criminal Justice Task Force of Roosevelt County," January 1977, in Frank I. Sanchez Papers, UNM.

33. "Chief Byrd and His Mini-Revolution," n.d., clipping, in Bio—Byrd, Don file, ABCPL; "Police Race and Cultural Relations Seminar," March 13–17, 1972, in Emma Moya Collection, UNM. See also "Police Community Program Expanded," *Albuquerque Tribune*, August 31, 1968; "City 'Storefront' Offers Aid," *Albuquerque Journal*, July 4, 1972; and "Program Aims at Better Youth-Police Relationship," *Albuquerque Journal*, July 21, 1974.

34. "Police Community Program Expanded"; "Police Efficiency Sought," *Albuquerque Journal*, June 21, 1970.

35. Many of the police-community relations were summarized in two reports: "Short Summarization of the Final (Volume II) Recommendations of the Criminal Justice Program (ISRAD-UNM) Study of the Police Department," ca. January 1974; and "Albuquerque Urban Coalition Police Task Force," ca. January 1974, both in PTF, ABCPL. See also Alvaro Villescas to D. A. Byrd, December 21, 1972, in Police Task Force General Data file, PTF, ABCPL.

36. "Police Storefront Will Open Today at SE Center Site," *Albuquerque Journal*, June 30, 1971; "City 'Storefront' Offers Aid," *Albuquerque Journal*, July 4, 1971. Police also proposed placing a storefront in the Martineztown neighborhood, but it is unclear if this storefront ever began operations. See "Project _____," n.d., in Police Task Force General Data file, PTF, ABCPL.

37. Officer Frank Chavez to Don Byrd, December 21, 1972, in Police Task Force General Data file, PTF, ABCPL.

38. Bob Stover to Mr. Jack Kolbert, President (Albuquerque City Council), November 4, 1974, in Police Task Force 1974–75 (1) file, PTF, ABCPL.

39. Officer E. M. Rouse to Jim McCraw, including PAL goals proposal, February 22, 1974, in Agreement between AUC & PAL file, PTF, ABCPL. PAL has a pretty long history, the first group having been formed in New York City in 1914. See "History of

PAL," Police Athletic League, December 2015, www.palnyc.org/history. See also Brower, "Balling with the Boys in Blue."

40. "Albuquerque Urban Coalition Report," ca. March 1974, in Police Task Force 1974–75 (1) file, PTF, ABCPL.

41. "Albuquerque, New Mexico ($5000)," n.d.; and "Police-Youth Project Albuquerque Urban Coalition," n.d., both in Police Task Force General Data file, PTF, ABCPL; "Agreement," in Agreement between AUC & PAL file, PTF, ABCPL.

42. James L. McCraw to Kaiser Michael, January 11, 1974, PTF, ABCPL; and Albuquerque Urban Coalition Police Task Force Meeting Minutes, January 8, 1974, both in PTF, ABCPL.

43. "Progress Report, Police Youth Project," September 10, 1973, in Agreement between AUC & PAL file.

44. Mike Rouse to Frank Martinez, August 22, 1973; and James L. McCraw report, June 6, 1973, both in Agreement between AUC & PAL file, PTF, ABCPL.

45. Nick Bachus, PAL report, in Agreement between AUC & PAL file, PTF, ABCPL.

46. "Group Charges Police Brutality, Harassment," *Albuquerque Journal*, October 31, 1974; "Police Brutality, Harassing Charged," *Albuquerque Tribune*, November 5, 1974.

47. "Group Charges Police Brutality, Harassment."

48. "APD Not Surprised by San Jose Complaints," unknown newspaper, October 31, 1974, in San Jose/Police Community Project file, PTF, ABCPL.

49. "Improving Police-Community Links under Coalition Study," *Albuquerque Journal*, October 31, 1974; "Neighborhood Police Centers May Re-Open," unknown newspaper, n.d.; Frank H. Martinez to Sam H. Dunlap (an official with Rocky Mountain Bell), February 17, 1975; and Martinez to Ray B. Powell, November 11, 1974, all in San Jose/Police Community Project file, PTF, ABCPL.

50. "Valley Residents Ask Police Probe," *Albuquerque Journal*, October 4, 1974; "City Policeman's Suspension Is Cut," *Albuquerque Journal*, October 5, 1974.

51. "Public-Police Issue Turns Quiet," *Albuquerque Journal*, November 10, 1974; "Troubles Eased in San Jose," *Albuquerque Journal*, November 28, 1974.

52. Citizens for Improved Government to Dear Mr. Proprietor, n.d., in San Jose/Police Community Project file, PTF, ABCPL; "Riot Threat Letter Sent to Businesses," *Albuquerque Tribune*, October 31, 1974.

53. "Public-Police Issue Turns Quiet"; "Troubles Eased in San Jose"; "Police Protest Cancelled," *Albuquerque Journal*, November 1, 1974.

54. For analysis of hiring programs, see Carbado and Richardson, "Black Police"; Peyton, Weiss, and Vaugh, "Beliefs about Minority Representation"; Felker-Kantor, *Policing LA*, 239–45; and Sklansky, "Seeing Blue."

55. "General," n.d.; and Albuquerque Urban Coalition Minutes of Police Task Force Meeting, November 9, 1972, both in PTF, ABCPL.

56. James L. McCraw to Deputy Chief Chappell, November 28, 1972; Chappell to McGraw, December 20, 1972; "Meeting with Police," December 19, 1972; and McCraw to Herb Smith, April 3, 1973, all in PTF, ABCPL. See also Albuquerque Urban Coalition Police Task Force Meeting Agenda, which includes a "Summary of the Presentation by Sgt. Murray and Following Discussion on the Topic of the Police Academy," December 5, 1972, in PTF, ABCPL.

57. "Proposal for Albuquerque Police Department, Recruitment and Orientation of Minority Patrolmen," ca. 1973, in Police Task Force General Data file, PTF, ABCPL. For the response of businesspeople, see G. B. Kelley (ATSF Railway) to Frank H. Martinez, January 8, 1973; E. H. España (Mountain Bell) to James L. McCraw, February 23, 1973; and McCraw to D. A. Byrd, February 1, 1973, all in Police Recruitment Program file, PTF, ABCPL. For background on "minority recruitment," see Rowan and Griffin, "St. Paul (MN)—Police Department—Minority Recruitment Program"; and Margolis, "Who Will Wear the Badge?," 15–25.

58. J. H. Bowdich to James L. McCraw, containing police academy curriculum and class schedule, June 8, 1973, in Police Recruitment Program file, PTF, ABCPL.

59. Albuquerque Urban Coalition Police Community Relations Monitoring Committee Meeting Minutes, January 27, 1975, in PTF, ABCPL; James McCraw to Bob Stover, January 22, 1975, in San Jose/Police Community Project file, PTF, ABCPL.

60. "Police Personnel Report," January 21, 1974, in PTF, ABCPL.

61. "Police Personnel Report," emphasis in original.

62. Steven Gonzales, "Spanish Language Training for Policemen—Lessons Learned during a First Attempt," March 4, 1974, in PTF, ABCPL.

63. Bob V. Stover to Jack Kolbert, November 4, 1974, in Police Task Force 1974–75 (1) file, PTF, ABCPL.

64. Albuquerque Urban Coalition Police Community Relations Monitoring Committee Meeting Minutes.

65. "Police Chicano File Suit," *Albuquerque Journal*, July 21, 1973; *Chicano Police Officer's Ass'n v. Stover* (1980).

66. Santiago Tapia y Anaya to Governor Bruce King, June 28, 1971, in Reies López Tijerina Papers, UNM.

67. "Special Study on Ethnic Arrest Patterns, DWI Offense All Bernalillo County," March 8, 1974, in Alcohol Traffic Safety Program file, PTF, ABCPL.

68. James L. McCraw to Herb Smith, February 2, 1973, and November 28, 1972, in Alcohol Traffic Safety Program file, PTF, ABCPL.

69. "Alcohol Traffic Safety—Arrests for Driving While Intoxicated," ca. 1974, in Alcohol Traffic Safety Program file, PTF, ABCPL.

70. Edited and concurred text of APD and AUC meeting, ca. 1974, in PTF, ABCPL.

71. The Supreme Court determined the legality of stop and frisk in 1968 in *Terry v. Ohio*. Albuquerque began stop and frisk in 1970. See "Civil Rights Report Cites Inequities," *Albuquerque Journal*, April 29, 1970; and press release, September 30, 1974, in Police Task Force 1974–75 (1) file, PTF, ABCPL (quotation).

72. Frank H. Martinez to Bob Stover, May 16, 1975, in Police Task Force 1974–75 (1) file, PTF, ABCPL. This letter also contained the results of the AUC's survey. "Police Unit Seeks Donation of Dogs," *Albuquerque Journal*, December 31, 1975.

73. James McCraw to Frank Martinez, November 17, 1975, in Police Dogs file, PTF, ABCPL.

74. AUC meeting notes, n.d., in Police Dogs file, PTF, ABCPL.

75. "Police Favors Dog Squads," *Santa Fe New Mexican*, December 8, 1975; "Duke City Will Add Police Dogs," *Alamogordo (NM) Daily News*, December 9, 1975; "Proposal Mounted Again," *Albuquerque Journal*, November 19, 1976; "Police Get Go-Ahead to Saddle Up in City," *Albuquerque Journal*, March 8, 1977.

76. "Police Marchers Told 'No,'" *San Antonio News*, February 8, 1968.

77. "Bilingual Policemen Identified," *San Antonio News*, September 8, 1966; "Bilingual Police Get Badge," *San Antonio Light*, September 8, 1966.

78. "Police Academy Becomes Coed," *San Antonio Express-News*, January 12, 1974; "S.A. Police Academy Graduates First Women," *San Antonio Express-News*, August 3, 1974; "Eleven Women in Police Class," *San Antonio Light*, July 12, 1983; "More Female Officers Needed," *San Antonio Express*, September 3, 1983.

79. "Policewomen Walk Lonely Beat," *San Antonio Express-News*, August 28, 1983.

80. "Cops in Disguise," *San Antonio Express-News*, March 3, 1974.

81. "Corruption Saps Police Morale," *San Antonio Express*, July 4, 1976.

82. See Behnken, "'Dallas Way,'" 1–6, 15–18.

83. Dallas Police Department, *Training Manual*, 6.

84. Dallas Police Department, *Training Manual*, 44, 45, 47. See chap. 16 for "quelling a riot."

85. Dallas Police Department, *Training Manual*, 63.

86. Police Foundation, press release, May 11, 1971, in PTF, ABCPL.

87. "Minority Test Scores Low," unknown newspaper, n.d., in Newsclips–Cartoons folder, Dallas Police Archives, DPL. Dallas began hiring Black officers in the 1940s: "Three More Negro Policemen Now on Duty," *Dallas Express*, March 27, 1948.

88. Dallas Police Department, *Goals for Dallas*, 47–48 (quotation), 49.

89. Dallas Police Department, *Goals for Dallas*, 51–52.

90. C. M. Lynn to Mayor Fred Hofheinz, Progress Report for 1974, memo, April 3, 1975; and LEAA Grants, press release, March 17, 1975, both in Police folder, Mayor Fred Hofheinz Papers, HPL.

91. "Chicano Squad Hits the Streets to Solve Murders," *Houston Post*, October 12, 1980.

92. "Chicano Squad of the HPD—They've Earned Their Stripes on the Streets," *Houston Career Digest*, February 1, 1982. For more information see also Cristela Alonzo, host, *Chicano Squad*, Vox Media Podcast Network, 2021, https://podcasts.apple.com/us/podcast/chicano-squad/id1546383966.

93. "Police to Begin Cadet Screening," *Houston Post*, September 10, 1977; "Booking Rules Changed after Torres' Death, Chief Says," *Houston Post*, September 20, 1977; "Program Explains Hispanic Culture," *Arizona Republic* (Phoenix), February 4, 1980.

94. "Chicano Group to Help Police," *Houston Post*, August 21, 1977.

95. Pate et al., "Effects of Police Fear Reduction Strategies," 1.

96. Pate et al., "Effects of Police Fear Reduction Strategies," 9.

97. Pate et al., "Effects of Police Fear Reduction Strategies," 10.

98. Pate et al., "Effects of Police Fear Reduction Strategies," 12–13.

99. "The Paradox of Policemen Policing Policemen," *Los Angeles Times*, December 18, 1977.

100. "Police Bullets and Controversy," *Los Angeles Times*, December 18, 1977.

101. "Los Angeles: Civilian Review," in Human Rights Watch, *Shielded from Justice: Police Brutality and Accountability in the United States*, June 1998, www.hrw.org/legacy/reports98/police/uspo75.htm.

102. Statement of District Attorney John K. Van De Kamp re Final District Attorney/Attorney General Report on Destruction of "Other-Than-Sustained" Complaint Files by

the Los Angeles Police Department, February 6, 1978, 2–4, 4 (quotation), in Matter of the Los Angeles City Document Destruction folders, Hugh Manes Papers, UCLA.

103. Report on the Investigation of the Destruction of Complaint Files, February 6, 1978, 15, in Matter of the Los Angeles City Document Destruction folders, Manes Papers, UCLA; Felker-Kantor, *Policing Los Angeles*, 124–25.

104. City of Los Angeles Request for Authority to Destroy Obsolete Records, November 19, 1975, in Matter of the Los Angeles City Document Destruction folders, Manes Papers, UCLA.

105. Report on the Investigation of the Destruction of Complaint Files, 47–86.

106. Van De Kamp Statement.

107. Felker-Kantor, *Policing Los Angeles*, 104–7, epilogue.

108. "Angry Citizens Seek to Closely Monitor Police," *Los Angeles Times*, May 31, 1985; "Police Official Acknowledges 'Polarization,'" *Los Angeles Times*, June 1, 1985; "Acquittal in Second Trial for Officer's Slaying," Associated Press, July 16, 1987.

109. "Police Advisory Board to Consider Permanent Role," *Los Angeles Times*, January 21, 1987; "Citizens Give Views on New Police Review Board," *Los Angeles Times*, February 8, 1989; "City to Form Prop. G Police Review Board," *Los Angeles Times*, March 4, 1989; "Activist to Head New Police Board," *Times-Advocate* (Escondido, CA), April 26, 1989; San Diego County Grand Jury, *San Diego Community Review Board*.

110. "Panel Hears Debate on Change in Code," *San Antonio Express*, October 3, 1976.

111. "Hispanic Leaders, Law Officers Plan Cooperation Meeting," *Corpus Christi Caller*, March 23, 1979; "Chicanos, Law Officers Meet to 'Open Minds,'" *Dallas Times Herald*, March 24, 1979 (quotation).

112. "Recruiters Seeking More Latino Police," *Arizona Republic* (Phoenix), April 9, 1973.

113. Texas Advisory Committee to the United States Commission on Civil Rights, *Texas*, 22, Rodriguez-Mendoza (Amalia) Papers, APL.

114. Texas Advisory Committee to the United States Commission on Civil Rights, *Texas*, 33 (fig. 4.7), in Rodriguez-Mendoza (Amalia) Papers, APL.

115. Texas Advisory Committee to the United States Commission on Civil Rights, *Texas*, 41, in Rodriguez-Mendoza (Amalia) Papers, APL.

116. "Texas 'Justice,'" *Houston Post*, April 2, 1978.

CHAPTER 7

1. For background information, see Garcia and Marinari, *Whose America?*

2. "Public Enemy Number One"; Tom LoBianco, "Report: Aide Says Nixon's War on Drugs Targeted Blacks, Hippies," CNN, March 24, 2016, www.cnn.com/2016/03/23/politics/john-ehrlichman-richard-nixon-drug-war-blacks-hippie/index.html; Mallea, *War on Drugs*, 13; Andrew Glass, "Reagan Declares 'War on Drugs,' October 14, 1982," *Politico*, October 14, 2010, www.politico.com/story/2010/10/reagan-declares-war-on-drugs-october-14-1982-043552; Bertram et al., *Drug War Politics*, 111–15.

3. Hinton, *From the War on Poverty to the War on Crime*.

4. "City Resident Is Shot for Threatening Officer," *Arizona Republic* (Phoenix), December 27, 1979; "2 Police Brutality Suits Filed Here," *Phoenix Gazette*, October 23, 1980.

5. "Avondale Marchers Will Protest Police Actions in Christmas Day Fight," *Arizona Republic* (Phoenix), January 24, 1980; "Protest in Avondale Planned," *Phoenix Gazette*, January 25, 1980; "200 March on Avondale Police Station," *Arizona Republic* (Phoenix), January 27, 1980; "Police Action Protested," *Arizona Daily Sun* (Flagstaff), January 28, 1980; "200 Protesters March against Avondale Police," *The Westsider* (Goodyear, AZ), January 30, 1980; Echeverría, "Palabras, Promises, and Principles."

6. "2 Police Brutality Suits Filed Here," *Phoenix Gazette*, October 23, 1980; "Policeman Justified in Striking Suspect with Gun, Jury Says," *Arizona Republic* (Phoenix), May 27, 1982.

7. "The Chicanos," *Mesa Magazine*, November 1980.

8. "Chicanos."

9. "Chicanos."

10. "Pascua Patrol Looks for a Two-Way Street," *Tucson Citizen*, December 2, 1980.

11. "A Young Policeman Wins Respect, Eases Tensions in Victory Acres," *Arizona Republic* (Phoenix), April 22, 1981; "Assault Rate Declines after Liaison Program," *Arizona Republic* (Phoenix), October 21, 1981.

12. "The City's Top Cop Talks about Crime and Life on the Streets," *Arizona Republic* (Phoenix), September 6, 1981; "Phoenix Police Chief Defied Odds," *Arizona Republic* (Phoenix), July 22, 1981.

13. "Ortega," unknown newspaper, n.d., in Ruben Ortega folder, ASU.

14. "City's Top Cop Talks about Crime and Life on the Streets"; Geerken and Gove, "Deterrence, Overload, and Incapacitation"; National Institute of Justice, *Five Things about Deterrence*, 1–2; Clark, "Prison Overcrowding." See also Lahav and Guiraudon, "Comparative Perspectives on Border Control," 69.

15. "Arizona's Own J. Edgar Hoover," *Phoenix New Times*, February 3–9, 1993. See also "The Rise and Fall of Ruben Ortega," *Phoenix New Times*, June 19, 1991; and "Police Chief Angered over Forced Rehirings," *Phoenix Gazette*, n.d., in Ruben Ortega folder, ASU.

16. "Ortega Accused of Misconduct by Police Union," *Phoenix Gazette*, June 2, 1986; "Request for Ortega Probe Rejected," *Phoenix Gazette*, June 3, 1986.

17. "3 Current and 2 Former Suns Indicted on Drug Charges," *Los Angeles Times*, April 18, 1987; "Rise and Gall of Ruben Ortega."

18. Phil Latzman, "Maricopa's Former Top Prosecutor Reflects on AzScam 25 Years Later," radio interview, *KJZZ*, April 12, 2016, http://kjzz.org/content/290916/maricopas-former-top-prosecutor-reflects-azscam-25-years-later.

19. "Arizona's Own J. Edgar Hoover."

20. "S. L. Hires Arizonan as Police Chief," *Deseret News* (Salt Lake City), November 2, 1992.

21. "Hispanics, Euless Police Meet to Improve Relations," *Fort Worth Star-Telegram*, n.d., in Samuel Garcia Papers, Genealogy, Local History and Archives, Fort Worth Public Library, TX; "Wounded Euless Youth Tormented by Pain, Fear for Life," *Fort Worth Star-Telegram*, July 15, 1980.

22. "Police Shooting Dismissed," *Dallas Morning News*, n.d., in Garcia Papers, Genealogy, Local History and Archives, Fort Worth Public Library, TX.

23. "Burglary Suspect Shot Dead by Policeman," *San Antonio Light*, December 26, 1980.

24. "Rights Probe Launched," *San Antonio Light*, December 31, 1980.

25. "Family Says Slain Suspect's Ghost Still Around," *San Antonio Light*, December 28, 1980; "Witness Fears Police Altered His Story," *San Antonio Light*, January 25, 1981; "Four Testify in Santoscoy Death Probe," *San Antonio Express*, January 27, 1981; "FBI Enters Shooting Case," *San Antonio Light*, January 1, 1981.

26. "14 Protest Probe of Alien Killing," *San Antonio Light*, January 16, 1981; "The Santoscoy Case Revisited," *San Antonio Light*, December 27, 1981.

27. Raul Gonzalez Galarza to Mayor Lila Cockrell, January 15, 1981, City Council Meeting Minutes, in Municipal Archives and Records, San Antonio, TX. Special thanks to San Antonio archivist Donna Guerra for this letter and the many other documents she sent to me regarding the Hector Santoscoy case.

28. "Rights Probe Pushed," *San Antonio Light*, January 30, 1981.

29. "DA Defends Action in Police Shooting," *San Antonio News*, January 30, 1981.

30. "Grand Jury Doesn't Expect to Reopen Santoscoy Case," *San Antonio Express*, February 21, 1981; "Grand Jury Again No-Bills Cammack," *San Antonio Express*, February 27, 1981.

31. "State Joins Santoscoy Probe," *San Antonio Express*, February 5, 1981.

32. "Officer Defends Shooting," *San Antonio News*, January 29, 1981.

33. "Eureste Urges Santoscoy Justice," *San Antonio Light*, February 1, 1981.

34. "Santoscoy Cammack's Second Victim, OUED Says," *San Antonio Express-News*, January 18, 1981; "Marchers Protest Santoscoy Shooting," *San Antonio Express-News*, February 8, 1981.

35. "Protestors March for Justice for Santoscoy," *San Antonio Express-News*, March 1, 1981; "Santoscoy Protest Draws 200," *San Antonio Light*, March 1, 1981.

36. "Santoscoy a Martyr in Song," *San Antonio Express-News*, February 22, 1981; "Shooting of Santoscoy Re-Enacted in Milam Park," *San Antonio Light*, March 15, 1981.

37. Walter Martinez to Fred Martinez (Department of Justice), February 5, 1981; and Mexican American Democrats Resolution, January 26, 1981, both in Office of the Mayor, Lila Cockrell Records, 1970–81, Municipal Archives and Records, San Antonio, TX.

38. "Slain Mexican's Mom Pleads for Justice," *San Antonio News*, January 23, 1981; "Santoscoy's Relatives, Countrymen Plead for Justice," *San Antonio Express*, January 23, 1981.

39. "Santos Challenges Santoscoy Autopsy," *San Antonio Express*, February 9, 1981.

40. "Santoscoy Autopsy Raises New Questions," *San Antonio Light*, February 8, 1981; "New Autopsy: Santoscoy's Death Murder," *San Antonio News*, February 8, 1981; "New Santoscoy Protest Planned," *San Antonio Express*, March 11, 1981.

41. "Mexico Autopsy Results Blasted," *San Antonio News*, February 9, 1981.

42. Ruben C. Santos, MD, to Honorable Judge Ed Prado, September 8, 1981, in Police Department Vertical File, Texana/Genealogy Collection, San Antonio Public Library, TX; "New Probe Asked in Death," *San Antonio Express*, August 28, 1981; "Santoscoy Action Demanded," *San Antonio Light*, September 19, 1981; "Santoscoy Case Revisited."

43. "March to Commemorate Mexican Shot by Officer," *San Antonio Express*, September 24, 1981; "Protest against Police, Rights Abuse Staged," *San Antonio Express-News*, December 20, 1981; "Rally for Justice—San Antonio Coalition against Racism," December 19, 1981, in Mario Salas Papers, UTSA.

44. "Brown Berets in Protest," *San Antonio Express*, March 4, 1982.

45. "Federal Grand Jury Will Investigate Year-Old Santoscoy Shooting Case," *San Antonio Light*, December 15, 1981; "Federal Just Begins Santoscoy Probe," *San Antonio Light*, January 13, 1981.

46. "Santoscoy Hearing Concludes," *San Antonio Light*, January 15, 1982; "Cammack Probe Comes to an End," *San Antonio Light*, March 10, 1982; "S.A. Policeman Won't Face Federal Prosecution," *San Antonio Express*, March 10, 1982.

47. "Santoscoy Decision Blasted," *San Antonio Express*, March 11, 1982.

48. "Transvestite Issues Threat to Officer, Shot to Death," *San Antonio Light*, April 1, 1984; "Officer Kills Male Hooker," *San Antonio Express-News*, April 1, 1984. Special thanks to Jehan Nuñez al Faisal and Santos Nuñez Galicia for helping me revise this section.

49. "Officer Kills Male Hooker."

50. "Vigil Held for Slain Transvestite," *San Antonio Light*, April 9, 1984.

51. "Gay Activists Accuse S.A. Police of Bias," *San Antonio Express-News*, December 9, 1984.

52. For background on Páez, see "Fred Páez, Activist," Houston LGBT History.org, accessed May 21, 2023, www.houstonlgbthistory.org/banner1980.html. Special thanks to Wesley Phelps for pointing me toward this research material. See also Phelps, "Politics of Queer Disidentification"; Haight, "Silence Is Killing Us"; and Haight, "From Hate Crimes to Activism," 82–86.

53. "Unofficial Auxiliary to Assist Police," *Tyler (TX) Morning Telegraph*, April 11, 1980; Denny Nivens, "How the Montrose Patrol Protected Gays against Street Violence in 1970s Houston," *Out*, July 19, 2017, www.out.com/out-exclusives/2017/7/19/how-montrose-patrol-protected-gays-against-street-violence-1970s-houston.

54. Sears, *Rebels, Rubyfruit, and Rhinestones*, 223.

55. "GPC Secretary Fred Paez Shot and Killed," *TWT News*, July 4–10, 1980; "Fred Paez, June 28 1980, Age 27, Houston," Texas Obituary Project, accessed May 21, 2023, www.texasobituaryproject.org/070480paez.html.

56. "Gay Leaders Urge Calm after Slaying," *Fort Worth Star-Telegram*, June 29, 1980; "Gun That Killed Paez Couldn't Have Fired Accidentally, Expert Says," *Houston Post*, July 2, 1980; "Federal Investigation Sought in Shooting," *Longview (TX) News-Journal*, June 30, 1980; "Special Report, Update on Paez Death," *TWT News*, September 19–25, 1980.

57. "Sources Say Officer Was Drinking," *Houston Post*, July 8, 1980; "Paez Death Investigated," *TWT News*, July 11–17, 1980; "Officer May Have Been Drinking Heavily," *TWT News*, July 18–24, 1980.

58. "US Probe Asked in Slaying of Gay Political Worker," *Houston Chronicle*, June 30, 1980; "FBI Investigates Paez Killing," *Upfront America*, July 4, 1980; "FBI to Question Cop in Homosexual Death," *Tyler (TX) Morning Telegraph*, July 9, 1980; "Task Force Tackles Paez Killing," *Upfront America*, August 29, 1980.

59. "Killing of Gay Worker Protested," *Longview (TX) News-Journal*, July 23, 1980.

60. "Cop Indicted in Paez Killing," *Upfront America*, October 24, 1980; "Houston Cop Indicted for Gay's Death," *Austin American-Statesman*, October 16, 1980.

61. "Police Officer Acquitted," *Paris (TX) News*, September 6, 1981; "Jury Finds McCoy Not Guilty," *TWT News*, September 11–17, 1981; "Gays Not Happy with Verdict," *TWT News*, September 11–17, 1981; "Cleared Officer Returns to Job," *Longview (TX) News-Journal*, September 11, 1981.

62. "Fred Páez, Activist."

63. "Candidate's AIDS Plan Stirs Furor," *Tyler (TX) Courier-Times*, October 25, 1985; "'Shoot the Queers' Gaffe Proves to Be Financial Gold Mine," Associated Press, October 30, 1985, https://apnews.com/aadaa878d5b99509064e14c61bb6ddae6; Robert Reinhold, "The '85 Elections," *New York Times*, November 7, 1985; "Houston Mayor Easily Wins Re-Election," *Fort Worth Star-Telegram*, November 6, 1985.

64. For broader works on this subject, see Flavin, "Police and HIV/AIDSs"; Mogul, Ritchie, and Whitlock, *Queer (In)Justice*; Stewart-Winter, "Queer Law and Order"; and especially Hoppe, *Punishing Disease*; and Phelps, *Before Lawrence v. Texas*.

65. Roth, *Life and Death of ACT UP/LA*, 34–36; Limberg, "Murder of Donna Gentile," 16. See also Kane and Mason, "AIDS and Criminal Justice."

66. "Killing—A Tale of Confusion and Tragedy," *Los Angeles Times*, March 6, 1981; "Fatal Shooting by Deputies Tied to Language Problem," *Los Angeles Times*, July 22, 1981.

67. "Family Gets $1.3 Million in Wrongful Death Case," *Los Angeles Times*, July 24, 1986.

68. "A Street Cop Becomes O.C. Sheriff," *Los Angeles Times*, June 22, 2008.

69. CAPA Report 1971–81, in Coalition against Police Abuse folder, Muñoz Papers, UCLA.

70. CAPA Report 1971–81.

71. Campaign for a Citizens Police Review Board, "Why Do We Need a Citizen's Police Review Board?," flyer, ca. 1980, in Press Clippings re: Police Repression folder, Muñoz Papers, UCLA; "Police Review Drive Starts," *People's World Southwest*, January 12, 1980.

72. CAPA Report 1971–81; "The Brutality Squads," *Freedom Socialist*, Spring 1980.

73. "Chicano Appointed to Police Commission," *Los Angeles Times*, April 12, 1980.

74. "Huntington Park Officer under Investigation by D.A.," *Los Angeles Times*, November 9, 1986; "D.A. Investigates Alleged Misuse of Stun Gun," *Los Angeles Times*, December 14, 1986.

75. "Stun Gun Episode Told," *Los Angeles Times*, November 18, 1987; "Youth Testifies Police Used Stun Gun to Question Him," *Los Angeles Times*, November 19, 1987; "Ex-Officers Convicted of Torturing Teen into Confession," *News-Pilot* (San Pedro, CA), December 12, 1987.

76. "Law-Enforcement Agencies Abuse Hispanics at Border, Coalition Says," *San Diego Tribune*, December 22, 1984.

77. "Abuse of Hispanics Is Alleged," *San Diego Union*, December 22, 1984; "Group Calls for Probe of Police," *Imperial Valley (CA) Press*, December 24, 1984.

78. "Hotline Planned to Curb Hispanic Abuse," *National City Star News* (San Diego), December 23, 1984.

79. "Abuse of Hispanics Continues, Coalition Says," *San Diego Tribune*, January 2, 1985.

80. Summary of Testimony of Roberto Luis Martinez before the House Judiciary Sub-Committee on Criminal Justice for HR 2452, Federal Law Enforcement Officer Review Act, September 11, 1986; and Martinez to Rep. Jim Bates, September 23, 1986, both in Correspondence, 1985–91 folder, AFSC Records, UCSD.

81. "Border Unit Kills 2 Alleged Canyon Bandits," *San Diego Union*, December 2, 1987.

82. "San Ysidro," *Los Angeles Times*, December 22, 1987.

83. Behnken, *Borders of Violence and Justice*, 46.

84. Esteban Torres, Mel Levine, and Jim Bates to Honorable Gus Yatron, October 12, 1989, in Border Patrol Abuses and Shootings, 1984–2003 folder, Roberto Martinez Papers, UCSD. See also Jiménez, "Police Policies and Practices"; and Martín Salvador Rocha, "Human Rights Abuse in the United States: Border Violence in the Hands of the INS," report, California State University Long Beach, 1990, in Human Rights, 1990–2004 folder, Martinez Papers, UCSD.

85. "Border Patrol Agent Accused of Shooting Teen in Mexico to Begin Trial," *The Guardian*, March 20, 2018, www.theguardian.com/us-news/2018/mar/20/border-patrol-agent-accused-of-shooting-teen-in-mexico-to-begin-trial; Kristine Phillips, "U.S. Border Agent Who Repeatedly Shot Mexican Teen through a Fence Acquitted of Murder," *Washington Post*, April 24, 2018.

86. "Senior Citizens' Haven Pushed to Supplant Barrion," *Los Angeles Times*, October 15, 1984; "Blighted Area Out of Sync in Northridge," *Los Angeles Times*, October 15, 1984; "Bernson Legislation Aims at Eviction of Low-Income Tenants," *Los Angeles Times*, May 10, 1985; "Neighborhood Shocked by Eviction Plan," *Los Angeles Times*, August 8, 1985.

87. "Letters, Petition Back Eviction at Bryant-Vanalden," *Los Angeles Times*, n.d., in Bryant-Vanalden (Northridge) Mass Eviction/"Re-Development" folder, Muñoz Papers, UCLA.

88. "Protesta contra plan de desalojo masivo en Northridge" (Protest against massive eviction plan in Northridge), *La Opinión* (Los Angeles), August 10, 1985; "Snyder dice malinterpretaron declaración" (Snyder says declaration misinterpreted), *La Opinión* (Los Angeles), August 10, 1985; "Snyder sorprendido por reacciones de Hispanos" (Snyder surprised by Hispanic reaction), *La Opinión* (Los Angeles), August 10, 1985; "Bryant-Vanalden Plan Faces Rising Protest," *Los Angeles Times*, August 12, 1985; "Bryant-Vanalden's Residents Mobilize to Resist Eviction," *Los Angeles Times*, August 20, 1985.

89. "Blighted Area Out of Sync in Northridge," *Los Angeles Times*, n.d.; Southern California District Communist Labor Party, "Police Harass (Six) Tenants," flyer, n.d.; and "Inquilinos abusados por la policia" (Tenants abused by the police), n.d., all in Bryant-Vanalden (Northridge) Mass Eviction/"Re-Development" folder, Muñoz Papers, UCLA. See also "Plagued Units to Get More Patrols," *Los Angeles Times*, August 28, 1985; and "Bryant-Vanalden Strategy Criticized," *Los Angeles Times*, September 1, 1985.

90. "Bernson Bryant-Vanalden Proposals Hit Multiple Snags," *Los Angeles Times*, April 21, 1986; "Developer Acts to Buy, Fix Up Bryant-Vanalden Apartments," *Los Angeles Times*, October 9, 1986; "L.A. City Council Expected to OK Bryant-Vanalden Area Renovation," *Los Angeles Times*, November 24, 1986; "Redevelopment OKd for Bryant-Vanalden," *Los Angeles Times*, November 27, 1986.

91. "Inspectors Sweep Bryant-Vanalden as L.A. Drafts New Cleanup Plan," *Los Angeles Times*, February 28, 1986; "Renewal Brings Class, Confusion to Neighborhood," *Los Angeles Times*, December 6, 1987; "Bryant-Vanalden Project Developer Quits as Manager," *Los Angeles Times*, June 4, 1988; "Developer Given 3 Weeks to Upgrade Housing Project," *Los Angeles Times*, March 16, 1989.

92. "Spanish booklet," in Community Service folder, L. A. Murillo Papers, USC. See also "L. A. Murillo," list of accomplishments, n.d.; "Biography," September 2003; and "Copy," n.d. (quotation), all in Community Service folder, L. A. Murillo Papers, USC.

93. Pablo Torres card, n.d., in Correspondence Related to Community Service & Air Force folder, L. A. Murillo Papers, USC.

94. Philip B. Davis to Mr. and Mrs. Vigil, November 16, 17, 1981; and Henry Zuniga to Davis, November 18, 1981, both in Frank I. Sanchez Papers, UNM.

95. "Mistaken Police Raid Sparks $2 Million Suit," *Albuquerque Journal*, December 14, 1984; "Roswell Couple Files Arrest Suit," *Carlsbad (NM) Current-Argus*, December 17, 1984.

96. "City Leaders Consider Counteraction in Suit," *Roswell (NM) Daily Record*, December 16, 1984; "Raid at Wrong Address Brings Suit against City," *El Paso Times*, December 17, 1984.

97. "Couple Win $150,000 Settlement in Rights Suit," *Albuquerque Journal*, November 1, 1985.

98. Voluntary Statement of Helen G. Gonzales, January 20, 1986; and Voluntary Statement of Jim Gonzales, January 20, 1986, both in Frank I. Sanchez Papers, UNM.

99. "National Progress Report, 1981," in American G. I. Forum (1981–83) folder, Garcia Papers, Genealogy, Local History and Archives, Fort Worth Public Library, TX.

CHAPTER 8

1. *Moreno v. Shriver*, No. CV 92-3444-WKD, May 4, 1993, in Peter Moreno vs. David Shriver folder, Hugh Manes Papers, UCLA.

2. The first nadir came in the early twentieth century; see Behnken, *Borders of Violence and Justice*, chap. 5.

3. See Harcourt, *Illusion of Order*.

4. See Provine, *Unequal under Law*; Balko, *Rise of the Warrior Cop*; and Felker-Kantor, *DARE to Say No*.

5. National Council of La Raza report on Los Angeles, ca. 1980, 44–45, in National Council de la Raza—Police Practices, 1983 folder, American Friends Service Committee—United States–Mexico Border Program Records, UCSD; Felker-Kantor, *Policing Los Angeles*, 105–7.

6. National Chicano Human Rights Council, "Los Angeles Report: Concerns in the Aftermath of the Recent Unrest," May 1992, 7, in "Los Angeles Report: Concerns in the Aftermath of . . . Unrest" folder, ASU.

7. "Los Angeles Report: Concerns in the Aftermath of the Recent Unrest," 1.

8. "Los Angeles Report: Concerns in the Aftermath of the Recent Unrest," 12–18; National Chicano Human Rights Council, press release, May 27, 1992, both in "Los Angeles Report: Concerns in the Aftermath of . . . Unrest" folder, ASU.

9. "Denuncian abusos en la frontera" (They denounce abuses on the border), *La Opinión* (Los Angeles), April 19, 1990; "Abuso en la frontera" (Abuse on the border), *La Opinión* (Los Angeles), April 24, 1990; "Border Patrol Abuse Tales Stir Call by Rights Group for Civilian Review Board," *San Diego Tribune*, June 8, 1991.

10. "1993/1994 INS/Customs/Border Patrol Complaints San Diego," report of the American Friends Service Committee, July 15, 1995, in American Friends Service Committee, 1991–99 folder, Roberto Martinez Papers, UCSD.

11. Director, Office of Operations to All Personnel, Office of Operations, memo, March 22, 1995, in Community Policing folder, L. A. Murillo Papers, USC.

12. "Community Policing Problem Solving Workbook," ca. 1995, in Community Policing Problem Solving Workbook folder, L. A. Murillo Papers, USC.

13. See, e.g., DiPietro, "STEPping into the 'Wrong' Neighborhood"; Sekhon, "Police and the Limit of Law"; and Harmon, "Why Arrest?"

14. "Police Get First Book to Go By," *San Antonio Express-News*, September 26, 1984.

15. "City Detectives Moving Out to Police Substations," *San Antonio Express-News*, November 19, 1992; "'Storefront' Program Gives Police a Sense of Community," *San Antonio Express-News*, March 14, 1993; "Police Rubbing Elbows," *San Antonio Express-News*, March 5, 1995.

16. "A Case for a Citizens' Police Review Board," Frontline 2000 proposal, May 2, 1992, in Topics, Police Brutality—Citizens' Police Review Board Report 1992, Mario Salas Papers, UTSA; Alexander E. Briseño to mayor and city council, memo, May 28, 1992, in Topics, Police Brutality—Newsclippings and Newsletters, 1950–2004, Salas Papers, UTSA.

17. "Oversight of Police to Change," *San Antonio Light*, January 8, 1993; "Police Union Submits Civilian Review Plan," *San Antonio Express-News*, July 19, 1993.

18. "Police Review Panel Slate Gets Nod," *San Antonio Express-News*, January 12, 1996.

19. "Review of Force," *San Antonio Express-News*, October 11, 2007; "SAPD Slated for Review," *San Antonio Express-News*, November 1, 2007; "FBI Reviewing Complaints about S.A. Cops," *San Antonio Express-News*, March 2, 2008; "Report Slams Way S.A. Police Treat Gays," *San Antonio Express-News*, September 23, 2005.

20. "Tactics under Fire," *San Antonio Express-News*, March 9, 2008.

21. "Arrest of Mexican Aliens in Austin Now Running about 44 Each Month," *Austin American*, October 29, 1969; "Austinite Files Suit Claiming Police Violated Civil Rights," *Austin American*, January 24, 1973.

22. "Rules of the Community-Police Relations Advisory Council," January 1981, in Police Department: Police-Community Relations Task Force folder, APL.

23. EAPAC, memo, July 17, 1996; and "Historical Summary of the East Austin Police Advisory Council (EAPAC)," July 15, 1996, both in Police/Crime Charlie Sector East Austin folder, Camacho Family Papers, APL.

24. "Model Policing," *Austin Chronicle*, September 6, 1996; "Keep Community Policing," *Austin American-Statesman*, September 7, 1996.

25. "Budget Would Move More Police to Streets," *Austin American-Statesman*, September 10, 1996; "Neighbors Need Police," *Austin American-Statesman*, October 7, 1996.

26. "Results of the Chandler Survey," 1, Office of Arizona Attorney General Grant Woods, 1997, in Results of the Chandler Survey, 1997 folder, ASU; Romero, "Racial Profiling and Immigration Law Enforcement."

27. "Results of the Chandler Survey," 5–6.

28. Romero and Serag, "Violation of Latino Civil Rights."

29. "Results of the Chandler Survey," 2.

30. "Results of the Chandler Survey," 13, 19, 27–28; "Scars Slow to Heal," *East Valley Tribune* (Phoenix), August 19, 2007.

31. "Results of the Chandler Survey," 30–34, quotations at 33, 34.

32. "Diversity Programs Ease Rancor over Chandler Roundup," *East Valley Tribune* (Phoenix), August 20, 2007.

33. "Chandler Roundup Spurs Suit," *Arizona Republic* (Phoenix), August 18, 1997; "Suit over Chandler Roundup Expands," *Arizona Republic* (Phoenix), December 3, 1997; "Plaintiffs' Lawyers Seek Mediator for Chandler Illegals Roundup Suit," *Arizona Republic* (Phoenix), April 15, 1998; "Chandler Roundup Deal Sought," *Arizona Republic* (Phoenix), October 15, 1998; "Settlement Not Enough to Heal Scars of Roundup," *Arizona Republic* (Phoenix), February 14, 1998.

34. See, e.g., O'Hear, "Third-Class Citizenship."

35. Kevin Drum, "A Very Brief History of Super-Predators," *Mother Jones*, March 3, 2016, www.motherjones.com/kevin-drum/2016/03/very-brief-history-super-predators.

36. Federal Bureau of Investigation, "Aggravated Assault Reported by Population, 2021–25," Crime Data Explorer, accessed May 21, 2023, https://cde.ucr.cjis.gov/LATEST/webapp/#/pages/explorer/crime/crime-trend. See also Cooper and Smith, *Homicide Trends*; and Friedman, Grawert, and Cullen, "Crime Trends: 1990–2016."

37. Federal Bureau of Investigation, "Aggravated Assault." At the time of this writing the data for 2023 had not been fully analyzed or finalized. See Ken Dilanian, "The U.S. Crime Rate Is Still Dropping, FBI Data Shows," *NBC News*, March 19, 2024, www.nbcnews.com/news/crime-courts/us-crime-rate-still-dropping-says-fbi-rcna144100. It should be noted that violent crime rates rose slightly during the COVID-19 pandemic while the property crime rate declined, an aberration that likely resulted from this unique historical moment.

38. Andrew Sandoval-Strausz notes succinctly that the rise in various crime trends had relatively little to do with the Latino/a/x population. See Sandoval-Strausz, *Barrio America*, 282–84.

39. Clinton, "Statement on Signing the Departments of Commerce, Justice, and State, the Judiciary, and Related Appropriations Act, 1994," 1837; "Clinton Crime Bill Focuses on Cops, Guns," *Arizona Daily Sun*, August 11, 1993.

40. See, e.g., Thomas Frank, "Bill Clinton's Crime Bill Destroyed Lives, and There's No Point Denying It," *The Guardian*, April 15, 2016.

41. "Crime Increase Costs Mayor Job," *Chicago Tribune*, February 25, 1994.

42. "The Region: Houston," *Fort Worth Star-Telegram*, July 26, 1994; "Kill City," *LA Weekly*, December 8, 1994.

43. "Austin's Police-Assistance Program in Crossfire," *Austin American-Statesman*, December 8, 1995. See also "84,246 Grant to Help Austin Fight Gangs," *Austin American-Statesman*, March 28, 1995.

44. "Cities Win Grants to Hire More Police," *Fort Worth Star-Telegram*, December 20, 1994.

45. "Gallup First NM City to Land Police Funds," *Carlsbad (NM) Current-Argus*, February 9, 1994.

46. "Crime Bill Likely to Send $2.6 Million to N.M.," *Santa Fe New Mexican*, October 7, 1994.

47. "Rio Rancho Will Get Seven More Cops," *Albuquerque Journal*, October 8, 1994.

48. "Bingaman Backs Policing Project," *Albuquerque Journal*, March 9, 1994.

49. "Mayor's Budget Pushes for More Cops on Beat," *Albuquerque Journal*, March 27, 1994; "Mayor to Give Budget Hard Sell," *Albuquerque Journal*, April 2, 1994.

50. "Union Sees Value in Police Plan," *Albuquerque Journal*, May 7, 1994. The community policing program continued after Stover retired under the leadership of Chief

Joe Polisar. See "Polisar Committed to Community," *Albuquerque Journal*, July 5, 1994; "Local Community Policing Effort to Continue," *Albuquerque Journal*, August 12, 1994; and "Community Policing Takes Time, Experts Say," *Albuquerque Journal*, October 19, 1994.

51. "Is an Anti-Crime Tax Needed," *Albuquerque Journal*, July 2, 1995.

52. "Mesa Seeking $54.2 Million for Police, Water in Bond Vote," *Arizona Republic* (Phoenix), March 19, 1994; "White House Releases Funds for 87 New Officers in Arizona," *Arizona Republic* (Phoenix), December 20, 1994.

53. "Phoenix to Speed Up Hiring of 30 Officers," *Arizona Republic* (Phoenix), October 13, 1993.

54. "President Chooses 'Top Cop,'" *Tucson Citizen*, December 20, 1994.

55. See "Arizona Crime Rates, 1960–2019," Disaster Center, accessed June 12, 2025, www.disastercenter.com/crime/azcrime.htm; and "Homicides Up by Half Last Year," *Tucson Citizen*, March 29, 1990. The increase resulted from the state's expanding population, which jumped from 2,715,357 in 1980 to 5,130,632 in 2000.

56. "Venture Capitalist Riordan Enters Race for Mayor," *Los Angeles Times*, November 19, 1992; Felker-Kantor, *Policing Los Angeles*, 174, 217.

57. "Police-Hiring Plan on Council Agenda," *Los Angeles Times*, March 24, 1992.

58. "City Council Approves More Police Officers," *Pasadena (CA) Star-News*, November 24, 1993.

59. "California Crime Rates, 1960–2019," Disaster Center, accessed May 21, 2023, www.disastercenter.com/crime/cacrime.htm.

60. "Justice Dept. Moves to Fund Hiring of Police," *Los Angeles Times*, August 27, 1994; "$12 Million to Hire More Police Goes to Southland," *Los Angeles Times*, October 13, 1994; "West Hollywood to Get 7 New Deputies," *Los Angeles Times*, October 20, 1994; "Give Valley a New Police Division, Alarcon Urges," *Los Angeles Times*, October 26, 1994.

61. "Clinton Grant to Fund 710 LAPD Officers," *Los Angeles Times*, May 15, 1996.

62. "392 Communities Receive Aid to Hire More Police Officers," *The Signal* (Santa Clarita Valley, CA), October 13, 1994.

63. Eisen and Chettiar, "Complex History of the Controversial 1994 Crime Bill."

64. Dara Lind and German Lopez, "16 Theories for Why Crime Plummeted in the US," *Vox*, May 20, 2015, www.vox.com/2015/2/13/8032231/crime-drop.

65. Mitchell et al., "Assessing the Effectiveness of Drug Courts on Recidivism"; Kaye, *Enforcing Freedom*, 10–11, 17–25; Behnken, Arredondo, and Packman, "Reduction in Recidivism."

66. Snyder, "Arrest in the United States, 1990–2010."

67. Bureau of Justice Statistics, "Drugs and Crime Facts, Drug Law Violations, Enforcement" and "Drugs and Crime Facts, Drug Law Violations, Pretrial, Prosecution, and Adjudication"; Matthew Friedman and James Cullen, "JustFacts: What Clearance Rates Say about Disparities in Crime and Prosecution," Brennan Center for Justice, September 30, 2016, www.brennancenter.org/our-work/analysis-opinion/justfacts-what -clearance-rates-say-about-disparities-crime-and; Cooper and Smith, *Homicide Trends in the United States*; Tyler and Boeckmann, "Three Strikes and You Are Out, but Why?"

68. Ann Devroy, "Clinton Retains Tough Law on Crack Cocaine," *Washington Post*, October 31, 1995.

69. Tapia, "U.S. Latino Arrest," 50; Malavé and Giordani, *Latino Stats*, 93–104. See also "The Alarming Lack of Data on Latinos in the Criminal Justice System," Urban Institute, December 2016, https://apps.urban.org/features/latino-criminal-justice-data.

70. Lofstrom et al., *New Insights into California Arrests*; Lofstrom et al., *Racial Disparities in California Arrests*.

71. Division of Correctional Policy Research and Internal Oversight Office of Research, *Offender Data Points*, 14; "California Profile."

72. Arizona Department of Public Safety, *Crime in Arizona, 2015*. Latino/a/x people are also counted as White, making an accurate figure hard to tabulate.

73. "Arizona Profile."

74. Jeff Proctor and Elaina Jameson, "NM Lacks Criminal Justice Data on Race, Ethnicity," New Mexico in Depth, March 11, 2019, http://nmindepth.com/2019/03/11/nm-lacks-criminal-justice-data-on-race-ethnicity.

75. "New Mexico Profile."

76. Hartney and Vuong, *Created Equal*, 12.

77. "Texas Profile"; "Race and Imprisonment in Texas."

78. "Drug War, Mass Incarceration and Race (English/Spanish)"; "Color of Justice." See also Banks, "Beyond Profiling."

79. "The Rampart CRASH Unit: Blood on the Hands of the LAPD," *Revolutionary Worker*, October 3, 1999, https://revcom.us/a/v21/1020-029/1024/lapd.htm; "L.A. Police Mired in Misconduct Scandal; Mexican-Americans Numb to the Violence," *Baltimore Sun*, March 13, 2000.

80. Behnken, *Borders of Violence and Justice*, 148, 220.

81. "Survivor of 2nd Shooting Says He Was Framed," *Los Angeles Times*, September 18, 1999; "Family Sues LAPD in Shooting," *Desert Sun* (Palm Springs, CA), November 24, 1999.

82. "Scandal Shows Why Innocent Plead Guilty," *Los Angeles Times*, December 31, 1999.

83. Charles Rappleye and Joseph Trevino, "The Dirty Shooting," *LA Weekly*, December 1, 1999, www.laweekly.com/the-dirty-shooting; Matt Lait and Scott Glover, "Shooting Scenes Rigged, Perez Says," *Los Angeles Times*, February 10, 2000; Don Knowland and Gerardo Nebbia, "The Los Angeles Police Scandal and Its Social Roots," *World Socialist Website*, March 13, 2000, www.wsws.org/en/articles/2000/03/lapd-m13.html.

84. Harry Weinstein and Jim Newton, "Civil Rights Lawyers Form a Gathering Storm for L.A.," *Los Angeles Times*, March 1, 2000.

85. "LAPD Files Internal Misconduct Charges against Rampart Officers," *Los Angeles Times*, July 26, 2000.

86. "LAPD Clears 2 Officers in Rampart Case," *Los Angeles Times*, May 31, 2001.

87. "City Fights Scandal Lawsuits, Saying Time Might Have Run Out," *Hanford (CA) Sentinel*, April 26, 2000.

88. Los Angeles Board of Police Commissioners, *Report of the Rampart Independent Review Panel*; Los Angeles Police Department, "Consent Decree Overview"; Felker-Kantor, *Policing Los Angeles*, 241–43.

89. Marquez, *Black-Brown Solidarity*, 162–63.

90. Jake Bernstein, "Are You Experienced? Video of a Police Killing Produces Shockwaves in Baytown," *Texas Observer*, May 29, 2002, www.texasobserver.org/597-are-you

-experienced-video-of-a-police-killing-produces-shockwaves-in-baytown; Marquez, *Black-Brown Solidarity*, 164; Aguilar, interview.

91. Marquez, *Black-Brown Solidarity*, 164 (first quotation); Bernstein, "Are You Experienced?" (second quotation); "4th Baytown Officer in Torres Case Off Patrol," *Houston Chronicle*, March 23, 2002.

92. Benavides, interview; "Justice Sought after Man Dies in Custody with Video," *Houston Chronicle*, March 4, 2002.

93. Marquez, *Black-Brown Solidarity*, 165–67.

94. "No Indictment in Mexican's Death," *Longview (TX) News-Journal*, May 3, 2002; "Baytown Police Officers Cleared of Arrest Death," *Tyler (TX) Morning Telegraph*, June 7, 2002.

95. "Torres Aftermath Leaves Deep Wounds in Baytown," *Houston Chronicle*, June 13, 2002; "Rights Groups Pushes for Inquiry," *Austin American-Statesman*, July 1, 2002; "Widow Sues for Wrongful Death in Police Incident," *Fort Worth Star-Telegram*, July 5, 2002; "Baytown Reaches Settlement in Wrongful Death Lawsuit," *Plainview (TX) Herald*, August 26, 2003, www.myplainview.com/news/article/Baytown-reaches-settlement-in-wrongful-death-8771585.php; Hilda Martinez, interview.

96. "Off-Duty Officer Fatally Shoots 15-Year-Old," *Houston Chronicle*, November 1, 2003; *City of Houston v. Vargas* (2006).

97. *Escobar et al. v. City of Houston et al.* (2006); "FBI Reviewing Two Teen Shooting Deaths," *Fort Worth Star-Telegram*, November 28, 2003.

98. "FBI Reviewing Police Shooting Deaths of Two Teens," *Houston Chronicle*, November 26, 2003.

99. "HPD Officer Is Cleared in Teen Boy's Death," *Houston Chronicle*, January 24, 2004.

100. "Houston Police Officer Who Killed Teen Is Fired," *Houston Chronicle*, February 13, 2004; "Ruling: Houston Officer Fired in Teen's Death Must Be Reinstated," *Houston Chronicle*, September 7, 2004.

101. "Family Sues HPD, Officer, Theater over Fatal Shooting," *Houston Chronicle*, November 4, 2003; "Multiple Probes Focus on the Police Shooting of Missouri City Youth," *Houston Chronicle*, November 10, 2003; "More Changes in HPD Training Likely," *Houston Chronicle*, June 2, 2008.

102. "Houston Police Officer Who Shot Teen Indicted on Murder Charge," *Houston Chronicle*, March 10, 2004.

103. Christopher Zoukis, "Houston Police Officer Sentenced to 60 Days for the Shooting Death of an Unarmed Teenager; Parents Sue," Prison Legal News, April 20, 2018, www.prisonlegalnews.org/news/2018/apr/20/houston-police-officer-sentenced-60-days-shooting-death-unarmed-teenager-parents-sue.

104. "Police Shootings Spur Calls for More Training," *Odessa (TX) American*, December 28, 2003; "Unarmed and Dangerous," *Houston Chronicle*, November 24, 2013.

105. "Officer Charged with Murder in Teen's Death," *Fort Worth Star-Telegram*, March 12, 2004; "Former HPD Officer Found Guilty in Unarmed Boy's Shooting Death," *Houston Chronicle*, January 18, 2005; "Judge Gives Officer 60 Days for Shooting Boy," *Houston Chronicle*, January 20, 2005.

106. "Review Finds Officers Seldom Punished in Shootings," *Houston Chronicle*, July 26, 2004.

107. "HPD Killing of Boy Prompts Rule, $1.5 Million Payout," *Houston Chronicle*, May 29, 2008; "Child's Tragic Death Leads to Change at HPD," *Houston Chronicle*, November 22, 2008.

108. "Complex Drug Probe Triggered SWAT Raid," *Arizona Daily Star* (Tucson), May 27, 2011.

109. "SWAT Team Returns Fire, Kills Man," *Arizona Daily Star* (Tucson), May 6, 2011.

110. "Man Killed by SWAT Did Not Shoot at Deputies," *Arizona Daily Star* (Tucson), May 20, 2011.

111. "SWAT Team Fired 71 Shots in Raid," *Arizona Daily Star* (Tucson), May 11, 2011; "SWAT Raid Fatal Drama Is Revealed in 911 Call," *Arizona Daily Star* (Tucson), May 14, 2011.

112. "Sheriff's Dept. Puts a Lid on Guerena-Shooting Info," *Arizona Daily Star* (Tucson), May 18, 2011.

113. "Attorney: SWAT Raid Found Guns, Body Armor," *Arizona Daily Star* (Tucson), May 20, 2011.

114. "Complex Drug Probe Triggered SWAT Raid," *Arizona Daily Star* (Tucson), May 27, 2011; "All Four Homes in Raid Tied to Guerena Family," *Arizona Daily Star* (Tucson), May 28, 2011; "Killing by SWAT Team Tucson Raises Questions," *Arizona Republic* (Phoenix), May 28, 2011.

115. "Dupnik: Raid Stemmed from 20-Mo. Probe," *Arizona Daily Star* (Tucson), June 1, 2011; "Records: Guerena's Brother Was Center of Drug-Trafficking Probe," *Arizona Daily Star* (Tucson), June 3, 2011.

116. "SWAT: We Said 'Open Up' at Least Twice," *Arizona Daily Star* (Tucson), June 4, 2011.

117. "Probe Clears 5 SWAT-Raid Officers," *Arizona Daily Star* (Tucson), June 14, 2011. Dupnik disclosed that Jose Guerena had a previous run-in with the Pinal County Sheriff's Office for alleged drug possession, for which he was never charged, as proof of his involvement in the drug scheme. Dupnik was not aware of that previous run-in at the time of the raid.

118. "Guerena Family: Finding Was Biased," *Arizona Daily Star* (Tucson), June 17, 2011 (quotation); "SWAT Victim's Widow Asks $20M," *Arizona Daily Star* (Tucson), August 13, 2011; "Widow Sues over Fatal SWAT Raid," *Arizona Daily Star* (Tucson), November 2, 2011; "$3.4M Settles Deadly '11 Raid," *Arizona Daily Star* (Tucson), September 20, 2013. See also "SWAT Team's Shooting of Marine Vet Causes Outrage," *Arizona Daily Sun* (Tucson), November 28, 2011.

119. "3 Arrested in Drug Case Connected to Man in 2011 SWAT Raid," *Arizona Daily Star* (Tucson), March 9, 2012; "Family's Ties to Alleged Pot Ring Detailed," *Arizona Daily Star* (Tucson), June 10, 2012.

120. "Man Gets Probation, Jail for His Role in Family Drug Outfit," *Arizona Daily Star* (Tucson), June 26, 2013; "15 Weekends of Jail in Marijuana Case," *Arizona Daily Star* (Tucson), July 23, 2013; "Man Guilty of Trying to Launder Money, Is Given Probation," *Arizona Daily Star* (Tucson), June 3, 2014.

121. "Highly Trained SWAT Teams Hold the Line between Order and Chaos," *Arizona Daily Star* (Tucson), October 4, 2013.

122. "Sheriff's Dept. Must Learn from Guerena Killing," *Arizona Daily Star* (Tucson), September 29, 2013.

123. Fernanda Echavarri, "Complex Drug Probe Triggered SWAT Raid," *Arizona Daily Star* (Tucson), May 27, 2011.

124. "Killing by SWAT Team Tucson Raises Questions," *Arizona Republic* (Phoenix), May 28, 2011.

125. Radley Balko, "Jose Guerena's Family Sues Pima County over SWAT Raid Killing," *Huffpost*, August 17, 2011, www.huffpost.com/entry/jose-guerena-pima-county -lawsuit_n_926454.

126. Emily Bregel, Becky Pallack, and Britain Eakin, "Police Militarization Debated in Arizona, Too," *Arizona Daily Star* (Tucson), August 24, 2014, https://tucson.com /news/blogs/police-beat/police-militarization-debated-in-arizona-too/article_c4bd5ecb -845b-5400-be3d-0ddb0a2871e5.html.

127. "Man Dies in San Jose Officer-Involved Shooting," *Fox KTVU*, July 5, 2016, www .ktvu.com/news/man-dies-in-san-jose-officer-involved-shooting; David Louie, "Family Questioning Police Tactics in Fatal Shooting San Jose," *ABC 7 News*, July 5, 2016, https://abc7news.com/news/family-questioning-police-tactics-in-fatal-shooting-san-jose /1414809.

128. "Why Did Police Kill a Suicidal Teenager in the Heart of Silicon Valley?," *Splinter*, November 28, 2016, https://splinternews.com/why-did-police-kill-a-suicidal -teenager-in-the-heart-of-1793863975.

129. Santa Clara County District Attorney's Office, *Report on the Fatal Shooting*; "Santa Clara County," *San Francisco Examiner*, August 16, 2017.

130. Robert Salonga, "Federal Civil Trial Underway in 2016 San Jose Police Shoot-ing," *San Jose (CA) Mercury News*, June 18, 2019, www.mercurynews.com/2019/06 /18/federal-civil-trial-underway-in-2016-san-jose-police-shooting; Christie Smith, "'He Didn't Deserve to Die,'" *NBC Bay Area*, July 8, 2017, www.nbcbayarea.com/news/local /san-jose-wrongful-death-complaint-lawsuit-shooting-death-18-year-old-anthony-nunez /25501.

131. *Nunez v. City of San Jose* (2019); "2 Officers Used Excessive Force in Fatal Shooting of 18-Year-Old," *NBC Bay Area*, July 2, 2019, www.nbcbayarea.com/news/local /2-officers-used-excessive-force-in-fatal-shooting-of-18-year-old/151849; "Jury Finds 2 San Jose Officers Liable for Excessive Force," *Visalia (CA) Times-Delta*, July 5, 2019; "Federal Civil Jury Finds Two San Jose Cops Liable for Excessive Force in Fatal 2016 Police Shooting," *San Jose (CA) Mercury News*, July 2, 2019.

CONCLUSION

1. "Police Investigating Shooting of Teen," *San Francisco Examiner*, October 24, 2013; "Shooting of Boy by Deputy Questioned," *Sacramento Bee*, October 25, 2013. See also "Andy Lopez—What Now? Making Sense of Senseless Loss," *Sonoma County Gazette* (Santa Rosa, CA), October 13, 2013.

2. *Estate of Lopez v. Gelhaus* (2017).

3. *Estate of Lopez v. Gelhaus* (2017).

4. "Santa Rosa, Calif. Deputy Erick Gelhaus, Who Shot Boy Carrying Toy Assault Rifle, Was a Firearms Instructor, Gun Range Master, Iraq Veteran," *New York Daily News*, October 29, 2013.

5. "Shooting of Boy by Deputy Questioned"; "Decision to Shoot Boy Made in 10 Seconds," *Sacramento Bee*, October 26, 2013; "FBI to Look into Shooting of 13-Year-Old with BB Gun," *Fresno Bee*, October 27, 2013; "Fatal Shooting of Boy, 13, Sparks Protest," *Fresno Bee*, October 30, 2013; "Deputy Shot Boy before Partner Left Car," *Fresno Bee*, October 31, 2013.

6. "Mother of Slain Boy Files Claim against County," *Sacramento Bee*, November 1, 2013; "Marchan por asesinato de niño en California" (March for murder of a child in California), *El Universal* (Mexico City), November 2, 2013.

7. "Law Enforcement Mum on Slaying of Boy," *Sacramento Bee*, November 8, 2013; "Andy Lopez Citizen Task Force Forming," *Petaluma (CA) Argus-Courier*, November 14, 2013.

8. "Deputy Return Angers," *Fresno Bee*, December 12, 2013.

9. "No Charges for Cop in Santa Rosa Teen Shooting," *San Francisco Examiner*, July 8, 2014; "Protesters Decry Decision to Not Prosecute Deputy in Boy's Death," *Los Angeles Times*, July 9, 2014.

10. "FBI Won't Charge Deputy Who Killed Youth in 2013," *Sacramento Bee*, July 3, 2015.

11. "Payout Reached in Teen's Slaying," *Los Angeles Times*, December 19, 2018.

12. "Focus Now on Police Task Force," *Petaluma (CA) Argus-Courier*, July 10, 2014; E. A. Barrera, "Council to Eye Police Review Proposal," *Petaluma (CA) Argus-Courier*, March 12, 2015; "County Weighs Office to Oversee Sheriff in Wake of Teenager's Shooting," *Tulare (CA) Advance-Register*, May 14, 2015; Independent Office of Law Enforcement Review and Outreach, "History," County of Sonoma, 2022, https://sonomacounty.ca.gov/IOLERO/History.

13. Veronica Rocha, "Driver Killed by CHP during Illegal Street Racing Probe Is Identified as Canoga Park Man," *Los Angeles Times*, July 5, 2016; "CHP Shots at Vehicle Unsafe, Experts Say," *Sacramento Bee*, July 6, 2016.

14. "Enhanced Body-Camera Video Showing Antonio Arce Shooting," *Arizona Republic* (Phoenix), January 30, 2019, www.azcentral.com/videos/news/local/tempe/2019/01/30/enhanced-body-camera-video-showing-antonio-arce-shooting/2726521002; Bree Burkitt, "No Charges for Tempe Police Officer Who Shot and Killed 14-Year-Old Antonio Arce," *Arizona Republic* (Phoenix), January 31, 2020; Bree Burkitt, "Tempe Approves $2 Million Settlement for Family of 14-Year-Old Killed by Police," *Arizona Republic* (Phoenix), June 25, 2020.

15. Julie Bosman and Neil MacFarquhar, "Video Is Released of Chicago Police Fatally Shooting 13-Year-Old," *New York Times*, October 27, 2021; Kim Foxx, "No Charges for Officers in Fatal Shootings of Adam Toledo, Anthony Alvarez," *NBC Chicago*, March 15, 2022, www.nbcchicago.com/news/local/chicago-politics/no-charges-for-officers-in-fatal-shootings-of-adam-toledo-anthony-alvarez/2783566.

16. John Paul Barajas and Gavin Nesbitt, "SAPD Fires Officer Who Shot Teen outside McDonald's Restaurant, Releases Video of Incident," KSAT-TV, October 5, 2022, www.ksat.com/news/local/2022/10/05/sapd-fires-officer-who-shot-teen-outside-mcdonalds-restaurant-releases-video-of-incident; John Paul Barajas and Ivan Herrera, "Erik Cantu Jr. Back Home More Than 7 Weeks after Being Shot by SAPD Officer, Family Says," KSAT-TV, November 22, 2022, www.ksat.com/news/local/2022/11/22/erik-cantu-back-home-more-than-7-weeks-after-being-shot-by-sapd-officer-family-says; Michael

Karlis, "Erik Cantu, San Antonio Teen Shot by Now-Former Police Officer, Readmitted to Hospital," *San Antonio Current*, December 6, 2022, www.sacurrent.com/news/erik-cantu -san-antonio-teen-shot-by-now-former-police-officer-readmitted-to-hospital-30500936.

17. Maya Yang, "Texas Police Fires Officer Who Shot a Teen Sitting in His Car in a Fast Food Parking Lot," *The Guardian*, October 8, 2022, www.theguardian.com/us -news/2022/oct/08/texas-police-fires-officer-shot-teenager; Jeanine Santucci, "Ex-Texas Cop Indicted by Grand Jury in Shooting of Unarmed Teen Eating McDonald's Ham- burger," *USA Today*, December 1, 2022, www.usatoday.com/story/news/nation/2022 /12/01/san-antonio-texas-james-brennand-shooting-erik-cantu/10813474002; Dillon Collier and Erica Hernandez, "Ex-SAPD Officer Brennand No Longer Facing Attempted Murder Charge after Reindictment," KSAT-TV, March 7, 2024, www.ksat.com/news /ksat-investigates/2024/03/07/ex-sapd-officer-brennand-no-longer-facing-attempted -murder-charge-after-reindictment. Sadly, Erik Cantu has had a host of problems since his shooting. See Dillon Collier and Erica Hernandez, "Erik Cantu Re-Arrested, Accused of Skipping Drug Tests, Driving on Suspended License," KSAT-TV, November 21, 2024, www.ksat.com/news/ksat-investigates/2024/11/21/erik-cantu-re-arrested-accused-of -skipping-drug-tests-driving-on-suspended-license.

18. Houston and Los Angeles are two noteworthy examples of this process. Jen Rice, "Houston Passes $5.1 Billion Annual Budget, Using Federal Aid to Plug Deficit," *Hous- ton Public Media*, June 2, 2021, www.houstonpublicmedia.org/articles/news/politics /2021/06/02/399679/houston-passes-5-1-billion-annual-budget-using-federal-aid-to -plug-deficit; Josie Huang, "LAPD Budget," *LAist*, August 23, 2023, https://laist.com /brief/news/criminal-justice/la-council-approves-major-hike-lapd.

19. *United States v. City of Albuquerque* (2020); "Albuquerque Police Has Revised Its Use-of-Force Policies," Associated Press, January 27, 2023, https://apnews.com/article /new-mexico-albuquerque-b83fb2458aa1f1dcf2e05409dfd10913. There is a great deal of information on the federal monitoring of the Albuquerque Police Department, see US Attorney's Office, District of New Mexico, *Investigation*.

20. Michael Haederle, "In Albuquerque, an Uproar over Shootings by Police," *Los Angeles Times*, April 14, 2012; Garrett Archer, "Phoenix Police Ranks #1 in Deadly Use of Force Compared to Other Major Departments," KNXV-TV ABC15 Arizona, March 14, 2022, www.abc15.com/news/in-depth/phoenix-police-ranks-1-in-deadly-use-of-force -compared-to-other-major-departments; Tara Pohlmeyer, "Facts about Police Violence in Texas," Progress Texas, June 2, 2020, https://progresstexas.org/blog/facts-about-police -violence-texas.

CODA

1. National Institute of Justice, "Research on Body-Worn Cameras."

2. Jalen Brown, "How Advances in Open-Sourced Data Can End Police Brutality," *Forbes*, April 20, 2021, www.forbes.com/sites/forbesfellows/2021/04/20/how-advances -in-open-sourced-data-can-end-police-brutality.

3. Rashawn Ray, "What Does 'Defund the Police' Mean and Does It Have Merit?," Brookings Institution, June 19, 2020, www.brookings.edu/blog/fixgov/2020/06/19 /what-does-defund-the-police-mean-and-does-it-have-merit.

4. Mathew Brown, "Barack Obama Criticizes Progressives over 'Defund the Police,' Saying Slogan Can Drive Away Moderates," *USA Today*, December 2, 2020; Ben Leonard, "Biden Draws Bipartisan Applause for Calls to 'Fund the Police,'" *Politico*, March 1, 2022, www.politico.com/news/2022/03/01/state-of-the-union-2022-fund-police-00013065.

5. Howard Henderson and Ben Yisrael, "7 Myths about 'Defunding the Police' Debunked," Brookings Institution, May 19, 2021, www.brookings.edu/blog/how-we-rise/2021/05/19/7-myths-about-defunding-the-police-debunked.

6. Christina Jedra, "Here's What Happens When Social Workers, Not Police, Respond to Mental Health Crises," *Honolulu Civil Beat*, March 1, 2021, www.civilbeat.org/2021/03/heres-what-happens-when-social-workers-not-police-respond-to-mental-health-crises; Christina Jedra, "Consider Shifting Police Funds to Social Services, Police Commission Says," *Honolulu Civil Beat*, March 17, 2021. See also Jackson Beck, Melissa Reuland, and Leah Pope, "Behavioral Health Crisis Alternatives: Shifting from Police to Community Responses," *Vera*, November 2020, www.vera.org/behavioral-health-crisis-alternatives.

7. Katherine Landergan, "The City That Really Did Abolish the Police," *Politico*, June 12, 2020, www.politico.com/news/magazine/2020/06/12/camden-policing-reforms-313750. See also Kaba and Ritchie, *No More Police*. There have been strong criticisms of the new policing model in Camden. See Brendan McQuade, "The 'Camden Model' Is Not a Model; It's an Obstacle to Real Change," *Jacobin*, July 4, 2020, https://jacobin.com/2020/07/camden-new-jersey-police-reform-surveillance.

8. For a few examples, see Mychal Denzel Smith, "Incremental Change Is a Moral Failure," *The Atlantic*, September 2020; Michael Brenes, "Police Reform Doesn't Work," *Boston Review*, April 26, 2021; and Mariame Kaba and Andrea J. Ritchie, "Why We Don't Say 'Reform the Police,'" *The Nation*, September 2, 2022. These articles make some excellent points, especially regarding why reforms fail. See also Worden and McLean, *Mirage of Police Reform*, esp. chaps. 1, 10.

9. Alex Vitale offers a compelling assessment of the promise and limitation of a variety of reform efforts. See Vitale, *End of Police*.

10. "President Biden's Executive Order on Police Reform: What You Need to Know," PORAC, July 1, 2022, https://porac.org/article/president-bidens-executive-order-on-police-reform-what-you-need-to-know.

11. Val Van Brocklin, "Warriors vs. Guardians. A Seismic Shift in Policing or Just Semantics?," Police1, May 7, 2019, www.police1.com/21st-century-policing-task-force/articles/warriors-vs-guardians-a-seismic-shift-in-policing-or-just-semantics-EXBkY2pEWCHi6Mni; McLean et al., "Police Officers as Warriors or Guardians"; Stoughton, "Law Enforcement's 'Warrior' Problem."

12. Peter Espinoza and Michael Romano, "It's Time to Reform Sentencing Enhancements," *CalMatters*, May 26, 2021, https://calmatters.org/justice/2021/05/its-time-to-reform-sentencing-enhancements; Dagenais et al., "Sentencing Enhancements and Incarceration"; Frase and Roberts, *Paying for the Past*. For the gang enhancement law, see California Code, Penal Code - PEN § 186.22.

13. "How Police in This Small West Virginia Town Received a $1M Armoured Truck," *The Independent*, June 20, 2020.

14. Charlotte Lawrence and Cyrus J. O'Brien, "Federal Militarization of Law Enforcement Must End," ACLU, May 12, 2021, www.aclu.org/news/criminal-law-reform/federal-militarization-of-law-enforcement-must-end.

15. Flamm, "From Harlem to Ferguson" (quotation); "From 'War on Crime' to War on the Black Community," *Boston Review*, June 21, 2016; Hinton, *From the War on Poverty to the War on Crime*.

16. Sarah Childress, "The Problem with 'Broken Windows,'" *Frontline*, June 28, 2016, www.pbs.org/wgbh/frontline/article/the-problem-with-broken-windows-policing; O'Brien, Farrell, and Welsh, "Looking Through Broken Windows"; Shankar Vedantam, host, *Hidden Brain*, podcast, Chris Benderev, Tara Boyle, Renee Klahr, Maggie Penman, and Jennifer Schmidt, "How a Theory of Crime and Policing Was Born, and Went Terribly Wrong," NPR, November 1, 2016, www.npr.org/2016/11/01/500104506/broken-windows-policing-and-the-origins-of-stop-and-frisk-and-how-it-went-wrong. See also Harcourt, *Illusion of Order*.

17. *Graham v. Connor* (1989); "SWAT Shooting of Guerena Ruled 'Reasonable and Justified,'" KOLD-TV 13, February 28, 2018 (quotation), www.kold.com/story/14901148/swat-shooting-of-guerena-ruled-reasonable-and-justified.

18. "Top 5 Negative Impacts of Arizona's 'Papers Please' Law," Center for American Progress, April 20, 2012, www.americanprogress.org/article/top-5-negative-impacts-of-arizonas-papers-please-law; Peter Slevin, "Ariz. Measure on Immigration Puts Police in Tight Spot," *Washington Post*, April 30, 2010; Viveca Novak, "Arizona's 'Papers Please' Law," FactCheck.org, June 3, 2010, www.factcheck.org/2010/06/arizonas-papers-please-law.

19. Ram Subramanian and Leily Arzy, "State Policing Reforms since George Floyd's Murder," Brennan Center for Justice, May 21, 2021, www.brennancenter.org/our-work/research-reports/state-policing-reforms-george-floyds-murder; Joe D'Antonio, "The United States Needs National Use of Force Standards," Friends Committee on National Legislation, September 8, 2020, www.fcnl.org/updates/2020-07/united-states-needs-national-use-force-standards.

20. Coyne and Hall, "Four Decades and Counting"; Alicia Inez Guzmán, "The War on Drugs Failed, but the Suffering It Caused Continues," *Rolling Stone*, November 30, 2021; "Biden Should End America's Longest War"; Mohammad and Fulkerson, "'War on Drugs.'"

BIBLIOGRAPHY

PRIMARY SOURCES

Manuscript and Archival Collections

ARIZONA
Tempe
    Arizona State University, Chicano Research Collection
        FR-34 Chicano folder
        Guadalupe, Arizona folder
        The Hanigan Case, Vol. 1: March 30, 1977–Nov. 24, 1977 folder
        The Hanigan Case, Vol. 2: Jan. 4, 1978–Dec. 24, 1979 folder
        The Hanigan Case, Vol. 3: Jan. 11–July 31, 1980 folder
        Ignacio Fontes Ruiz folder
        Lawrence Koslow folder
        "Los Angeles Report: Concerns in the Aftermath of . . . Unrest" folder
        Police Brutality folder
        Results of the Chandler Survey, 1997 folder
        Ruben Ortega folder
CALIFORNIA
Davis
    University of California, Davis, Special Collections Department
        Mario G. Obledo Papers
Los Angeles
    University of California, Los Angeles, Special Collections
        Hugh Manes Papers
        Rosalio Muñoz Papers
        Sleepy Lagoon Defense Committee Records, 1942–45
    University of Southern California, Special Collections

LA County Sheriff's Dept's Records on the Investigation
     of the Homicide of Ruben Salazar
L. A. Murillo Papers

San Diego

University of California, San Diego, Special Collections and Archives
     American Friends Service Committee—United States–
          Mexico Border Program Records
     Herman Baca Collection
     Roberto Martinez Papers

San Marino

Huntington Library
     John Anson Ford Papers, 1928–71

NEW MEXICO

Albuquerque

Albuquerque and Bernalillo County Public Library, Special Collections
     Albuquerque Urban Coalition Records
          Police Task Force Collection
     Bio—Byrd, Don file
     NM Associations—Black Berets file
University of New Mexico, Center for Southwest Research and Special Collections
     Emma Moya Collection
     Francisco E. Martínez Papers
     Frank I. Sanchez Papers
     Gloria Montoya Chavez Papers
     Reies López Tijerina Papers
     US Marshal Papers

TEXAS

Arlington

University of Texas, Arlington, Special Collections
     Migrant Farm Workers Organizing Movement Collection
     Pancho Medrano Papers

Austin

Austin Public Library, Austin History Center
     Camacho Family Papers
     John Norman Vasquez folder
     Mexican Americans, Brown Berets folder
     Police Department: Police-Community Relations Task Force folder
     Rodriguez-Mendoza (Amalia) Papers
Lyndon Baines Johnson Presidential Library
     Texas Governor John Connally Papers
     White House Central Files
University of Texas School of Law, Tarlton Law Library
     William Wayne Justice Papers

Dallas

Dallas Public Library, Texas Dallas History and Archives Division
     Arrest/Jail Log Books (female), Women's Holdover, 11/20/1953–5/31/1954

Dallas Police Archives
Dallas Police Department Reports, 1961
Fort Worth
Fort Worth Public Library, Genealogy, Local History and Archives
Samuel Garcia Papers
Houston
Houston Public Library, Houston History Research Center
Ben T. Reyes Papers
Constable Raul C. Martinez Papers
John J. Herrera Papers
Judge Woodrow Seals Papers
LULAC Council #60 Papers
Mayor Fred Hofheinz Papers
Mayor Louie Welch Papers
Mexican-American Small Collections
Moody Park Riot Papers
Small Collections 47
Liberty
Texas State Library and Archives Commission, Sam Houston
Regional Library and Research Center
Texas Governor Price Daniel Records
San Antonio
Municipal Archives and Records
City Council Meeting Minutes
Office of the Mayor, Lila Cockrell Records, 1970–81
San Antonio Public Library, Texana/Genealogy Collection
Police Department Vertical File
University of Texas, San Antonio, Special Collections
José Angel Gutiérrez Papers
Judge Albert A. Peña Papers
Mario Salas Papers

Legal Cases

ARIZONA
Garcia v. City of South Tucson, 131 Ariz. 315 (1981)
Garcia v. South Tucson, 135 Ariz. 604 (Ariz. Ct. App. Mar. 3, 1983)
State v. Miranda, 401 P.2d 721 (Ariz. 1965)
CALIFORNIA
Estate of Lopez v. Gelhaus, 871 F.3d 998 (9th Cir. 2017)
Katzev et al. v. County of Los Angeles (52 Cal. 2d 360), June 24, 1959
Nunez v. City of San Jose, 381 F.Supp.3d 1192 (N.D. Cal. 2019)
Peter Moreno v. David Shriver, No. CV 92-3444-WKD, May 4, 1993
NEW MEXICO
Chicano Police Officer's Ass'n v. Stover, 624 F.2d 127, No. 78-1591 (1980)
Cordova v. City of Albuquerque, 86 N.M. 697, 526 P.2d 1290 (1974)

Cordova v. Larsen, 2004-NMCA-087, 136 N.M. 87, 94 P.3d 830 (May 19, 2004)

Duran v. Apodaca, C.A. No. 77-721-C (D. N.M. 1977)

Duran v. King, C.A. No. 77-721-C (D.N.M. 1980)

State v. Canales, 78 N.M. 429, 432 P.2d 394 (1967)

State v. Couch, 193 P.2d 405 (N.M. 1946)

State v. Garcia, 83 N.M. 51, 487 P.2d 1356 (N.M. Ct. App. 1971).

United States v. City of Albuquerque, No. CIV 14-1025 JB\SMV (D.N.M. June 12, 2020).

TEXAS

Cain v. State, 549 S.W.2d 707 (1977)

City of Houston v. Vargas, Civil Action No. 01-04-01173-cv (Mar. 16, 2006)

Escobar et al. v. City of Houston et al., Civil Action No. 04-1945 (Sept. 29, 2007)

Ruiz v. Estelle, 503 F. Supp. 1265 (S.D. Tex. 1980)

UNITED STATES

Allee v. Medrano, 416 U.S. 802 (1974)

Canales v. Baker, 406 F.2d 685 (10th Cir. 1969).

Escobedo v. Illinois, 378 U.S. 478 (1964)

Graham v. Connor, 490 U.S. 386 (1989)

Hernandez v. Texas, 347 U.S. 475 (1954)

Lozano v. Smith, 718 F.2d 756 (5th Cir. 1983)

Martinez v. Winner, 771 F.2d 424 (10th Cir. 1985)

Medrano et al. v. Allee et al., Civil Action No. 67-B-36,
    US District Court, Southern District of Texas (June, 26, 1972)

Miranda v. Arizona, 384 U.S. 436 (1966)

Ruiz v. Collins, Civil Action No. H-78-987
    (U.S. District Court, Southern District, 1992)

Ruiz v. Estelle, 161 F.3d 814 (5th Cir. 1998)

Ruiz v. Johnson, Civil Action No. A. H-78-987, 154 F.Supp.2d. 975 (2001)

Ruiz v. Scott, Civil No. H-78-987 (U.S. District Court, Southern District, 1998)

Tennessee v. Garner, 471 U.S. 1 (1985)

Terry v. Ohio, 392 U.S. 1 (1968)

United States v. Denson, 588 F.2d 112 (5th Cir. 1979)

United States v. Denson, 603 F.2d 1143 (5th Cir. 1979)

United States v. Hayes, 589 F.2d 811 (5th Cir. 1979)

Newspapers, Magazines, TV Stations, and News Sites

ABC7 News

Abilene (TX) Reporter-News

Alamogordo (NM) Daily News

Albuquerque Journal

Albuquerque News

Albuquerque Tribune

Amarillo (TX) Globe

Arizona Daily Star (Tucson)

Arizona Daily Sun (Flagstaff)

Arizona Republic (Phoenix)

Arrow—CSU Pueblo (CO)

Associated Press

The Atlantic

Austin American

Austin American-Statesman

Austin Chronicle

Austin Statesman

The Baffler

Baltimore Sun
Boston Review
Boulder (CO) Weekly
Brownsville (TX) Herald
CalMatters
Carlsbad (NM) Current-Argus
CBS News Los Angeles
CCR Newsletter (Committee on
    Chicano Rights, CA)
Chicago Daily Tribune
Chicago Tribune
Chicano Communications Training
    Project (newsletter)
Clovis (NM) News-Journal
CNN
Corpus Christi Caller
Corpus Christi Caller-Times
Corpus Christi Times
Daily Sentinel (Grand Junction, CO)
Daily Texan (Austin; student newspaper)
Dallas Express
Dallas Morning News
Dallas News
Dallas Times Herald
De Kalb (IL) Daily Chronicle
Del Rio (TX) News-Herald
Deming (NM) Headlight
Denver Police Bulletin
Denver Post
Deseret News (Salt Lake City)
Desert Sun (Palm Springs, CA)
The Dispatch (Moline, IL)
East Valley Tribune (Phoenix)
El Diario de la Gente (Boulder, CO;
    student newspaper)
El Gallo (Denver)
El Grito del Norte (Española, NM)
El Grito Special Bulletin (Española, NM)
El Malcriado (CA)
El Mundo (Las Vegas)
El Obrero
El Paso Herald
El Paso Herald-Post
El Paso Times
El Pueblo

El Servidor (Seguin, TX)
El Sol (Houston)
El Sol de Texas (Dallas)
El Universal (Mexico City)
Forbes
Fort Collins Coloradan
Fort Worth Star-Telegram
Forumeer
Fox KTVU
Freedom Socialist
Fresno Bee
Frontline
FUCK
Gallup (NM) Independent
Gatesville (TX) Messenger and Star-Forum
G.I. Forum Bulletin
Goliad Advance-Guard (Beeville, TX)
Greeley (CO) Daily Tribune
The Guardian
Hanford (CA) Sentinel
Honolulu Civil Beat
Houston Career Digest
Houston Chronicle
Houston Informer
Houston Post
Houston Press
Houston Public Media
Huffpost
Iconoclast (Dallas)
Imperial Valley (CA) Press
The Independent
Jacobin
Justicia
Kansas City (MO) Times
KMID-TV (Odessa, TX)
KNXV-TV ABC15 Arizona
KOLD-TV (Tucson, AZ)
KSAT-TV (San Antonio, TX)
La Causa (Los Angeles)
La Cucaracha (Pueblo, CO)
La Fuerza (Austin, TX)
LAist
La Opinión (Los Angeles)
La Raza (Los Angeles)
Las Cruces (NM) Sun-News

Las Vegas Optic
La Voz de la Alianza
LA Weekly
Longview (TX) News-Journal
Look
Los Angeles Daily News
Los Angeles Herald Examiner
Los Angeles Times
LULAC News
Marshall (TX) News Messenger
Mesa Magazine
The Militant
Milwaukee Sentinel
The Monitor (McAllen, TX)
Mother Jones
The Nation
National City Star News (San Diego)
NBC Bay Area
NBC Chicago
NBC Los Angeles
New Mexico Review
New Times Weekly
News-Pilot (San Pedro, CA)
New York Daily News
New York Times
Odessa (TX) American
Out
Oxnard (CA) Press Courier
The Pantagraph (Bloomington, IN)
Papel Chicano (Houston)
Paris (TX) News
Pasadena (CA) Star-News
People's World Southwest
Peoria Times (Tempe, AZ)
Petaluma (CA) Argus-Courier
Phoenix Gazette
Phoenix New Times
Plainview (TX) Herald
Politico
Prison Legal News
recordnet.com
Revolution
Revolutionary Worker
Rocky Mountain News (Denver)
Rolling Stone
Roswell (NM) Daily Record

Sacramento Bee
Salt Lake City Tribune
San Angelo (TX) Standard Times
San Antonio Current
San Antonio Express
San Antonio Express-News
San Antonio Informer
San Antonio Light
San Antonio News
San Bernardino County (CA) Sun
San Diego Tribune
San Diego Union
San Francisco Examiner
San Jose (CA) Mercury News
Santa Fe New Mexican
Seattle Times
The Signal (Santa Clarita Valley, CA)
Silver City (NM) Daily Press
Sonoma County Gazette (Santa Rosa, CA)
Southern Illinoisan (Carbondale)
Southern School News
Spectrum News 1
Splinter
Spokesman-Review
State Press (Tempe, AZ; student newspaper)
St. Louis Post-Dispatch
Tejano News Magazine
Texas Catholic Herald (Dallas)
Texas Monthly
Texas Observer
Time
Times-Advocate (Escondido, CA)
Tucson Citizen
Tucson Daily Citizen
Tulare (CA) Advance-Register
TWT News
Tyler (TX) Courier-Times
Tyler (TX) Morning Telegraph
Upfront America
USA Today
Valley Evening Monitor (McAllen, TX)
Valley Morning Star (McAllen, TX)
Victoria (TX) Advocate
Visalia (CA) Times-Delta
VIVA (Denver; newsletter)
Vox

Washington Post   The Worker
The Westsider (Goodyear, AZ)   World Socialist Website
Westword (Denver)

Government Documents

CALIFORNIA

California Code. Penal Code - PEN § 186.22, January 1, 2019. https://codes.findlaw
    .com/ca/penal-code/pen-sect-186-22.html.
Division of Correctional Policy Research and Internal Oversight Office of Research.
    Offender Data Points for the 24-Month Period Ending in June 2018. California De-
    partment of Corrections and Rehabilitation, January 2019.
Governor's Commission on the Los Angeles Riots. *Violence in the City—An End or a
    Beginning? A Report by the Governor's Commission on the Los Angeles Riots.* State of
    California. December 2, 1965.
Lofstrom, Magnus, Justin Goss, Joseph Hayes, and Brandon Martin. *Racial Dispari-
    ties in California Arrests.* Fact sheet. Public Policy Institute of California, October
    2019. www.ppic.org/publication/racial-disparities-in-california-arrests.
Lofstrom, Magnus, Brandon Martin, Justin Goss, Joseph Hayes, and Steven Raphael.
    New Insights into California Arrets: Trends, Disparities, and County Differences.
    Report. Public Policy Institute of California, December 2018. www.ppic.org
    /publication/new-insights-into-california-arrests-trends-disparities-and-county
    -difference.
Los Angeles Board of Police Commissioners. *Report of the Rampart Independent
    Review Panel.* Executive summary, November 16, 2000. https://clearinghouse.net
    /doc/10835.
Los Angeles Police Department. "Consent Decree Overview." Los Angeles Police
    Foundation and LAPD (online), 2025. www.lapdonline.org/office-of-the-chief-of
    -police/constitutional-policing/consent-decree-overview.
San Diego County Grand Jury. *San Diego Community Review Board on Police Practices
    (CRB).* City of San Diego, 2018. www.sandiegocounty.gov/content/dam/sdc
    /grandjury/reports/2017-2018/CRBReport.pdf.
Santa Clara County District Attorney's Office. "DA Report: SJPD Officers Lawfully
    Shot and Killed Suicidal Man Who Pointed Gun at Police." Press release. August
    15, 2017. www.sccgov.org/sites/da/newsroom/newsreleases/Pages/NRA2017
    /A-NunezOIS-Porter.aspx (page discontinued).
Santa Clara County District Attorney's Office. *Report on the Fatal Shooting of Anthony
    Nunez on July 4, 2016.* August 15, 2017. https://files.santaclaracounty.gov/2024-05
    /report-on-the-fatal-shooting-of-anthony-nunez-on-july-4-2016.pdf?VersionId=
    73mv5yVmPu.QontGH4XR4xE9eJUEtJyP.

NEW MEXICO

New Mexico Sheriff and Police: A Monthly Review of Police Programs and Activities 31,
    no. 7 (July 20, 1936). Albuquerque: S. A. Mitchell.
New Mexico Supreme Court. Committee on Uniform Jury Instructions. *New Mexico
    Uniform Jury Instructions.* Charlottesville, VA: Michie, 1966.

Office of the Attorney General of the State of New Mexico. *Report of the Attorney General of the February 2 and 3, 1980 Riot at the Penitentiary of New Mexico.* Part 1, *The Penitentiary, the Riot, the Aftermath.* State of New Mexico, June 1980.

Office of the Attorney General of the State of New Mexico. *Report of the Attorney General of the February 2 and 3, 1980 Riot at the Penitentiary of New Mexico.* Part 2, *The Last Ten Years, Conditions Leading to the Riot, Conclusions and Recommendations, and Report of the Citizens Advisory Panel.* State of New Mexico, September 1980.

TEXAS

Dallas Police Department. *Goals for Dallas, Compared with Goals for Black Dallas and Mexican American Objectives.* DPD, November 1978.

Dallas Police Department. *Training Manual on Community Tensions.* DPD, ca. 1960.

Texas Advisory Committee to the United States Commission on Civil Rights. *Texas: The State of Civil Rights, Ten Years Later, 1968–1978.* Washington, DC: Government Printing Office, 1980.

Texas Attorney General's Office. *Summary of Civil Rights Investigations by the Texas Attorney General's Office of Incidents Resulting in Death, John L. Hill, Attorney General of Texas, 1975–1978.* Austin: Attorney General's Office, 1978.

UNITED STATES

Bureau of Justice Statistics. "Drugs and Crime Facts, Drug Law Violations, Enforcement." US Department of Justice, June 1, 2001. www.bjs.gov/content/dcf/enforce.cfm (page discontinued).

Bureau of Justice Statistics. "Drugs and Crime Facts, Drug Law Violations, Pretrial, Prosecution, and Adjudication." US Department of Justice, June 1, 2001.www.bjs.gov/content/dcf/ptrpa.cfm (page discontinued).

Bureau of the Census. "We, the American Hispanics." Department of Commerce, September 1993. www2.census.gov/library/publications/decennial/1990/we-the-americans/we-02r.pdf.

Clinton, William J. "Statement of Signing the Departments of Commerce, Justice, and State, the Judiciary, and Related Agencies Appropriations Act, 1994." In *Public Papers of the Presidents of the United States: William J. Clinton. Book 2, August 1 to December 31, 1993.* Washington, DC: Government Printing Office, 1994.

Commission on Civil Rights. *Mexican Americans and the Administration of Justice in the Southwest.* Report. Washington, DC: Government Printing Office, March 1970.

Commission on Civil Rights. *Stranger in One's Land.* Clearinghouse Publication no. 19. Washington, DC: Government Printing Office, May 1970.

Congress. House of Representatives. "Brutality by Law Enforcement Agencies: Case Summaries (by State)." In *U.S. Commission on Civil Rights Authorization Extension: Hearings before the Subcommittee on Civil and Constitutional Rights of the Committee on the Judiciary, House of Representatives, Ninety-Fifth Congress, Second Session on H.R. 10831, U.S. Commission on Civil Rights Authorization Extension, March 1, 6, 9, and April 14, 1978.* Washington, DC: Government Printing Office, 1978.

Congress. House of Representatives. *Prison Inmates in Medical Research: Hearings before the Subcommittee on Courts, Civil Liberties, and the Administration of Justice of the Committee on the Judiciary, House of Representatives, Ninety-Fourth Congress,*

First Session, on H.R. 3603 to Limits Use of Prison Inmates in Medical Research,
September 29 and October 1, 1975. Washington, DC: Government Printing Office,
1976.

Congress. Senate. "Civil Rights Improvements Act of 1977." *Hearings before the*
Subcommittee on the Constitution of the Committee on the Judiciary, United States
Senate, Ninety-Fifth Congress, Second Session, on S. 35, February 8 and 9 and May 2
and 3, 1978. Washington, DC: Government Printing Office, 1978.

Congress. Senate. *Hunger and Malnutrition in America: Hearings before the Subcom-*
mittee on Employment, Manpower, and Poverty of the Committee on Labor and Public
Welfare, United States Senate, Ninetieth Congress, First Session, July 11 and 12, 1967.
Washington, DC: Government Printing Office, 1967.

Congress. Senate. *Migrant and Seasonal Farmworker Powerlessness: Part 6-A, August*
1, 1969: Hearings Before the Subcommittee on Migratory Labor of the Committee
on Labor and Public Welfare, United States Senate, Ninety-first Congress, First and
Second Sessions on Farmworker Legal Problems. Washington, DC: Government
Printing Office, 1970–71.

Cooper, Alexia, and Erica L. Smith. *Homicide Trends in the United States, 1980–2008.*
US Department of Justice, Bureau of Justice Statistics, NCJ 236018, November
2011. www.bjs.gov/content/pub/pdf/htus8008.pdf.

Lentzner, Harold R., Randall P. Harvey, and Siretta L. Kelly. *Hispanic Victim: A Na-*
tional Crime Survey Report. US Department of Justice, Bureau of Justice Statistics,
NCJ 69261, August 1981. https://bjs.ojp.gov/library/publications/hispanic-victim
-national-crime-survey-report.

Margolis, Richard J. *Who Will Wear the Badge? A Study of Minority Recruitment Efforts*
in Protective Services. US Commission on Civil Rights, Clearinghouse Publication
no. 25. Washington, DC: Government Printing Office, 1971.

National Institute of Justice. *Five Things about Deterrence.* US Department of Justice,
NCJ 247350, May 2016. www.ojp.gov/pdffiles1/nij/247350.pdf.

National Institute of Justice. "Research on Body-Worn Cameras and Law Enforcement." US Department of Justice, January 7, 2022. https://nij.ojp.gov/topics
/articles/research-body-worn-cameras-and-law-enforcement.

Pate, Antony M., Mary Ann Wycoff, Wesley G. Skogan, and Lawrence W. Sherman.
"The Effects of Police Fear Reduction Strategies: A Summary of Findings from
Houston and Newark." Final Draft Report submitted to the National Institute of
Justice, February 10, 1986.

"Public Enemy Number One: A Pragmatic Approach to America's Drug Problem."
Richard Nixon Foundation, June 29, 2016. www.nixonfoundation.org/2016/06
/26404.

Snyder, Howard N. "Arrest in the United States, 1990–2010." Bureau of Justice Statistics, October 2012. www.bjs.gov/content/pub/pdf/aus9010.pdf.

US Attorney's Office. District of New Mexico. *Investigation into Albuquerque Police*
Department. US Department of Justice, December 16, 2022. www.justice.gov
/usao-nm/apd.

Walker, S. *Critical History of Police Reform.* US Department of Justice report, NCJ
42802, 1977. www.ojp.gov/ncjrs/virtual-library/abstracts/critical-history-police
-reform.

Data from Policy Groups and Advocacy Organizations

Arizona Department of Public Safety. *Crime in Arizona, 2015*. Arizona Department of Public Safety, Access Integrity Unit, 2016. www.azdps.gov/sites/default/files/2023 -09/Crime_in_Arizona_2015.pdf.

"Arizona Profile." Prison Policy Initiative. Accessed May 21, 2023, www.prisonpolicy.org /profiles/AZ.html.

Barrera, James. "The Political Repression of a Chicano Movement Activist: The Plight of Francisco E. 'Kiko' Martínez." In *Chican@: Critical Perspectives and Praxis at the Turn of the 21st Century* (selected papers from the 2002–4, 29th, 30th, and 31st Annual Conferences of the National Association of Chicana and Chicano Studies).

"California Profile." Prison Policy Initiative. Accessed May 21, 2023. www.prisonpolicy .org/profiles/CA.html.

"The Color of Justice: Racial and Ethnic Disparity in State Prisons." The Sentencing Project, October 13, 2021. www.sentencingproject.org/publications/color-of-justice -racial-and-ethnic-disparity-in-state-prisons/#IV.%20Drivers%20of%20Disparity.

Currie, Haver C. "Papers concerned with Mexican-Americans in Austin and Travis County." Vol. 1. Regional Research Associates, 1976.

"The Drug War, Mass Incarceration and Race (English/Spanish)." Drug Policy Alliance, January 25, 2018. www.drugpolicy.org/resource/drug-war-mass-incarceration-and -race-englishspanish (page discontinued).

Eisen, Lauren-Brooke, and Inimai M. Chettiar. "The Complex History of the Controversial 1994 Crime Bill." Brennan Center for Justice, April 14, 2016. www.brennancenter .org/our-work/analysis-opinion/complex-history-controversial-1994-crime-bill.

Friedman, Matthew, Ames C. Grawert, and James Cullen. "Crime Trends: 1990–2016." Brennan Center for Justice, 2017. www.brennancenter.org/sites/default/files /publications/Crime%20Trends%201990-2016.pdf.

Gross, Zenith, and Alan Reitman. *Police Power and Citizens' Rights: The Case for an Independent Police Review Board*. New York: American Civil Liberties Union, 1966.

Hartney, Christopher, and Linh Vuong. *Created Equal: Racial and Ethnic Disparities in the US Criminal Justice System*. National Council on Crime and Delinquency, March 2009. www.racialviolenceus.org/Articles/created-equal.pdf.

Lofstrom, Magnus, Brandon Martin, Justin Goss, Joseph Hayes, and Steven Raphael. *New Insights into California Arrests: Trends, Disparities, and County Differences*. Public Policy Institute of California Report, 2018.

Morales, Armando. "Police Deadly Force: Government-Sanctioned Execution of Hispanics." In "Crimen y Justicia: Crime and Justice for Hispanics Symposium." National Council of La Raza Symposium, Racine, WI, June 28–30, 1979.

"New Mexico Profile." Prison Policy Initiative. Accessed May 21, 2023. www.prisonpolicy .org/profiles/NM.html.

"Race and Imprisonment in Texas: The Disparate Incarceration of Latinos and African Americans in the Lone Star State." Justice Policy Institute, 2005. www.justicepolicy .org/images/upload/05-02_rep_txraceimprisonment_ac-rd.pdf.

"Symposium Goal and Objective." In "Crimen y Justicia: Crime and Justice for Hispanics Symposium." National Council of La Raza Symposium, Racine, WI, June 28–30, 1979.

"Texas Profile." Prison Policy Initiative. Accessed May 21, 2023. www.prisonpolicy.org /profiles/TX.html.

Oral Histories

Aguilar, Fred. "The Luis Alfonso Torres Case." Interview by Civil Rights in Black and Brown Oral History Project. Baytown, TX, July 12, 2016. https://crbb.tcu.edu/clips /2492/the-luis-alfonso-torres-case.

Benavides, Eva. "Forming the United Concerned Citizens Committee." Interview by Civil Rights in Black and Brown Oral History Project. Baytown, TX, July 20, 2016. https://crbb.tcu.edu/clips/2721/localizing-the-community.

Crespo, Manuel. Interview by Houston Public Library staff. January 8, 1980. Oral History Collection, Houston History Research Center, Houston Public Library, Texas.

Crespo, Manuel. Interview by Thomas Kreneck. August 21, 1980. Oral History Collection, Houston History Research Center, Houston Public Library, TX.

Flores, Lidia. Interview by Selina Kristal Ramos, March 23, 2018. Alfonso Loredo Flores Collection, Special Collections and University Archives, University of Texas Rio Grande Valley, Edinburg. https://scholarworks.utrgv.edu/alfonsoloredoflores/1.

Gutiérrez, José Angel. Interview by author. October 30, 2009.

Martinez, Hilda. "Outcome of the Luis Alfonso Torres Case." Interview by Civil Rights in Black and Brown Oral History Project. Baytown, TX, July 15, 2016. https://crbb.tcu .edu/clips/5714/outcome-of-the-luis-alfonso-torres-case.

Martinez, Raul C. Interview by Thomas Kreneck. April 13, 1989. Oral History Collection, Houston History Research Center, Houston Public Library, TX.

Medrano, Francisco "Pancho." Interview by George N. Green and Carr Winn. 1971. Special Collections, University of Texas, Arlington.

Montes, Carlos. "The Brown Beret: Young Chicano Revolutionaries." Interview by *Fight Back!* staff. August 2, 2009. https://fightbacknews.org/articles/brownberetsEW.

Montes, Carlos. Interview by David P. Cline. Alhambra, California, June 27, 2016. Civil Rights History Project Collection, Archive of Folk and Culture, American Folklife Center, Library of Congress, Washington, DC. www.loc.gov/item/2016655430.

Salas, Mario. Interview by author, November 20, 2009.

Truan, Carlos. Interview by José Angel Gutiérrez. 1998. Center for Mexican American Studies, no. 84, University of Texas, Arlington.

SECONDARY SOURCES

Achor, Shirley. *Mexican Americans in a Dallas Barrio*. Tucson: University of Arizona Press, 1978.

Agee, Christopher Lowen. *The Streets of San Francisco: Policing and the Creation of a Cosmopolitan Liberal Politics, 1950–1972*. Chicago: University of Chicago Press, 2014.

Alexander, Michelle. *The New Jim Crow: Mass Incarceration in the Age of Colorblindness*. New York: New Press, 2020.

Alvarez, Luis. *The Power of the Zoot: Youth Culture and Resistance during World War II*. Los Angeles: University of California Press, 2008.

Appier, Janis. *Policing Women: The Sexual Politics of Law Enforcement and the LAPD.* Philadelphia: Temple University Press, 1998.

Aynes, Richard L. "Behavior Modification: Winners in the Game of Life." *Cleveland State Law Review* 24, no. 3 (1975): 422–62.

Bailey, Richard. "The Starr County Strike." *Red River Valley Historical Review* 3, no. 1 (1979): 42–61.

Balko, Radley. *Rise of the Warrior Cop: The Militarization of America's Police Forces.* New York: PublicAffairs, 2021.

Balto, Simon. *Occupied Territory: Policing Black Chicago from Red Summer to Black Power.* Chapel Hill: University of North Carolina Press, 2019.

Banks, R. Richard. "Beyond Profiling: Race, Policing, and the Drug War." *Stanford Law Review* 56, no. 3 (2003): 571–603.

Barajas, Frank P. *Curious Unions: Mexican American Workers and Resistance in Oxnard, California, 1898–1961.* Lincoln: University of Nebraska Press, 2012.

Behnken, Brian D. *Borders of Violence and Justice: Mexicans, Mexican Americans, and Law Enforcement in the Southwest, 1835–1935.* Chapel Hill: University of North Carolina Press, 2022.

Behnken, Brian D. "The 'Dallas Way': Protest, Response, and the Civil Rights Experience in Big D and Beyond." *Southwestern Historical Quarterly* 111, no. 1 (2007): ix–29.

Behnken, Brian D. *Fighting Their Own Battles: Mexican Americans, African Americans, and the Struggle for Civil Rights Movement in Texas.* Chapel Hill: University of North Carolina Press, 2011.

Behnken, Brian D. "The Next Struggle: African American and Latino/a Collaborative Activism in the Post–Civil Rights Era." In *Civil Rights and Beyond: African American and Latino/a Activism in the Twentieth-Century United States,* edited by Brian D. Behnken, 195–216. Athens: University of Georgia Press, 2016.

Behnken, Brian D. "'We Want Justice!': Police Murder, Mexican American Community Response, and the Chicano Movement." In *The Hidden 1970s: Histories of Radicalism,* edited by Dan Berger, 195–213. Piscataway, NJ: Rutgers University Press, 2010.

Behnken, Monic P., David E. Arredondo, and Wendy L. Packman. "Reduction in Recidivism in a Juvenile Mental Health Court: A Pre- and Post-Treatment Outcome Study." *Juvenile and Family Court Journal* 60, no. 3 (2009): 23–44.

Bender, Steven. *Greasers and Gringos: Latinos, Law, and the American Imagination.* New York: New York University Press, 2003.

Berger, Dan. *The Struggle Within: Prisons, Political Prisoners, and Mass Movements in the United States.* Oakland, CA: PM Press, 2014.

Bertram, Eva, Morris Blachman, Kenneth Sharpe, and Peter Andreas. *Drug War Politics: The Price of Denial.* Los Angeles: University of California Press, 1996.

Blackwell, Maylei. *¡Chicana Power! Contested Histories of Feminism in the Chicano Movement.* Austin: University of Texas Press, 2011.

Blue, Ethan. *The Deportation Express: A History of America through Forced Removal.* Berkeley: University of California Press, 2021.

Braddy, Haldeen. "The Pachucos and Their Argot." *Southern Folklore Quarterly* 24, no. 4 (1960): 255–71.

Brienen, Martin W., and Jonathan D. Rosen. *New Approaches to Drug Policies: A Time for Change.* London: Palgrave Macmillan, 2015.

Brilliant, Mark. *The Color of America Has Changed: How Racial Diversity Shaped Civil Rights Reform in California, 1941–1978.* New York: Oxford University Press.

Brower, Eric A. "Balling with the Boys in Blue: How Police Athletic Leagues Affect Attitudes toward Police." Working paper, May 2, 2017. www.siena.edu/files/resources /balling-with-the-boys-in-blue-how-police-athletic-.pdf.

Burgan, Michael. *Miranda v. Arizona: The Rights of the Accused.* Minneapolis, MN: Compass Point Books, 2007.

Bustillos, Crystal Jewel. "Targeting Minorities: An Inductive Exploration of the FBI's Impact on Social Movements (1960s–1970s)." Master's thesis, University of Texas, El Paso, 2012.

Bynum, Katherine. "Civil Rights in the 'City of Hate': Black and Brown Organizing against Police Brutality in Dallas." In *Civil Rights in Black and Brown: Oral Histories of the Liberation Struggles in Texas,* edited by Max Krochmal and J. Todd Moye, 221–44. Austin: University of Texas Press, 2021.

Campney, Brent M. S. "'A Bunch of Tough Hombres': Police Brutality, Municipal Politics, and Racism in South Texas." *Journal of the Southwest* 60, no. 4 (2018): 787–825.

Campney, Brent M. S. "The Most Turbulent and Most Traumatic Years in Recent Mexican-American History: Police Violence and the Civil Rights Struggle in 1970s Texas." *Southwestern Historical Quarterly* 122, no. 1 (2018): 33–57.

Campney, Brent M. S. "Police Brutality and Mexican American Families in Texas, 1945–1980." *Annals of the American Academy* 694 (March 2021): 108–21.

Cano, Luis Rey. "Pachuco Gangs in Houston—a Postwar Phenomenon." *Agenda: A Journal of Hispanic Issues* 9, no. 1 (1979): 17–20.

Carbado Devon W., and L. Song Richardson. "The Black Police: Policing Our Own." *Harvard Law Review* 131, no. 7 (2018): 1979–2025.

Chase, Robert T. "Cell Taught, Self Taught: The Chicano Movement behind Bars— Urban Chicanos, Rural Prisons, and the Prisoners' Rights Movement." *Journal of Urban History* 41, no. 5 (2015): 836–61.

Chase, Robert T. "We Are Not Slaves: Rethinking the Rise of Carceral States through the Lens of the Prisoners' Rights Movement." *Journal of American History* 102, no. 1 (2015): 73–86.

Chase, Robert T. *We Are Not Slaves: State Violence, Coerced Labor, and Prisoners' Rights in Postwar America.* Chapel Hill: University of North Carolina Press, 2019.

Chavez, Leo R. *Latino Threat: Constructing Immigrants, Citizens, and the Nation.* Stanford, CA: Stanford University Press, 2008.

Clark, Charles S. "Prison Overcrowding: Will Building More Prisons Cut the Crime Rate?" *CQ Researcher* 4, no. 5 (1994): 97–120.

Coyne, Christopher J., and Abigail R. Hall. "Four Decades and Counting: The Continued Failure of the War on Drugs." *Policy Analysis* (CATO Institute) no. 811, April 12, 2017. www.cato.org/policy-analysis/four-decades-counting-continued-failure-war -drugs.

Cunneen, Chris. *Defund the Police: An International Insurrection.* Bristol, UK: Policy Press, 2023.

Dagenais, Elan, Raphael Ginsburg, Sharad Goel, Joseph Nudell, and Robert Weisberg. "Sentencing Enhancements and Incarceration: San Francisco, 2005–2017." *Stanford Computational Policy Lab,* October 17, 2019, 1–14.

DiPietro, Samuel. "STEPping into the 'Wrong' Neighborhood: A Critique of the *People v. Albillar*'s Expansion of California Penal Code Section 186.22(a) and a Call to Reexamine the Treatment of Gang Affiliation." *Journal of Criminal Law and Criminology* 110, no. 3 (2020): 623–54.

DiSalvo, Daniel. "The Trouble with Police Unions." *National Affairs*, no. 54 (Winter 2023). www.nationalaffairs.com/publications/detail/the-trouble-with-police-unions.

Doty, Roxanne Lynn. *The Law into Their Own Hands: Immigration and the Politics of Exceptionalism.* Tucson: University of Arizona Press, 2009.

Dowling, Donald C. "*Escobedo* and Beyond: The Need for a Fourteenth Amendment Code of Criminal Procedure." *Journal of Criminal Law and Criminology* 56, no. 2 (1965): 143–57.

Dulaney, W. Marvin. *Black Police in America.* Bloomington: Indiana University Press, 1996.

Dulaney, W. Marvin. "Whatever Happened to the Civil Rights Movement in Dallas, Texas?" In *Essays on the American Civil Rights Movement*, edited by Marvin Dulaney and Kathleen Underwood, 66–95. College Station: Texas A&M University Press, 1993.

Echeverría, Darius V. *Aztlán Arizona: Mexican American Educational Empowerment, 1968–1978.* Tucson: University of Arizona Press, 2014.

Echeverría, Darius. "Palabras, Promises, and Principles: Arizona Police Prejudice, Profiling, Patrolling, and Preserving the Peace in the 1970s." *Border-Lines Journal* 3 (Spring 2009): 38–63.

Elizondo, Sergio D. *Muerte en una estrella / Shooting Star.* Houston: Arte Publico, 2013.

Elmore, Maggie. "In the Shadow of the Law: The Hanigan Case and the Genesis of the Immigrant Rights Movement." *Journal of American History* 111, no. 2 (2024): 309–31.

Escobar, Edward J. "Bloody Christmas and the Irony of Police Professionalism: The Los Angeles Police Department, Mexican Americans, and Police Reform in the 1950s." *Pacific Historical Review* 72, no. 2 (2003): 171–99.

Escobar, Edward J. *Race, Police, and the Making of a Political Identity: Mexican Americans and the Los Angeles Police Department, 1900–1945.* Berkeley: University of California Press, 1999.

Escobar, Edward J. "The Unintended Consequences of the Carceral State: Chicana/o Political Mobilization in Post–World War II America." *Journal of American History* 102, no. 1 (June 2015): 174–84.

Escobedo, Elizabeth R. *From Coveralls to Zoot Suits: The Lives of Mexican American Women on the World War II Home Front.* Chapel Hill: University of North Carolina Press, 2015.

Escobedo, Elizabeth R. "The Pachuca Panic: Sexual and Cultural Battlegrounds in World War II Los Angeles." *Western Historical Quarterly* 38, no. 2 (2007): 133–56.

Esparza, Jesús Jesse. "Chale con la Guerra: The Chicano Antiwar Movement in Houston, 1965–1975." In *Rewriting the Chicano Movement: New Histories of Mexican American Activism in the Civil Rights Era*, edited by Mario T. García and Ellen McCracken, 116–47. Tucson: University of Arizona Press, 2021.

Farber, David. "The Advent of the War on Drugs." In *The War on Drugs: A History*, edited by David Farber, 17–36. New York: NYU Press, 2021.

Felker-Kantor, Max. "The Coalition against Police Abuse: CAPA's Resistance Struggle in 1970s Los Angeles." *Journal of Civil and Human Rights* 2, no. 1 (2016): 52–88.

Felker-Kantor, Max. *DARE to Say No: Policing and the War on Drugs in Schools*. Chapel Hill: University of North Carolina Press, 2024.

Felker-Kantor, Max. *Policing Los Angeles: Race, Resistance, and the Rise of the LAPD*. Chapel Hill: University of North Carolina Press, 2018.

Flavin, Jeanne. "Police and HIV/AIDSs: The Risk, the Reality, the Response." *American Journal of Criminal Justice* 23, no. 1 (1998): 33–58.

Floyd, Jami. "The Administration of Psychotropic Drugs to Prisoners: State of the Law and Beyond." *California Law Review* 78, no. 5 (1990): 1243–85.

Forman, James, Jr. *Locking Up Our Own: Crime and Punishment in Black America*. New York: Farrar, Straus and Giroux, 2017.

Fortner, Michael Javen. *Black Silent Majority: The Rockefeller Drug Laws and the Politics of Punishment*. Cambridge, MA: Harvard University Press, 2015.

Frase, Richard S., and Julian V. Roberts, *Paying for the Past: The Case against Prior Record Sentence Enhancements*. New York: Oxford University Press, 2019.

Gallardo, Roberto. "On the Thin Blue Line: Examining the Mexican American Officer Experience in the Los Angeles Police Department." PhD diss., University of California, Riverside, 2018.

Gamino, Eric. "Racialized Policing on the South Texas–Mexico Border: Mexican American Police Officers' Racialization of Latin-Origin Unauthorized Immigrants." PhD diss., Texas A&M University, 2016.

Garcia, Ignacio M. *White but Not Equal: Mexican Americans, Jury Discrimination, and the Supreme Court*. Tucson: University of Arizona Press, 2008.

García, Juan R. *Operation Wetback: The Mass Deportation of Mexican Undocumented Workers in 1954*. Santa Barbara, CA: Praeger, 1980.

Garcia, Maria Cristina, and Maddalena Marinari, eds. *Whose America? U.S. Immigration Policy since 1980*. Urbana: University of Illinois Press, 2023.

García, Mario T. *The Chicano Generation: Testimonios of the Movement*. Oakland: University of California Press, 2015.

García, Mario T. *Mexican Americans: Leadership, Ideology, and Identity, 1930–1960*. New Haven, CT: Yale University Press, 1989.

García, Mario T., and Sal Castro. *Blowout! Sal Castro and the Chicano Struggle for Educational Justice*. Chapel Hill: University of North Carolina Press, 2011.

Garcia, Matt. *A World of Its Own: Race, Labor, and Citrus in the Making of Greater Los Angeles, 1900–1970*. Chapel Hill: University of North Carolina Press, 2002.

Geerken, Michael, and Walter R. Gove. "Deterrence, Overload, and Incapacitation: An Empirical Evaluation." *Social Forces* 56, no. 2 (1977): 424–47.

Gilmore, Ruth Wilson. *Abolition Geography: Essays towards Liberation*. New York: Verso, 2022.

Gómez-Quiñones, Juan, and Irene Vásquez. *Making Aztlán: Ideology and Culture of the Chicana and Chicano Movement, 1966–1977*. Albuquerque: University of New Mexico Press, 2014.

Goodman, Adam. *The Deportation Machine: America's Long History of Expelling Immigrants*. Princeton, NJ: Princeton University Press, 2020.

Griffith, Beatrice. "Who Are the *Pachucos*?" *Pacific Spectator* 1, no. 3 (1947): 352–60.

Guajardo, Antonio G., Jr. *The Milwaukee Police and Latino Community Relations, 1964–2000: The Role of Latino Officers*. Lanham, MD: Lexington Books, 2020.

Guariglia, Matthew. *Police and the Empire City: Race and the Origins of Modern Policing in New York*. Durham, NC: Duke University Press, 2023.

Gutiérrez, José Angel. *FBI Surveillance of Mexicans and Chicanos, 1920–1980*. Lanham, MD: Lexington Books, 2020.

Gutiérrez, José Angel. *Tracking King Tiger: Reies López Tijerina and the FBI*. East Lansing: Michigan State University Press, 2019.

Guzmán Hays, Veronica. "Brown Bodies and Police Killings: The Case of José Campos Torres, Jr. and Anti-Mexican Violence in Houston in the 1970s." Master's thesis, Texas A&M University, Corpus Christi, 2020.

Haight, Christopher P. "From Hate Crimes to Activism: Race, Sexuality, and Gender in the Texas Anti-Violence Movement." PhD diss., University of Houston, 2016.

Haight, Christopher P. "The Silence Is Killing Us: Hate Crimes, Criminal Justice, and the Gay Rights Movement in Texas, 1990–1995." *Southwestern Historical Quarterly* 120, no. 1 (2016): 20–40.

Harcourt, Bernard E. *Illusion of Order: The False Promise of Broken Windows Policing*. Cambridge, MA: Harvard University Press, 2001.

Harmon, Rachel A. "Why Arrest?" *Michigan Law Review* 115, no. 3 (2016): 307–64.

Hernández, Kelly Lytle. *Migra! A History of the U.S. Border Patrol*. Los Angeles: University of California Press, 2010.

Hernández, Osmín Rodrígo. "¡Justicia for Santos! Mexican American Civil Rights and the Santos Rodríguez Affair in Dallas, Texas, 1969–1978." Master's thesis, Texas Christian University, 2016.

Hinojosa, Felipe. *Apostles of Change: Latino Radical Politics, Church Occupations, and the Fight to Save the Barrio*. Austin: University of Texas Press, 2022.

Hinton, Elizabeth. *America on Fire: The Untold History of Police Violence and Black Rebellion since the 1960s*. New York: Liveright, 2022.

Hinton, Elizabeth. *From the War on Poverty to the War on Crime: The Making of Mass Incarceration in America*. Cambridge, MA: Harvard University Press, 2016.

Hoppe, Trevor. *Punishing Disease: HIV and the Criminalization of Sickness*. Oakland: University of California Press, 2018.

Hornblum, Allen M. *Acres of Skin: Human Experiments at Holmesburg Prison*. New York: Routledge, 1998.

Jett, Brandon T. *Race, Crime, and Policing in the Jim Crow South: African Americans and Law Enforcement in Birmingham, Memphis, and New Orleans, 1920–1945*. Baton Rouge: Louisiana State University Press, 2021.

Jiménez, Maria. "Police Policies and Practices: The Case of the Border Patrol." *Immigration Newsletter* 17, no. 4 (1988): 5–6.

Johnson, Jenell. *American Lobotomy: A Rhetorical History*. Ann Arbor: University of Michigan Press, 2014.

Justice, William Wayne. "The Origins of *Ruiz v. Estelle*." *Stanford Law Review* 43, no. 1 (1990): 1–12.

Kaba, Mariame. *We Do This 'til We Free Us: Abolitionist Organizing and Transforming Justice*. Chicago: Haymarket Books, 2021.

Kaba, Mariame, and Andrea Ritchie. *No More Police: A Case for Abolition*. New York: New Press, 2022.

Kane, Stephanie, and Theresa Mason. "AIDS and Criminal Justice." *Annual Review of Anthropology* 30 (2001): 457–79.

Kang, S. Deborah. *The INS on the Line: Making Immigration Law on the US-Mexico Border, 1917–1954*. New York: Oxford University Press, 2017.

Kaye, Kerwin. *Enforcing Freedom: Drug Courts, Therapeutic Communities, and the Intimacies of the State*. New York: Columbia University Press, 2020.

King, Shannon. *The Politics of Safety: The Black Struggle for Police Accountability in La Guardia's New York*. Chapel Hill: University of North Carolina Press, 2024.

Kohler-Hausmann, Issa. *Misdemeanorland: Criminal Courts and Social Control in an Age of Broken Windows Policing*. Princeton, NJ: Princeton University Press, 2019.

Kohler-Hausmann, Julilly. *Getting Tough: Welfare and Imprisonment in 1970s America*. Princeton, NJ: Princeton University Press, 2017.

Krochmal, Max, and J. Todd Moye, eds. *Civil Rights in Black and Brown: Oral Histories of the Liberation Struggles in Texas*. Austin: University of Texas Press, 2021.

LaChance, Daniel. *Executing Freedom: The Cultural Life of Capital Punishment in the United States*. Chicago: University of Chicago Press, 2016.

Lahav, Gallya, and Virginie Guiraudon. "Comparative Perspectives on Border Control: Away from the Border and Outside the State." In *The Wall around the West: State Borders and Immigration Controls in North America and Europe*, edited by Peter Andreas and Timothy Snyder, 55–80. Lanham, MD: Rowman and Littlefield, 2000.

LeBrón, Marisol. *Policing Life and Death: Race, Violence, and Resistance in Puerto Rico*. Los Angeles: University of California Press, 2019.

Limberg, Jerry Kathleen. "The Murder of Donna Gentile: San Diego Policing and Prostitution. 1980–1993." Master's thesis, California State University, San Marcos, 2012.

Madrid-Barela, Arturo. "In Search of the Authentic Pachuco: An Interpretive Essay." *Aztlán* 4, no. 1 (1973): 31–60.

Malavé, Idelisse, and Esti Giordani. *Latino Stats: American Hispanics by the Numbers*. New York: New Press, 2015.

Mallea, Paula. *The War on Drugs: A Failed Experiment*. Toronto, ON: Dundurn, 2014.

Mantler, Gordon K. *Power to the Poor: Black-Brown Coalition and the Fight for Economic Justice, 1960–1974*. Chapel Hill: University of North Carolina Press, 2013.

Marin, Christine. "They Sought Work and Found Hell: The Hanigan Case of Arizona." *Perspectives in Mexican American Studies* 6 (1997): 96–122.

Marquez, John D. *Black-Brown Solidarity: Racial Politics in the New Gulf South*. Austin: University of Texas Press, 2013.

Martínez, Elizabeth. "The 'Kiko' Martinez Case: A Sign of Our Times." *Crime and Social Justice* 17 (Summer 1982): 92–95.

Martinez, Monica Muñoz. *The Injustice Never Leaves You: Anti-Mexican Violence in Texas*. Cambridge, MA: Harvard University Press, 2020.

Mazón, Mauricio. *The Zoot Suit Riots*. Austin: University of Texas Press, 1984.

McCollom, James P. *The Last Sheriff: A True Tale of Violence and the Vote*. Berkeley, CA: Counterpoint, 2017.

McLean, Kyle, Scott E. Wolfe, Jeff Rojek, Geoffrey P. Alpert, and Michael R. Smith. "Police Officers as Warriors or Guardians: Empirical Reality or Intriguing Rhetoric?" *Justice Quarterly* 37, no. 6 (2020): 1096–118.

McWilliams, Carey. *North from Mexico: The Spanish-Speaking People of the United States.* Santa Barbara, CA: Praeger, 1948.

Mitchell, Ojmarrh, David B. Wilson, Amy Eggers, and Doris L. MacKenzie. "Assessing the Effectiveness of Drug Courts on Recidivism: A Meta-Analytic Review of Traditional and Non-Traditional Drug Courts." *Journal of Criminal Justice* 40, no. 1 (2012): 60–71.

Moffitt, Terrie. "Adolescence-Limited and Life-Course-Persistent Antisocial Behavior: A Developmental Taxonomy." *Psychological Review* 100, no. 4 (1993): 674–701.

Mogul, Joey L., Andrea J. Ritchie, and Kay Whitlock. *Queer (In)Justice: The Criminalization of LGBT People in the United States.* New York: Beacon, 2011.

Mohammad, Fida, and Gregory Fulkerson. "The 'War on Drugs': A Failed Paradigm." In *New Approaches to Drug Policies: A Time for Change,* edited by Martin W. Brienen and Jonathan D. Rosen, 229–50. London: Palgrave Macmillan, 2015.

Montejano, David. *Sancho's Journal: Exploring the Political Edge with the Brown Berets.* Austin: University of Texas Press, 2012.

Moore, Nina M. *The Political Roots of Racial Tracking in American Criminal Justice.* New York: Cambridge University Press, 2015.

Morris, Roger. *The Devil's Butcher Shop: The New Mexico Prison Uprising.* Albuquerque: University of New Mexico Press, 1983.

Navarro, Armando. *The Cristal Experiment: A Chicano Struggle for Community Control.* Madison: University of Wisconsin Press, 1998.

Navarro, Armando. *La Raza Unida Party: A Chicano Challenge to the U.S. Two-Party Dictatorship.* Philadelphia: Temple University Press, 2000.

Nieto, Adriana. "Running the Gauntlet: Francisco 'Kiko' Martínez and the Colorado Martyrs." In *Enduring Legacies: Ethnic Histories and Cultures of Colorado,* edited by Arturo J. Aldama, 365–78. Boulder: University Press of Colorado, 2011.

O'Brien, Daniel T., Chelsea Farrell, and Brandon C. Welsh. "Looking through Broken Windows: The Impact of Neighborhood Disorder on Aggression and Fear of Crime Is an Artifact of Research Design." *Annual Review of Criminology* 2 (2019): 53–71.

O'Hear, Michael. "Third-Class Citizenship: The Escalating Legal Consequences of Committing a 'Violent' Crime." *Journal of Criminal Law and Criminology* 109, no. 2 (2019): 165–236.

Olden, Danielle R. *Racial Uncertainties: Mexican Americans, School Desegregation, and the Making of Race in Post–Civil Rights America.* Oakland: University of California Press, 2022.

Olivas, Michael A. "*Hernandez v. Texas*: A Litigation History." In *"Colored Men" and "Hombres Aquí": Hernández v. Texas and the Emergence of Mexican-American Lawyering,* edited by Michale A. Olivas, 221–22. Houston: Arte Publico Press, 2020.

Oropeza, Lorena. *The King of Adobe: Reies López Tijerina, Lost Prophet of the Chicano Movement.* Chapel Hill: University of North Carolina Press, 2019.

Oropeza, Lorena. *¡Raza Sí! ¡Guerra No! Chicano Protest and Patriotism during the Viet Nam War Era.* Los Angeles: University of California Press, 2005.

Orozco, Cynthia. *No Mexicans, Women, or Dogs Allowed: The Rise of the Mexican American Civil Rights Movement.* Austin: University of Texas Press, 2009.

Pagán, Eduardo Obregón. *Murder at the Sleepy Lagoon: Zoot Suits, Race, and Riot in Wartime L.A.* Chapel Hill: University of North Carolina Press, 2003.

Parenti, Christian. "Guarding Their Silence: Corcoran Guards Acquitted of Rape." In *Prison Nation: The Warehousing of America's Poor*, edited by Tara Herivel and Paul Wright, 252–57. New York: Routledge, 2003.

Payne, Darwin. *Big D: Triumphs and Troubles of an American Supercity in the 20th Century*. Dallas: Three Forks, 2000.

Perino, Justina Cintron. *Citizen Oversight of Law Enforcement*. Chicago: American Bar Association, 2006.

Perkinson, Robert. *Texas Tough: The Rise of America's Prison Empire*. New York: Metropolitan Books, 2010.

Peyton, Kyle, Chagai M. Weiss, and Paige E. Vaugh. "Beliefs about Minority Representation in Policing and Support for Diversification." *Proceedings of the National Academy of Sciences* 119, no. 52 (2022): e2213986119.

Phelps, Michelle S. *The Minneapolis Reckoning: Race, Violence, and the Politics of Policing in America*. Princeton, NJ: Princeton University Press, 2024.

Phelps, Wesley G. *Before Lawrence v. Texas: The Making of a Queer Social Movement*. Austin: University of Texas Press, 2023.

Phelps, Wesley G. "The Politics of Queer Disidentification and the Limits of Neoliberalism in the Struggle for Gay and Lesbian Equality in Houston." *Journal of Southern History* 84, no. 2 (2018): 311–48.

Phillips, Michael. *White Metropolis: Race, Ethnicity, and Religion in Dallas, 1841–2001*. Austin: University of Texas Press, 2006.

Pihos, Peter C. "The Local War on Drugs." In *The War on Drugs: A History*, edited by David Farber, 131–58. New York: NYU Press, 2021.

Prenzler, Tim, and Garth den Heyer, eds. *Civilian Oversight of Police: Advancing Accountability in Law Enforcement*. New York: CRC, 2016.

Provine, Doris Marie. *Unequal under Law: Race in the War on Drugs*. Chicago: University of Chicago Press, 2008.

Pulido, Laura. *Black, Brown, Yellow, and Left: Radical Activism in Los Angeles*. Berkeley: University of California Press, 2006.

Raymond, Virginia Marie. "Mexican Americans Write toward Justice in Texas, 1973–1982." PhD diss., University of Texas, Austin, 2007.

Reiner, Robert. *The Politics of the Police*. New York: Oxford University Press, 2010.

Rivas-Rodríguez, Maggie. *Texas Mexican Americans and Postwar Civil Rights*. Austin: University of Texas Press, 2015.

Rivera, George, Jr. "Nosotros Venceremos: Chicano Consciousness and Change Strategies." *Journal of Applied Behavioral Science* 8, no. 7 (1972): 56–71.

Robles, David. "Chicano Revolt and Political Response: Grassroots Change in the South Texas Town of Pharr after the 1971 Riot." PhD diss., University of Texas, El Paso, 2018.

Robles, David. "'It Was Us against Us': The Pharr Police Riot of 1971 and the People's Uprising against *El Jefe Político*." In *Civil Rights in Black and Brown: Oral Histories of the Liberation Struggles in Texas*, edited by Max Krochmal and J. Todd Moye, 131–50. Austin: University of Texas Press, 2021.

Rodriguez, Marc Simon. *Rethinking the Chicano Movement*. New York: Routledge, 2015.

Rodriguez, Melanie Lorie. "Racial Injustice in Houston, Texas: The Mexican American Mobilization against the Police Killing of Joe Campos Torres." PhD diss., University of Texas, El Paso, 2017.

Romero, Leo M. "Sufficiency of Provocation for Voluntary Manslaughter in New Mexico: Problems in Theory and Practice." *New Mexico Law Review* 12, no. 2 (1982): 747–89.

Romero, Mary. "Racial Profiling and Immigration Law Enforcement: Rounding Up of Usual Suspects in the Latino Community." In *Deviance and Social Control: A Sociological Perspective*, edited by Michelle Inderbitzin, Kristin A. Bates, and Randy R. Gainey, 468–84. Los Angeles: Sage, 2013.

Romero, Mary, and Marwah Serag. "Violation of Latino Civil Rights Resulting from INS and Local Police's Use of Race, Culture and Class Profiling: The Case of the Chandler Roundup in Arizona." *Cleveland State Law Review* 52, no. 75 (2005): 75–76.

Rosales, F. Arturo. *Chicano! The History of the Mexican American Civil Rights Movement.* Houston: Arte Público, 1997.

Roth, Benita. *The Life and Death of ACT UP/LA: Anti-AIDS Activism in Los Angeles from the 1980s to the 2000s.* New York: Cambridge University Press, 2017.

Rowan, R. H., and J. S. Griffin. "St. Paul (MN)—Police Department—Minority Recruitment Program." *Police Chief* 44, no. 1 (1977): 18–20.

Salinas, Lupe S. *U.S. Latinos and Criminal Injustice.* East Lansing: Michigan State University Press, 2015.

Samora, Julian, Joe Bernal, and Albert Peña. *Gunpowder Justice: A Reassessment of the Texas Rangers.* Notre Dame, IN: University of Notre Dame Press, 1979.

San Miguel, Guadalupe. *Brown, not White: School Integration and the Chicano Movement in Houston.* College Station: Texas A&M University Press, 2005.

Schrader, Stuart. *Badges without Borders: How Global Counterinsurgency Transformed American Policing.* Oakland: University of California Press, 2019.

Sears, James T. *Rebels, Rubyfruit, and Rhinestones: Queering Space in the Stonewall South.* New Brunswick, NJ: Rutgers University Press, 2001.

Sekhon, Nirej. "Police and the Limit of Law." *Columbia Law Review* 119, no. 6 (2019): 1711–72.

Sklansky, David Alan. "Seeing Blue: Police Reform, Occupational Culture, and Cognitive Burn-In." In *Police Occupational Culture: New Debates and Directions*, edited by Megan O'Neill, Monique Marks, and Anne-Marie Singh, 19–46. Oxford: Elsevier JAI, 2007.

Smiley, Calvin John. *Defund: Conversations toward Abolition.* Chicago: Haymarket Books, 2024.

Snow, Robert L. *Policewomen Who Made History: Breaking through the Ranks.* Lanham, MD: Rowman and Littlefield, 2010.

Stoughton, Seth. "Law Enforcement's 'Warrior' Problem." *Harvard Law Review Forum* 128, no. 6 (2015): 225–34.

Stuart, Gary L. *Miranda: The Story of America's Right to Remain Silent.* Tucson: University of Arizona Press, 2004.

Suddler, Carl. *Presumed Criminal: Black Youth and the Justice System in Postwar New York.* New York: New York University Press, 2019.

Tapia, Mike. "U.S. Latino Arrest: An Analysis of Risk by Nativity and Origin." *Hispanic Journal of Behavioral Sciences* 37, no. 1 (2015): 37–58.

Thompson, J. Phillip. "Broken Policing: The Origins of the 'Broken Windows' Policy." *New Labor Forum* 24, no. 2 (Spring 2015): 42–47.

Tijerina, Reies López. *They Called Me "King Tiger": My Struggle for the Land and Our Rights*. Houston: Arte Público, 2000.

Treviño, Jesús Salvador. *Eye Witness: A Filmmaker's Memoir of the Chicano Movement*. Houston: Arte Público, 2001.

Sandoval-Strausz, A. K. *Barrio America: How Latino Immigrants Saved the American City*. New York: Basic Books, 2019.

Stewart-Winter, Timothy. "Queer Law and Order: Sex, Criminality, and Policing in the Late Twentieth-Century United States." *Journal of American History* 102, no. 1 (2015): 61–72.

Tyler, Tom R., and Robert J. Boeckmann. "Three Strikes and You Are Out, but Why? The Psychology of Public Support for Punishing Rule Breakers." *Law and Society Review* 31, no. 2 (1997): 237–66.

Umbreit, Mark, and Marilyn Peterson Armour. *Restorative Justice Dialogue: An Essential Guide for Research and Practice*. New York: Springer, 2011.

Urbina, Martin Guevara, and Sofía Espinoza Álvarez. *Hispanics in the U.S. Criminal Justice System: Ethnicity, Ideology, and Social Control*. Springfield, IL: Charles C. Thomas, 2018.

Urbina, Martin Guevara, and Sofía Espinoza Álvarez. *Latino Police Officers in the United States: An Examination of Emerging Trends and Issues*. Springfield, IL: Charles C. Thomas, 2015.

Valencia, Reynaldo Anaya, Sonia R. García, Henry Flores, and José Roberto Juárez Jr. *Mexican Americans and the Law: ¡El Pueblo Unido Jamas Sera Vencido!* Tucson: University of Arizona Press, 2004.

Vargas, Zaragosa. *Labor Rights Are Civil Rights: Mexican American Workers in Twentieth-Century America*. Princeton, NJ: Princeton University Press, 2004.

Vigil, Ernesto B. *The Crusade for Justice: Chicano Militancy and the Government's War on Dissent*. Madison: University of Wisconsin Press, 1999.

Vitale, Alex S. *The End of Policing*. New York: Verso, 2021.

Walker, Samuel. *A Critical History of Police Reform: The Emergence of Professionalism*. Lanham, MD: Lexington Books, 1977.

Wang, Jackie. *Carceral Capitalism*. South Pasadena, CA: Semiotext(e), 2018.

Watson, Dwight D. "Murder on the Bayou: The Demand for Justice following the Death of José Campos Torres." In *Social Justice, Poverty and Race: Normative and Empirical Points of View*, edited by Paul Kriese and Randall E. Osborne, 57–70. Amsterdam: Rodopi, 2011.

Watson, Dwight D. *Race and the Houston Police Department, 1930–1990: A Change Did Come*. College Station: Texas A&M University Press, 2005.

Weitz, Mark A. *The Sleepy Lagoon Murder Case: Race Discrimination and Mexican-American Rights*. Lawrence: University Press of Kansas, 2010.

Williams, Roy H., and Kevin J. Shay. *And Justice for All: The Untold History of Dallas*. Fort Worth, TX: CGS Communications, 1999.

Wilson, Steven Harmon. "*Chicanismo* and the Flexible Fourteenth Amendment: 1960s Agitation and Litigation by Mexican American Youth in Texas." In *Seeking Inalienable Rights: Texans and Their Quest for Social Justice*, edited by Debra A. Reid, 147–68. College Station: Texas A&M University Press, 2009.

Wilson, Steven Harmon. *The Rise of Judicial Management in the U.S., District Court, Southern District of Texas, 1955–2000.* Athens: University of Georgia Press, 2003.

Worden, Robert E., and Sarah J. McLean. *Mirage of Police Reform: Procedural Justice and Police Legitimacy.* Oakland: University of California Press, 2017.

Zapata, Joel. "The South-by-Southwest Borderlands Chicana/o Uprising: The Brown Berets, Black and Brown Alliances, and the Fight against Police Brutality in West Texas." In *Civil Rights in Black and Brown: Oral Histories of the Liberation Struggles in Texas*, edited by Max Krochmal and J. Todd Moye, 93–114. Austin: University of Texas Press, 2021.

INDEX

Page numbers in italics refer to illustrations.

Bray, Lynn, 172–73, 174, 176, 222
Brennand, James, 220, 221
Briggs, Al, 51
Briscoe, Dolph, 91, 103
broken windows policing, 10–11, 143, 151, 194, 198, 215; critique of, 232, 234
Brown Berets, 7–8, 47, 75–76, 79, 92, 115, 130, 176; Austin chapter of, 115–16; Dallas chapter of, 79; experiences with police abuse of, 40, 43, 65; formation of, 38–39, 39; involvement in investigations of, 129; protests by, 41, 42, San Antonio chapter of, 76–77, 179, 180; ten-point program of, 40. *See also* Black Berets (Albuquerque)
Brunson, Perry, 98, 99–100, 101. *See also* Falcón, Ricardo
Bryant-Vanalden urban renewal program, 170, 187–88, 200
Bustamante, Antonio D., 108, 111
Butler, Richard, 209–10
Byrd, Don, 48, 52, 150–51, 153, 156, 222. *See also* Albuquerque Police Department

CAHOOTS (Crisis Assistance Helping Out on the Streets), 227–28
Cain, Darrell, 1, 11, 79–80, trial of, 82. *See also* Rodriguez, Santos
Caldwell, Harry, 84, 86, 87, 162–63. *See also* Torres, Jose "Joe" Campos
California, 3, 16–17, 34–35, 71; Clinton Crime Law and, 204–5; criminal justice reform in, 71, 165, 166, 184–85, 188–90; criminal justice system in, 20, 21–22, 38, 145; incarceration in, 131, 137–38; Mexican Americans in law enforcement in, 4, 34–35; police violence in, 16–18, 70–71, 131, 184, 187, 193, 195–96, 214, 217, 220; protests in, 38–39, 112–13; state investigations in, 21, 22. *See also* Brown Berets; Bryant-Vanalden urban renewal program; Coalition against Police Abuse (CAPA); Los Angeles, CA; San Diego, CA; Sleepy Lagoon case; Zoot Suit Riots

California Citizens' Committee on Civil Disturbances in Los Angeles, 21–22
California Highway Patrol, 188–90, 220; El Protector Program, 189, 189, 190
Caló, 16. *See also* pachuco phenomenon
Cammack, James, Jr., 76, 177–80. *See also* Phillips, Bobby Jo; Santoscoy, Hector
Campaign for a Citizens Police Review Board, 185
Campos, Victor, 33
Canales, Rito, 38, 49, 57, 58, 59, 61, 62, 150, 221, 222; anti-carceral activism of, 51, 55; background of, 50–51; killing of, 51, 55; killing of, 51–52; post-killing investigation of, 52–54; protests in support of, 55–56. *See also* Chapa, Tim; Cordova, James Antonio
Cano, Luis, 89
Cantrell, S. T., 176
Cantu, Erik, 220–21, 293n17
CAPA. *See* Coalition against Police Abuse (CAPA)
Caravana por Justicia, 109, 110
Carbonneau, Arthur, 209, 210, 216
CARE (Control and Rehabilitation Effort), 138, 139
Carroll, Bob, 51
Carter, Jimmy, 91, 111, 113; administration of, 67, 108, 130–31
Casseb, Solomon, 127
Castro, Sal, 40, 41
Castro, Vickie, 39
Castroville, TX, 94, 101–2
CCBG (Concerned Citizens for Better Government), 152, 153
Cedillo, Joe, Jr., 1, 2, 5, 6, 92; killing of, 77–78
Challapalli, Krishnakumari, 130
Chandler, AZ, 199–200, 202
Chandler Roundup, 199–201
Chapa, Tim, 51, 54–55, 58, 59, 62, 248n69, 248n75
Chauvin, Derek, 233
Chavez, Cesar, 46–47
Chavez, Gus, 172, 173

García Loya, Manuel, 6, 105–6, 107–8, 111, 117. *See also* Hanigan, George; Hanigan, Patrick; Hanigan, Thomas; Herrera Mata, Bernabe; Ruelas Zavala, Eleazar

Gelhaus, Erick, 217, 218–19

Gill, Abel, 1, 2, 70

Glendale, AZ, 132–33

Gonzales, Philip, 191

Gonzales, Rodolfo "Corky," 56, 57, 62, 109, 112. *See also* Crusade for Justice

Gonzales, Rudy, 56

Gonzales, Steven, 154–55

Gonzalez, Henry B., 84, 103

Gonzalez Galarza, Raul, 178

Granado, Florencio "Freddie," 99–100; death in Boulder bombing of, 58

Green, Joe, 152, 153

Guadalupe, AZ, 148, 173

Guerena, Alejandro, 212

Guerena, Gerardo, 212

Guerena, Jose, 210–11, 215, 221, 223, 225; biased news reporting about, 211, 212; death of, 211; as example of hypermilitarized policing, 213–14; inaccurate information from Sheriff Dupnik about, 212, 290n117

Guerena, Vanessa, 212–13

Guerrero, Frank, 64

Guillen, Bernardino, 69

Gutierrez, Dean, 198

Gutiérrez, José Angel, 43; creation of MAYO by, 76; Raza Unida Party and, 101

Guzman, Sergio, 90–91

Haile, Roy Bartee, 46, 47

Hanigan, George, 6, 105, 106

Hanigan, Pamela, 109

Hanigan, Patrick, 105; attempt to shift blame to Thomas Hanigan by, 110–11; federal trials of, 108–11; state trial of, 106–7; torture of Manuel García Loya, Bernabe Herrera Mata, and Eleazar Ruelas Zavala by, 105–6

Hanigan, Thomas, 105; federal trials of, 108–11; state trial of, 106–7; torture of Manuel García Loya, Bernabe Herrera Mata, and Eleazar Ruelas Zavala by, 105–6

Hanigan case, 6, 67, 95, 105–6, 117, 222

Hanigan Case Coalition, 107, 108; Caravana por Justicia, 109, *110*

Haro, Juan, 57–58, 59, 62; trials of, 58. *See also* Quintana, Antonio

Harrelson, R. V., 24

Harris County Constables, 7, 32

Harris County grand jury, 183, 209, 210

Harris County Sheriff's Office, 7, 30

Hauck, William, 127

Hayes, Dorothy, 102, 103

Hayes, Frank, 94, 95, 101–2; murder of Ricardo Morales by, 102; protests against, 102; trials of, 103. *See also* Morales, Ricardo

Heard, Percy, 25, 26. *See also* Latin American Squad

Helm, Eugene, 118, 128. *See also* Bexar County Boy's School

Hernandez, Adan, 129

Hernandez, Marcelino, 129

Hernandez, Pablo, 177, 178

Hernandez, Paul, 115, 116

Hernandez, Pete, 121, 122, *122*, 126

Hernandez, Urban, 162

Hernandez v. Texas (1954), 9, 120, 121, 141, 144, 222

Herrera, John J., 24–25, 26–27, 30, 35, 121, 122

Herrera Mata, Bernabe, 6, 105–6, 107, 111, 117. *See also* García Loya, Manuel; Hanigan, George; Hanigan, Patrick; Hanigan, Thomas; Ruelas Zavala, Eleazar

Hinostro, Robert, 35

Hirsch, Thomas, *88*, 89

Hofheinz, Fred, 84

Hogue, Carol, 57, 59, 60

Holguin, Elisa, 33–34

Holguin, Theresa, 151

Hollander, Nina, 179, 180
Houston, TX, 6–7, 15, 24, 223; civil rights protests in, 47, 84–85, 86–87, 89, 129; gay rights movement in, 182–83. *See also* Moody Park
Houston Police Department, 6–7, 24–25, 27, 79, 82; attempts to halt activism by, 47, 89; Chicano Squad and, 155, 162; Clinton Crime Law and, 203; Community Organizing Response Team (CORT) of, 163; hiring of Mexican American officers by, 32; Intelligence Division of, 46–47, 156; Internal Affairs Division of, 163; Jose "Joe" Campos Torres killing and, 83–85; killings of Eli Escobar and Jose Vargas and, 209–10; Latin American Squad of, 25–26, 221; reform of, 120, 161, 163, 210, 216, 222. *See also* Cortez, Elpidio; Houston 12; Martinez, Raul C.; Moody Park Rebellion; Páez, Fred; Torres, Jose "Joe" Campos
Houston 12, 47, 62
Huchens, Sandra (née Jones), 184
Hudson, C. V., 182
Huntington Park, CA, 7, 185–86
Hurst, Elva, 129

Immigration and Naturalization Service (INS), 112, 113, 188, 201; Border Crime Prevention Unit, 170, 186–87. *See also* US Border Patrol
Immigration Reform and Control Act (1986), 170
incarceration, 8, 119, 121–22, 205–6, 215; abolition of, 10, 12, 120, 239n16, 239n18; in jails, 18, 24, 25, 34, 96, 102, 159, 188; and prison industrial complex, 11, 126, 134, 135, 136, 140, 168, 203, 231; in prisons, 18, 24, 51, 55, 61, 82, 86, 89, 94, 97, 102, 103, 111, 119, 124, 134, 137–38; problems with, 120, 126–27, 128–29, 131, 132–33, 135–37, 185; reform of, 120–21, 122, 132–33, 134–35. *See also* Bexar County Boy's School; Duran, Dwight;

Lopez, Jesus "Jess"; New Mexico State Penitentiary Riot; Ruíz, David Resendez; Sanchez, Eddie
Independent Office of Law Enforcement Review and Outreach (IOLERO), *218,* 219–20, 229
Indigenous peoples, 110, 112, 148, 173

Jachimczyk, Joseph, 85
Jacobs, Donovan, 165
Jameson, Lois, 124–25. *See also* Miranda, Ernesto Arturo
Janish, Joseph, 83, 86
Jelso, Joseph, 73
Jimenez, Angelina, 190–91
Jimenez, Pablin, 190–91
Johnson, James, 1, 77–78. *See also* Cedillo, Joe, Jr.
Johnson, Lyndon Baines, 170, 231
Johnson, Robert, 78–79
Jones, Byron, 208
Joya, Raymond, 170–71, 172, 191
justice, extralegal, 2, 5, 6, 105, 107, 110, *110,* 111
justice, legal, 2–3, 6–7, 8, 17, 119, 140, 206; Chicano activism and, 38–39, 56–57, 120, 122, 124, 126; Mexican American service in, 34, 35–36; as opposed to Mexican American rights, 60–61, 73; unfair operation of, 75, 98–99, 101, 103, 107, 144. *See also* law enforcement; police, violence
Justice, William, 140
juvenile delinquency, 15, 16, 17, 19, 20, 22–23, 27, 35–36

Kennedy, Don, 150
Kennedy, Edward "Ted," 45
Kern, Clairville V. "Buster," 30
Ketelaar, Roger, 172
Kilbourne, H. Wells, 73
King, Bruce, 48–49, 53, 135, *136*
King, Martin Luther, Jr., 11, 239n20
King, Rodney, 132, 196, 197
Kinney, Louis, 83, 85

KKK. *See* Ku Klux Klan

Kloss, Gene, 129

Knoll, Barry L., 123–24

Ku Klux Klan, 46, 95, 111, 112, 117, 186, 192; border watch by, 111–12; protests against, 113–16, *114*

La Fuerza de los Barrios, 176

La Raza Unida Party, 75, 91, 99

Larson, Wayne, 51, 52. *See also* Canales, Rito; Cordova, James Antonio

Latin American Squad, 25–26, 221. *See also* Houston Police Department

Latino/a/x people, 186, 187–88, 195, 196, crime and, 205–6, 215, 286n38; demographics of, 3, 6, 238n3

law enforcement: and hiring of Mexican American officers, 32–34, 153, *158*, 159, 160–61, 174; investigations or studies of, 20, 21, 42–43, 53–54, 56–57, 59–60, 62, 64–65, 144–46, 154–55, 167, 192; and officer fatalities or injuries, 29, 57, 79, 95, 97, 104, 165; organization of, 4, 6–7, 8, 119, 165, 194–96, 202–3, 205, 215, 223; reform of (*see* reform, police); violence committed by (*see* violence, police). *See also* Arizona; California; Colorado; justice, legal; New Mexico; "papers, please" policing; Texas; *and names of specific police departments and county sheriff's offices*

Law Enforcement Assistance Act. *See* Omnibus Crime Control and Safe Streets Act (1968)

law enforcement–perpetrated homicides, 1, 2, 79–80, 83, 94, 102. *See also* violence, police

League of United Latin American Citizens (LULAC), 24, 25, 27, 67, 85–86, 121, 162–63, 166, 167, 176, 208

legal defense committees, 91; Carlos Villarreal Defense Committee, 181–82, 192; Committee to Defend the Rebellion, 89; Danny Vasquez Defense Committee, 91; Francisco E. Martínez

Defense Committee, 60, 61; Free the Moody Park 3, 89; Houston 12 Defense Committee, 47, 62; Sleepy Lagoon Defense Committee, 18–19

ley fuga (law of flight), 5, 53, 65, 77, 84, 207, 220, 233

Leyvas, Henry, 17, 18

Leyvas, Rudy, 20

LGBTQIA+ community, 170, 181, 182, 183, 191

Lichtenstein, Alvin, 61

Límon, María, 115, 116

Logan, Fred, 76

Looney, Paul, 1, 77, 78. *See also* Cedillo, Joe, Jr.

Lopez, Andy, 217–18, *218*, 219, 220, 222, 229

Lopez, Fred, 39

Lopez, Jesus "Jess," 132–34

Lopez, Rodrigo, 219

Lopez, Sujey, 219

Los Angeles, CA, 2, 6–7, 14, 15, 36, 223; city government investigations of police violence in, 20–22, 42–43; civil rights protests in, 40, 41, 42; gay rights movement in, 183; Reyes Martinez killing in, 131–32; Mexican American officers in, 35, 243n82; 1992 uprising in, 132, 196–97; pachuco/zoot suit hysteria in, 16–18, 22; records destruction incident, 164–65; Watts Rebellion in, 38–39, 163, 164, 196. *See also* Sleepy Lagoon case; Zoot Suit Riots

Los Angeles County, 22, 23, 24, 27; Los Angeles County Jail, 18

Los Angeles County Sheriff's Department, 1, 7, 23; Clinton Crime Law and, 204–5; reform of, 188–90; violence by, 41, 42, 70–71, 184, 193, 196

Los Angeles Police Department: attempts to halt activism by, 41, 42, 165; Clinton Crime Law and, 204–5; police violence by, 42, 131, 184, 195–96, 223, 206–7; Rampart Scandal and, 196, 206, 207; reform of, 163–64, 184, 185, 188–89; Scanning, Analysis, Response, and Assessment (SARA), 197–98, 215

Love, Eula Mae, 132
Lozano, Larry Ortega, 129–30, 222
Lucero, David, 56
LULAC. *See* League of United Latin American Citizens (LULAC)
Lustig, William, 185–86

Malley, Clyde, 135
Mancias, Adela, 115, 116
Maricopa County Sheriff's Office, 148, 171
Marmion, Ralph, 149, 222
Marquez, Lawrence, 73, 152
Martinez, Ben, 50
Martínez, Francisco E. "Kiko," 58, 62, 99, 100, 221, 250n113; flight and capture of, 59–61; Winnergate and, 60–61
Martinez, Glen, 156
Martinez, Jaime, 114
Martinez, Luis "Junior," 38, 57, 61
Martinez, Raul C., *31*, 32
Martínez, Rene, 80–81
Martinez, Reyes, 58, 131–32, 141
Martinez, Roberto, 186
mass incarceration, 11, 126, 134, 135, 136, 140, 168, 203, 231
Mata, Manuel, 78
Mauricio, Yvonne, 199
MAYO (Mexican American Youth Organization), 46, 75–76
McCoy, Kevin, 182–83
McCraw, James, 157
McFate, Yale, 124–25
McNutt, Ralph, 51–52, 53
McWilliams, Don, 85
Medellin, David, 176, 177
Medrano, Francisco "Pancho," 44–45, 79, 80
Mendez Pulido, Ignacio, 187
Mendez-Ruiz, Juan, 113
Mendoza, Ramon, Jr., 34
Mendoza, Ramon S., Sr., 34
Mesa, AZ, 34, 124, 172, 174, 176, 191, 204
Mesa, Vincent, 99, 100
Messina, L. Michael, 54
Metzger, Tom, 112

Mexican-American Police Command Officers Association, 166–67, 174
Mexican Americans, 1–2; abuse from justice system of, 3–4, 5–6, 17–18, 19–20, 24, 27–28, 40, 52, 57, 59–60, 66, 78, 80, 83, 131–32, 220–21; brownness and, 5, 82, 113, 161, 170, 195, 199; civil rights activism of, 4–5, 8–9, 38–39, 46, 55, 64, 66–67, 81–83, 86–87, 102, 109–10, 132, 184; demographics of, 3, 24; as not opposed to policing, 3, 7–8, 8–9, 30, 35, 38, 56, 92, 120, 168, 221–22; perceptions of criminality of, 15, 19, 20, 26–27, 36; service in criminal justice system of, 9–10, 25–26, 30–32, 33–36, 153, 155, 159, 162, 166, 173, 174–76; whiteness and, 4–5
Mexican American Youth Organization (MAYO), 46, 75–76
Mexico: citizens and police violence in US, 24, 30, 35, 105, 177–78, 186–87, 196–97, 201; consulate of, 24, 107, 178–79; escape of Mexican Americans to, 60, 98; government of, 24, 98, 107, 169, 178–79; Mexico City, 14–15, 91, 98; Piedras Negras, 177; Nogales, 187. *See also* Mexicans
Miles, Robert, 78
Minez, Jose, 79
Miranda, Ernesto Arturo, 124–25, 126, Miranda Warning and, 9, 126
Miranda v. Arizona (1966), 9, 12, 120, 122, 124, 125–26, 222
mob justice, 105, *110. See also* justice, extralegal
Montag, Gustav, 42
Montenegro, Alberto, 68
Montenegro, Daniel, 68
Montenegro, Edward, 68, 69
Montenegro, Javier, 68
Montenegro, Jose, 68
Montenegro, Maria, 68
Montero, Jim, 162
Montes, Carlos, 8, 39, *39*, 40
Moody Park, 86, 87, 129, 161
Moody Park Rebellion, 87–89, *88*

Rodriguez, Robert (Huntington Park police officer), 185
Rodriguez, Robert (Oxnard police officer), 35
Rodriguez, Santos, 1, 2, 9, 11, 79–80, 82, 91, 92, 108, 120, 140, 161, 221, 222, march for, 80–82. *See also* Dallas Disturbance
Rodriguez, Thomas, 79
Rodríguez, Valentin, 77
Roma Chavez, Octavio, 187
Romero, Robert, 181–82
Ronstadt, Peter, 147–48
Rosa, Robert, 128. *See also* Bexar County Boy's School
Rosales, Rado, 89
Roswell, NM, 150, 190, 191
Roybal, Edward, 108, 113
Rubio, Emmett, 151, 222
Ruelas Zavala, Eleazar, 6, 105–6, 107, 111, 117. *See also* Hanigan, George; Hanigan, Patrick; Hanigan, Thomas; Herrera Mata, Bernabe; García Loya, Manuel
Ruíz, David Resendez, 120, 139–40, 141
Ruiz, Ignacio, 29
Ruiz, John, 25, 26
Ruiz, Richard, 147
Ruiz, Rodolfo, 56
Ruiz v. Estelle (1980), 140

Saavedra, Ike, 71, 72–73
Salas, Luis, 29
Salazar, Jose, 51, 52
Salazar, Ruben, 5, 42
Saldana, Juan Manuel, 206–7
San Antonio, TX, 45, 76–77, 87, 91, 166, 171, 178–79, 223; civil rights protests and, 113–14; gay rights movement in, 181, 183; jails in, 127. *See also* Bexar County Boy's School
San Antonio Police Department, 102, 220; hiring of Mexican American officers by, 158, 159; police violence by, 76, 159, 177, 181, 198, 19, 220–21; reform of, 198, 199; Tactical Response Unit (TRU)

of, 199. *See also* Santoscoy, Hector; Villarreal, Carlos
Sanchez, Beltran, 42
Sánchez, David, 39, 39, 40–41, 43
Sanchez, Eddie, 120, 138–39, 141
Sánchez, Frank (activist), 150
Sánchez, Frank (zoot-suiter), 25
Sanchez, Guillermo, 42
Sanchez, Ralph, 151
Sanchez, Rudy, 80–81
Sanchez y Baca, Felipe, 34
San Diego, CA, 34, 70, 113, 165, 166, 183, 185–86
San Diego Police Department, 165, 186
Sandoval, Mateo, 78
Sandoval, Ruben, 67, 92, 167, 180, 198; Babich case and, 74; Hanigan case and, 109–10; Santoscoy case and, 178–79
San Jose, CA, 70, 214
San Jose, NM, 151, 152
Santa Fe, NM, 49, 134, 135–37; Clinton Crime Law and, 203. *See also* Penitentiary of New Mexico
Santiago, Nina, 157
Santleben, Alvin, 103
Santos, Ruben, 179, 180
Santoscoy, Alicia, 179
Santoscoy, Hector, 168, 179–80, 191, 198, 222; killing of, 177–78
San Ysidro, CA, 112
Scanning, Analysis, Response, and Assessment (SARA), 197–98, 215
Schemmel, Michael, 217, 219
Schomburg, A. H., 24
Seals, Woodrow, 45
Seeber, Paul, 73, 152
Semaan, Fred, 180
Serrano Collier, Josephine, 35
Shipton, Carl, 113
Shriver, David, 193–94
Sinohui, Jose H., Jr., 66–67, 69, 222
Sinohui Sanchez, Anna, 67
Sleepy Lagoon case, 17, 19, 23
Smith, Craig, 70
Snyder, Stephen, 57
Solar, Michael, 208